Tim R. Swartz's Big Book of...

INCREDIBLE ALIEN ENCOUNTERS

A Global Guide to Space Aliens,
Interdimensional Beings
And
Ultra-Terrestrials

Helen Hovey

Publisher's Dedication

To: Helen Hovey, lifelong friend and confidant – and Tim R. Swartz, ace flying saucer man with a graphic's touch.

Tim R. Swartz

Inner Light - Global Communications

PO Box 753
New Brunswick, NJ 08903

MRUFO8@HOTMAIL.COM

Tim R. Swartz's Big Book of...

INCREDIBLE ALIEN ENCOUNTERS

By Tim R. Swartz, Timothy Green Beckley, Sean Casteel

Contributors:

Brian Allan, Hakan Blomqvist, Barry Chamish, Scott Corrales, Maria D' Andrea, Preston Dennett, Ben and Paul Eno, Olavo T. Fontes, M.D., Adam Gorightly, T. Allen Greenfield, Rick Hilberg, Cynthia Hind, Hercules Invictus, William Kern, Erica Lukes, Philip Mantle, Aleksandar Petakov, Brent Raynes, Paul Dale Roberts, Malcolm Robinson, Susan Demeter-St. Clair, Brad and Sherry Steiger, Diane Tessman, Nigel Watson, Charles J. Wilhelm, Linda Zimmermann

Published in the United States of America By
Inner Light/Global Communications
Box 753, New Brunswick, NJ 08903

Staff Members:
Timothy G. Beckley: Publisher
Carol Ann Rodriguez: Assistant to the Publisher
Sean Casteel: General Associate Editor
Tim R. Swartz: Formatting, Graphics and Editorial Consultant
William Kern: Editorial and Art Consultant

www.ConspiracyJournal.com

Email: MrUFO8@hotmail.com

INCREDIBLE ALIEN ENCOUNTERS

CONTENTS

INCREDIBLE ALIEN ENCOUNTERS

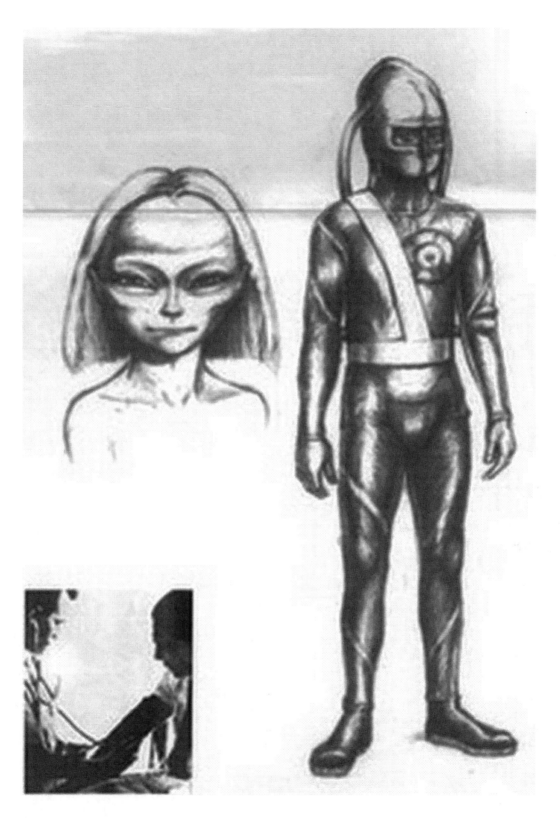

Illustrations of the humanoids that abducted Villa Boas on October 16, 1957.

Timothy Green Beckley's "*UFO UNIVERSE*" magazine.

ESTABLISHING A UFO PRINT LEGACY

By Timothy Green Beckley

There is now a void in UFO publishing that concerns me, makes me unhappy, but for which hopefully there is a positive solution.

Canadian artist Gene Duplantier did some of the incredible art for Tim's first UFO Zine, "The Interplanetary News Service Report."

Starting in 1964, when I put out my first mimeographed zine, *"The Interplanetary News Service Report,"* I was an admitted newbie, wet behind those little green ears, with no deep insight into the overall picture as far as the UFO phenomena goes. But let's admit it: What sort of research material did I have to draw on? At the age of ten I started reading everything I could get my hands on concerning what just had to be an "alien invasion," friendly or not.

I think for 35 cents I picked up a magazine in 1957 called *"True Space Secrets."* It had a garish red and yellow cover and was printed on some ridiculously cheap paper. To this day I think the publisher of "Confidential" was behind it, or they had the same art director at least. The pulp had the usual poorly written articles; one I remember was entitled, "Are The Chinese From Outer Space?" The UFO photos were probably fake, and do you know the same ones are still being published to this day?

The purchase of this magazine coincided with my first UFO sighting, in the summer of 1957, of two brightly lit "discs" above the cloud cover which circled in the sky near my home in New Brunswick, New Jersey.

Unsatisfied with this rather garish publication with its sensationalist cover lines (I learned later I could write better ones and did so professionally), I hunted for additional material and came across "*Fate Magazine*," which was well worth the cover price. This digest had started out with an article by flying saucer "originator" Kenneth Arnold in 1948 and on occasion still provides a dwindling print audience with a volume to hold in their shaking hands (it being no doubt an older audience, as opposed to those reading it on their Kindle).

Beckley put down less than a buck for *"True Space Secrets,"* thinking at the tender age of ten that he would learn something from its contents. Wrong!

There were a couple of paperbacks I scooped up. "*Flying Saucers From Outer Space*," by Donald E. Keyhoe, in the pages of which the retired Marine Corps Major postulated that these glittering flying discs were coming here from outer space, though he refused to speculate on who was piloting them, being more concerned with pestering the Air Force to release their top-secret documents which he just knew they had to be hiding!

Then there was "*Flying Saucers Have Landed*," written by a Polish immigrant named George Adamski, who told a thrilling, but hard to believe, tale of meeting a space being from Venus and later taking several trips into outer space. His thing was "cosmic philosophy," which was helping to introduce the New Age movement that was beginning to thrive in California and along the West Coast.

(From left to right) Beckley's early inspirations – John Keel, Gray Barker and Jim Moseley.

There was also Frank Edwards, a news journalist who did a nightly radio broadcast till he was kicked off the air because he talked too much about flying saucers, which the show's national advertiser (a labor union) did not like at all. Edwards aimed for a mass audience with his pocket sized editions which contained dozens of short stories about all sorts of paranormal topics. His work focused a great deal on UFOs, which was an audience-grabber for the same price as a double dipped ice cream cone. You may still have a dusty copy of "**Stranger Than Science**" which you got through your middle school "*Weekly Reader*" book club.

For about five years, TGB wrote a column for Ray Palmer's "Flying Saucers." Beckley's "On The Trail Of The Flying Saucers" covered every aspect of the UFO topic.

Eventually, well into my teens, "*The Interplanetary News Service Report*" was becoming a burden.

In those days – i.e., the mid to late Sixties – there were no quick copy services, so you had to print everything yourself on some sort of duplicating apparatus. You had to ink the mimeograph or ditto machine, print each side of the page, stack up the printed pages, collate them by hand, staple the pages together and affix postage (only seven or eight cents in those days as opposed to the 55 cents for a one ounce newsletter, which by postal code has to go inside an envelope, for which you need to add another nickel).

Yes, I would rather have been dating girls!

Along about 1966 came Mr. James W. Moseley, who was publishing a fairly "professional" UFO magazine with headquarters in midtown Manhattan. There was even a listing for his magazine, *"Saucer News,"* in the yellow pages. I had met him at several UFO meetings he held on a regular basis around Times Square and had worked myself into a position of being an able-bodied assistant. At some point he offered to take my subscriptions and combine them with his *"Saucer News"* readership rolls, giving him a massive circulation of around 10,000, though he never did sell the magazine on newsstands.

JWM hired me as his Managing Editor, and I stayed in that position till he folded the magazine some time later, taking over his office on Fifth Avenue while he moved to Florida to sell pre-Columbian antiques (much more profitable than putting out a UFO tract).

In his Fifth Avenue office, Tim holds the third issue of his flying saucer newspaper. "UFO Review" was distributed from coast to coast and overseas. Photo by Jeff Goodman.

As for myself, I got into rock and roll and the entertainment business (see my book *"David Bowie, UFOs, Witchcraft, Cocaine and Paranoia - Full Color Version: The Occult Saga of Walli Elmlark - The 'Rock and Roll' Witch of New York"*), opened up the New York School of Occult Arts and Science, wrote a column, *"On The Trail of the Flying Saucers,"* for my mentor Ray Palmer's widely-distributed *"Flying Saucers From Other Worlds Magazine,"* and, before too long, was on the newsstands with *"UFO Review,"* best known as the "World's Only Flying Saucer Newspaper," with an impressive print run of 33,000.

I was putting NICAP and APRO, two prestigious UFO groups, to shame with my "massive" circulation, as opposed to their rather dismal number of readers. *"UFO Review"* lasted close to a decade, I believe, as I added other tabloids to my publishing "empire," such as *"Joe Franklin's Memory Lane News,"* a Sci-Fi paper called *"Tomorrow,"* which I think only lasted, I have to admit, two or three issues.

Other low end publishers heard of my ability to put together a magazine on a shoestring and hired me to package such "you-never-heard-of-them" magazines with titles like: *"Moped Action," "Front Page Disasters," "Afternoon Soap Opera,"* and a number of KISS and Peter Frampton "one-shots."

The late punk rock star Helen Wheels (sister of Peter Robbins, and a UFO abductee in her own right) displays one of her favorite publications. Missing from picture – her pet boa.

Along came Al Weiss, who had made a splash with a couple of martial arts magazines. He had money to spend and wanted to put out a UFO magazine. His distributor told him it would sell. (They must have been crazy?) Weiss hired me. Who else knew the ropes about magazine publishing and UFOs combined? There was a press run of 175,000 copies on the first issue. Most of them never got on sale. The publisher took a hosing with this miscalculation and cut the print run to 50K from there on out. The magazine was sold – or given away might be a better term – to collect a debt to a larger publishing firm. We continued publishing "UFO Universe," and its sister publications, "Unsolved UFO Sightings," "UFO Files," "Angels and Aliens," and whatever else we could fill the racks with, for eleven years before the bottom fell out of the magazine publishing business. This same publisher had been putting out a total of around 35 magazines, but the newsstands continued to close along with most book stores, one right after another. In fact, there isn't an actual newsstand in New York City that I know about, Barnes and Noble being about the only place you can buy an actual printed magazine. And nothing on this sort of topic outside of "Fortean Times" from the UK and a couple skeptics magazines.

Sad news for those who like to hold a book, turn the pages of a magazine, or even spill coffee on them. There are, of course, a number of very well produced magazines in e-book format to which we contribute, including "Phenomena" edited by Brian Allan and Steve Mera out of the UK, as well as "Unexplained Mysteries," also from the UK. And a publication from Australia which we just found out about, though they have printed over three hundred issues, called "UFO Encounter." The information-packed e-zine is filled with sightings reports from Down Under as well as well-researched classic cases, a couple of which we have drawn upon for purposes of this book.

Still wet behind his Venusian ears, Beckley looks in awe at an almost life-size portrait of Orthon, the space brother Adamski is said to have met in the desert.

And so, while one could get easily depressed over a lack of printed material on the subject, we, as probably the world's largest niche publisher of UFO and paranormal books, have decided to take matter into our own hands and on a regular basis (hopefully maybe three or four times per year) come out with a new title similar to "*Incredible Alien Encounters*."   Noted UFO/paranormal researcher, Tim R. Swartz, along with the help from some of the best researchers in our well established stable of writers, have brought together some of the most fantastic and bizarre UFO and alien encounters from across the globe for this book and your reading pleasure.

The topics may vary, but we have long gotten past reporting on "simple lights in the sky," since we now realize that UFOs mean something different to just about everyone. There may be some – a few – spaceships, some interdimensional beings popping through portals and wormholes, time travelers, hollow earth dwellers, some Nazi saucer pilots hiding out at the South Pole undetected (or maybe Uncle Sam knows all about them since they allowed five thousand Nazis to come into this country after WWII under Project Paper Clip.) And let's not forget the undersea creatures Preston Dennett has written about, probably more than anyone else. And leaping lizards, and misplaced Bigfoot, and the Space Brothers, and their Tall White friends. And I dare not mention the dreaded Men-in-Black who might well put us all out of business.

But have no fear – come hell or high water, we will be here to guide you in your search to discover the truth about UFOs. It's been an interesting journey and we are glad you could join us and welcome others to hop on our rocket ship right out of here.

To all the independent researchers reading this – we welcome your support and your written contributions. We are looking for solid cases, particularly those involving close encounters and ultra-terrestrial pilot sightings. Just drop me a line and let me know what you have. We would love to look all kinds of material over.

So let's get on with the ever-loving cup and saucer show. . .

mrufo8@hotmail.com

Mr. UFO's Secret Files -- YouTube.com

Exploring the Bizarre -- KCORradio.com

www.ConspiracyJournal.com

EUROPE

MYSTERY OF THE BLACK SUN ON STARR HILL
By Timothy Green Beckley

Much to the dismay and confusion of military authorities and community leaders, sightings of Unidentified Flying Objects persist regularly, like clockwork, above the tiny, isolated town of Warminster, England. Being over four to five decades after "The Thing," as it was known, first appeared, many of the witnesses have moved or passed away, including my close journalist friend, Arthur Shuttlewood.

On several occasions, in various books and magazine articles, I have mentioned how I was apparently successful in an attempt to communicate with a light that appeared overhead, whose origins could not honestly be determined, though our fearless leader on Starr Hill that night insisted that it was a "bogie," as the military often classified such hovering and darting orbs.

Residents here have come to accept, as a matter of course, strange flying machines, the observations of which continued – at the peak of the flap – at the astounding rate of two per week. Since December of 1964, hundreds of responsible individuals have spotted clusters of diamond-brilliant UFOs over this desolate area on Salisbury Plain. Shapes reported vary widely, from "glowing spheres" to enormous "cigars" with lighted windows.

According to *"Warminster Daily"* editor, Arthur Shuttlewood — himself a confirmed believer after numerous close encounters — UFOs sighted near this British community have recently taken on a new, even more puzzling quality. "Events of the last few months have helped to steadily convince me," says Shuttlewood, "that a sizeable portion of what has transpired in and around Warminster is of a non-physical nature, totally defying the acknowledged laws of science. We now have strong evidence that the phenomenon is simply fading into and out of our earthly plane of existence.

"Perhaps," states the veteran newsman, "entering into another realm or dimension."

The deceased reporter for the community's conservative daily maintained what most UFOlogists now take for granted – that there is a paranormal element of this mystery, and that under certain circumstances these "invisible" UFOs and their crew members can be seen with the aid of photographic equipment or by individuals who happen to visually catch them while they are in the process of making a transformation from visibility to invisibility.

While visiting Warminster's Starr Hill author/publisher Tim Beckley took this picture in complete darkness. Between the two skywatchers can be seen a strange light coming down from the sky and bobbing in the background. There were no houselights, headlights, or planes to account for this "invisible-to-the-naked-eye" phenomenon.

Citing a particular instance in which he was involved, Shuttlewood willingly recounted the following episode: "A group of 30 skywatchers had gathered on Starr Hill — a vantage point from which UFOs can be seen on a regular basis — when a dynamic, metallic craft came from out of nowhere, floating in our direction. Before our very eyes, within mere moments, the vessel simply vanished — literally dissolving into thin air! Not able to move a muscle, we all stood in silent awe, unable to believe what our senses told us had happened. Looking back at it, the flying saucer had been there one second — and poof! — the next moment it was gone, as if someone had extinguished a gigantic light bulb in an otherwise darkened room.

"Minutes later, this same object reappeared bit by bit, in a different portion of the sky, seemingly rebuilding its molecular structure. Soon it hovered there in all its former splendor for everyone to gaze upon."

A startling photograph taken by an unsuspecting visitor at high noon, at the foot of Starr Hill, depicts an object — a dark, ominous shape — which the human eye was unable to detect. "I had heard of the sightings in Warminister," says John Wright of Walthamstow, Essex, "and so I decided to visit the area. I spent some time there during the month of August, accompanied by two friends. It was not until we returned home, however, and developed some photographs of the region that I noticed anything unusual. There, on two different frames of 35mm film, was a gigantic black globe, the likes of which I have never seen in my entire life. At first, I thought the film might have been defective, or that there was a light leak in the camera. Imagine my surprise when I had the equipment thoroughly checked out, and discovered that there was absolutely nothing wrong with it. Somehow — I have no explanation to offer — my camera managed to take a picture of something our eyes at the time the photos were taken were not able to see."

Asked if he had noticed anything at all unusual at the time the photos were taken, Wright states that he was aware only of the deathly silent and brooding atmosphere of the hill's surroundings. "It was very unnatural. You couldn't hear a sound — not a bird or a cricket. We thought to ourselves that this was extremely odd, but managed to shrug it off."

Invisible "black sun" photographed above Starr Hill as English town was infested with strange flying devices.

According to Arthur Shuttlewood, a close examination of the film by experts failed to turn up any signs of a hoax. "There is no possible way these photographs could have been tampered with — faked. They have held up under scrutiny. No one is able to offer a reasonable explanation as to how they were taken or what the object is. The UFO seems to be rising from a clump of trees some 600 yards away from the percipients. The exact same area has been the scene of repeated UFO activity for the longest period.

"It is here," maintains the journalist, "that transparent UFOnauts – the creatures who pilot these ships – have reportedly been seen on several occasions. In addition, the mysterious sound of heavy footsteps on the ground has been noted, though no one was visible to account for them."

Photo-Shopped picture of Arthur Shuttlewood walking in area where the outline of giants could be seen.

Shuttlewood adds that he, himself, was privileged to encounter these beings during the winter of 1972, not more than fifty feet away from the barn shown in the Wright photo. It was about 8:30 p.m.

"I was on the hill, along with a half dozen other individuals," Shuttlewood says, "including a former police officer and a bank executive. Suddenly, we heard thumping noises from a clump of bushes to our left. We imagined the noises were being made by a wild animal, but soon realized this was not so. Another sound caused us all to look at the hedgerow to our left. That's when we saw the three giant figures standing at the edge of a field, a distance away. They were all eight feet tall, had domed heads, no apparent necks, wide shoulders tapering to slim waists, and long arms that dangled at their sides. Their outlines were clearly discernible, even thou it was dark."

As the startled observers attempted to leave the area, the transparent "creatures" followed them, gliding several inches above the ground.

"You could see right through them," Shuttlewood maintains. "And although we finally lost our fear and attempted to communicate with them, they did not respond. A member of our party walked right up to one of these beings and was able to pass right through the eerie form. The figures vanished as the lights of approaching cars moved in our direction."

A recent episode involved Sally Pike, daughter of retired Police Superintendent John Rossiter, who gave the following details of her earth-shattering experience: "Both my husband and I have had rather unnerving experiences at Cradle Hill" — an area located a quarter of a mile from Starr Hill. "One solo watch came to an abrupt end when I became slightly apprehensive and, on turning, saw quite clearly the outline of a tall male figure striding up the road in the bright moonlight.

"He seemed to be about seven feet tall, with extremely long arms which hung limply at his sides. He seemed to have no neck, his head appeared to rise directly from his shoulders. His body itself, only the outline being solid, was almost transparent and silvery. I admit to a feeling of fear, although I don't know why."

Mrs. Pike says she refrained from telling her husband Neil about the strange events, for fear he would not believe her. Unbeknownst to Mrs. Pike, her husband was to encounter a similar being several days later. "As I approached the white metal gates which lead to the summit of Cradle Hill, I had to adjust my eyes to the existing light, since it was rather late in the evening. Seconds later, I saw them — three giant figures, standing in a line. At first they were mere shadowy, ghostlike outlines. But as I peered through the quiet darkness, they sharpened their form until they appeared almost solid. The only unusual thing was that their bodies ended at the mid-section, no legs or feet being visible. The starkly defined outline of their upper halves was crystal clear, the interiors transparent. Their heads were long and slightly pointed at the top."

Wondering if his eyes were playing tricks in the eerie and deceptive half-light, Neil aimed the beam of a flashlight he was carrying at one of the tall figures.

The cover of "UFO Prophecy - Visions From The Town Haunted by Flying Saucers." Updated book with photos and text by Shuttlewood and others.

Immediately the giant disintegrated – vanished – only to reappear at another spot near the solitary watcher.

"I flashed my searchlight onto the two other forms, and the same horrifying thing happened. The ghostly trio was now much closer to me, their faces featureless, black and fearsome. It was at this nerve-wracking moment, alone on a weird hill except for my even weirder 'companions,' that I decided to run."

Neil Pike says he fled, rushing for his sports car and coasting downhill as fast as possible. He had only been on Cradle Hill for three minutes, but that was long enough for him to realize the enormity of what had happened. "There is no doubt that I came face-to-face with the unknown! I was petrified. These are the only words I can use to describe my experience."

Research done by Shuttlewood showed at the time that a total of seventeen people had seen these gigantic transparent figures on Cradle and Starr Hills. Sixty others heard the heavy, thudding footsteps of the notorious "invisible walkers" who apparently haunted this area.

Shuttlewood insisted before his untimely passing that, "There is something going on in Warminster that is beyond our current understanding. It may be that an armada of spaceships and their crews are using our town as a landing base or way station. There is now substantial evidence to indicate that they are able to make themselves invisible upon command. We can only guess as to what their purpose might be. Let us hope it is a peaceful one!"

ADDENDUM

In this line of work you find out something new every day, especially if you're observant and well-read.

Just got a copy of Brent Raynes' book, "*John A. Keel: The Man, The Myths and the Ongoing Mysteries.*"

It's a wonderful read. I knew Keel well. Besides being on the board of directors of the New York Fortean Society, which JAK headed, he lived just down the block from me. We sometimes got together at "Ms. K's," a come-as-you are deli that featured meatballs on their menu for 25 years. We sometimes went to the movies to see camp films like "Killer Clowns From Outer Space." And, of course, we shared twisted tales of the strange and unknown.

Raynes relates an anecdote about Linda Scarberry's mother (witness to the Mothman in Point Pleasant, West Virginia) that involved invisibility: "All sorts of strange things plagued them (after their sighting): UFOs, doors opening and closing as though by invisible hands, mysterious footsteps, unexplained odors and ghostly apparitions. Linda once awakened to see the dark outline of a man standing at the foot of her bed." Linda, furthermore, told of hearing heartbeats coming from the empty cellar (they must have been awful loud). A member of my own family had a similar experience, having heard voices coming up the cement cellar stairs, though no one VISIBLE was down there! Invisible walkers, as I call them, are nothing new to UFO witnesses. Kenneth Arnold, the man who gave flying saucers their name, said the rocking chair on his porch would rock back and forth as if someone were seated in it. So take heed! You might be under observation even if you can't see who is spying on you.

As Motown artist Rockwell (with an uncredited but undeniable Michael Jackson in the background) sang: "Somebody's Watching Me!"

WANT TO LEARN MORE?

Join Facebook Group – Warminster UFO Research Group

Mr UFO's Secret Files: www.youtube.com/user/MRUFO1100

Attack of Warminster's "The UFO Thing!" 50th Anniversary Redux
Published on May 23, 2016 – www.youtube.com/watch?v=cTvyfoPO-lo

Warminster UK was known throughout the 1960s and 70s as THE TOWN HAUNTED BY UFOS and other strange anomalies. Thousands gathered to watch the sky and they were not disappointed in what they saw and heard. Exploring the Bizarre hosts Tim Beckley and Tim Swartz travel back in time with British researchers Steve Wills and Ben Emlyn-Jones to relive this monstrous flap, the largest in UK history. Sightings are still being made. You'll be amazed.

STRANGE SPIKED UFO ATTACKS SCOTTISH MAN

By Malcolm Robinson and Sean Casteel

The case of Scottish abductee Robert Taylor is an unusual one, even for a field that is continually steeped in high strangeness.

According to a UK-based website called *UFO Insight*, in an article written by Marcus Lowth, police would treat Robert Taylor's report regarding his apparent out-of-this-world encounter as a case of "criminal assault."

"This would make the incident the only UFO or alien abduction case," Lowth writes, "to be part of a criminal investigation. It is highly probable that one of Scotland's most famous UFO encounters, sometimes referred to as the 'Dechmont Woods Encounter,' involved the alien abduction of Taylor.

On the morning of November 9, 1979, 61 year old Robert Taylor, a forestry worker for the Livingston Development Corp, in West Lothian, Scotland, encountered a "strange dome-shaped" UFO, hovering over a clearing.

"Many have undertaken investigations into the events of November 9, 1979, near Livingston. All agree Taylor himself is a very solid and credible witness. Essentially, most people believe him to be telling the truth entirely. Perhaps the fact that Scotland has more than the average of such sightings makes the account even more interesting."

Author Malcolm Robinson examines the UFO landing area at Dechmont Woods.

The well-credentialed UFO researcher, author and media personality, Malcolm Robinson, also based in the UK, undertook a detailed investigation into the experience of Robert Taylor. Robinson has written a book on the strange events called "The Dechmont Woods UFO Incident, An Ordinary Day, An Extraordinary Event."

"As we have learned," Robinson writes, "the police were called out to investigate this case. They treated this as an assault by 'person' or 'persons' unknown, as they had to take it seriously. Yes, it was way out from the norm of their normal police line of work, but nonetheless, a member of the community had been assaulted by someone or 'something.' And, at the end of the day, it was at the police's responsibility to find out what had gone on, and, as such, visited the location to conduct their enquiry."

RECOUNTING WHAT HAPPENED TO TAYLOR

Lowths' *UFO Insight* article recounts what happened to Taylor, who was attending to his routine duties as a foreman forester employed by the Livingston Development Corporation.

Taylor drove to Dechmont Woods accompanied by his dog. He decided to pull his vehicle to the side of the road so he could stretch his legs and allow his dog to do the same. He did so, on a quiet road near to the M8 motor way.

"As he made his way into the woodland at the roadside," Lowth writes, "a 'flying dome' came into his line of sight. It appeared to be floating, slightly above the tops of the trees. The craft was close enough that he could make out the rough sandpaper-like texture of the black metallic material. An aroma of 'burning brakes' suddenly seemed to fill the air. He noticed two objects that had fallen to the ground from the main craft.

"Of more concern to Taylor," Lowth continues, "he could feel a pulling sensation on his body – as if the craft was dragging him towards it. It was then he realized his hips had 'rods' attached to them that had shot out from the small objects. He began to panic and pull back from it, but his body didn't respond."

The next thing he knew, he was alone in the clearing in the woods. The object had vanished. After gathering his thoughts, Taylor returned to his vehicle, which was still there where he had left it. But his relief was short-lived. The car refused to start, as if drained of power by an unknown source.

He would continue his journey on foot. When he arrived home, his family was aghast at his torn clothing, as well as the cuts and bruises on his face and arms.

His wife asked him what had happened, and he replied that he had been attacked by a spaceship. She, being unsure what to do, called Taylor's employer and boss, Malcolm Drummond. He would always declare that Robert was not a person to "make up stories!" He had no doubts whatsoever of Taylor's genuineness or lack thereof.

When the police were contacted, they had Taylor take them back to the site of the encounter so they could see it for themselves. His torn trousers went off for scientific analysis. The examiners concluded that the damage to his clothes appeared to be in line with a machine-like object gripping and pulling him. Every indication so far was that he was telling the truth.

No less a personage than Nick Pope, a UFO researcher and former Ministry of Defence UFO Project Director, claims that this case offers "no middle ground." Pope believes Taylor is genuine witness who had "little to gain and much to lose" by telling of the incident.

"Robert Taylor passed away in 2007," Lowth writes, "but there remains an interest in his story. Not least because of its apparent authenticity. Taylor never once altered his version of events at any point after the incident."

In an appendix to his book, Robinson provides the official police statement on the case, word for word. A portion of the report follows here.

Robert Taylor shows an illustration of the landed UFO and bizarre spheres that attacked him on November 9, 1979.

THE OFFICIAL POLICE STATEMENT ON THE INCIDENT

Incident at Dechmont Woods, Livingston, West Lothian, on Friday 9th November 1979.

Robert John Taylor, (Author's Comment, actually Robert David Taylor) 61 years, born 25.7.1918, is employed by Livingston Development Corporation as a foreman forester operating from the depot at Rosebank, Livingston.

On Friday 9th November 1979, at 7.45am, Mr. Taylor commenced work at Rosebank, Livingston and attended to some routine tasks. He thereafter went home to Broomieknowe Drive, Deans, Livingston, for breakfast. About 10.10am he left home to continue work and he drove the Bedford pickup truck to the west side of Dechmont Woods, Livingston, where he parked it on a pathway there. It was his intention to carry out a routine inspection of the woods and the surrounding fences and gates. He walked with his dog through the wooded area in a north-easterly direction for a distance of about half a mile, and on reaching a large clearing of some 25 yards x 25 yards, approximately 600 yards north from Dechmont Law, which is in a fairly isolated position, he states he saw a large dome-shaped object on the ground in front of him. He describes the dome-shaped object as being about 30 feet high, grey in colour, changing to translucent continually with a flange around the middle on which there were situated several antenna (sic) with objects similar to rotors on top. It had several round porthole type apertures on the dome shape above the flange.

As Mr. Taylor stood and watched this object, he alleges that two smaller objects appeared from underneath it and approached him in a rolling action, at a vast rate of speed. He describes these objects as being shaped like sea mines with approximately 6 legs attached thereto. These objects arrived one on either side of Mr. Taylor, and he was aware of a strong pungent smell which was overpowering. He states that as he was lapsing into unconsciousness (sic) he was aware of being seized on either side of his legs at the top of his thighs and on feeling pressure under his chin with a burning sensation on it. Mr. Taylor then recollects falling forward, hearing a 'whooshing' sound as if an object was taking off and his dog barking. When he came round, Mr. Taylor felt extremely weak and unsteady on his feet. He half crawled, half staggered to his vehicle and on reaching it, he endeavoured to use the radio to notify his office, but found himself unable to speak. He could not co-ordinate his actions and in an attempt to reverse his vehicle it ran off the pathway and became bogged down in the soft earth.

Mr. Taylor thereafter walked home, a distance of about half a mile, reaching there about 11:15am. His wife, Mary Stevenson or Taylor (66) was at home and she speaks to (sic) his face and clothes being dirty and that he was pale and exhausted looking. When she asked him what had happened, Mr. Taylor replied that he had been attacked by a 'spaceship thing', made mention of a smell and intimated that he required to have a bath. Mrs. Taylor did not detect and smell anything from her husband on his clothing, but she observed that his trousers were slightly torn on the outside of both legs just below the side pockets. Mr. Taylor described to his wife the object he had seen as being like a large spinning top and the smaller objects which had attacked him as being round.

APPENDIX 4

JOHN WARK.   Bathgate

                                                                    Bathgate.
JOHN WARK.   Detective Constable,
                            states:-

I am 34 years of age and have completed 15 years Police Service.

On Friday, 9th November, 1979, I attended at Dechmont Woods, Livingston, where a Unidentified Flying Object had been sighted. On arriving at the locus Detective Inspector McDonald pointed out marks that had been made on the ground. This area of ground had been fenced off, and measuered (sic) approximately 19 feet by 25 feet.

The marks consisted of two tracks, each measuring 10 feet by 1 foot wide. tracks were 7 feet apart. Each track was circled by 20 holes in the ground measuring 3½ins in diameter and 4ins in depth. These holes went into the ground at an angle. I took measurements and photographs of the marks on the ground.

Later at Bathgate Police Station, I prepared a

PRODUCTION No.   sketch plan

of the marks on the ground at Dechmont Woods, Livingston.

The sketch plan is attached to the report.

Police report by Detective John Wark.

INCREDIBLE ALIEN ENCOUNTERS

Malcolm Kenneth Drummond (58), Landscape Forestry Manager, 'Deanbank', Deans South, Livingston, who is in charge of Mr. Taylor, was summoned to the house and learning of the incident, went to the locus; he saw nothing at this time. Mr. Drummond arranged for the Bedford pickup truck, which Mr. Taylor had been driving, to be uplifted and he thereafter returned to Taylor's home; the truck was undamaged.

Gordon James Harvey Adams, M.B., Ch.B, Health Centre, Blackburn, the family doctor, attended at 4 Broomieknowe Drive, Livingston, and examined Mr. Taylor who was complaining of a headache. The only visible injuries found were a graze to his left thigh and a graze under his chin which was barely visible. Dr. Adams found no signs of head injury or brain compression and his temperature and blood pressure were normal. However, as a precautionary measure, Dr. Adams decided to send Mr. Taylor to Bangour General Hospital, Uphall for a head X-ray and an interview with a psychiatrist. Before going to hospital however, Mr. Taylor insisted on returning to the locus with Mr. Drummond. Both men returned to the clearing at locus and there found marks on the ground which appeared to be fresh and could not be accounted for. Following this, both men returned home. Mr. Taylor was conveyed to Bangour General Hospital for examination while Mr. Drummond notified the police at Livingston of the matter. Mr. Taylor, after being taken to Bangour Hospital, signed himself out before examination, having waited approximately 2 hours without being seen by a doctor. About 2.00pm, same date, Detective Inspector MacDonald, with other officers, visited the locus. The weather at this time was dry but it was extremely cold. The grass within the woodland clearing was fairly long. Within the central area of the grass, were two tracks which appeared to have been made by a track laying vehicle. However, no marks were found leading to and from the tracks. The tracks were 10 feet long, 1 foot wide and seven feet apart. The tracks appeared to be reasonably fresh, but rain water was lying on them, which suggested that the marks had not been made that morning. Surrounding the tracks and running between the tracks were a number of small holes. These holes which were all similar and appeared fresh went into the ground at a slight angle for a depth of about 3 inches and they were wide enough to admit the breadth of four fingers.

The clothing worn by Mr. Taylor at the time of the incident has been examined by Lester Knibb and Jennifer Hendry of the forensic science laboratory Force Headquarters, but nothing of significance was found other than the tears previously mentioned with a corresponding tear on the left leg of his underpants. Despite extensive enquiries made, no information has been gained which could indicate what in fact made the marks on the ground at the locus. Mr. Taylor is a respected member of the community and is described as a conscientious (sic) and trustworthy person not likely to invent such a story. It should be noted however, that about 14 years ago he suffered from meningitis and on the 3rd July of this year after complaining to his doctor of severe headaches, he was admitted to the City Hospital Edinburgh for examination. Nothing was found and he was discharged after a few days. After 5 days after this incident, Mr. Taylor was revisited by Dr. Adams. He was found to be well, but declined the doctor's wish that he be seen by a neurologist.

Author's Comment.

Let us take a look at Robert Taylor's official statement to the police about what he encountered.

APPENDIX 5

THE OFFICIAL TESTIMONY OF ROBERT TAYLOR GIVEN TO THE POLICE.

ROBERT (DAVID) TAYLOR, 61 years, born 25.7.1918 at Bonshead near Pitlochry, Foreman Forester (sic) 4 Broomieknowe Drive, Deans, West Lothian.

States: *"I am a foreman forester (sic) employed by Livingston Development Corporation".*

"On Friday 9th November 1979, I started work at 7:45am at Rosebank Nurseries and my first job was to take a caravan and squad to a wood near Bellsquarry. I returned to the nursery and filled out some time sheets for the previous day. I filled up my vehicle, a Bedford pick up with petrol, then went home for my breakfast. I left my home about 10:10am and drove to Woodlands Park and onto Dechmont Woods where I parked the vehicle at the first clearing. I then walked to the second wood and walked down the 'ride' to a part where it meets the transverse 'ride'. At this

point there is a clearing measuring about 75 X 50 yards. It is covered in grass. This would be about 10:30am".

"As I cleared the trees and entered the clearing, I saw this object in front of me. I can describe this object as follows. It was about 30 feet high, but not as high as the trees. It was grey in colour although I got the impression that the top of the dome shape changed from grey to translucent continually. The top of the object was dome shaped and had a flange around the middle on which were situated (sic) several antenna (sic) with objects similar to rotors on the top. There were also several round porthole type apertures on the dome shape above the flange. I do not know what the bottom of the object was like. As I stood and watched the object, I saw two smaller objects appear from underneath it and come shooting over towards me at a fast rate of speed. These objects were shaped like sea mines with about six legs attached thereto. These spheres rolled towards me from one leg to another and they both arrived at my side. At this time I was aware of a strong pungent smell which was overpowering. Although I was lapsing into subconscious (sic) I was aware of being grabbed on either side of my legs at the top of my thighs. I also felt pressure under my chin. I fell forward but was not conscious of being dragged forward. The next thing I knew was a whooshing sound and my dog, which had been running in the trees barking. I do not know if this happened before I lost consciousness or after I came round. When I did come round there was nothing there although I felt extremely weak (sic) and unsteady on my feet. I dragged myself up and half crawled, half staggered to my vehicle".

"On reaching my vehicle I tried to use the radio but could not speak. I tried to drive my vehicle but could not coordinate my actions and as a result of my attempts I got the vehicle bogged down. I then walked home in a dazed condition and when I got to my house I spoke to my wife about the smell and she ran a bath for me and I had a bath. My wife then telephoned my boss Mr. Drummond and he came to the house to see me. I asked him to go to the locus and he did. My doctor, Dr. Adams was summoned and he attended at the house and examined me. I was found to be suffering from a graze on the top of my left thigh. While the Dr. was there, my boss returned and told me that there was nothing to be seen at the locus. However, with the doctor's *permission, I went to the locus with Mr. Drummond and showed him where the machine was. On the ground, I could see several marks where it had been.*

Robinson quotes Detective Constable Ian Wark, the principle police investigator on the case as saying, "Well, as far as the marks on the ground are concerned, I think that some type of machine landed there. I don't think they were put there or were manmade. Something made those marks. To this day, we have no idea."

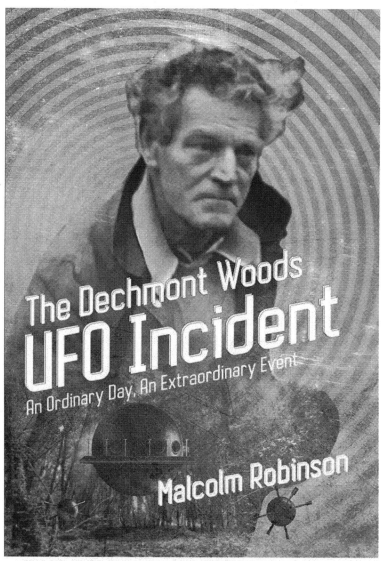

Malcolm Robinson's wonderfully well-researched book, "*The Dechmont Woods UFO Incident: An Ordinary Day, An Extraordinary Event*," is available at Amazon.com. People can contact Malcolm at malckyspi@yahoo.com

CURRICULUM VITAE.

Name: Malcolm Robinson.

(Founder of Strange Phenomena Investigations) 1979

Date of Birth: 01/05/ 57.

I've been interested in the strange world of UFOs and the paranormal for as long as I can remember and in 1979 I formed my own research society entitled, **Strange Phenomena Investigations, (SPI).** Since forming this society, I have moved down to Hastings in East Sussex where I have started up a sister branch to SPI, entitled, **Strange Phenomena Investigations England).** SPI Scotland is now in the hands of a fellow researcher. The aims of SPI are basically to collect, research, and publish, accounts relating to most aspects of strange phenomena, and to purposely endevour to try and come up with some answers to account for what at present eludes us.

Articles by me, have appeared in many of the world's UFO and paranormal magazines. I have assisted many of the U.K's National and Regional newspapers in connection with stories concerning ghosts, poltergeists and UFOs. I have also been interviewed by many of the U.K's major (and minor) radio stations regarding the above mentioned subjects. I have travelled extensively throughout the U.K. on research projects, and I have lectured to various clubs and societies throughout Scotland and England, and I am pleased to say that I have represented my country at International UFO conferences.

My television work has seen me appearing on Scottish Television, BBC Reporting Scotland News. Scottish Television news (STV), American television's **'Sightings'** programme. I have also worked for Japanese television, German television (Twice, ARD and PRO 7). Mexican television. Australian television. Italian television and Australian television. And I have appeared twice on the Michael Aspel show, **'Strange But True'.**

I have also appeared on Grampian television, and completed documentaries for BBC Scotland, **(Cracking Stories)** and the BBC 2 programmes, **'Strange Days'** and **'The Right To Differ'.** Both Lorraine Kelly and Eammon Holmes also interviewed me live (twice) at the G.M.T.V. Television studios in London in regards to a ghost case that our society had been working on. I have also appeared on the **Disney Channel and LWTV's 'Ultimate Questions'.** Plus the **Chris Moyles** Channel 5 show, and also UK Horizons **'Paranormal Files'.** I also did a show with Melinda Messenger **(Loose Lips).** And have assisted **Mentorn TV** for a programme for the Discovery Channel.

In June 2015 I was interviewed live on **This Morning** programme by Amanda Holden and Philip Schofield. I have also completed documentaries for the Paranormal and Unexplained channels for SKY Television. I was featured on the **BBC One Show** in May 2019. I also appeared on Channel 5's Conspiracy programme aired July 2015. These are but some, of the many T.V. shows that I have participated in over the years. I was the very first Scottish UFO researcher to speak in Laughlin Nevada USA in February 2009. I was the first Scotsman to speak on UFOs in France (Strasbourg) a fact that I am very proud of. I was also the first Scotsman to lecture on UFOs in Holland in November 2009. I am also one of the few people on this planet to have gone down into the murky depths of Loch Ness in a submarine. I have written seven books. UFO Case Files of Scotland (Volumes 1 & 2) 'Paranormal Case Files of Great Britain (Volume 1, 2 and 3) 'The Monsters of Loch Ness' (The History and the Mystery). The Dechmont Woods UFO Incident, (And ordinary day, an extraordinary event) My goal in life is to continue researching cases pertaining to the strange world of UFOs and the paranormal, and to hopefully provide some form of answer to account for what at present eludes us.

Malcolm Robinson, Strange Phenomena Investigations (ENGLAND), Flat 5, Unicorn House, Croft Road, Hastings, East Sussex, England, United Kingdom. TN34 3HE.   Mobile: 07949 178 835.

e-mail: malckyspi@yahoo.com   Facebook: www.facebook.com/malcolm.robinson2

Robert Taylor indicates the location where he was confronted by a UFO at Dechmont Woods in Livingston.

UFO LANDING AND OCCUPANTS IN NORMANTON, WEST YORKSHIRE, ENGLAND

A Look Back At An Old Case

By Philip Mantle

When I look back now, I am amazed to find that I have been involved in UFO research and investigation for thirty years. Over those years I have been a member of six UFO groups, four of which were in the UK and two overseas. I've always had an interest in all things "paranormal," but for some reason UFOs gained my full attention in the late 1970's. I've been asked many times which UFO case most impresses me. Is it the UFO crash at Roswell? Or the events at Rendlesham forest in 1980? My answer to this question is none of those. Without doubt, the UFO case that has most impressed me is one that I investigated with Mark Birdsall when we were both part of the Yorkshire UFO Society. Mark now owns and edits the successful *EYE SPY* magazine and he was part of the hugely successful *UFO MAGAZINE* with his late brother, Graham Birdsall, for many years. I doubt if you have ever heard of the following case that Mark and I investigated, but I remember interviewing the witnesses like it was only yesterday.

The following account was first published in the July/August issue of *QUEST* magazine, at the time the hand printed publication of the Yorkshire UFO Society (YUFOS).

On Friday, the 13th of October, 1986, I had been featured in the regional newspaper the Wakefield Express. The article in question told of my involvement with YUFOS and it encouraged its readers to report any UFO sightings to us. We had a number of observations reported to us but one stood out among the others. I was telephoned by a lady by the name of Mrs. Westerman. She began by stating that "I wouldn't believe her." She repeated this several times before she eventually told me that she and a number of her children had witnessed the landing of a UFO near her house in Normanton, West Yorkshire, a few years earlier – complete with humanoid occupants outside it in a nearby field. I quickly took her contact details and, along with Mark Birdsall, arranged an appointment to see her and conduct an interview.

It wasn't long before Mark Birdsall and I interviewed her at her home in Normanton. There were seven witnesses to the events in question, six of whom were the children of Mrs. Westerman. In 1986 Normanton had a large mining community, all of which has gone now. It lies just a few miles outside of the city of Wakefield and the M62 and M1 motorways run close by.

Mrs. Westerman stated that the date of the incident was the summer of 1979. She could not remember the date but speculated that it could have been May or June. Mrs. Westerman went on to inform us that on the day in question she was at home doing the washing. It was a sunny afternoon and a perfect day to get the washing done. Her children were outside playing a ball game and enjoying the sun. They were not on school holiday so it must have been a weekend.

Quest Magazine in 1986. The original hand made publication that detailed the UFO landing at Normanton.

It was around mid-afternoon when her eight year old daughter suddenly ran into the house shouting and crying and telling her mother to "come quick, an aeroplane had just landed in the field." The Westerman't house was an elevated property and was near the end of a cul-de-sac and beyond that were some fields which contained electricity pylons.

Mrs Westerman switched off her washing machine and ran outside. Just a matter of a few hundred yards away, in the fields adjacent to her house, she saw an object on the ground. It was a dull grey colour and had the appearance of a "Mexican hat." Around the object stood three very tall "men," all of whom appeared to be dressed in silver suits. These men seemed to be pointing a dark instrument at the ground.

The children and Mrs Westerman made their way over the field towards this object and stopped at a fence. The men walked to the rear of the object and it rose vertically, stopped in mid-air, and then shot off at an angle at a high rate of speed. Needless to say, they were speechless.

This was a brief description given by Mrs Westerman but we also took advantage of speaking to some of the children as well. Unlike Mrs Westerman, they had actually seen the object come in to land as well. The children were interviewed separately and their story was very consistent. This is what they had to say:

The children had been playing ball behind the house where Mrs. Westerman lived. Eight-year-old Sandra told us how the ball they were playing with had been thrown up into the air as part of the game. As she went to catch the ball, she observed a strange object in the sky. Sandra shouted to the rest of the children to look and

Artist impression by David Sankey of the 1979 UFO landing case.
Copyright David Sankey (www.davidsankey.com)

pointed skyward. They all observed a silvery coloured object, disc-shaped, with a rim around the perimeter. The object was at low level and was seen just above the electricity pylons. It suddenly stopped in mid-air just a few hundred feet up, hovered for a few seconds, before slowly landing in the field. Sandra immediately set off at this point to get her mother.

While Sandra went to fetch her mother, the other children ran towards the landed object but stopped when they reached a fence the enclosed the field. The object itself wasn't very big, perhaps as long as a large Volvo car. However, the "men" around the object all seemed to be very tall and the object in their hand looked similar to a torch. These three very tall humanoids had been seen to emerge from the rear of the landed object. Their heads and face were covered by some kind of "visor." Their silver suits had no zippers, buttons or seams; they had gloves or mittens covering their hands and were wearing a wedged shaped boot. None of these men appeared to communicate with each other and their actions were slow and precise.

Original artist impression: Featured in the 1986 publication is this on-site sketch of the entities by Mark Birdsall.

It was at this point that Mrs. Westerman and her daughter Sandra caught up with the other children. They continued to observe this strange spectacle for about a minute or so. Suddenly, one of the humanoid figures looked up and noticed Mrs. Westerman and the children all standing behind the fence. Now these three very tall men quickly walked away behind the object and were never seen again. A few seconds later the object silently rose from the ground, stopped in mid-air, before moving off at an angle at high speed. All seven individuals were amazed by what they had just seen and Mrs. Westerman, the only adult there, had to calm the children down. All seven witnesses hardly spoke about this incident down the years and had never told anyone outside of the family about it until relating it to me and Mark Birdsall.

All six children related similar accounts to us. There were minor discrepancies, but we expected to find that from different people and several years after it had happened. All of the children were of the opinion that the dark object the men had in their hands and were moving about looked like a torch but it had no light and gave off no sound. The "uniforms" the men were wearing were metallic silver and they would crease when the men moved. All of the witnesses stated quite clearly that both upon landing and departure this object never made a sound.

The location of this event is interesting. The field lies at the end of the houses, which in turn are part of a large housing estate. There are many electricity pylons in the field, making it very difficult for such things as helicopters to land. At our interview, a young man by the name of Andrew Lewis was invited to attend by Mrs. Westerman. He was a friend of the children at the time and, although he did not observe anything unusual himself, he arrived shortly afterwards and confirmed how excited they all were. Another friend was Danny Shore. He was one of the seven original witnesses and was thirteen years old at the time. He estimated that the whole incident lasted no more than between five and ten minutes.

Both Mark and I visited the location and were impressed by the credibility of the witnesses. At no time did they call the object a "spaceship" or a "flying saucer," and there was no way Mrs. Westerman wanted any publicity – she would not even allow us to take her photograph. They were honest, hard-working, down-to-earth people. The children's accounts were consistent and all seven witnesses were in no doubt that they had observed something out of the ordinary. Both Mark and I could find no reason for them to concoct such a story. Mrs. Westerman did say that she was amazed that no one else had seen the object. It was a sunny day and it flew at low level over the housing estate.

So there you have it. This is the one UFO case that most impresses me above all others. Why? Well it's not just because I was involved in it, and it is not necessarily what the witnesses related to us. Instead, it is the witnesses themselves. Normanton had a large miner's community. In fact, Mrs. Westerman's husband worked at a local colliery. My late father worked down the mines all his life and I grew up with people very much like Mrs. Westerman. Added to that, and despite our best efforts, neither Mark Birdsall nor I could find any rational explanation for this event. It either happened as they reported it to us or they were lying, and we could find no evidence of the latter.

This incident has now led me to begin a long-term study of alleged UFO landing reports in the UK. I would therefore like to hear from anyone else, either witness or UFO researcher, who has any information regarding UFO landings in the UK.

I can be contacted on email at: philip.mantle@gmail.com, other methods of contacting me can be located via our blog at: http://flyingdiskpress.blogspot.co.uk/

• • • • • • • • • •

ABOUT THE AUTHOR: Philip Mantle is an internationally published author, lecturer and broadcaster on the subject of UFOs and lives in West Yorkshire, England.

Philip Mantle

ALL IN THE ALIEN FAMILY – THE PINK PANTHER, ET STYLE

By Nigel Watson

Stefan Lobuczek has had a lifetime of strange experiences and alien encounters, which seem to run in his family. Unlike many abductees who are spiritually uplifted by their alien contacts, Stefan's experiences are deeply troubling to him.

He told me in no uncertain terms that, "I do not like them. I hate them. What gives them the right to take me and others? I hate them for that. My feelings haven't changed over the years. I'd be very happy to forget about it, but I can't."

Back in 1964, when he was only five years old, he remembers going into his parents' bedroom to shout at them to get rid of the strange people in his room.

This early memory only came to him after a series of nightmares in 1973, which prevented him from sleeping at night and made him frightened of the dark. He realized that, "I was conditioned not to remember by those who had taken me. They had implanted a false memory in the form of a nightmare. This prevented me from seeing the truth beyond its barriers."

MEETING THE PANTHER

Stefan was eleven years old when he had a major alien experience. At the time he only remembered finding a strange book and feeling a strange presence in his bedroom.

As an adult, he recalls that on the first night he felt a strange presence. Then, a beam of intense light lifted him through his bedroom window and deposited him inside a nearby UFO.

Stefan Lobuczek claims to have had a lifetime of strange experiences and alien encounters.

Here Stefan found himself naked on a metal examination table. Looking down on him were several aliens. He said, "There were the tall thin ones, which I always think of as the Pink Panthers, but without the tail; they had big black eyes and they floated about a lot. The other beings, of which there seemed to be more short, grey and wrinkly and had a pungent odour I can't begin to describe."

A silver object was put in his arm and he felt a terrible pressure inside his head. And an alien, who looked like a Pink Panther cartoon character, reassured him via telepathy that he would be returned home soon.

Another memory of this, or a similar abduction two nights later, involved him being taken down a long corridor. He said, "The lighting was blue and was concealed in the recess either side of the walk way. The walls narrowed to the ceiling. I remember running my fingers along the wall and it felt metallic, silky smooth and was cold to the touch. The corridor led to a dark holding area where I was left and the door closed. I was in the room with other children. None of us spoke and I felt sick and very cold."

A striking part of his alien memories is of seeing several clear cases holding human body parts and a cylindrical case containing a severed Neanderthal head.

After writing about these encounters on his website, a person contacted him to say that he had seen a UFO hovering over Stefan's home during the period when he had his encounters. This indicates to Stefan that there is more to his early experiences than just imagination or fantasy.

The same group of Pink Panther-type aliens seem to have kept a regular watch on his life and have made contact on many occasions since he was five.

Often his childhood memories come at unexpected moments. One memory was triggered a few years ago when he was looking at an old family photograph taken in the garden of their home in Birmingham in June 1965. As he looked at it he realized this was the exact spot where he had dragged his older brother in the middle of the night, sometime in 1964.

Photograph of Stefan and his family taken in the garden of their Birmingham home in June 1965. Stefan (front row, second from right), remembered that this was the same location where he and his older brother had a bizarre experience in 1964.

Stefan said: "Then I remembered us both being surrounded by the brightest of light; nothing could be seen through it to the outside of it. I have no further recollection of the events that followed.

"My granddad, my two sisters and I share these strange encounter experiences but it wasn't until I saw that photograph that I knew that my brother was also implicated in this bizarre nightmare of events."

DRIVING LESSONS

One night in 1986, he saw a bright light in the sky as he was driving down a country lane. He suddenly forgot about driving down this lane and was startled to see a rabbit in his car headlights. Shocked out of his trance, he got out of his car and realized he was lost.

He got back in his car, and as he reversed into a field he saw a grey-type alien standing by the gate. Knowing they are not very pleasant characters, he drove off as fast as possible.

In the middle of 2009, he was warned indirectly not to openly talk about his experiences, but he is not intimidated. In defiance of these warnings, he gave a speech into his research into Electronic Voice Phenomenon (EVP) at the Unitarian Society for Psychical Studies Annual Conference on 04 September 2010.

As an indication that he should have heeded the warnings, he said that after the conference:

"On the way back, just a little after midnight Sunday, 05 September 2010, between Great Hucklow and Buxton, the car suddenly started to change modes from CD, to radio and Aux input and also in volume, the Sat Nav was also going crazy in a way not consistent with loss of satellite data. I remember vaguely stopping the car and getting out of the vehicle. It was very dark and there were woods either side of the road. The car stereo going crazy had made it hard to concentrate on driving safely and it wouldn't power off.

"So by pulling over and turning off the ignition, I thought this might somehow reset the sound system. The next thing I remember I'm outside the car for no apparent reason, the car door is open yet the courtesy light isn't illuminating the interior.

"I then felt very sick for no apparent reason and vomited. Then, as if no time had passed, I'm standing outside my car miles away in a lay by somewhere on the A38 (my route home) feeling sick. It then seemed to take ages to navigate back home and when I got home at about 2:45 AM I continued to be sick. This journey should have taken me no more than an hour and fifteen minutes. I cannot account for an hour plus added to my journey time."

It is Stefan's view that the aliens come from outer space and can use different dimensions to visit us as they will. What most upsets him is the recurring childhood memory of the limbs and severed head he saw onboard the UFO. These alien experiences and nightmares attack him at random, literally out of the blue, and he sees them as a lifelong plague. Why they are here and why they are doing this is a constant mystery to him as well as to the rest of us.

FAMILY ENCOUNTERS

Stefan's youngest sister remembers that, when he was 11 years old and she was 5 years old, she woke up one night because a bright light was shining through the curtains. It seemed as bright as day in her room and she could hear people moving about in the house. The same thing happened again two nights later. This seems to confirm Stefan's alien encounter at that time. She also said that their older sister at that time had a dream of being on an operating table in a spacecraft. When Stefan asked her about this, she became upset and refused to talk about it.

A STRANGE WIND

In recent years, Stefan's youngest sister was woken in the middle of the night because the bedroom curtains were blowing about. Assuming the window was open, she got up to close it, but found it was closed. Looking outside she saw a funnel of wind that came towards her and entered her mouth.

The next instant she found herself downstairs with her arms outstretched like Jesus on the cross. On her right she saw an angel and on the left a jester. She felt impelled to say the Lord's Prayer; after stumbling over the words she finally got it right. At that moment, the jester turned into an angel, and she was levitated backwards up the stairs. The funnel of wind left her mouth as she banged against the landing wall, and then she woke up in her bed.

MISSING TIME

When Stefan's Granddad was courting a girl in Poland before World War II, he saw a bright light in the forest after leaving her home. He walked towards the light to see what it was, and then he suddenly found himself walking in the opposite direction. Looking at his watch he found it was two hours later than he expected.

$$C \ (E=mc^2) \text{ The Collective consciousness of energy exchange}$$

Stefan Lobuczek

EBE Hybrid.

INCREDIBLE ALIEN ENCOUNTERS

REMOTE VIEWING

When Stefan was 22 years old, he worked nights at a car parts warehouse in Nuneaton, which was built over an old coal mine. Here the staff reported several strange events, but the most outstanding occurred one Friday night at 10pm.

At the time, he regarded it as an Out-of-the-Body Experience, but now thinks it an example of remote viewing. He was operating a computer ordering system, and, when he was satisfied that it was running properly, he placed three chairs together and went to sleep. Then, he says:

"The next thing I remembered was walking out of data control into the open plan office area. I could see Alex the security guard fast asleep. I went into the computer room but don't remember opening the door. I proceeded to the paper console and, as it was at waist level, I leant over it to view how many orders were left to process. I would normally place my hands either side of the console for support but don't remember seeing my hands. This didn't seem abnormal at the time. I took visual note of the orders left to process and proceeded back through the door into the open plan office. Again, don't remember actually opening the door.

"I could see Alex still fast asleep, but now he was snoring quite loudly. I proceeded to data control to go back to sleep. However, when I got there, I could see someone else fast asleep. After a moment's viewing and the subsequent shock, I realized that I was the person asleep. Now, just like people claim when they die, my whole life seemed to flash before me and I just freaked, thinking I had died.

"Then, as if I was on the end of a very powerful elastic band under tension, I shot back into my body. I sort of filled up from boots to head with such a force that I sat bolt upright and banged my head on the desk that my head was asleep under."

PORTRAITS OF ENCOUNTERS

Kim Carlsberg's experiences and thoughts about them are very similar to Stefan Lobuczek's. She also regards them as beings from another dimension who are able to travel to our planet, and become real and solid in form when we see them.

Kim sees them during dreams or through screen memories that protect her from the full impact of these encounters. For example, they take the form of owls or other animals.

When working on the "Baywatch" TV show in 1988, she saw a moon-like UFO and a week later had a horrifying encounter when she woke up on an operating table inside a UFO.

Since then she has had many other encounters with the aliens, and in her previous book, "***Beyond My Wildest Dreams: Diary of an Alien Abductee,***" she describes these encounters, including giving birth to hybrid babies.

These experiences seem to run in her family, and she thinks there are a range of aliens that can instantly visit us from their home planets. She has had dreams of fleets of UFOs in our skies, which indicate the possibility they might physically invade us one day. Otherwise they seem to stick to contacting individuals and their families via dreams, telepathy and mind manipulation.

In her latest book, "***The Art of Close Encounters,***" she has collected the testimonies of abductees and illustrations of their experiences. As might be expected, most of these cases are from the USA, but she does include some intriguing British alien experiences.

Stephen Martin, for example claims he has seen tall lizard-like beings. He said:

"I saw two of these giant fellows during the same encounter that I saw praying mantis-like beings. At about nine feet tall, these guys kinda stuck out from the crowd.

"...I saw a huge brown dusty desert. I was told that this world spins on its side, so this area of the planet always faces the planet's main star. This desert is locked in perpetual day, so its inhabitants have learned to build their towns and cities underground. I saw buildings actually carved into the side of canyon walls and cliff sides."

Helen Sanderson thinks "Draconian" beings live under Glastonbury. One encounter took place with a Draconian who told her "We were ninety meters below ground in what I know to be one of the empty magma chambers of a long-dead volcano."

<u>REFERENCE</u>

'The Art of Close Encounters' website at:

www.closeencounterspublishing.com

ABOUT THE AUTHOR: Nigel Watson has researched and investigated historical and contemporary reports of UFO sightings. He has written for numerous books, publications and websites such as *Fortean Times*, *Strange Magazine*, *Paranormal Magazine* and *Wired*. He is the author of such books as: *"Portraits of Alien Encounters"* (1990), *"Supernatural Spielberg"* (with Darren Slade, 1992) and editor/writer of *"The Scareship Mystery: A Survey of Phantom Airship Scares, 1909-1918"* (2000). He has also contributed to the books: *"Alien Bloodlust: Are There Vampires in Space?"*, and *"Screwed By The Aliens"*, both published by Inner Light/Global Communications. His latest book is: *"Alien Abductions in the USA"*, published by McFarland.

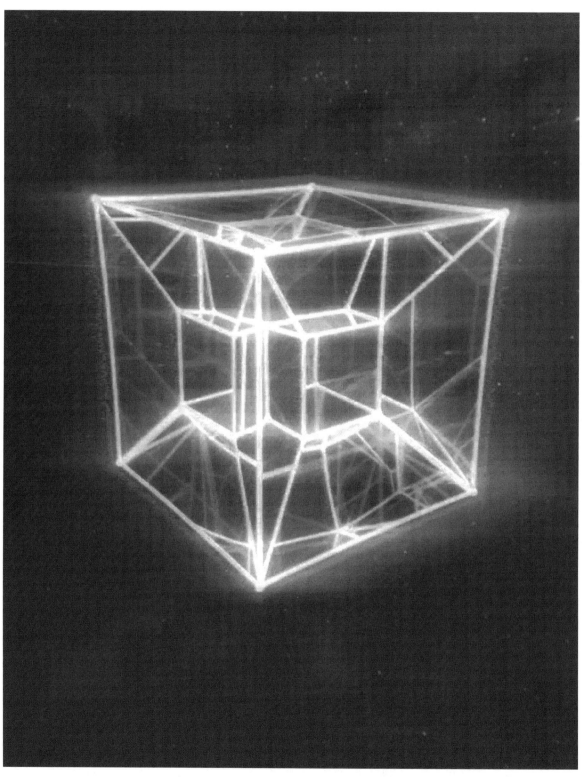

The Tesseract is a three dimensional representation of a four dimensional object.
Is it possible that the image could cause a weakening of reality?

THE STRANGE AFFAIR OF JAMES MARTIN

By Brian Allan

PUBLISHER'S NOTE: As a result of a very early close encounter with the otherworld, Brian Allan has had an abiding interest in UFO's and all kinds of paranormal and occult phenomena throughout his life. Although he had initially confined his interest in the subject to a passive role, involving study via books etc., it is only in the past forty years or so that he actually became involved in an active "hands on" basis. During this period of time he has witnessed at first hand some genuinely remarkable phenomena and has also met some truly remarkable and talented people. He has written twelve books, all dealing with various aspects of the paranormal in one way or another, and he is currently the editor of the online publication, *"Phenomena Magazine."* He has also been privileged to receive the Strange Phenomena Investigations prestigious Tartan Skull award for services to Ufology and the paranormal in Scotland. All back issues of *"Phenomena Magazine,"* which is absolutely free, can be accessed at www.phenomenamagazine.co.uk

· · · · · · · · · ·

"We are part of a symbiotic relationship with something which disguises itself as an extra-terrestrial invasion so as not to alarm us." Terrence McKenna

James had his encounters during the 1990s and they lasted over a number of years; unfortunately, they also brought his marriage to breaking point. There is a clear link between what happened to James and the experiences recounted by shamans and others who have ingested psychoactive substances, i.e. that had visions, and so did James. The method he employed was discovered by accident and was the result of a sustained lack of sleep combined with the consumption of quantities of amphetamines. He is at great pains to stress that he did not take large quantities of this chemical, nor was it over a long period of time. He also indicated that when he resumed a normal sleep pattern and stopped taking the amphetamines, the visions stopped. However, during this period in his life, he began to see what could, depending on the context, easily be interpreted as either extraterrestrials or indeed fairies, because the similarities were remarkable.

He witnessed "spacecraft" of various shapes, both saucer-shaped and spherical, emerging from an earth bank, travel down what seemed to be a "runway" of sorts (it was lined on both sides with tiny but bright lights). Some flew off into the air while others settled into the trees surrounding the area. He also saw some of the craft on the ground with the occupants gathered around them carrying out various tasks. In every case, other than a very few humans (or humanoids), the occupants and all the other entities he observed were all quite small.

As already mentioned he described the spacecraft as both saucer-shaped and spherical and both types were silver in colour, hinting at them being metallic in nature. He also commented on their propulsion systems.

James Martin reported that he saw "spacecraft" of various shapes, both saucer-shaped and spherical.

"The only ones I witnessed were the saucer and the sphere. The sphere showed nothing visible. The saucer; on the under-belly an orange flame would start to lick around in a circular motion, speeding up until it became an orange glow. The saucer would rise into the air then [there was] a flash, very bright, leaving two rings of white light momentarily hanging in the air as the saucer vanished."

James also described some of the entities he saw: "A grey type with a small box/trunk instead of a mouth and a short, stocky-type being with a bald head and visible vertebra running across the skull from forehead to nape of the neck. The ones I saw a lot [of were] similar to greys, but with long necks with visible vertebrae, large spherical black eyes and 3 fingers and a thumb. I once heard them speak in deep 'growling' voices and [the] language [was] not recognizable.

"There was an apparent hierarchical system, soldiers, armed, and those wearing silver metallic skullcaps, which ended in a v shape between the eyes. The skullcap was patterned in glyphs similar to Egyptian (hieroglyphs). The aliens types not skull capped would always be wearing white overalls when working on any of the craft, I'm not sure if these were also the pilots. I got the impression the craft were also sentient. And finally as I said, I did see humans as well. [Ibid]

"But here's the 'biggy,' the whole deal involves kingdoms. The kingdoms I saw had a human-type king with [a] crown, plus princesses. And last, one morning I was privy to an appearance in the sky about a mile away of, I think, 4 or 5 heads and shoulders of these last described alien types, but not with skullcaps.

"They just appeared, seemed to watch me for a few minutes, then went. I think they may have been 'THE GODS', (James's emphasis,) I don't know. When we were living in a small cottage in Bradford I saw in the private garden about 30 or 40 different craft [of] all shapes and sizes in the trees [and] in the garden. Right in the middle of the garden [were] 3 angels, human with the huge wings exactly like the religious paintings etc. They just stood there smiling. I did the same; I was in shock and in awe. Then they faded, [but] the craft stayed for hours [Ibid]."

Intriguingly, he also mentions that he witnessed one of the spacecraft "die" (his description). During this process, its bright silver finish faded, turned brown and the device gradually "vanished." He described it like this: *"It materialised down the runway okay but instead of drifting into a tree it drifted to the ground. The hatch opened [and] 5 aliens got out, they went off to [a] rest area then 5 humans, naked, got out and ran their hands frantically over the saucer. It changed from silver to grey then started to [turn] brown; it was at this point they left it. One of the other saucers then floated down and they got inside. After their rest they went and stood behind an orange screen one at a time; they appeared to shrink into nothing. I went to the melting saucer which was now just a mound giving off intense heat. Within I think an hour there was no sign it had ever been there, apart from [some] flattened grass with a slight discoloration."*

One must ask just exactly what did James actually witness? One curious similarity between what James witnessed and what has been seen in the vicinity of the Neolithic burial ground of Cairnpapple Hill in Scotland, are the appearance of "glowing rings" hanging in mid air above the burial site. Is this some sort of circumstantial corroboration for both sightings? In addition there are other points of convergence between James's encounters and the occurrences at Utah's Sherman Ranch. Even taking this into account, there is still an undercurrent of curiosity asking if it was all a hallucination produced by a combination of lack of sleep potentiated through the consumption of amphetamines, or was it something else entirely? This is of course possible, but what he describes, although highly detailed, is no more fantastic or unlikely than many other reported encounters with these strange and unearthly beings.

Is this yet one more example of Terrence McKenna's opening observation about some entity disguising itself to avoid alarming us? To help us appreciate James's state of mind, we should be aware that lack of sleep allows certain brain chemicals to build up. Amongst others, this includes serotonin, which is one of the main neurotransmitters associated with mood and also one closely associated with altered states of awareness; small wonder then that most ghost sightings and E/T encounters are at night when we are tired. Most people have experienced feelings of unease and "edginess" when tired, or have caught glimpses of movement from the corner or the eye. James appears to have accidentally succeeded in achieving a similar state to the shamans and mystics who deliberately exploit the properties of specific plant compounds to achieve transcendence and contact.

Another fairly common symptom when encounters with alternate realities are experienced is an odd separation or dislocation from reality; I have experienced this bizarre feeling myself on several occasions when involved in cases involving cleansings (or exorcisms to use the more emotive term). When the entity leaves, there is a feeling of complete stillness; a strange and tangible quality of silence not normally found in everyday life. There is also a clear impression that, although one can see other people in the vicinity, no one is there with you. I am aware that this sounds almost schizophrenic, but it is an accurate, if subjective, impression.

It seems to be an element of what the respected British paranormal researcher, Jenny Randles, called, *"The Oz factor,"* which frequently occurs in some classes of encounters with non-human entities, I stop short of calling them extraterrestrial because there is no convincing evidence that they are. Another facet of the Oz Factor is the frequent discovery that time has in some way been altered; this is known as "missing time." Just why this should occur is as yet unknown and, while it might well be created by the conditions necessary for anomalous encounters to occur, it might equally be the result of misinterpreted neurological malfunctions, although this would obviously not explain aspects involving the physical relocation of the experiencers.

NON-PHYSICAL PORTALS

What defines a non-physical portal? Surely this encompasses transitions accomplished without the use of any physical mechanism, although as we have seen the term "mechanism" may be difficult to isolate and define in terms of our understanding of what technology is. This definition must therefore include the use of hallucinogens and other methods designed to induce altered states, but it should also take into account such artefacts as labyrinths which were used as aids to contemplation and meditation. Although this is undoubtedly true, is it possible that the design of the labyrinth emulates the circular motion of the "fairy dance"?

Mysterious "glowing rings" have been spotted hovering over the Neolithic burial ground of Cairnpapple Hill in Scotland.

If this is so, then is the similarity accidental or based on ancient arcane lore and an instinctive use of "technology" in the widest sense of the word? In addition, a wide range of phenomena appear to manifest in window areas with no clear reason why, although there are many viable theories The range of entities encountered, be they "the Faerie" or "Skinwalkers," have many features in common with the inhabitants of Ted Holiday's Goblin Universe and John Keel's ultra-terrestrial dimensions. Also in common with both of them: they have the same claims to reality. One other aspect of what we see here is the distinct possibility that these entities are here right now and coexisting beside us.

This is not a fanciful as it might at first appear; bear in mind that when the famous explorer, Captain James Cook, first made landfall in the South Pacific, it is claimed that the islanders literally could not see the large boats in which Cook and his men had arrived. They could see the small vessels in which the sailors rowed ashore, but not the main craft. They were unable to do so because they had no frame of reference by which to judge what was there. All they could discern was, at best, large waves and at worst absolutely nothing at all. It was not until they had been taken out to them and touched then that they actually "saw" them.

Nor is this an isolated case. Native American tribes, when first shown paintings, could not see any images, only a confusing array of colours. They had to be told what was there and only then did the images become visible. So it may be with us, a relatively sophisticated civilisation, so tied into our own perceptions that we cannot see what is in front of us. They may be here hiding in plain sight and it is only by the use of mind-altering chemicals either ingested or injected, or even produced in our brains by physical techniques, that they become visible to us; unfortunately the effects on the viewer are quite unpredictable.

Be that as it may, from what data is available, as already suggested, there appear to be significantly stronger magnetic fields in the vicinity of window areas and, as we have seen in the case of Cairnpapple Hill, there is, in addition, a large and complex microwave tower, which is an excellent possible source of raw energy. The wide range of the phenomena, which are by no means confined to purely UFO sightings, tend to support a particular group of hypotheses suggesting that most, if not all of the happenings at the various sites, have a common root cause sometimes referred to as the psychosocial hypothesis.

This view assumes that UFO's and their associated phenomena are identical in every meaningful sense to paranormal events like hauntings, apparitions and poltergeist manifestations. Indeed, it can be argued that there is even a spiritual aspect to many of the encounters and it is clear that they have occurred since human beings walked the face of the Earth. With the advent of religion, they were considered as creatures of either God or Satan, when in reality they are neither – they originate in the spaces behind convention and thrive in the cracks in the façade of reality. As far as proof goes, except for the experiments carried out by the US Department of Mines, in all the cases presented here nothing can be conclusively proved one way or another, which makes this an easy target for skeptics and debunkers. Like the belief in a Creator God, it may be a matter of faith alone.

THE TESSERACT

A further example of the portal phenomenon may be found in the construction of a geometric figure called the Tesseract, sometimes known as the "Hypercube."

Resembling a cube within a cube, when actually constructed as a wire-frame object, the figure is said to be a three dimensional representation of a four dimensional object. From a personal point of view, I can state that on at least one occasion when I was looking at the image of a Tesseract on a computer monitor, for an instant I was not seated looking at the drawing, *I was inside the image looking out.*

The sensation was both unsettling and alarming and I was compelled to quickly push myself away from the monitor; the sensation could not have lasted for more than a fraction of a second, but it was very real and disorienting. Whether or not this was some transient effect produced by involuntary meditation or whether it was a weakening of reality caused by the image itself is obviously open to question, but it seems to have parallels with the arcane figures and symbols traditionally used to operate magical rituals. I have not tried to replicate what occurred with the Tesseract.

• • • • • • • • •

ABOUT THE AUTHOR: Brian Allan has had an abiding interest in paranormal and occult phenomena in all their varied forms for as long as he can remember. Although he has experienced strange and unusual encounters from a very early age, he initially confined his interest in the subject to a passive role involving studying the subject via books etc, and it is only in the past thirty years or so that he actually became involved on a "hands on" basis. During this period of time Brian has been privileged to meet some genuinely fascinating and spiritual people and witness at first hand some truly wondrous sights. Brian has also written and had twelve books published, all dealing with the paranormal in one way or another. Currently Brian is the editor of Phenomena Magazine and a regular speaker on the conference circuit.

His most recent book is: "***Project Phenomena: Evaluating the Paranormal.***"

ALIEN ODDITIES IN HISTORIC FRENCH UFO WAVE

By Timothy Green Beckley & Sean Casteel

"It was made in the 1680s in France and the design on one side certainly looks like it could be a flying saucer in the clouds over the countryside," said Kenneth E. Bressett, a former President of the American Numismatic Association and owner of the curious coin.

The French have a history of UFOs. The average citizen doesn't mock the subject. Going back to the early and mid-1950s aliens of one type or another – usually small, but tough as nails, humanoids – were landing and fighting the French as if it were the end of the Great War. A lot of these dramatic incidents made it into the press and the subject was more or less taken seriously from the get go. Landing pads were found in the soil out in the countryside and mushrooms and other vegetation was growing to exceptional size after being zapped by the extraterrestrials, or however we wish to define the place of their origin. The French have always had their UFO experts – for example Jacques Vallee – and numerous authors whose sensationalistic words no doubt kept many a French reader up late at night. So when the French government decided in March of 2007 to release some of its classified UFO files, your typical Parisian might not have been overly impressed, but the rather effete *Washington Post* did take notice.

"On an August day," an article in the paper begins, "two children tending a herd of cows outside a village in central France reported seeing 'four small black beings' fly from the ground and slip headfirst into a sphere that shot skyward in a flash of light and left behind a trail of sulfuric odors.

"The alleged extraterrestrial sighting, described by the French government as 'one of the most astonishing observed in France,' is among 1,600 UFO case files spanning the last half century that the country's space agency opened to the public for the first time Thursday (March 22, 2007)."

In what the venerable American newspaper called "an unprecedented move," the voluntary decision to release the files in France made available more than 100,000 pages of witness testimony, photographs, film footage and audiotapes from its secret UFO archives.

Most Western countries, the article said, the U.S. included, consider such records classified matters of national security.

UFOs STILL AN OPEN QUESTION

Within three hours of posting the first cases, the French space agency's web server crashed, overwhelmed by the flood of viewers seeking a first glimpse of the official government evidence on a subject long a target of both fascination and ridicule. The material dates back as far as 1954 and is being posted to enhance scientific research into what the French government calls "unexplained aerospace phenomena."

"The data we are releasing," said Jacques Patenet, who heads the Group for the Study and Information on Unidentified Aerospace Phenomena, "doesn't demonstrate the presence of extraterrestrial beings. But it doesn't demonstrate the impossibility of such a presence either. The question remains open."

Patenet also said that a few dozen cases among the 1,600 to be opened to the public "are very intriguing and can be called UFOs."

Most of the cases in the files were determined to be caused by atmospheric anomalies or the mistaken perception of such things as airplane lights or simply hoaxes. One file case described how investigators proved that a man was lying about being abducted by aliens when blood tests failed to prove he had recently experienced the weightlessness of space travel.

Jacques Patenet heads the Group for the Study and Information on Unidentified Aerospace Phenomena.

FRENCH CHILDREN ARE VISITED

"In one of the cases investigators consider most credible," the article continues, "a 13-year-old boy and his 9-year-old sister were watching over their family's cows near the village of Cussac on August 29, 1967, when the boy spotted 'four small black beings' about 47 inches tall, according to documents released Thursday. Thinking they were other youngsters, he shouted to his sister, 'Oh, there are black children!'

"But as they watched, the four beings became agitated and rose into the air, entering the top of what appeared to be a round spaceship, about 15 feet in diameter, which hovered over the field. Just as the sphere rose up, one of the passengers emerged from the top, returned to the ground to grab something, then flew back to the sphere. The sphere rose silently in a spiral pattern, then 'became increasingly brilliant' before disappearing with a loud whistling sound. It left a 'strong sulfur odor after departure,' the report said."

The children raced home in tears and their father called the local police, who duly noted the sulfur smell and the dried grass left behind when the sphere took off. Investigators said they were impressed at how consistent the stories told by the children and other witnesses were under further questioning. The investigators concluded that, "No rational explanation has been given to date of this exceptional meeting."

AIR FRANCE SIGHTING

One of the most detailed inquiries involved the report of an Air France crew flying near Paris on January 28, 1994.

"Three crew members spotted a large, reddish-brown disk 'whose form is constantly changing and which seems very big in size.' As the passenger plane crossed its trajectory, the object 'disappeared on the spot.' Radar signatures confirmed an object of the same size and location described by the crew and led investigators to conclude that 'the phenomenon is not explained to date and leaves the door open to all the assumptions.'"

MORE COMMENTS FROM PATENET

Patenet, the lead investigator for the French space agency's team, said he and his colleagues receive about 100 new cases every year, of which only 10 percent lead to further investigations.

"In 99 percent of the cases," he said, "the witnesses are perfectly sincere. They saw something. Most of the time, what they saw is a perfectly natural phenomenon that has been perceived in an erroneous way."

Patenet said he has never seen a UFO, though he believes it is unlikely that we are alone in the universe.

"But the probability of various civilizations coming across each other is also very slim," he said. To read some of the French files in English, go to http://geipan-english.blogspot.com/

A STRUGGLE WITH HELMETED HUMANOIDS

A French tabloid illustrates Marius Dewilde's strange encounter, adding to the sensationalism of the event.

The publication *Nord Éclair*, September 16, 1954, announced the encounter of Marius Dewilde. On the night of September 10, 1954, Dewilde was at home in Quarouble, Nord, France. His house was built near some train tracks. At 22:30, his dog started to bark desperately. Dewilde went outside with a flashlight and the dog itself. He walked towards the tracks, where he saw an object some 6 or 7 meters away from him. Behind him, he could hear some steps. When he pointed the flashlight, Dewilde saw two small humanoid figures who were as short as children. When the light was pointed to their heads, it was reflected as if they were wearing a mirror helmet or some kind of shiny material.

Suddenly, a light beam shot off the object he saw on the tracks and left him totally paralyzed. He slowly looked back and saw a door opening in the object behind him. The beings boarded the object and it took off towards the sky, changing its colors as it flew.

When he recovered his ability to move, he attempted to tell his wife and then his neighbor what he had just seen, but neither of them had seen nor heard anything. He then tried the local police, who sent some police officers to his home. Dewilde could not approach the point where everything happened because it made him feel sick, giving the officers a certainty that his story was not a hoax. Also, objects which are energized by batteries, like Dewilde's flashlight and telephone, stopped working. Before sunrise, investigators were already thoroughly covering the scene of the strange event.

AFTERMATH

The Evening Star, October 19, 1954, reported the encounter of Marius Dewilde and the other minor incidents that happened on the following days. When people were investigating the location of the object's appearance, an approaching train produced a very loud noise when passing by, making it stop. A six meter depression was found on the exact point where the object had landed, and was immediately said to be the cause of the noise.

During daylight, more details were discovered: the small rocks placed under the train tracks were all carbonized on the depression. The pieces of wood between the steel lines also featured some symmetric marks.

The incident was made famous by the local magazine *Radar*.

More small incidents were added to this main happening: Dewilde suffered from respiratory problems, his dog died three days after the encounter, three cows died on farms nearby (and their autopsies revealed that their blood had been totally and unexplainably removed). Also, several local people claimed sights of objects and creatures similar to the ones witnessed by Dewilde.

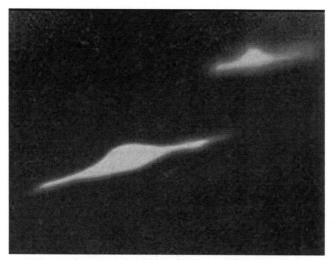

Here comes the fleet? Well, at least two UFOs recorded over Chantureine, France in 1973.

A SWEDISH UFO MYSTERY – HUMAN ABDUCTIONS AND THE APPEARANCE OF THE DREADED MEN IN BLACK

By Hakan Blomqvist

Art by Carol Ann Rodriguez

PUBLISHER'S NOTE: We have been exchanging information with this very special Swedish UFO group, which may house the only full time UFO library in the world, where my papers and files will probably go after my passing. This chapter was written a couple years back but is just as germane today. The Men In Black (MIB) have been active since the first reports started coming in back in the 1890s.

Håkan Blomqvist (co-founder, archivist and chairman of the AFU board) was born in Karlstad, Sweden, in 1952. University studies at Stockholm University: history of religion, philosophy, ethnology. Now he is a librarian at the Norrköping Public Library.

Håkan has been a member of UFO-Sweden since 1970, first as chairman of a local group, UFO-Södertälje. In 1973 he co-founded Arbetsgruppen för ufologi which, in January 1980, transformed into the Archives for UFO Research Foundation. Håkan has been a board member of UFO-Sweden since 2008 and is presently the vice-chairman of this national group. At the archives Håkan specializes in the personal and organizational files kept from paranormal activists, groups and organizations.

Published works: *"UFO – I myt och verklighet"* (*UFO in myth and reality*), NTB-Parthenon, 1993, 133 p. *"Främlingar på vår jord. UFO-kontakter i Sverige"* (*Aliens on earth. UFO contacts in Sweden*), Parthenon, 2009, 129 p. *"En resa i tiden: UFO-Sveriges historia 1970-2010"* (*A travel in time: The history of UFO-Sweden 1970-1995*), *"UFO-Sverige,"* 2010. 102 p. Hundreds of articles in various magazines and newspapers.

Special interests: Contactee cases, psychological and religious aspects of the UFO phenomenon. The theosophical/esoteric tradition and its connections to the UFO phenomenon. Building of archives for the preservation of paranormal history. Check out his regular blog in Swedish on ufology and the work at AFU.

As you read Hakan's report, please note that "Helge's" real name was later revealed to be Richard Höglund.

• • • • • • • • • •

Håkan Blomqvist

During my years as an active UFOlogist in Sweden I have come across several UFO contact cases. In the beginning of the 1970s, I heard frequent rumors of a remarkable case involving the infamous men in black. Although being very skeptical, I started collecting notes from various sources. This was not easy, as several of the people involved were reluctant to reveal what they knew. Because of the sinister aspects of the case, they had no wish to become mixed up in it again.

As the years passed, some of the main witnesses became close friends of mine, and so more and more I learned of the full details of the case. Today my file on the case has grown to large proportions. Still, I probably would never have presented this case save for an unusual coincidence. In 1979 a similar but totally unrelated MIB case emerged from an unexpected source. This incident confirmed much of the data I had acquired earlier. I understand that there will be grave doubts regarding this information, but I am honestly presenting the facts as I know them.

INCREDIBLE ALIEN ENCOUNTERS

THE SOURCES

Most of the information has been obtained from three different second hand sources. All of them were closely related to the witness "Helge's" (actual name Richard Höglund) original experiences. Personally I have only had a short telephone conversation with Helge, in 1973. He then stated that he was not allowed to tell anything and that people would be shocked if they knew of these things. The initial experience was first presented by Ernst Linder, then chairman of I Foloqiska Sall, a Stockholm-based lecture group now discontinued. Linder was the first person who heard of the case and made the initial investigations.

HEALED BY UFO ENTITIES

Helge is an ordinary Swedish worker, age now around 60, rock blaster by profession. He is a down-to-earth man and an atheist. The only difference from the commonplace is that he is very telepathic, which has gotten him into trouble several times because he can see when a man is lying and he doesn't hesitate to say so. In December 1985, Helge was severely troubled by a stone in his kidneys. On December 9th, the day before his operation, he felt a sudden urge to take a long walk on a frozen lake in the vicinity of his home. At that time he lived with his wife in a small town not far from Gothenburg. He took his dog along and started out on the lake.

Suddenly, the· dog began to run in circles like he was mad. Helge had to put him in leash. There was a whining sound in the air. As Helge looks up he observes an object about 8m in diameter and 3m in height. It was saucer-shaped and translucent but not like glass. He could see figures moving inside. The object came closer to the ground in a spiraling movement. It stopped before touching the ice and a dark tube was lowered from under the object. This tube was seemingly made of a soft material since it moved in the wind. He felt a breeze o£ hot air with a clear smell of hyacinth reaching him.

Helge first thought that this must be a Russian machine but soon changed his mind. From the tube, four entities floated down like in an invisible elevator and walked up to him. They were three men and one woman. Except for wearing translucent overalls, they were totally naked. One of the men seemed old while the others were younger. They were of normal height, had very large, dark, somewhat slanted eyes and perfect teeth. Their skin had no blemishes and there was absolutely no hair on their bodies, not even genital hair. Helge was especially fascinated by their ears, which were large and pointed. He could almost see into their heads, he thought. The men seemed very strong, wrestler types with bull necks. As a whole, they had a slight oriental look about them. The entities were covered by the clear plastic overalls which looked like they were held out from the body by air pressure.

Helge became very confused, but not afraid. They began a conversation through signs and drawings in the snow. The entities were very fascinated by his hair. He had to remove his cap several times, and they laughed and pointed. When he tried to touch their overalls, they quickly moved back. They didn't want him to touch them. With a small black package, they sprayed a gas-like substance on everything before they touched it, even the dog. The dog didn't like this as the gas had a strong smell about it. Helge even smelled of hyacinth several days afterwards, which made his wife wonder if he had already bought flowers for the coming Christmas.

"Helge's" (actual name Richard Höglund) observed a saucer-shaped object and its occupants on December 9, 1985.

Art by Carol Ann Rodriguez

The sign conversation on the ice went on for a while, and Helge' tried to explain several things, like hunting and dancing. The female alien played with the dog, which Helge thought strange since it was normally very aggressive towards strangers. All the time it looked as if they walked on an unseen layer. They didn't touch the ground. When the girl patted the dog, she also leaned her knee against this invisible layer. The entities had a broad black bracelet with a yellow button on their left wrists which they touched occasionally and which seemed to have some connection to their weightlessness. The older man explained that he knew about the pygmies and showed how they hunted with bow and arrow. He also made it clear that his people would come in great armadas in the future. After some conversation, the older man returned to their ship and fetched an object in the shape of a cylinder or a microphone. He let this object glide along the back of Helge who suddenly felt relieved from his kidney pains which had troubled him for fifteen years. Helge said the object felt warm and vibrated against his skin.

When the conversation had lasted for about one hour, it grew darker and then Helge noticed that the vehicle was surrounded by a blue phosphorescent light. The craft sort of vibrated. Except for the dark cylinder beneath, it was semi-transparent. It consisted of two shells, of which the outer shell rotated. The inside seemed very Spartan-like, no chairs, but only three shining cylinders standing on the floor. Terminating the conversation, the entities entered the craft, which took off with enormous speed. Helge noticed that it changed color from blue to orange as it flew away.

When the doctors had Helge x-rayed on the following day, they were very confused as the stone was gone. Subsequently all x-ray plates were checked by a doctor in Stockholm who confirmed that no stone was visible on the plates taken after the contact experience. This doctor has since moved to Switzerland and I have been unable to trace him.

THE SECOND CONTACT

In August 1966, about ten months after the first experience, Helge felt a strong urge to go back to the lake where he had his initial contact. The urge was very strong, almost as if someone else drove the car. As he arrives at the lake, he finds the same craft hovering a few feet above the water's surface (it's now summer). Beside "the ship" a man is standing in the air, as if weightless. There is a slight breeze causing ripples on the lake. Helge spots a small skiff and starts out through the reeds towards the craft. He recognizes the man as one from the initial meeting. This "man" starts to talk but the sounds he makes are not synchronized with his lip movements. They seem instead to come from inside the craft (and are slightly delayed?).

Helge is informed that he must go to the Bahamas as their contact man, and he is given a metal plate always to wear. He says it is impossible for him to go to the Bahamas since he doesn't speak English and is an uneducated man. Besides he has a wife to care for at home. Obviously, however, Helge has no choice, he is ordered to go. Post-contact he digs a hole in the wood and buries the metal plate there.

He tells his wife what has happened and they decide to sell everything they have and even to kill their dog, which was very dear to them. In March 1967, they take off for the Bahamas. They are told to go to a certain place on Little Exuma. Helge makes one mistake however. He forgets his plate. Nothing happens in the Bahamas and they are forced to return home. They feel ashamed to resettle in their old home town. Instead they .make contact with a brother of Helge's living in Stockholm. From their remaining funds, they buy a house trailer and settle down south of Stockholm, where Helge finds work as a rock blaster once more.

A peculiar episode happened on the plane traveling from England to Nassau in the Bahamas. Helge noticed 14 peculiar looking people who looked like Catholic priests and who all disappeared when they arrived at their destination. Beforehand, one of them identifies himself as Father Rapas and indicates that they will be seeing him again.

Helge and his wife try put their involvement with this group of individuals – aliens or not – behind them. They obtain an apartment south of Stockholm, through friends who were members of "JE - Fologiska Sallskapet." He met several of the leading members of that group and one of them, a wealthy building contractor, offered to finance the trips to the Bahamas. Helge decides to fetch the plate he has hidden in the lake.

On his way up from Gothenburg, he stops at a gas station. There, an old man comes up to him and asks if he is going towards Stockholm. Helge felt somewhat tired and thought it would be nice to have someone to talk to so he accepts the passenger. The man is dressed in a black cape, boots, and a big black slouch ha£. After a while he asks Helge if he doesn't recognize him. Helge denies this but suddenly it dawns on him that this is one of the priests that he saw on the plane for Nassau. The man introduces himself as Father Rapas. He is working for the overlords, which he preferred to call them, who had contacted Helge on the previous occasions. Rapas suggests a coffee-break at a motel. They sit down at a table and Rapas takes off his hat and puts it on the table, but orders nothing to drink.

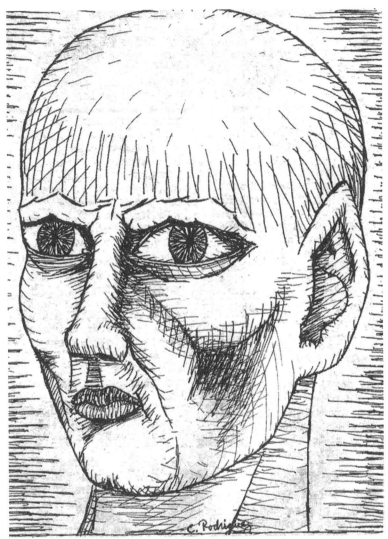

Richard Höglund noticed that the UFO occupants were completely hairless and he was especially fascinated by their ears, which were large and pointed.
Drawing by Carol Ann Rodriguez

At this point Helge begins to feel very confused about the whole thing. Perhaps I'm going crazy and this man doesn't exist at all, he thinks. When a young boy passed their table, Helge gives the big hat a push and it falls to the floor. The boy, thinking it is he who has done it, picks up the hat and apologizes. Rapas obviously is real, Helge thinks. Helge is given instructions on how to proceed the next time he goes to the Bahamas. This time he must not forget his plate. The plate in question was 7 x 4.5 cm in size and about 1 cm thick with a rough backside. It was made of a material like aluminum and was engraved with three rows of cryptic symbols, possibly a kind of identity card. The plate occasionally became so hot that Helge kept it wrapped up in asbestos. He also claimed it gave him rashes. (This reminds me of Albert Bender, who received a metal disc that became so hot he couldn't hold it and also the Aarno Heinonen contacts reviewed in AFU Newsletter 18 and 19). As they traveled a few more miles, Rapas suggested that he take the wheel for a while.

Helge wonders if this is wise, since Rapas seems to be very old; Helge suggests about 60 or 70 years of age. Well, if you double that some ten times you will be closer to the truth, is Rapas' answer. Anyway, they change seats and Rapas proves to be a good driver, perhaps a little too good. He drives like Helge's old Volvo Amazon was a racing car. Helge tries to calm him by telling him that the police may have checkpoints here and there. But Rapas says he can feel where they are. Helge falls asleep and when he wakes up Rapas is gone and the car is parked beside the road outside Sodertalje. On the driver's seat is a package of fruit.

THE NEW GENERATION

Several Swedish UFOlogists were now becoming interested in the Helge case, and lots of rumors circulated. A small group grew up around Helge, who returned to the Bahamas, this time carrying his plate. The building contractor financed this trip. Money was to be mailed to Helge through a school teacher in Nykoping -Tryggwe Glantz. In January 1968, a meeting is held in Nykoping. The gathered people are informed of a letter from Rapas, written through Helge and dated January 1, 1968.

In the letter, Rapas outlines the basics for an organization to be started by the Swedish group. This course of action has been confirmed by the overlords. The organization is to be called "The New Generation." The New Generation was intended to be a peace organization. I quote from the claimed letter from Rapas: "We detest you. That is why we believe in the youth, they are the only ones whose hands are not soiled with the blood of others. Your catchword shall be: Freedom from violence - from hunger - we are all brothers and sisters. You who have supported him (Helge) shall not be forgotten, you shall reap a hundredfold, but if someone hurts him or his devoted wife, I say they shall be revenged sevenfold."

PUBLISHER'S NOTE - We should mention at this point that this organization known as The New Generation sounds remarkably like similar groups of supposed extraterrestrials said to have settle among us on Earth. In particular the members of the UMMO and Friendship groups. For additional information, we suggest delving into a copy of *"Alien Strongholds – UFO Bases On Earth,"* which will serve to enlighten you on the topic.

The group also received the "Rapas Rules," 65 philosophical points. For example, point 15 says: "If you have helped a poor man with your last money and dressed him with your own clothes, given him your last food and he rises up and wants to knock you down, toss him into the lake, he is worth nothing else." Point 17: "If there should be interplanetary people among you, which I believe is rather rare, don't let them go to heaven, but bring them down to Earth again and demand more work of them."

Most members of the group felt uneasy about the whole thing. There were too many threats in the background. Something was not right, they thought. The building contractor had been told to pay thousands of crowns without knowing what he really supported. When Helge returns from his second Bahamas sojourn, the group breaks up and Helge feels betrayed and secludes himself.

THE BAHAMAS RETREAT

Helge's second trip to the Bahamas had fared better; while this time he didn't forget his plate. It all happened around the New Year of 1967-68. Father Rapas had told Helge what to do when he came to the island Little Exuma. On New Year's Eve he went to the harbor and contacted an elderly black man, Joe, who owned a boat. There was also a girl by the name of Li. They started towards a small island, presumably called Wennergren Island, where they entered a mountain through an opening.

This was the base. Here Helge saw various kinds of entities: giants, hermaphrodites and dwarves. He was shown the evolution of Earth and its civilization in a three dimensional picture. During this experience, he collapsed three times and had to be revived by Rapas. Helge was also shown a collection of weapons from all ages. From this mountain center "The New Generation" organization would spring, according to Rapas. Here Helge was to enter some kind of school.

Although the Swedish group broke up, Tryggwe Giantz continued for a while to promote The New Generation. He was interviewed by the Swedish daily "Folket" and their article was published on June 1, 1968. Tryggwe claimed that they already had 600 members. The movement was referred to as a "worldwide peace movement in the spirit of Martin Luther King, originated by the West Indian Peacemaker Rapaz." In the autumn of 1968, the organization had plans for a great meeting where Harry Belafonte, Ralph Abernathy and Coretta King would appear. This meeting never took place. Rapas is referred to as a wealthy industrialist this time. During a trip around the world, he saw so much misery that he decided to use his wealth for charity purposes, all claims according to the "*Folket*" article.

CIA AGENT KILLED BY THE BROTHERS

Since the building contractor now had withdrawn his economic support, Helge had to rely on his contacts "from space." Obviously this group had unlimited economic resources. One day a man from a car firm visited Helge and gave him a new car. He said it was paid for and was to be delivered to Helge.

Before the third trip to the Bahamas, Helge contacted a friend who was to take care of the apartment, pay the rent and care for the flowers. The payment for this service would be sent from the Bahamas to a special bank account. Helge paid in just five crowns on this account before he and his wife went. On the very day that they went to the Bahamas, someone paid 1,000 crowns into this account. Every week it increased by a few hundred crowns, but the receipts never said who put the money there. No money ever arrived from the Bahamas. When Helge and his wife returned they were very anxious, as they thought they must owe their friend a lot of money. When their friend explained that there was always money in the account, they first thought he had given them himself but later realized that some of their UFO-connected contacts must have made payments.

On his further trips Helge only met one type of entity. They had thin, pointed features, deeply tanned, with a somewhat oriental look, long tapering fingers and dark eyes. They all seemed very perfect, not a blemish on their skin. In the Bahamas, Helge also met others of their earthly contacts. There was a Russian and one Afro-American, named Loftin, with whom he made good friends. One day Little Exuma was swarming with CIA agents. Loftin had informed the CIA of the base. Later Loftin was found dead with a bullet hole in his head. He had been killed for treason. Since the CIA now knew of the Bahamas base, it was moved to a place outside Mexico City. From now on, Helge boarded the plane for Mexico City instead of Nassau. In this way the contacts are still going on as far as I have been informed.

THEY HAVE NO FEELINGS

People who have been in touch with Helge through the years naturally ask him why he doesn't stop working for these entities. His answer is that he cannot, or he will go the same way as Loftin did. There is a way in but no way out.

INCREDIBLE ALIEN ENCOUNTERS

In August 1976, a friend of mine talked to Helge on the phone. He then said: "What I have gotten into is negative. You become very isolated. I warn you from going deeper into this." During the first few years, in the 1960s, Helge thought he owed them some help in return for their healing of him.

Later he said: "You don't know what kind of a hell I'm into." In case he couldn't take it anymore, he had a pill that he carried around. Helge got very little information from the aliens. If he asked something they would return the next day after consulting their overlords. Still Helge's Russian friend said that Helge seemed to know more about them than he had found out after working for them for twenty years. They seemed totally without feelings; death and torture did not disturb them in the least. In some ways, though, they seemed stupid, not even telepathic, according to Helge. They claimed they came from another planet and were here to prevent a third World War, but Helge eventually thought differently.

One of my informants saw several photographs taken by Helge in the Bahamas. The entities couldn't be photographed, though. Instead there was a lighted square where one of them had been. Helge remembers one episode when he sat on a bench, talking to one of them. Suddenly a stranger walks by and Helge felt very embarrassed as it appeared as though he was talking to himself. These people have the ability to disappear into thin air. In most MIB encounters, there is some form of mind-tampering. What we do find here, though, are mythic elements, like the visit to the mountain retreat perhaps had been mentally induced?

A peculiar feature was that they never slept or ate, but they did drink. Also, Helge never met any women among them. While in the Bahamas, he was allowed to use one of their phantom cars. He drove an odd type of black Cadillac, which seemed fresh inside as if it were new. Nor could the car be crashed.

Where do they come from? What do they really want? The only way to get away from them is to sell yourself to the highest bidder. They control the corrupt politicians. They are working on an international basis like a form of global Mafia.

They move among us without any apparatus and have obviously been here for a long time. There are MIB reports from as far back as the 19th century. My personal speculation is that these entities somehow belong to this Earth but are of a different evolution. In theosophical literature there are frequent mentions of two other physical evolutions sharing this Earth with us. They are possibly neither good nor evil but can be used by those who know how. Perhaps John Keel is right when he concludes: "We have not been viewing the masters, only the slaves."

IMPORTANT UPDATE TO SWEDISH CONTACT AND MIB CASE

Empirical evidence in the Richard Höglund case

In the American magazine *UFO Report* 1977, John Keel wrote a very interesting article, *The Contactee Key*, presenting some of his conclusions and advice from several years of field investigation. He noted the great mistake made by the early UFO organizations, APRO and NICAP, in regarding all contactees as hoaxers and consequently missing a lot of valuable data: "Had these groups applied some fundamental logic to the situation they might have realized their approach was wrong... By publicly dissociating themselves from the contactees, the early ufologists left this fruitful aspect entirely in the hands of the government." (*UFO-Report*, vol. 4, no. 4, August 19970).

John Keel (in the middle) during his visit to Sweden 1976.

What John Keel discovered during his field investigations was that some contactees were actually genuine and did encounter visitors from somewhere and that this aspect of the UFO enigma required a different approach than ordinary mainstream UFO research. Jacques Vallee, in his *Messengers of Deception*, let the character Major Murphy define this problem facing ufologists: "What makes you think UFOs are a scientific problem?... science has certain rules. For example it has to assume that the phenomenon it is observing is natural in origin rather than artificial and possibly biased. Now, the UFO phenomenon could be controlled by alien beings. If it is, added the Major, then the study of it doesn´t belong in science. It belongs in Intelligence. Meaning counter espionage." (p. 68).

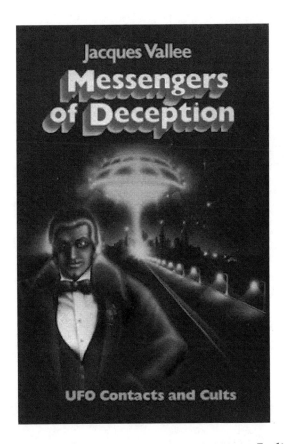

During my many years of contactee investigation I discovered that in a few physcial contactee cases there was independent or circumstial evidence that the contactee really was meeting "strangers," whoever they were. Lou Zinsstag found this out regarding George Adamski and ufologist Ted Bloecher changed his mind on contactees when he discovered a similar situation in the Woodrow Derenberger case.

Based on these experiences what I find rather frustrating in mainstream UFO research, at least in Sweden, is the large amount of time spent by field investigators on ordinary UFO observations and misidentifications. In my view a complete waste of time and money that will never solve the UFO enigma. I have for years tried, without much success, to convince active ufologists in Sweden to forget misidentifications and reports with very little empirical data and concentrate one hundred percent on close encounters and contact cases. My advice is as ever, try to be more of a UFO detective or intelligence agent than investigator of lights in the sky.

One of the most intriguing and complicated UFO contacts I have ever investigated is the Richard Höglund case, summarized by Timothy Good in his latest book *Earth - An Alien Enterprise*. I will not repeat the summary here as you can find the case here and on several of my blog entries. But I would like to give a few details of the circumstantial evidence indicating a genuine contact.

Richard Höglund

1. Disappearance of kidney stones.

Richard claimed to have been healed from his kidney troubles with an instrument placed on his back during the first contact on December 9, 1965. The pain left him instantly when the alien visitor held an instrument to his back. There were x-rays taken both before and after this incident. I received written statements from three medical doctors involved with the x-rays. They confirmed that no stone was visible on the plates after December 9, 1965, but there is a possibility that the stones could have left the body in a natural way. According to one of the doctors, Karl Erik Swenson, the later plates after the incident seems to indicate a man who never had any kidney stones.

Karl Erik Swenson M.D. Richard´s physician.

2. Telephone interference

Two of Richard´s friends, Gösta and Sture Johansson, many times experienced strange telephone problems talking to Richard. Often when Gösta Johansson called Richard on the phone, the line was broken and a harsh voice simply said "it is wrong", always the same voice. Sometimes when talking on the phone a clicking sound was heard and then Richard became very nervous and wanted to end the conversation. Once the clicking sounds could be heard after the conversation had ended and the phone was dead. Then a call came and when Gösta answered the same voice only said "it is wrong". Gösta Johansson was convinced that Richard´s phone was tapped.

Gösta Johansson 1986.

3. Invisible entities

Once on the Bahamas Richard was sitting on a bench talking with one of his alien visitors. Some people are passing by and suddenly Richard found himself talking aloud alone and the visitor had gone. He felt very embarrassed of the situation. Obviously the aliens could make themselves invisible. In the beginning of the 1970s, the couple, Sture and Turid Johansson, became involved with Richard´s activities. On a Monday evening, around midnight, when the couple had gone to bed, Turid was awakened by the sound of their front door opening and someone walking around with heavy steps in the apartment. Believing she has forgotten to lock the door, Turid goes up only to find the door closed and no one there. She goes to bed again and then the heavy steps are heard once more, like someone is walking around in the rooms. She wakes up her husband. They look for some intruder to no avail and after a while no footsteps are heard.

During a telephone conversation with Richard a few days later, Turid mention the name Var de Cartino, the name of one of the alien visitors. Richard answers: "Yes he was here for three days and he visited you one evening and said you had a nice apartment." Then Richard gives a detailed description of Sture and Turid´s apartment, although he had never been there.

Richard Höglund in Nassau, Bahamas

4. Travels

Richard was often gone from home, sometimes for months. He claimed that the space people picked him up in their craft, often visiting the base hidden in the Bahamas and also Mexico. Richard complained once to Gösta Johansson that he was not allowed by his contacts to visit the Olympic Games in Mexico in 1968. Gösta noticed that sometimes in the middle of the Winter he found Richard with a deep suntan when he returned to Sweden. Richard was a retired rock blaster with very little money. He couldn´t have gone on regular flights around the world based on his meager income.

5. Gunvor Höglund´s Bahamas encounter

Richard´s wife Gunvor was not allowed to participate in the meetings with the alien visitors but she observed them many times when they came to their home. But once, at a restaurant in Nassau, Bahamas, she was introduced to one of Richard´s contacts: "It was a small and crowded premise. Richard recognized one of his contacts and they came to our table. I watched this man and he looked at me.. He had a brown suit, a sort of suntan, not very tall and rather thin, a southern look in appearance. And he wasn´t very tall. My God, I thought, your suit is too large. He greeted me but we didn´t shake hands... His gaze was very intense and hypnotic. He smoked and left the rest of the cigarette on the table and then went away. I saved the cigarette butt as evidence."

Gunvor Höglund

6. Reluctant contactee

Richard was a reluctant contactee. He was given no message but ordered to start a Peace Movement in Sweden. This failed and he was reprimanded because other contactees had succeeded in founding organizations that made a lot of money. Richard didn´t trust the alien visitors and noticed that they were not of high morals. He was actually afraid of them but felt compelled to continue working for them. From a psychological viewpoint his thoughts and reactions are interesting, speaking in favor of a genuine contact.

When investigating contactee cases like Richard Höglund it is important to be aware of different alternatives in interpretation and try to find corroborative evidence supporting the claims. In my book on the Höglund case I presented several possibilities: The contact claims as a cover story for criminal activity or espionage, a hoax for making money from gullible followers, fictional story as a result of drug abuse, mystic visionary experiences with no physical evidence, the contactee a mental case, mythmaker or fantasy prone personality. During one period Richard's friends, Sture and Turid Johansson, speculated that because of his many travels, he was a courier in the international drug trade, but they later came to accept his contacts as genuine.

When ufologists become involved in contactee cases like this the advice and experiences of John Keel and Jacques Vallee will prove invaluable. This is a world very different from investigating and documenting misinterpretations of Venus and airplanes.

While on a trip to the Bahamas, Richard Höglund was taken to an underground base where he was shown various kinds of extraterrestrial entities: giants, hermaphrodites and dwarves. Art by Carol Ann Rodriguez.

• • • • • • • • •

WANT TO LEARN MORE? VISIT THE AUTHOR'S BLOG

https://ufoarchives.blogspot.com

Hercules Invictus has dedicated his earthly sojourn to studying, sharing and applying the legacy and lessons of the ancient alien Gods of Greek Mythology who still reside on Mount Olympus.

INCREDIBLE ENCOUNTERS WITH THE WORLD BEYOND

By Hercules Invictus

PUBLISHER'S NOTE: Those who have accepted Incredible Encounters as part of their "chosen path" are prone to rationalize their lifelong channelings of the bizarre in a variety of terms. Hercules Invictus is one of the most profound writers we are honored to have in our stable of regular contributors. And while much of the practices of wizardry are shrouded in darkness for self-protection, Hercules is willing to share his cosmic wisdom as it applies to the legacy and lessons of the Celestial Gods of Greece – the ancient aliens of mythology – whom he still remains in communication with, "hiding out" on Mount Olympus. Invictus has had many subtle experiences that some might be prone to place in the category of life after death or out-of-body occurrences. As with Maria D'Andrea, these experiences revolve around beings whom we might consider "invisible," but, if you are sensitive, you have the ability to peer into their domain just like they can peer – and materialize at times – into ours. You can learn about some of these incredible encounters Hercules has had here, and ponder his cosmic wisdom through his other writing as well as his podcasts on the Internet.

· · · · · · · · · ·

The hour was ungodly and I was bone tired. Clad mostly in fur and leather (and brandishing a huge steel sword), I regally sat on the passenger bench in the empty train as if I were a barbarian king in a Mead Hall surrounded by my loyal Thanes.

En route to my apartment, where Queens and Brooklyn met and mated, I reflected on my life thus far and proclaimed it great. Though facing many challenges (as we all do at all times) I was openly living the Mythic Hero's Journey (my Spiritual

Path of choice), my eccentricities were accounted as assets by my employers, I was esteemed in my profession (Workforce Development), was actively engaged in exploring the paranormal and had my own fringe TV show on UHF and Public Access.

I have adventured under several names over the years, each one a cultural (or sub-cultural) aspect of Hercules, my divine ancestor, operant archetype, tutelary deity, overshadowing entity and Higher Self. At the time I was enamored with all things Northern European, both factual and fictive. As Thor is the Norse equivalent of Hercules, and the Barbarian is the primary expression of Herculean adventure in heroic fantasy, I became Thor the Barbarian to fully experience both aspects at once.

My overall message was simple: If I – being quite atypical in my creative self-expression and what I wanted out of life – can earn a conventional living, climb professional career ladders, actively (and very publicly) pursue (and actualize) my dreams while serving the common good – just imagine what YOU can accomplish unhampered by such strangeness! My mission was to awaken and empower the divine creative spark that dwells within us all, allowing it the opportunity to express itself.

UFO over Temple of Poseidon in Greece.

INCREDIBLE ALIEN ENCOUNTERS

My show, though local, was popular in the New York Metropolitan area, and not a day went by when I was not recognized and hailed as I wended my way through the concrete canyons of the Big Apple seeking adventure (accompanied by my modern day minstrels, all armed with mini-dv cams).

And I was on my way to bigger and better things. NJN (the PBS of New Jersey) had me on as a guest several times and subsequently there was talk of my starring in a regularly scheduled series. Through them I could already be heard pontificating on a wide variety of vocational topics in mall-kiosks throughout the Garden State. While that was going on, I was also approached by folks who wanted to air my show in 300 cities throughout the nation. There were also opportunities to be rebroadcast on Digital TV and the Internet.

Yes, after years of dancing to the tune of a different drum, things were finally looking up and I felt content and fulfilled. I felt myself relaxing, surrendering to the exhaustion that permeated my being.

And then I died.

NEITHER HERE NOR THERE

I felt myself leaving my body with my last breath. I rose, catching a last glimpse of myself with an omni-directional vision I never knew I possessed. I looked undignified in death and found, to my surprise, that I was not in the least bit disturbed by the prospect of leaving my body behind. Briefly I wondered what would happen to the loved ones I was abandoning but I received a wordless reassurance, a certainty that they would all be fine.

And then I merged into an all-pervading golden white light. As my consciousness incrementally faded, I heard someone say, "You were indeed very difficult."

Flashes of my life at seemingly random points in time reconfigured into patterns of behavior and communicated recurring themes I could not previously discern. I had to admit that, yes, I could indeed be very difficult . . . and had certainly been so with the Invisibles. Throughout my life they had been there with me, and for me, but I was far from cooperative (or appreciative) even though I knew that they were present, as I could often sense and sometimes see them. Right before my passing, for instance, I knew that I was physically unwell. I suspected I had pneumonia, as I had had pneumonia before and knew how it felt, but I still pushed myself way past my physical limits. I ignored all inner prompting (from Them) to seek treatment, take a break or slow down. Because, honestly, how could I? Things were happening and there was so much to do!

I was in the Light and of the Light while this review and reveal process was going on. But I was not alone. I telepathically communicated to my Companion that I understood what was revealed to me and that I accepted total responsibility for everything I ever did and all that was ever done to me. Then I accepted total responsibility for all the timeless tales that I lived and projected on to others. I now knew that they were all of my own choosing. Consciousness faded once again as I re-merged with the Light.

TO BE AND WHERE TO BE

Greek and Roman statues that look like the occupants of UFOs to some.

At some point later, and quite suddenly, I found myself in a vast white room with many others. We were all dressed in immaculate white robes . . . or were we? At times it seemed that we were all Beings of Light. Some were engaged in enigmatic activities that I could not fathom. Others, like myself, were not.

The room was so bright that I could not make out any details. And it frequently shifted to conform to whatever I expected it to be. It was an ancient Greek Amphitheater with Corinthian columns. No, it was the interior of a UFO. No, it was actually a shiny Star Ship manned by wise and benevolent Space Brothers (and Sisters).

In any case, I was seated across from an older and wiser Being of Light who may (or may not) have had a well-combed mane of white hair. We were communicating through thought exchange. He was very patient with me and very lovingly answered my questions.

I must have asked about the true nature of the place we were in because he answered, "Don't concern yourself with what it looks like. What does it feel like to you?"

"It feels like a place of arrival and embarkation, like a Bus Terminal."

He smiled and said "Very good."

As I have a strong personal preference for and resonance with all things Olympian, this place of coming and going became the Holy Mountain of my ancestors. It transformed into the Olympus of my Primal Vision and remained so, becoming more 'real' with each passing moment. Winged gods and goddesses, nude or loosely draped with gold embroidered white sheets, continuously landed here or took to the skies.

I finally understood the true nature of this place. This was Home.

Has the author traveled in a chariot of fire? All our readers want to know.

"So, what is next?" I inquired.

"Elysium" he replied. "You accomplished all that you intended to do, accepted full responsibility for everything that you experienced, internally and externally, and forgave all karmic debt."

I knew all about Elysium. Called Devachan by the Theosophists, it is a place of rest, rejuvenation and personal fulfillment. It is a state of mind where everything you have ever dreamed of, or wished for, will happen and continue happening until you no longer want it to.

Elysium sounds (and actually is) a wonderful place to be − perhaps one of the best places in creation − but I knew that I was not ready to return there.

"Understood," said the Elder, now a full-fledged Olympian god. "Will you remain here with us?"

Tempting as it was to tarry there for a while, I said "No, I want to go back. I want to continue adventuring on Gaia. There are incarnate souls of my acquaintance I still want to meet up with and things I'd still like to experience − with them and on my own." Endless possibilities raced through my mind, and I felt both elated and very much alive. I was totally at peace with my decision.

As consciousness faded, I heard the older Olympian (now bearded and sitting on a Heavenly Throne) regally intone:

Remember! You already are that which you most wish to be.

You already have everything you need to create anything you want.

All you need to do is decide what you want to create.

THE ADVENTURE CONTINUES

I re-emerged in this world when my alarm went off. I felt great physically but I did not remember arriving home, getting undressed, collapsing in my bed or falling sleep. Was my recent Near Death Experience naught but a strange dream? No, I could not dismiss it as such.

INCREDIBLE ALIEN ENCOUNTERS

Through meditation I reconstructed the previous day and went about checking the details against the memories of all those I knew who crossed my path. Everything had happened as I remembered, save that no one recalled my being unwell.

Further inquiry led me nowhere. Even the cryptic utterances of the Invisibles weren't helpful. What was I to make of this experience? I certainly did not know at the time, but it certainly changed me.

My relationships with the people already in my life at the time of my death transformed. I grew much closer to some and more distant with others. I was especially happy to be here and watch my son grow into the wonderful individual he is. I subsequently met and have worked with many awesome people who immediately felt familiar when our paths first crossed.

In addition, I knew that I was here because I myself wanted to be here. I knew that I was continuously watched and guided. And that I had a bunch of awesome things on my To Do List that I really wanted to anchor and actualize in this world. In truth, I have been actively engaged in the process of making them happen since the day I re-awoke on Gaia.

I am Hercules Invictus. I am the Voice of Olympus. I am currently recruiting Argonauts to help me usher in a new Age of Heroes.

Sound familiar? Does it strike a chord? If so, contact me and we'll talk.

Onwards!

© Hercules Invictus

Hercules is currently involved with several social causes, teaches, conducts workshops and hosts *The Elysium Project*, *Pride of Olympus* and *Voice of Olympus* podcasts. He also writes for magazines on occasion, has published two e-books and has regularly contributed Olympian content to Timothy Beckley's paranormal anthologies. Hercules most recently established the Order of the Golden Fleece and has been recruiting Argonauts to help him usher in a new Age of Heroes. For more information please Friend him on Facebook, visit his website: http://www.herculesinvictus.net or e-mail him at hercules.invictus@gmail.com.

"Space Gods of Ancient Greece and Rome" is a valuable asset for those studying the history of UFOs in the Mediterranean.

BRIEF CATALOG OF INCREDIBLE ENCOUNTERS WITH UFO BEINGS IN GREECE

THE ATALANTI CASE – THE GREEK ROSWELL

The Atalanti case is considered the most important UFO incident in Greece. Some researchers refer to it as the "Greek Roswell" as it raised the awareness of the Greek public on the UFO phenomenon. On the night of September 2nd 1990, a fleet of around 12 to 17 UFOs was observed in multiple locations over mainland Greece. After flying over the Peloponnese (South of mainland Greece) the fleet made a turn and headed towards the North.

At 9:30 pm, while over the town of Atalanti (150 kilometers northwest of Athens) one of the UFOs parted from the fleet formation. The witnesses mentioned that the craft seemed to have some problem, it changed its color to red and appeared to have caught fire. At the same time, three explosions were heard (other reports speak of loud metallic sounds). The craft landed at the top of a hill where the Prophet Is Elias Church is (726 meters) situated outside of the village of Megas Platanos (a few kilometers from Atalanti). Locals looking at the incident from a distance of approximately one kilometer reported what was happening at the top of the hill to the police but the location was not easily accessible during night time.

Once the malfunctioning unknown craft landed, the rest of the fleet also landed around it as if to protect it. The gathering of all the craft on top of the hill lit up the area, allowing witnesses to see. Witnesses, mostly local farmers, describe the objects as round and having the size of a tractor. According to a witness that approached closer to the landing location, the beings were described as short and humanoid and appeared to be working on repairing the craft. The incident lasted from 9:30 pm until

3:00 am the next day. The humanoids were able to repair the craft and all of the fleet flew off together.

Locals visited the location the next morning. The grass was burned and some smoke was coming off the ground. Some collected cables, metallic parts and a sponge-like artifact. A close by pine tree had the lower part of its trunk burned. A witness that touched the trunk had his hand burned.

A month later, the Greek military published a report. The report focused on the equipment found. According to the report, the pieces found included a plug made of copper with a diameter of 11cm and Arabic writing on it; a multi-pin cable made of copper connected to the plug; the cable's insulation (a silk-like material); a burnt plastic cover; a steel ring and three 10 cm steel bars, each one with a switch featuring the Greek letter Φ. The report concluded that the pieces probably belonged to an old satellite. But satellites do not land and take off again!

Courtesy historydisclosure.com

On the night of September 2, 1990, a fleet of around 12 to 17 UFOs were seen in multiple locations over mainland Greece. This amazing incident is often referred to it as the "Greek Roswell" as it raised the awareness of the Greek public on the UFO phenomenon.

INCREDIBLE ALIEN ENCOUNTERS

BEG. MAY 1939, PENTELIKON MOUNTAIN, ATTICA, GREECE, ANTONIS PRIFTIS:

Brief summary of the event and follow-up:

One Ioannis Yannopoulos reportedly said that in Pentelikon Mountain, Attica, Greece, early in May 1939, at 23:00, Antonis Priftis was coming down the mountain, taking his sheep back to the fold, when he suddenly saw a bright mushroom-shaped object hovering above some nearby trees. The object had bright searchlights around its rim below and was illuminating the area.

Two strange beings seemed to descend to the ground on one of the beams of the "searchlights." They wore "diver's suits," or were described as "sponge divers." They walked towards the witness and stopped about three meters away from him. They did not talk to him, but the witness felt "voices inside his head."

The creatures asked repeatedly for him to go with them, but the witness refused. They also told him that they had come many times to the same spot and that they would come back again.

After that, they went back to the "flying mushroom" in the same manner. The object's light seemed to dim and it started gaining height. After a while the object disappeared with great speed, leaving behind it a bright trail.

http://ufologie.patrickgross.org/ce3/index.htm

JUNE 24, 2001, PELOPONNESE, GREECE, MR. G. P.:

Brief summary of the event and follow-up:

The Greek paranormal researcher, spaceflight journalist and science fiction author, Thanassis Vembos, reported on his website that on June 24, 2001, at 01:50 in the night, Mr. G. P., a University professor, was watching TV at his home. His wife and small son were asleep in their rooms. His daughter was away. When he turned off the TV set, he saw that the kitchen light was on. He went to turn it off, and then felt cold, like there was a cold wind blowing. Turning back, he came face to face with a 1.90 meters-tall lanky humanoid wearing something like a tight-fit blue overall with "wave-like patterns." Its face had very vague human characteristics, having bumps where facial characteristics should be. The witness said it looked like a computer graphic.

The creature started to move with big leaps, "like the leaps of the hurdles' athletes," but in "slow motion," like "a dancer with his toes not touching the ground." It went out of the kitchen and entered the lavatory – the door was open. The witness chased it but the lavatory was empty. Then he saw it again, coming out of his daughter's room and disappearing into the kitchen. Then, for a third time, the creature came out from the lavatory and vanished into the living room. After that, it was not seen again. He had the impression that the creature was "running away from something," or "hunted by something and wanted to avoid any contact." The closest distance between the witness and the humanoid was two meters. He also had the impression that the creature was "something solid, moving in an ethereal way."

The witness felt shocked after the 30 seconds experience. He had heard no sound, nor smelt any odor during the incident. He could not say if the sense of cold persisted during the whole incident. The witness had at least two experiences with apparitions in his previous lifetime: once in 1974, when a strange woman knocking at his door asking for money vanished into thin air, and another one in 1986 when he saw for five minutes his dead mother-in-law inside a bus. Thanassis Vembos indicates that this report was from of his investigation.

http://ufologie.patrickgross.org/ce3/index.htm

MAY 1978, ATHENS, ATTICA, GREECE, YANNIS K.:

Brief summary of the event and follow-up:

Greek ufologist Thanassis reported in 1989 that on 7 Lazarinou street, New Filothei neighborhood in Athens, Greece, on May 1978, at about 2 a.m., Yannis K., 17-year-old, suddenly woke up and was unable to move. He then saw three human-like figures approaching his bed from the balcony area. The three persons came closer and one of them sat on the bed. The person that remained standing was a female with bushy hair, wearing a blouse with skirt. The second person was a tall, heavy-set man with short hair; he wore black gloves and a black close-necked top. The third was a young blond haired girl, tall and with unnaturally long fingers. She wore a black blouse and skirt.

The young girl removed her blouse; she wore no bra and then engaged in sexual intercourse with the boy. Later the girl dressed and all three went out an apparently closed balcony door.

SUMMER 1936, HALANDRI, ATHENS, GREECE, MARIA K. AND 5 OR 6 OTHER CHILDREN:

Brief summary of the event and follow-up:

From second-hand sources, it seems that in his 2000 book about UFOs in Greece, Greek ufologist Makis Podotas was the first to tell that in the summer of 1936, in Halandri, Athens, Greece, twelve-year-old Maria K., shortly before lunchtime at noon, was playing with five or six other children in an area where the population was scattered, and where today stands Hygeia hospital, Kifissias avenue.

Suddenly, the place was invaded by clouds of dust. The children stopped playing, checked what caused the dust, and saw an egg-shaped silver-colored object a little larger than a plane. It landed and rested on "little legs" at about 100 or 150 meters from them. They saw no door on the object, but saw that on the ground, under the craft, was a small humanoid with long white hair wearing white equipment and a wide belt on which small lights shone.

The creature turned to the children for a moment. After that, it waved a hand as if to greet the children, then disappeared suddenly. A muffled squeal or a loud hiss was heard and the object took off vertically between clouds of dust, then climbed into the sky until it was out of sight. The very shocked children did not play anymore. Then their parents called them for lunch and all of them told what had happened. The families did not believe the children, thinking they were putting on a hoax.

http://ufologie.patrickgross.org/ce3/index.htm

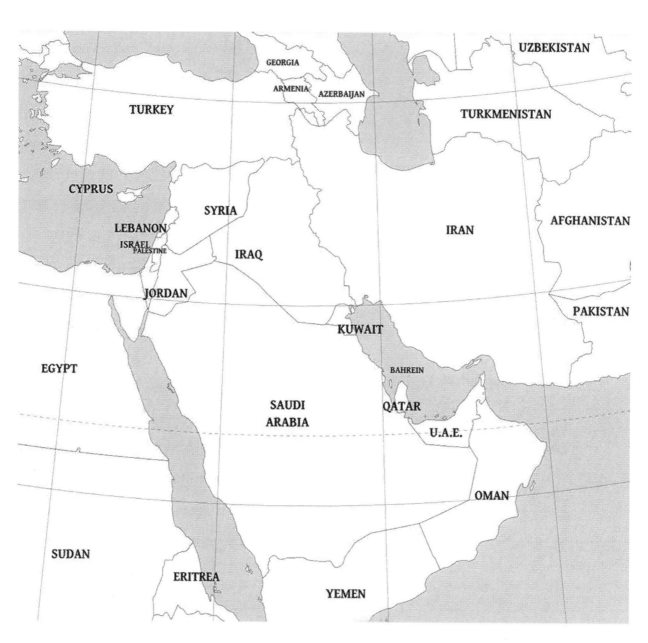

 MIDDLE EAST

UFOS IN THE PERSIAN GULF

By Timothy Green Beckley

During the opening volley of the Persian Gulf War, the CNN anchor in Tel Aviv scrambled to grab his gas mask as a brightly lit object descended from the sky off in the distance; its fiery contrail picked up by TV cameras and broadcast worldwide. In an excited tone of voice, the CNN anchor could be heard over the drone of air raid sirens to say, "We don't know if it's a SCUD attack, an enemy plane, a comet, or a UFO."

At first, this might seem like a very strange comment − but evidence shows quite clearly that UFOs have played an important part in several previous wars, and, furthermore, they are nothing new to this area of the world, having been seen time and time again throughout the Persian Gulf, from Israel to Iran. As it turned out, the fiery object falling from the heavens was in reality a Russian satellite burning up upon reentering the Earth's atmosphere. But for a short while, at least, it did have everyone worried that it might be an enemy attack.

To summarize the situation, during World War II UFOs were observed by Allied as well as the Axis forces, each side thinking that they were the secret weapons of their opposition. On many occasions, peculiar balls of light − seemingly under intelligent control − would pace our airplanes while they went on bombing runs over Germany. During World War II, UFOs were called "Foo Fighters." After the conflict in Europe, mysterious cigar-shaped objects began appearing regularly over Sweden. Nicknamed "Ghost Rockets," they attracted the attention of our military, with General MacArthur telling the press that they definitely were not anything the U.S. had developed. In the early days, it was thought that the Russians might have been testing a circular craft based upon captured German technology, but this theory was quickly put to rest by German scientists working in this country, who insisted that the objects being sighted in Europe could not possibly be anything that Hitler had been developing during the closing days of the war.

In Korea many American pilots found themselves face-to-face with an aerial menace that they could NOT shoot down, for these craft seemed to have a sort of "force field" around them that protected them should they be fired upon. Likewise, in Vietnam, the situation got so far out of hand that one general said during a press conference that many of our soldiers were seeing UFOs, but they definitely weren't ours and they weren't theirs either!

Being that most of the governments of the Persian Gulf practice some form of censorship, it is not all that frequent that news leaks out about UFO encounters in this part of the world. Yet, through various U.S. government and military sources, we are able to piece together a UFO story that needs to be told.

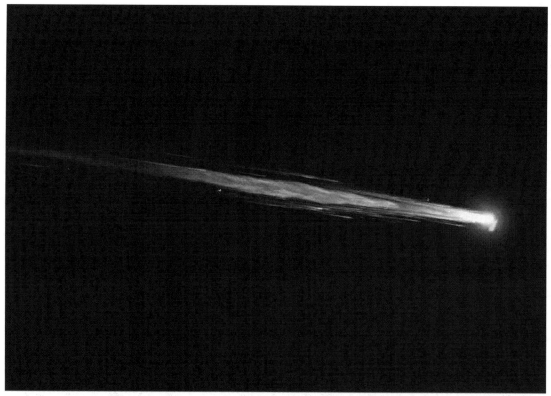

A Russian satellite burning up over Israel sparked fear of an attack, or even a UFO during the opening days of the Persian Gulf War.

UFOS IN IRAN

During the time that Iran had the U.S. Embassy under siege in 1979, UFO sightings were very heavy throughout the area. Many Iranian leaders, it seems, were apparently convinced that the United States military was responsible for the invasion of its air space in a "deliberate provocation to frighten the Iranian public." In an interview given to the Islamic Revolution, an official newspaper of the Ayatollah Khomeini, an army "political-military expert" is quoted as saying that these reports "are true" and represent "part of a psychological warfare operation that the United States has started." The military spokesman adds that, "The nature of these objects is top secret and only a few people in the U.S. know about it." In several instances, the Iranian Air Force has engaged in cat and mouse maneuvers with the UFOs. "In this way," states the story in Islamic Revolution, "the power of our air defense is lessened."

On the night of September 19, 1976, Iranian fighter jets attempted to engage a UFO, but lost all instrumentation, including weapons control.

In a wire service story flashed worldwide by the highly respected Reuters News Bureau, it was disclosed that "reports of UFOs have been broadcast (over Iranian radio) almost every day since the U.S. raid, which ended in disaster in the Central Iranian Desert." The report adds that the "militant students occupying the U.S. Embassy said they had fired on a suspicious, unmarked helicopter which flew over the American compound."

It should be noted that similar unidentified "mystery" helicopters with no markings have repeatedly appeared in association with UFO sightings in the U.S., particularly in instances of animal mutilations, which have been attributed to aerial intruders. Various UFO investigators are convinced of a direct link.

Interestingly, before political tensions started to build in Iran, that nation was experiencing a large number of UFO encounters, perhaps as a symbolic warning of the troubles that would soon plague this country. What is likely the best known case ever from the Persian Gulf involves two Iranian Air Force F-4 Phantom jets who, in September, 1976, were sent airborne to try and identify an unidentified object that had invaded the airspace above the capitol city of Teheran.

The UFO reportedly hovered at an altitude of 5,000 feet and was seen from the control tower of the Mehrabad Airport, flashing colored lights that alternated blue, red, orange and green. The craft was very large and was just standing still over the city.

The jets approached within about thirty miles of the UFO when their instrumentation and communications equipment went dead. One of the jets tried to fire a missile at the object, but the missile refused to fire for some unexplainable reason. At one point during the intercept attempt, the UFO shot out a smaller disk-shaped craft that moved in on the jets but veered off at the last second, leaving the pilots quite shaken.

The incident was reported to the American government, and, while details have been released under the Freedom of Information Act, no solution has ever been forthcoming as to what the object might have been – other than a real UFO.

FROM CHALUS TO ISFAHAN BY UFO

In all honesty, we can't tell you whatever became of Gholam Reza Bazargani, but we'd certainly like to be able to interview him today to see if we can't get more details concerning an event which caused quite a stir when it was published in the Iranian press on April 7, 1976.

It all began when 19-year-old Gholam Reza Bazargani, belonging to a wealthy and respectable family of Chalus, decided to take a stroll in the nearby woods on Sizdehbedar day.

It ended two days later in Isfahan, leaving in its trail a score of baffled policemen, puzzled psychiatrists, an unidentified flying object (UFO) and a lot of mystery.

19-year-old Gholam Reza Bazargani claimed that while out taking a walk, a UFO swooped out of the sky and four "beings" emerged and captured him.

According to Bazargani's report to the Isfahan police, he was whisked away by a UFO on Sizdehbedar day while strolling through the forests, and landed in far away Isfahan on Sunday morning.

While the authorities immediately placed Bazargani under psychiatric examination to determine his sanity, other reports from villagers in Marvine and Lanjan near Isfahan poured in as if to confirm the young man's claims.

According to police officials in Isfahan, a number of people from these villages reported seeing what they described as a "flying saucer." Similar reports were also received from other individuals and groups from the same region. The time of observations in all these reports coincided with Bazargani's claims.

In Chalus, meanwhile, the police had launched a massive search for Bazargani, but there was no trace whatsoever of the young man. According to Bazargani, while he was walking alone deep in the forest on Friday he suddenly saw a UFO emerge from the sky, fly straight towards him and stop directly above him. He said he was unable to move as he watched four "beings" come out of the spaceship and take him inside it. He claims that he spent some time under the scrutiny of the "beings" before passing out. "The next thing I remember is that I woke up back on Earth early in the morning, not in the lush Caspain forests, but surrounded by barren lands," he said. He somehow found his way to Isfahan later the same day. After spending a day with the police and psychologists, he travelled back to Chalus.

Although most authorities are skeptical about the whole affair, they are still mystified by so many identical reports coming from varied people. All the doctors, including those at the Red Lion and Sun Society hospital in Isfahan, who examined Bazargani have given a clear report as to his health, both physical and mental.

For the next several months UFOs were in the sky all over Iran. Jet fighters from the Imperial Air Force were even chased on several occasions by brightly lit objects, and thousands of Iranians spotted the discs while outdoors. On September 25, 1976 the Tehran Journal published the following.

INSIDE THE FLYING SAUCER

The Ettela'at offices continued to be flooded with reports from people who claimed to have seen flying saucers. After last week's report of a UFO being chased by jets of the Imperial Iranian Air Force, newspaper offices were swamped by people claiming to have seen a "bright thing in the sky." One man claimed yesterday that he had actually been kidnapped by strange beings and taken inside a flying saucer. Ahmad Bani Ahmad, 56, a researcher in Iranian history, said he had been reluctant to tell the story of his encounter with beings from another planet earlier because he thought people would make fun of him.

But now, after the UFO was seen by so many people, he no longer fears ridicule. He said that last weekend, he and his wife were visiting Tabriz Lake. "My attention was caught by a glittering body that landed about 100 yards from my car. My wife and I were terrified. The round object was about four or five meters across and there was a small window in the side. Two beings similar in shape to Egyptian mummies stepped out."

UFOS STOP OIL PUMPS IN KUWAIT

On November 10, 1978, a UFO landed in an old field in Kuwait and stopped drilling operations for 15 minutes. The incident was witnessed by seven oil company workers who maintain that the object was larger than a 747 Jumbo Jet. Official State Department documents of the incident state the following;

"UFO sightings cause security concern in Kuwait. A series of UFO sightings caused the GOK to appoint an investigatory committee of experts from the Kuwait Institute for Scientific Research. The Committee's Report, which was released January 20, described eight sightings from November to December 14. A number of the early sightings took place near oil company facilities north of Kuwait City. Release of the report was something of a media event as it coincided with front page stories of yet another UFO sighting over Kuwait City, which included photographs in local newspapers."

Another official document released under the Freedom of Information Act states in part. . ."A senior Kuwait Oil Company official told us the UFO which first appeared over the northern oil fields seemingly did strange things to KOC's automatic pumping equipment. This equipment is designed to shut itself down when there is some failure which may seriously damage the petroleum gathering and transmission system and it can only be re-started manually. At the time of the UFOs appearance, the pumping system automatically shut itself down and when the UFO vanished the system started itself up again."

Kuwait oil field: Did a UFO cause this fire?

UFOS INVADE BAHRAIN

In a letter to Tim Beckley, Haitham Ameen, who lives in Manama, the capitol of the Kingdom of Bahrain, says his country has undergone an intensive UFO wave over the years.

Ameen points out that the object that eventually landed in Kuwait was first seen passing over his nation, which is made up of 34 islands in the Arabian Sea. According to Ameen, the second UFO ever sighted over Bahrain was on Friday, August 24, 1979. "At 11:40 P.M. Bahrain's Harbor Master and his Manager of Customers, each saw a strange object in the sky. They both claim that the object exploded into four segments, spewing out red balls of flame.

"Their sighting was made at the same time pilots from 29,000 to 35,000 feet reported seeing a UFO. The object was reportedly elongated, with pulsating green and white lights in front and left behind a trail of sparks in the sky. Officials of British Airways, Kuwait Airways, Scandinavian Airlines, and Qantas all logged the sighting, and some of the pilots said they saw not one, but a total of four different UFOs. At the same time the object(s) was being observed from the air, residents on the beach saw several metallic fragments fall into the area between Bahrain and Qatar."

Disturbed over the similarity of the sightings, the government of Bahrain quickly called for an official investigation to find out more about the UFO. "They estimated the UFO to have traveled at 6,500 mph, and a Senior Air Force Traffic Control Officer said that the UFO followed a ragged course when it was sighted. He also said it moved in its own tangent and therefore it could not have been a meteor or a shooting star, as they follow the Earth's movement, which the UFO did not. "A check of the Bahrain Airport control tower log gives the following details (all times are GMT).

20.35: British Airways Flight 3610 reports light crossing right to left 110 nautical miles northwest of Bahrain.

20.40: Kuwait Airways Flight 370, reports light 80 nautical miles away breaking up into three or four sections (later confirmed by Doha Central Tower).

20.45: Possible UFO sighting in Eastern Sector, near Dubai, heading South. Four UFOs, orange with orange tail, reported by Scandinavian Airlines, Qantas Flight 1 and British Airways Flight 601.

The world has changed a whole lot since the bulk of this material was collected. Correspondence with researchers and witnesses have ceased for fear that those involved in UFO research might end up in prison – or far worse! My book *"The Riddle of Hangar 18"* was published in Iran, but I am sure all copies have been banned and probably turned into ashes at a book burning of Western literature. Once the citizens of these nations have again been allowed to think for themselves, and not see everything under the guise of religion or national heritage, we might find out some very interesting information in regard to the visit of Ultra-terrestrials or "dimension hoppers."

As the actual physical combat and the war of political words continues, it will be interesting to see if UFOs crop up in any future news stories, or if such events will be censored. UFOs have always had an intensive interest in our global conflicts and there is no reason to believe these otherworldly craft won't be keeping a close eye on any earthly conflict that will confront us in the future – God forbid!

ABOUT THE AUTHOR: Fifty years and fifty bursting file cabinets later, Timothy Green Beckley is well deserving of the status of a true pioneer in the UFO/paranormal fields. Beckley started his writing career early on. His published articles have appeared in *Fate, Beyond Reality, Saga, and UFO Report.* For many years he served as a stringer for the Enquirer and edited over 30 newsstand publications, including *UFO Universe*, which lasted for over 11 years before almost everything became digital. He has appeared on a multitude of radio and TV shows going back as far as the Long John Nebel program, in the 1960s, and recently on William Shatner's "Weird or What?" program. Currently he is co-host of the podcast "Exploring the Bizarre" on the KCOR Digital Radio Network.

```
GROSS MARGARET A
79 KUWAIT 496
                    UNCLASSIFIED
UNCLASSIFIED
PAGE 01
ACTION NSA-37      KUWAIT 00496  2909207
INFO  OCT-01  EUR-12  ISO-00  OES-03  NASA-02  NSF-02  DOE-15
      SOS-02  CIAE-00  PM-05  P-02  INS-10  L-03  NSAE-00
      NSC-05  PA-02  SP-02  SS-15  NAS-01  /005 Y
                              ---------132479  2909207 /11
R 2006062 JAN 79
FM AMEMBASSY KUWAIT
TO SECSTATE WASHDC 2964
INFO AMEMBASSY ABU DHABI
AMEMBASSY DOHA
AMEMBASSY LONDON
AMEMBASSY MANAMA
AMEMBASSY MUSCAT
SECDEF WASHDC
USCINCEUR
USICA WASHDC
UNCLAS KUWAIT 00496
CINCEUR ALSO FOR POLAD
E.O. 12065: N/A
TAGS: MPOL, PINS, MASS, SOPN, TGEN, KU
SUBJECT: "UFO" SIGHTINGS CAUSE SECURITY CONCERN IN KUWAIT
1. A SERIES OF "UFO" SIGHTINGS ON NOVEMBER 9 CAUSED THE
GOK TO APPOINT AN INVESTIGATORY COMMITTEE OF EXPERTS FROM
THE KUWAIT INSTITUTE FOR SCIENTIFIC RESEARCH (KISR).
THE COMMITTEE'S REPORT WHICH WAS RELEASED JANUARY 20 DESCRIBED
EIGHT SIGHTINGS FROM NOVEMBER TO DECEMBER 14. A NUMBER OF
THE EARLY SIGHTINGS TOOK PLACE NEAR A KUWAIT OIL COMPANY
GATHERING CENTER NORTH OF KUWAIT CITY. RELEASE OF THE
COMMITTEE'S REPORT WAS SOMETHING OF A MEDIA EVENT AS IT
COINCIDED WITH JAN 21 FRONT PAGE STORIES OF YET ANOTHER "UFO"
SIGHTING OVER KUWAIT CITY, WHICH INCLUDED PHOTOGRAPHS IN
LOCAL NEWSPAPERS.
UNCLASSIFIED
UNCLASSIFIED
PAGE 02      KUWAIT 00496  2909207
2. THE KISR COMMITTEE REJECTED THE NOTION THAT THE
"UFO'S" WERE ESPIONAGE DEVICES BUT REMAINED EQUIVOCAL
ABOUT WHETHER THEY WERE OF EXTRATERRESTRIAL ORIGIN.
THE KISR COMMITTEE REPRESENTATIVE, BATIR ABU ID, TOLD
EMBOFF THAT THE SCIENTISTS DID NOT KNOW ENOUGH ABOUT THE
PHENOMENA TO SAY WITH CERTAINTY THAT THEY WEREN'T
"SPACESHIPS." THE REPORT WENT
ON TO RECOMMEND THAT THE GOVERNMENT TAKE ALL POSSIBLE
MEASURES TO PROTECT KUWAIT'S AIR SPACE AND TERRITORY AS
WELL AS THE COUNTRY'S OIL RESOURCES.
3. SOME LOCAL WAGS HAVE MADE LIGHT OF THE FIRST UFO
SIGHTINGS WHICH CAME NEAR THE END OF THE LONG AND
TRADITIONALLY EXUBERANT HOLIDAY CELEBRATIONS OF ID-AL-
ADHA. HOWEVER WE HAVE LEARNED RECENTLY OF AN EVENT
COINCIDENT WITH ONE OF THE UFO SIGHTINGS WHICH HAS
              UNCLASSIFIED
                                                    PAGE
```

Unclassified document reveals security concerns over UFOs being seen over Kuwaiti oil fields.

ISRAELI MOSSAD & INTERPOL UFO REPORT

By Paul Dale Roberts

Did Aliquis of Israeli Mossad and Hospes of Interpol Witness a UFO in South Africa? Is Aliquis with the Israeli Mossad and is Hospes with Interpol? You decide. Note: Israeli Mossad is aka The Institute for Intelligence and Special Operations and Interpol is aka International Criminal Police Organization. Could Aliquis and Hospes belong to these two groups and were they on assignment in South Africa for these organizations? Read on.

At 10:00 PM January 1, 2011, I may have received a phone call from operatives of the Israeli Mossad and Interpol, but of course, again, it could have been a prank international call. I report it as it comes to me. Here is that report.

Paul: Hello? Aliquis: (speaker phone)

Hello Paul, we just had a UFO sighting that was kind of unusual and want to make a report. (Accent).

Paul: Sure, go ahead. What is your name?

Aliquis: Call me Aliquis. My partner here is Hospes.

Paul: What are your full names? Where are you calling from? This is a very unusual number.

Hospes: No full names please (British accent?). We are here at Annadale, South Africa and we see something unusual. We can't explain it. Do you take UFO reports?

Paul: Yes, HPI takes UFO reports. How did you find me?

Aliquis: We read your UFO stories on the Internet; you are easy access to reach. This morning at 8am we see two UFOs. One UFO chased the other UFO and shot a beam at the other UFO. One UFO keeps its beam on the other UFO and moves it along and up into the clouds. The clouds parted and we could see the blue sky.

Paul: It is 10pm here and it's still Jan 1st. It must be Jan 2nd over there, correct?

Hospes: Yes, correct.

Paul: So, you are saying the one UFO shot out a trajectory beam at the other UFO and it appeared it was towing the other UFO with a beam?

Hospes: Yes.

Paul: What kind of work do you two do? And do you live in South Africa?

Aliquis: No, I am from Israel and my friend is from England. We are on assignment here in South Africa.

Paul: What kind of assignment?

Aliquis: I cannot comment on that.

Paul: What are the weather conditions? I have to ask you what kind of work do you do, for the establishment of your character for this report.

The Israeli Mossad agency contacted Paul Dale Roberts.

Hospes: Aliquis is an intelligence officer and I work in a Criminal Analysis Department. Some rain, partly cloudy at times, some thunder and we saw some lightning.

Paul: Hospes, sounds like he is from England and if he works for a Criminal Analysis Department, then most likely he works for Interpol?

Hospes: I cannot disclose that. Have there been any other sightings in South Africa?

Paul: Yes, South Africa is sometimes a hotbed for UFO sightings. I believe in 1965 some constables saw a UFO land in South Africa and in 1974 two men were abducted by a UFO. Many sightings take place in South Africa. Did you see any lights on the UFOs, and what were the shapes?

Hospes: Disc-shaped and they were both pulsating red. We were maybe 10 miles from the UFOs when we saw them.

Paul: Did they change color?

Hospes: No.

Paul: Was there any sound emitting from the crafts?

Hospes: No.

Paul: Were there any aircraft nearby?

Hospes: Not that we can see.

Paul: Were you two the only ones that saw it?

Hospes: From what we can tell, yes.

Paul: Do you think there was some kind of misidentification, perhaps these were conventional aircraft and what you saw was a light emitting from one plane to another and the other plane followed the other plane into the clouds?

Aliquis: No, we are experienced observers, we know what aircraft look like, we make no mistakes. And my organization has not made any mistakes, only when we didn't capture Mengele.

Paul: What? Mengele? The former German SS officer that was on the run, the Angel of Death? Israel Mossad was after Mengele. Are you Mossad?

Aliquis: (Laughing) Paul...you are a funny man. Even if I was, I would not be able to disclose that.

Paul: Okay, I think I have everything for my report. If you think of anything else or come across any other witnesses, please contact me again.

Aliquis: We will.

Personal Note from Paul:

I do believe that Aliquis and Hospes saw something in South Africa, something that they will never forget. Many prestigious men and women of all walks of life have seen UFOs. Here are some quick case examples. Major General Wilfried De Brouwer, a very distinguished Belgium military officer has reported sightings of UFOs. As of November 29, 1989 a total of 143 UFOs have been reported in Belgium alone. Federal police at Lake Gileppe witnessed a UFO shoot out 2 red light beams with a red ball at the spearhead of both beams, in the horizontal plane.

Neil Daniels a United Airlines pilot Captain for 35 years with 30,000 flying hours under his belt and holds the distinguished flying. Neil in 1977 saw a UFO with his co-pilot and flight engineer. They observed a perfect round brilliant light at their wing tip, only a mere 1000 yards away from their United DC-10 that was enroute to Boston Logan from San Francisco.

With credible witnesses like this, I scoff at the critics. These men know what conventional aircraft look like. When they say they saw a UFO, I have a strong tendency to believe them. When I hear someone faced with witnesses like this and say they are skeptical, I say SHUT UP and listen! Okay let's move on. In 1982 a Portuguese Air Force pilot named Julio Guerra looked out his cockpit window and saw a low-flying metallic disc. He was the Captain of Portugalia Airlines. He only saw this one UFO, but it changed his life forever. General Parviz Jafari of the Iranian Air Force on Sept 18, 1976 was flying over Tehran and encountered two UFOs. The UFOs did not show up on radar and at one point of time Jafari was preparing to shoot down the UFOs with his AIM-9 heat seeking missiles. All instruments on the plane stopped working, communication disabled, weapon control panel went out as he observed the UFOs that went 10 degrees to the right, 10 degrees to the left and 10 degrees back to the right, something that a jet can't even do! When the UFOs were gone, all instruments on the plane came back on and were in working order.

Commandant Oscar Santa Maria Huertas of the Peruvian Air Force witnessed UFOs, the list goes on and on and on! Did you know the FAA investigated a UFO that chased a Japanese 747 across the Alaskan sky for 30 minutes on November 7, 1986? Prestigious people from all around the world have witnessed UFOs or discovered the government knew more about UFOs than they want to admit, ask former head of British Defense Ministry's UFO Investigative Unit Nick Pope. Ask Fife Symington III, former governor of Arizona what he thinks those Phoenix Light were, and, believe me, he does not think they are flares!

It's just a matter of time, when we realize 1. We are not alone. 2. Extraterrestrials kick-started the human race and have been with us since the beginning of time. 3. Our governments knew about UFOs all along and suppressed it from the people. The day of enlightenment will be here soon.

. . . .

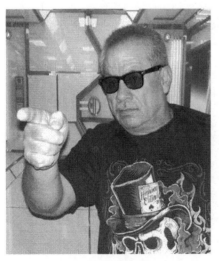

ABOUT THE AUTHOR: Paul Dale Roberts is a Fortean investigator who delves into ALL things paranormal – from Mothman, to the Chupacabra, UFOs, Crop Circles, Ghosts, Poltergeists, Demons and more. Roberts is the HPI (Hegelianism Paranormal Intelligence – International) Owner. www.facebook.com/groups/HPIinternational

Significant investigations by HPI are the Skinwalker Ranch in Utah, looking for Natalee Holloway's ghost in Aruba, UFOs and Bigfoot at Mount Shasta, UFOs and USOs at Monterey Bay, Area 51, Guatemala City – Guatemala.

Roberts now writes for online magazines such as "Chatterbrew Magazine": chatterbrew.com; "Lorena's Angels": www.lorenasangels.com; "Ceri Clark's All Destiny Magazine". Roberts was recently picked up by "Paranormal Magazine UK" and works for the online national news site "Before It's News."

**Did ancient Israelites establish contact with even more ancient aliens?
Art by Jim Nichols/UFO Universe.**

RETURN OF THE GIANTS

By Barry Chamish

PUBLISHER'S NOTE: While Paul Dale Robert's experience with the Israeli Mossad may seem unique, encounters with UFOs and their crews, i.e., ultra-terrestrials, are nothing new, especially if you go back to Biblical times with the tales of Enoch and Ezekiel. Barry Chamish, though now deceased, was a collector of the abnormal and unexplained throughout the Middle East, specializing in abductions, close encounters and what he termed the "return of the giants." He was a frequent contributor to *"UFO Universe"* and publications in Israel. The following constitutes a smidgen of his field investigations.

· · · · · · · · ·

ISRAEL AWAKENS TO THE INVASION

During the spring of 1980, I was a soldier in the anti-aircraft brigade of the Israeli Air Force. My duty was to operate two types of anti-aircraft missile. My unit was on training maneuvers in the bleak Sinai Desert and Private Adam Reuter was on sky-watch. While staring into the western skies with his binoculars, he called me over, saying, "I think I'm looking at a UFO." He handed me the glasses and I saw a large, well-lit, silvery object. Circling it were red objects that occasionally flew into the silver one, seemingly melding with it.

One by one, members of the unit were called to observe the sight until most had stopped digging their foxholes. Our officers intervened and everyone went back to their mundane military exercises. Everyone but Adam and I, who were severely reprimanded for slagging work. Nonetheless, we could not take our eyes off the sky.

Over the next three months, strange lights passed over our base. We had been trained to identify jets and helicopters of all kinds and how not to confuse them with

117

satellites. What we were seeing was nothing like anything taught in our sky-watching classes.

These were high-flying, soundless dots in the upper atmosphere that flew in squadrons, stopped in the middle of their flight, joined together then split off in different directions and turned at impossible angles. They were best described as manually controlled satellites. Since such a fleet of vehicles did not exist, we had no explanation for what we were seeing.

As the summer wore on, Adam and I were the sole advocates of the UFO theory and I especially was subjected to mockery. The most common theory among the unit was that a new weapons system was being tested, but, over time, that explanation did not suit even the most hardened critics.

One morning at assembly, the unit asked our officers to request an explanation from the Air Force. A few days after the request was submitted, a colonel from the Meteorological Division addressed us. His message was simple: "We don't know what you are seeing but we request that you do not tell outsiders since that only spreads rumors."

So the arguments over the lights continued and, as strongest advocate of the extraterrestrial visitation hypothesis, I was ribbed ruthlessly. This would not happen today. Back in 1980, very few Israelis had seen UFOs. The only major sightings were in Haifa in the early Fifties. Since then, Israel was mostly ignored by otherworldly civilizations.

The saucers have come to Israel.

UFO captured hovering over the Dome of the Rock at the Temple Mount Jerusalem

Despite the irritating kidding I was receiving, I began a little investigation. I was serving at a large air force base and pilots would occasionally lecture us on tactics for aiming and shooting our missiles. Once the lecture ended, I approached the pilots and asked them if they had ever chased UFOs. Because I was a fellow soldier, the pilots let down their guard. Two admitted that they had chased ships of unexplainable origin. One was glowing blue, and the pilot chased it over Haifa until it tired of the pursuit and sped off over the Mediterranean at a speed the pilot's state-of-the-art Phantom could never hope to achieve. The other chase was over Jerusalem. The object was twice as large as a Phantom, red and "disappeared before my eyes."

I am told that I was privileged to squeeze any information out of Israeli Air Force pilots. The person who told me so was Julie, a reporter for the official air force magazine, distributed to personnel throughout the country's air bases. We crossed paths in January, 1994. She was doing a story about the UFO wave for the magazine and we were interviewing the same people. She told me outright that there is a special unit within the air force investigating UFO incidents but, as far as anyone was concerned, it was non-existent. The air force would not help one of its own journalists get near the unit or its files. And pilots were ordered not to answer her questions.

There is, however, a former air force radar operator, who lives near Kadima and was briefly referred to before, who has been telling Ufologists a few interesting things. For instance, he told me, "The operators often get strange blips on their screens, such as objects flying at impossible speeds which shouldn't be there or objects making gravity-defying turns. These are reported and planes scrambled to chase them. I was personally responsible for two reports that led to chases. I saw the pictures the pilots took. They were of cigar shaped craft. The air force feels these craft are intruders and a security risk, so will not publicize incidents, partly to avoid panic and, in part, because there is no answer to them if they turn hostile."

Because the air force had effectively covered up UFO encounters and because there were so few sightings, until the late 1980s almost all Israelis viewed UFOs as pure science fiction. Then in 1988, two UFO incidents were well-filmed and documentary evidence was presented to the public.

On the 26th of February, 1988, Rosetta Kalphon was having a gathering at her apartment in Haifa on Israel's northern Mediterranean coast. Included among her fifteen guests was a professional photographer from Ashdod who had brought his video-camera with him.

As the evening drew to a close, all sixteen people stood on Rosetta's balcony and watched a spectacular UFO, while, for seventeen minutes, it was filmed professionally. Shortly after, journalists were invited to Rosetta's apartment to view the film.

Though I missed the occasion, I saw a frame of the film that was reproduced in a local paper called Kol Bo. The shot is outstanding, far clearer than Doron Rotem's blowup of Eli Cohen's videotape. The UFO is somewhat umbrella-shaped and on the side shown in the shot were eight smallish orange lights and, in the middle of them, an orange light twice their size.

I found the picture in Avi Grief's files while interviewing him in Haifa and hoped to see the original film while I was in the city. I managed to get Rosetta on the phone in the early evening. I told her I was writing a book on Israeli UFO experiences and her voice became very animated.

"It happened again," she said. "Two weeks ago, my apartment was filled with light and I went on the balcony. Opposite me, in the same place as in 1988, was a silver UFO as big as a house. I thought I was going crazy. What do they want with me already?"

On the 26th of June, 1988, the Israeli papers carried the account of Yossi Ayalon. Two nights before, at 1:30 AM, he stood on his balcony in Herzlia, ten miles north of Tel Aviv and saw a point of light appear on the horizon out of nowhere. "I called my wife out but the light had disappeared by then. Suddenly it reappeared as big and bright as the sun at dawn. I knew I was seeing something I'd never witnessed before, so I ran inside for my video camera and started filming."

Yossi did not call the police but rather sent the film to Israel Television for public scrutiny. He, however, refused to appear on television, explaining, "I never believed in UFO stories and I don't want to become a joke. But I just can't ignore what I filmed and saw." Nor could many viewers. Yossi's UFO is clearly round and, like many of the Israeli UFOs, emits a bright orange light. The roundness is broken by a dark colored square from the rim to the middle, taking up about 20% of the ship's size.

Thus, in 1988, two UFOs were videotaped in Israel and this evidence is important to me. The purpose of this work is to prove that UFOs and aliens visited Israel in its ancient past and returned again in 1987. Only by gathering the strongest physical evidence of the present could the more difficult biblical thesis be made plausible.

Although there are a number of UFO contactees in Israel, I vowed not to include their stories unless they were backed with physical evidence or corroborated by disinterested witnesses. Thus, with great dismay, I sat down to interview a UFO witness in Ramat Gan, a suburb of Tel Aviv, only to discover that he was a follower of an Indian mystic and made contact by putting himself in a trance. I politely turned down the offer of a sitting to meet the aliens via his mind.

Doron Rotem directed me to someone with "quite a story." On the phone, he told me he would not grant an interview until he had received permission from "them." As fascinating as his experience must be, I decided it would be out of context with the direction of reporting. I chose to concentrate on the physical to the almost complete neglect of the metaphysical. One of the most remarkable of the physical stories involved a chase right out of the movies.

Just before 3:00AM on the morning of December 6, 1991, Yossi Ben Maos was driving in a taxi outside the city of Bet Shean, in the Jezreel Valley approximately halfway between Haifa and Tiberius. It was then that he noticed that a strange vehicle emitting "a pleasing light" was pacing the taxi 150 meters opposite it. Yossi thought the craft must be some sort of glider carrying terrorists from Jordan, ten miles distant, to an attack. He and the driver decided to follow the glider to its destination and then call for the police. The craft stopped and hovered above the industrial zone of Bet Shean and there Yossi found a phone to make his report.

A squad car quickly arrived. The policeman took a look at the large object dangling in the air and immediately called his superior, Chief Inspector Yitzhak Mordechai, at home, woke him up and implored him to rush over. Mordechai told the policeman he was on his way and ordered him to call the army, air force, border guards and to alert the local kibbutzim.

Israeli police and army personnel opened fire on a UFO hovering over the Jezreel Valley in the early morning hours of December 6, 1991.

By the time Mordechai arrived, the industrial zone was filled with armed men. The UFO began moving slowly toward the Jordanian border, trailing a convoy of jeeps and police cars beneath it. The craft reached the border and turned back toward Israel.

After a half an hour of this eerie chase, the UFO settled in one spot, 150 meters in the air above Kibbutz Maoz Chaim. Beneath it were about a hundred armed men, many of whom thought it was a terrorist invader, though most understood by then that this was no earthly object. At about 5:00 AM someone gave the order to shoot. The shots were heard throughout the area and could not be covered up. The next day, the police blamed the army for shooting at the craft while army personnel accused the police of ordering the attack. The craft was not damaged by the fire and just at sunrise, an hour later, it rose into the sky and disappeared.

Thus, Ben Yossi Ben Maos and the unnamed cabbie witnessed the UFO for over three hours, while dozens of cops, soldiers and kibbutzniks stood under it for almost two and a half hours.

Doron Rotem interviewed a reserve soldier who as at the scene and his account is more expansive. According to the soldier, it wasn't just a few bullets that were shot but long rounds of small arms fire and shoulder-harnessed anti-aircraft missiles.

Yoram Torbatian says, "A lot of information about the Bet Shean attack is being covered up. The morning after the encounter Mordechai was telling the media what happened, truthfully. Later in the day, he was told to watch himself. After that, he wouldn't talk to anyone and won't to this day." If the Chief Inspector was open, it was for the public good. The UFO was witnessed by hundreds of Israelis and dozens had called radio stations demanding to know if a war had started, if there was a terrorist attack or just why they saw what they saw.

Mordechai gave a now famous radio interview, assuring the public that he had chased a UFO. "It wasn't a plane, it wasn't a helicopter or a meteor. It was a UFO." It is not known if his blunt report actually comforted the public but it certainly was blatant official confirmation of UFOs over Israel.

Reading Mordecchai's press quotes of that day is illuminating. In the morning, he told reporters, "After Yossi Ben Maos called the police, a squad car arrived and the policemen identified a mysterious glowing object moving eastward. At this point I had a car sent to me and began chasing the object until it stopped above Kibbutz Maoz Chaim. We stayed with it until almost six o'clock. When the sun rose, it left.

"The object was glowing and bright, it flew 200 meters above the ground and stood out clearly in the background of stars. It tipped from side to side until it balanced itself and then stayed in the same position, circling on its axis from left to right until it became steady. Then it stopped and hung in the sky. I don't believe it had hostile intentions.

"The craft seemed very curious about us. To tell the truth, I don't know what it was, but I saw what I saw and not for an instant but for two and a half long hours."

The official description of the night's events were reported in the Bet Shean police reports as, "A UFO incident."

Later in the day, Mordechai sat for an interview with Gabi Nitzan, a reporter for the daily, Chadashot. Already he was under scrutiny, as Nitzan reports: During the interview, Mordechai, under strict supervision from the spokeswoman of Israel Police's central headquarters, who "just happened to be with us, completely by accident," tried to obscure the incident. Before the spokeswoman could warn him about "correct talk," Mordechai admitted being deeply affected by the event.

Keeping in mind that Mordechai was under close scrutiny, his testimony is all the more important.

"A lot of policemen arrived, squad cars, patrol cars, security people from the kibbutzim, border guards, and army jeeps...It was a powerful experience, the first time

I've had to deal with anything like it. And make no mistake about it, a lot of men shared my experience. There's no doubt about what happened."

Nitzan got down to the question of who shot at the UFO, probably the main reason why the police spokeswoman was in the room. Mordechai gives no answer, so Nitzan asks, "Maybe it was the UFO that shot?" Mordechai answers as if there is no sarcasm in the question, "It never moved. Most of the time it just hung in the air above Kibbutz Maoz Chaim."

Spokeswoman or not, the police chief inspector of Bet Shean describes a large military operation and the use of armed force against the UFO. Israel's weapons seem to have had no effect on the UFOs whatsoever. Barely a month later on January 14, 1992, a couple from the southern city of Beersheva, Liza and Babar Alon, released a videotape of a UFO they had filmed two weeks earlier. The film clearly shows a glowing disc, dark in the middle, with a light circle following the rim, hanging above the skies of the Negev Desert. What distinguished the film was its length. The couple had managed to film the craft for a full forty-five minutes.

At 10 PM, on January 24, 1992, Israel was treated to the greatest UFO display of all. Israeli Ufologists call this UFO, "the mother ship." It traversed the country for two hours, beginning in the Haifa region, making appearances all along the densely populated coast, flying over Beersheva and the Negev before disappearing over Jordan.

Thousands of people witnessed the ship. What choice did they have? Reports put its length at that of two jumbo jets. Circling it were smaller craft that occasionally joined it, then were ejected into different flight patterns.

The best way to approach this incident is to quote some of the many reports printed in Israel's newspapers.

Ephi Sarid, photographer for Yediot Ahronot, who spotted the craft outside the Galilee city of Sfat; "I saw a huge light, and circling it were smaller lights. The length of the object wasn't clear but I estimated its width at 30 meters. It moved at high speed about 2 kilometers up. It was noiseless and lit up the whole sky."

Liran Shor, 16, from Haifa; "It flew low above the houses. It made no noise and that caught my attention. It was ellipsoid-shaped and huge, the length of two jumbo jets."

"The light was like burning embers, and it left an orange trail behind it. It lit up the whole street," said David Butrashvili, 32, high school physics and astronomy teacher. "It was ellipsoid-shaped, the length of two jumbo jets and travelled between 50 and 80 kilometers an hour."

Spaceships over Haifa, uploaded by Amf Amfik, March, 2016, YouTube.

Aran Mishelli, 13, Haifa: "It left a red, glowing trail behind it, inside of which there were two rockets spitting fire. Afterward, the big body split into three parts, two small, one big. They were white and left a red trail."

Pini Shechter, 17, Tiberius: "A small white ball flew ahead of the big ship and was connected to it by a white strip of light. The big ship left a fiery trail. The craft was about 35 meters in length and nine in height. Its color was white or red."

Tal Moran, 27, Haifa; "It was a huge ball of fiery light. Circling it were smaller balls and it left a trail of light. It was as big as several buildings and its predominant colors were red and white."

Rina Green, 42, Karmiel: "The craft was enormous. It flew at an altitude of a kilometer to a kilometer and a half and passed right over us. Its length was 200 meters and left a gigantic, fiery trail behind it."

Danny Kushner, 17, Rishon LeTzion: "I saw five lighted bodies flying in an arrow formation. Each left a white trail behind it."

Tel Aviv police patrolman: "I saw a huge, lit object falling from the skies over Tel Aviv. It split into three parts and disappeared."

Reserve soldier, stationed in the Negev Desert: "I saw seven huge red balls leaving trails behind them. They flew in formation with one leading them. The white vapor trails lit up the whole desert."

Menachem Shizef, Kiryat Shmoneh (Galilee region): "I saw a huge object made up of shiny points of light. It seemed like an enormous submarine constructed of sparkling lights."

The testimony, while often contradictory, agrees on a number of points. The UFO was enormous and left a bright trail behind it. Israeli Ufologists call it the mother ship because of the reports of smaller craft circling, joining, separating from or following it.

The ship took its time investigating Israel. It was reported as ten to twenty times larger than any other previous Israeli sighting. Yet the Israeli Air Force reported that it had not appeared on any of its radar screens. However, the same military minds could not deny the observations of thousands of people.

UFOs had been inspecting Israel for the past three years and now the mother of all UFOs made her appearance without shame. What was the mission and was there a message? A Haifa auto mechanic, Amiel Achrai, thinks there is both.

UFO HOVERS OVER HAIFA

In November, 1994, I sent a summary of the UFO landings and giant sightings between April-July 1993 to the television show "Sightings." By January, a "Sightings" crew was in place to record the incidents. As if the visitors knew about my plans, they returned after a long hiatus, just in time for "Sightings" to film some of the most convincing evidence of giants ever recorded.

In late December, Yossi Torner photographed a huge, round, orange UFO hovering over Haifa, which was reproduced in the large circulation newspaper, Yediot Ahronot. I called him to try and receive the original print and he informed me, "Yediot returned my whole roll of film but said they lost the negative of the UFO. I think they're lying and it was confiscated from me."

A week later, on the first Tuesday of 1995, Israel had an incident that must be included amongst the most powerful encounters of any nation. Herzl Consatini, the security chief of the village of Yatzitz, ten miles east of Rishon Letzion, heard an explosion which shook his friend Danny Ezra's house. He opened the front door to investigate and was confronted with "a giant, three meters tall, wearing grey clothes.

His face was hidden from view by an electronic-looking mist." Terrified, he slammed the door and told Ezra to look through his curtains. He took one glance and fainted.

Herzl called the police, who were reluctant to believe him but nonetheless, arrived within twenty minutes. They found deep, mysterious tracks outside Ezra's house. Thinking that terrorists had infiltrated the village, dozens of army trackers and snipers were called in. They found 8.5 kilometers of totally unexplainable tracks. The tracks were made by shoes which dug 35 cm. into the hard soil at the sole, and between 5 and 10 at the heel. Later testing of the ground by the police suggested that the creature had to have weighed over a ton to make such deep tracks.

The tracks were made in twos but, occasionally, a third round mark appeared between them. I guessed this was a walking stick of some kind. Sometimes the tracks were like a human gait, then there would be a twelve-foot gap before the tracks began again. At times, the creature which made them must have jumped or floated enormous distances.

The tracks led army trackers to the village of Karmei Yosef, which had been the center of UFO activity the year before. There, unidentified red lights hovered above the village and one villager claimed the lights sent a blue beam at her through her bedroom window. The trackers could make no guess at who or what made the prints in the ground, so the police called in the head of the regional office of the Nature Reserves Authority, who originally disclosed that the tracks were made by a camel. When it was revealed that the camel would have had to have been two-legged and wearing boots, he next guessed an antelope made the tracks. A flying antelope, it was noted. Finally, he admitted to Yediot Ahronot, "The tracks may well have been made by giants from outer space."

I travelled to Yatzitz four days later and was joined by several dozen curiosity seekers. More than 10,000 Israelis would eventually arrive to see the giant tracks. I met Danny Ezra first and can only say that he seemed to be in a daze still. He was not forthcoming about his experience. Herzl Consantini was enjoying his new fame (that, too, would end) and showed me his medical certificates. He was rushed to hospital the evening after his encounter with one gonad blown up "like a balloon." The doctor who signed the report wrote that the cause of the affliction was unknown but heavy doses of antibiotics brought down the swelling.

Herzl agreed to be filmed by "Sightings" and two young boys who had overheard the conversation told me they had something interesting to tell as well. The night after the incident, they had filmed a UFO over the village. The boys, Coby (13) and Itamar (11) Saadon filmed a white object, shaped like a child's spinning top, darting like a moth in the sky. In the background, the family dog was barking wildly and the boys' mother told me, "You should see what's around his doghouse."

We walked outside and saw a burnt circle of six feet diameter around the dog's pen. A foam cushion within was melted by the heat, yet there were no charcoals or anything hinting at fuel to be seen. "The dog has been terrified ever since," Coby explained.

Next to make headlines was the Gueta animal mutilations of Moshav Porat, two miles from Kadima. Rachel Gueta awoke and found her dog whining. Its eyes had been removed bloodlessly. Twenty minutes later, it died. She proceeded to the sheep pen and saw all three sheep dead. Their cheeks had been shaved and a two centimeter hole drilled through the bone. All blood had been drained and the animals would not rot, even five months after being thrown in the local dump. Next she went to her chicken coop and found all 35 birds frozen dead in their roosts. There had been no panic among them at the time of death. Outside the coop was a 4.5 meter crop circle, typical of the Kadima wave of 1993.

I phoned my producer at "Sightings" and told her the stories. She told me later she didn't believe me and there were discussions about canceling the filming because of my unreliability. My faxing her newspaper reports of the one ton Yatzitz giant saved the project. And to this day, I think the aliens decided to help me out. After the "Sightings" crew began its filming, those otherworldly forces provided us with almost live action.

On January 14, we visited Hanna Somech in Burgata. We were preceded by two days by a far more dramatic visitor. Hanna's daughter "felt" the presence of a giant watching over her bed and she ran the 100 yards from her house to her mother's, where, "I held my mother's hands all night." The next morning, they saw the circles from Hannah's house to her daughter's bedroom window. And so did we, two days later. I counted 18 circles big and small in the dark. Undoubtedly I missed some. There were counter-clockwise circles on the grass, in bushes and on high treetops. To cause a fraud, the trickster would have had to have hovered over twenty foot trees with a counter-rotating giant fan. The "Sightings" crew, incidentally, all skeptics about UFOs, grasped quickly enough that something as unexplainable as Yatzitz had occurred in Burgata.

Hanna related her encounter of June 1993 when she told a giant off for making her dog fly in the air and hurting it. She told the interviewer that there was another incident when she had seen a craft floating outside her door. She related being called to "in my head" by name at different times. But perhaps most significant of all, she admitted that 25 years before she had been pregnant and the fetus disappeared with no medical explanation. She provided the name of the doctor who attended her and offered to present written documentation. She now believes the lost pregnancy was related to the current visitations. (Batya Shimon of Rishon Letzion became pregnant after her July '93 encounter with a dozen giants. "There is no way it could have happened naturally," she insisted.)

On January 15, the giants or whoever or whatever again decided to help the "Sightings" project. A UFO was spotted over Kadima and in the morning a monster 18 meter circle was found. When we arrived, it was literally still warm. We put our hands within and they were covered in the red oil found during the 1993 wave. As usual, silicon was discovered and it later tested 99.35% pure by the University of Manchester (England) Materials Science laboratory. All the evidence of 1993 was presented just when the film crew needed it most. And when the filming ended, so did the incidents at Kadima for many months.

Israeli Ufologist Zvi Bighest photographed the filming at the circle, and when he developed the film later that day, something emerged that seemed to defy logic. In the background of the circle are two "beings" seemingly watching the humans examine their landing mark..

None of us remembered the objects being there. But Doron Rotem noted that tractors were in the area and might have been passing by. The photos were examined, enlarged and published in numerous magazines, including *"Fate Magazine"* and *"UFO Universe."* In each case, the editors ruled out any tractor shape and agreed that whatever they were, the two figures matched the bald, round-faced giants described by the witnesses.

The giants had returned. And this time they chose to leave no doubt about their presence. They left miles of impossible boot tracks in hard mud, they swirled circles in tall trees, they produced a huge, hard-to-miss landing circle and they may have allowed themselves to be photographed.

THE INVESTIGATION CONTINUES

Dec. 8, 1994.

Two weeks ago, I sent the manuscript of my book on recent Israeli UFO incidents, along with photographic and physical evidence, to Paramount Studios in Hollywood, where the "Sightings" program is produced. Today I received a call from the show's producer hiring me to arrange a few days shooting for the program beginning January 11.

December 22, 1994.

A Haifa resident, Yossi Torner, took a photograph of a large UFO over the city, and it appeared in the country's biggest circulation newspaper, "Yediot Ahronot." The newspaper refused to return the negative, claiming it had been lost. All other shots on the film are returned.

First week of January, 1995.

Tuesday and Saturday – After a lull of a year and a half, the aliens return to Israel. In 1993, strange giants over seven feet tall were seen and spoken to by four professional women in their late 30s, three in the area of Kadima, forty miles north of Tel Aviv, and one in Rishon Letzion, twenty miles south of the city.

On Tuesday evening at 8.30, two male residents of Yatzitz, a farm village ten miles east of Rishon Letzion, are terrified to see a giant outside the home of Herzl Casatini, the area security chief. Casatini describes the creature as nine feet tall, wearing shiny metallic clothing, its face obscured by a strange misty glow. He notifies the police, who arrive and find peculiar tracks outside his window. Fearing a terrorist incursion, dozens of army and security personnel are called in to investigate. They trace the tracks of two separate creatures for eight kilometers to the village of Karmei Yosef, which had been the scene of a week of UFO activity the year before.

The tracks sank 35cm into the hard ground, and estimates of the weight of whatever made them are in the range of a ton. The tracks are of shoes but the walker stepped on his soles, in tippy toe fashion. The heel sinks only 5cm. Investigators jumping on the ground can only make tracks of a few millimeters in depth. The tracks reveal a gait of from a few feet up to twelve feet, meaning the beings occasionally literally floated between steps. Casatini becomes very ill the next day with an enlarged gonad. Doctors have no explanation for his condition.

At 6.am on Saturday morning, Memuneh Guata, a fortyish resident of the farm village of Porat, three miles from Kadima, awoke to feed her animals. She ventured into the eerie silence to find carnage. Her dog breathed its last breath in her arms. Its eyes had been surgically removed without blood. Her thirty-five chickens were dead, literally frozen in their place. Her three sheep were dead, with perfectly round holes drilled in their cheeks. By May, they had still not rotted in the village dump, and were in a mummified state.

Jan. 11 1995."Sightings" cameraman Phil Lapkin arrives. His first two days are spent filming witnesses to the Haifa (Shikmona Beach) and Kadima landings. On the evening of his second day, a UFO is witnessed in Kadima by an American new immigrant and his son. Local researchers found the landing site in the morning and we arrive. The circle is huge, eighteen meters in diameter, and it still smells acrid. When we put our hands in the crushed grass, they are coated with the red fluid we assume is the same cadmium-based oil left in the Kadima circles of 1993. Also found were the shards of shiny material previously tested by the Israeli Geological Institute and found to be pure silicon. Some shards weigh over a pound. Ufologist Zvi Bighest photographs the area.

He develops the shots and from a distance bald, round-faced creatures appear in five of them. They appear to be observing us. Lapkin takes the photos back to America and we are still eagerly awaiting analysis. We all agree the images are hard to explain but are they really invisible aliens?

Jan. 15, 1995. We visit Hanna Samech, a witness, at her home in Burgata, two miles from Kadima. In June 1993, she saw her barking dog fly in the air and smash against her kitchen wall. She went outside to investigate but was prevented by an invisible shield. She then saw the giant alien and demanded to know what he did with her dog. He smiled wryly and replied that he could do the same thing to her if he wanted to but simply didn't feel like it. The alien's ship left a 4.5 meter circle with the red oil within.

Hanna's married daughter lives in a neighboring home fifty yards away. Three days before, the aliens visited her. There are circles about a meter in diameter from Hanna's front door to her daughter's bedroom window. I count eighteen of them. Whatever made the circles was a powerful force that crushed bushes and small trees. The alien stood over the daughter's bed and held her hand. Hanna claims on camera that the aliens have been visiting her for years and that when she was twenty-five, they removed her baby from her womb. She also stated that she is called by name telepathically from time to time.

February 1995. The "Sightings" staff inform me that the material is so strong that a decision has been made to broadcast four segments instead of the intended two. Two videotapes of UFOs had been verified as real, the oily grass within the Kadima circles had "conformed in molecular structure with circles found worldwide," and the silvery shards were indeed silicon-based but "with some very unusual characteristics."

March 1995. Two giants are witnessed again. In Afula, twenty miles east of Kadima, four astonished young women watched an oversized hairy bouncing head in their apartment garden for twenty minutes before the appearance of a seven foot giant in the adjacent parking lot sent them scurrying in terror. All witnesses felt the giant was female. A week later, a giant male was sighted by a young woman near Ramat Hasharon not far from Tel Aviv. Plaster casts taken at the site showed a similar track to that of the Yatzitz visitors.

On a Tuesday evening in mid-March, the popular national television program, "The Ruby Show," devoted an hour to the wave of sightings and strange occurrences. I was invited as a guest along with Casatini, Guata, Batya Shimon, who had two visitations in Rishon Letzion, and Jonathan G., the American immigrant who witnessed the January Kadima UFO. He brought a document with him from the Israeli Atomic Research Laboratory. Technicians there tested the shards and discovered them to be different from those of 1993. They were found to be 75.6% silicon but significant traces of a wide variety of elements, including barium, rhodium, titanium, iron and aluminium(aluminum) were found. Batya informed me that the aliens still call to her by name telepathically.

The show was something of a set-up, with three debunkers as guests. Nevertheless, in my opinion, the sincerity of the witnesses wins the day. I explain that unless fifteen people who didn't know each other yet described seeing the same type of giant formed a conspiracy, there were, in fact, giants roaming Israel. I added that reports of giants in Israel were last made in the time of King David and that the biblical giants were the enemies of God and Israel. I noted that the re-appearance of giants is not necessarily a reason to celebrate.

The show was supposed to have been broadcast two weeks later. But, two months later, the show has still not been seen. I phone every week to find out why, and am told that it will be shown the next week. It never is and I'm beginning to become suspicious. It is clear to me, as it is to all other Israeli Ufologists, as it is to the producers of "Sightings," that Israel is the scene of intense UFO activity, and the giants of the ships are leaving clues, including the shards, oils and tracks as well as permitting themselves to be photographed and seen.

Of the fifteen people who have seen the giants, thirteen have been women and all contactees have been married women. No one has been hurt by the giants except Herzl Casatini and it is likely he was not meant to be a witness. Nonetheless, the behavior of the tall visitors has been far from friendly and the goodness of their purpose is still in great doubt.

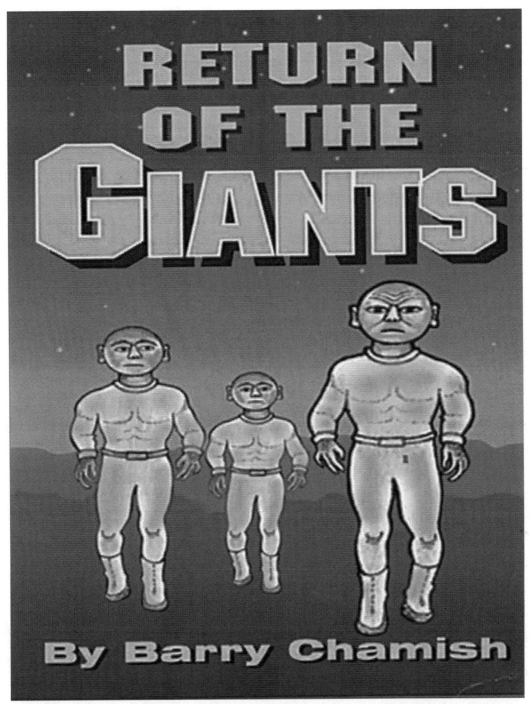

In his book, "*Return of the Giants,*" Barry Chamish writes that there are only two periods of recorded history when giants were reported in Israel: in biblical days and since 1993 in modern Israel.

INCREDIBLE ALIEN ENCOUNTERS

The respected American UFO abduction researcher Derrell Sims arrived in Israel in mid-January for five days of intensive work. His primary goal was to thoroughly test a Netanya household over three days but by the end of his trip, Sims also examined another abductee, Yossi Saguy.

SPIRITS ROAM A NETANYA APARTMENT

On Dec. 31 at 7:55 PM, Shoshana Bar-on, a fortyish mother and grandmother, was returning home from Tel Aviv by car with her live-in boyfriend Ilan Cohen. Both spotted an orange/red disk flying over the seaside cliffs of Netanya. Ilan stopped his car and both chased the object. They saw it break into three parts; one part further split into dozens of glowing plates which fell on the beach below.

Shoshana bent over the cliff and saw four typical small greys on the ledge below. She called Ilan over to look but he could not see the entities. She stood up and saw a nine foot long, clam-shaped craft appear opposite her. The top of the "clam" opened and she saw four entities, three in a row and a pilot sitting forward, seated in tight, tiny chairs.

One of the entities floated vertically from the craft and stunned Shoshana with his "white projector-like beams coming from his eyes." He approached her and rubbed her arm to the neck with a stubby, soft hand. She later recalled that his touch didn't feel bad. Nonetheless, she was screaming at Ilan to save her but he didn't hear anything. He watched her slowly collapse to the ground but could not run to pick her up because he was "frozen, magnetized to the spot."

Within a few minutes he found the strength to approach her but couldn't lift her because, "She felt like a concrete block buried in the ground." With much effort, he finally did manage to drag her away but she insisted he take her back "in a voice that wasn't her own." Ignoring her request, he pulled her to the road several hundred yards distant, where he flagged down a car which drove them to a nearby hospital.

At this point the story becomes strange enough to scare off any rational UFO investigator. Shortly after admitting Shoshana with a burnt face, Ilan decided he didn't like the treatment they were receiving and before being released, escaped the hospital with Shoshana, the police trailing right behind.

They made good their escape and returned to their apartment, where Ilan called a long list of local UFO researchers to attend, essentially, a press conference. Within an hour, about a dozen Ufologists surrounded the bed where Shoshana and Tali, Ilan's eleven year old daughter from a previous marriage, lay. Over the next week,

Ilan dragged the researchers on numerous wild UFO chases until all had written him off as berserk. Hearing a rumor that Maariv reporter David Ronen was about to print an unfavorable report of him, Ilan had a lawyer issue a restraining order against him, preventing publication of his piece.

Nonetheless, both Ilan and Shoshana appeared on television, Channel Two's 5 PM news program, and I was impressed by their story. I called the station and agreed to meet them the next day despite dire warnings within the UFO community.

Shoshana modestly related her story and told me of other phenomenon: a drilling sound in her left ear, horrid headaches, a pungent stench when the spirits entered the apartment, an ammonia-like taste in the mouth after, a needle puncture behind her ear. Her story was sincere and the puncture mark real. Ilan far too energetically added details. His daughter had been visited by spirits or whatever they were for the past year. They were stealing away her devotion to him and transferring it to them. He had videos made of the UFOs flying over the cliff and he returned to the encounter site and collected strange rocks left on the ground.

The rocks sold me. One was light and brown. When you lit it with a match it bubbled and melted. Drippings from the rock landed on the table and immediately turned hard and black. I had never seen a rock like that and didn't believe Ilan capable of creating one for a hoax.

I phoned my editor, Michael Hesemann, and gave my verdict that this was a powerful case. Accepting my conclusion, I was flattered that Hesemann quickly organized Sims' trip to Israel to investigate in depth.

He arrived on a Friday and Ilan gave a demonstration that was an immediate doubt-breaker. He took out a shiny rock found at the encounter site and placed it on an ice cube. Though it had not been heated and was at room temperature, it melted right through the ice and became almost as cold as it. Derrell and I agreed that we had never heard of a rock that does anything like this. Where did the heat come from?

Derrell next passed a black light over Shoshana. Explaining that fluorescence is a common feature of alien encounters, he found what he was looking for in her hands. Her palms and fingers glowed yellow green and near perfect fluorescent circles were found just below her thumb. The soles of her feet also displayed subdermal fluorescence.

We went to sleep, I relieved that I had not dragged Derrell ten thousand miles for nothing. The next day, Derrell began serious questioning, designed in part to trip

Soshana up. Ilan didn't approve of the approach, in fact was confused by it and became increasingly more intrusive.

With great difficulty, Shoshana drew, under Derrell's skilled guidance, accurate drawings of prototypical small greys about 90 cm in height and possessing arms that dangled below the knees. With even more difficulty Derrell succeeded in putting Shoshana under light hypnosis. She recalled the incident three times but each time she saw the "projector eyes" her face contorted and she snapped to with a painful headache.

As evening approached, I stood by the window and smelled a stench that shocked me. I yelled, "The smell, it's here!" It was like burnt tires and it came from nowhere. No electric appliance or any other source could explain its presence. It filled my sinuses and left a lingering, awful taste in my mouth. Derrell was next to smell it and did so on four other occasions in four other locations in the apartment. There was no logical explanation for it.

As the investigation continued, Ilan became impossible. Seeing that Shoshana and his daughter were the main foci of the research, he became totally intrusive and insulting when things weren't done his way. I was warned that this would happen but was unprepared for how irritating the behavior could be. I left the apartment in anger at 2 AM, vowing to return only for the final hypnotic session the next day.

Derrell warned Ilan that he would be the next to leave unless he removed himself while he was examining Shoshana and Tali. He acquiesced and Derrell gathered more vital evidence. A red ball of energy had entered Shoshana's bedroom the previous week and she told it to go away. Five minutes later it appeared outside her window. She had told me the same story previously only she ordered the ball away from Tali's room and it changed directions before leaving.

Tali's tales of abductions dovetailed with Shoshana's. The beings flew in a craft too small for Shoshana to fit it. They had a spare chair just big enough for her to fit into. The next day she told me she had to sit in the snug chair while flying or she would float around the little craft. She also added that when they took off, her stomach rose from the propulsion.

Tali was even more persuasive than Shoshana because of both her sharpness and her innocence. She knew the names of two of her abductors; Shimshon, the nice one and Makhluf, not as nice. When Derrell drew her a picture of a somewhat more elongated face, she recoiled from fear. She added details of the chairs Shoshana had drawn. Because Shoshana had only seen the craft at eye-level, she had not seen the legs of the chairs but she had seen arms with control buttons on them. Tali had seen the same arms and buttons but the legs as well. And both confirmed that the beings had rather stubby fingers.

Tali had described a site near a beachside hotel where she said the beings lived. Ilan insisted on taking Derrell to the location, though he had misgivings. Two nights before Ilan had taken us to the cliffs to point out UFOs which were clearly boats and planes. But this time he didn't disappoint. Telling Derrell to stand away, Ilan walked to a spot some yards distant and was quickly surrounded by unusually skittish alley cats. Something drew them to him in unexplainable numbers.

An added factor that must be considered is the location of Netanya, some ten miles west of the village of Kadima. Since 1993, this tiny area has seen five highly documented encounters with tall aliens, at least fifteen landing circles imbued with a red cadmium-based liquid and hundreds of craft sightings.

Our mutual conclusion was that the cases of Shoshana and Tali are genuine. Derrell believes Shoshana was not abducted, the craft's size would mitigate against that, but Tali was and on numerous occasions. We agreed that the case is a strong one but because of the difficulty, in fact, near impossibility of working properly, we would not want to do a repeat investigation.

NEXT VISIT, YOSSI SAGUY

On his next to last evening in the country, I had about 20 of Israel's top UFO researchers over to my home to meet Derrell. Yossi Saguy insisted on coming. He was a publicized abductee who knew I doubted his story. The problem began when I organized an episode for "Sightings" last September. I invited Saguy, who is a professional actor, to be interviewed. His agent phoned me not long after to discuss terms. An incident like that tends to plant doubts deeply.

However, most Israeli researchers accept Saguy's story of his beach house being invaded by robot-like creatures, who took a sperm sample from him and left appliances inoperable. They point to the dozens of witnesses who saw a craft over his building the night of the alleged abduction. Derrell demonstrated his techniques to the local investigators and put Saguy through a grilling interrogation. His verdict: "He passed with flying colors."

Thus ended Sims' five-day odyssey to Israel. This was the first time Israel's abduction stories had been examined by a worldwide expert in the field and all passed "with flying colors." Israel is indeed the focus of intense UFO abduction activity.

COLUMNIST DAVID RONEN

David Ronen is in an enviable position. Because he is the only UFO columnist for a major newspaper, Zman Tel Aviv, a weekend magazine of Maariv, he is the first address for Israeli UFO witnesses to contact. And David Ronen is one of the most honest, decent personalities in Israeli ufology.

Unfortunately, anti-UFO forces and plain old hucksters have exploited his sincerity in the past and it seems they're at it again. It was David who first broke the story of the Achihod "alien" in December of '96, one of the most embarrassing episodes in Israel's short UFO history. And this month he has broken two stories that are spreading fast. I hope to nip at least one story in the bud before it causes worse damage than even the Achihod fiasco.

The first story is that two individuals visited him with the same tattoo burned into their skin: that of an oval-eyed child-like figure. David reported that one of his visitors was an Israeli politician "known around the world." This has sparked massive speculation throughout Israel and the politician, who David cannot identify, nonetheless will be so identified soon since he is a high-ranking Knesset member who lives in Kiryat Ono. If he does not confirm the story, David will have a huge embarrassment on his hands... But maybe he will...when pigs can fly, and they barely walk in Israel.

David began April with an even bigger story. He claimed an alien had been photographed in Eilat and his article was accompanied by a computer depiction of a typical grey alien garnered from two photos he had received.

Here's the story David told me and his readers. On August 11, 1996, the Red Sea resort of Eilat was overflown by UFOs witnessed by hundreds of people. This is a fact. One Shimon Zohar took his video camera to a hill above Eilat's port to film the UFOs. He succeeded in capturing a UFO on film, but, when he played the cassette back at home, he saw an alien on the film, which he described as having "small eyes, and barely noticeable lips and nostrils."

He immediately called a group of people to see the film, including TV producer Yifat Dargesh and abductee/conference organizer Carlos Bin Nun. The former insisted she saw an alien "with big black eyes just like on the X-Files," while the latter cam-corded the film off the TV screen.

After the crowd left, David Ronen insists ten people saw the film; Zohar contacted his rabbi and invited him to see the film. The rabbi informed him that he had captured a demon on film and thus the cassette must be destroyed. Zohar obeyed and trashed the invaluable evidence. But he recalled that he had forgotten his camera tripod on the spot and returned the next night with one Benny Mazgini to recover it. While approaching the tripod, a UFO returned and Mazgini "was so frightened, I snapped two pictures automatically."

The UFO did not appear on the film but an alien did.

David had Bin Nun's two stills taken from Zohar's TV screen detailed by a computer graphics expert and what should appear then but a "grey" face replete with black, oval eyes. Now Israelis think that one of their countrymen photographed an alien and Maariv is being approached by worldwide networks. David told me, "CNN and NBC have already said they want the story. This is going global."

And, once again, Israeli Ufology is about to be humiliated. The story is ridiculous enough. Zohar destroys the original cassette but returns to recover his tripod with an associate who happens to have a camera handy.

They discover a 30 meter burnt circle around the tripod and just at that moment, the UFO decides to return. Luckily, Mazgini was so scared he clicked his camera twice and though he didn't actually see an alien, it showed up on his film when he developed it. But Mazgini was not prepared to let David Ronen actually see the photos. Ronen would have to make do with Bin Nun's second generation video reproduction of Zohar's original tape.

Now let us look at the personalities involved in this story.

* David Ronen - A good journalist, but too easily swayed by unscrupulous opportunists. Even after BUFORA - England tested the Achihod "alien" and found its carbon level the same as a lizard's, he refused to give up the fight. Eight months later, he published a laboratory test by police pathologist Dr. Yehuda Hiss concluding the creature was not of this world.

* Dr. Yehuda Hiss- This man has been totally disgraced for his role in covering up two of Israel's greatest scandals. The first was the Rabin assassination. While Israel police and three doctors who attended Rabin stated he was shot point blank, once from the front, and that his spine had been shattered, none of which the convicted murderer could have done, Hiss signed a final pathology report eliminating all the damning wounds. Second, early in Israel's history, the authorities kidnapped and sold 4500 babies, mostly from Yemenite immigrant parents. Last year, the Hebrew University of Jerusalem conducted DNA tests on an elderly Yemenite lady and a California woman who suspected she had been kidnapped from the woman and adopted in America. The tests matched and thus the kidnapping claims were verified. Dr. Hiss conducted his

own tests on behalf of the government, which supposedly nullified the results of Hebrew University. He was the last man on earth who would have given an honest testing of the Achihod alien lizard.

* Carlos Bin Nun - Coincidently or probably not, just as the Achihod fraud gathered momentum, Bin Nun's UFO conference took place in Eilat. A mystic speaker promised that the UFOs would land in Tel Aviv on Jan. 4 and announce their presence to the world. Definitely not coincidentally, the next day all the major newspapers announced the prediction and on the eve of Jan. 4, Israeli TV changed its prime time programming to make an utter mockery of the false prediction. Between Achihod and that horrible evening, legitimate Israeli Ufology was given a blow it should not have recovered from. Yet, so many powerful UFOs were filmed in 1997, that the public still could not ignore what was happening in their skies and sometimes, in their homes.

*Zohar and Mazgini - They know each other because they share deep debt. Mazgini is chairman of the Mortgage Victims Association of Eilat, which represents those who fell into debt because of the cutthroat mortgage policies of Israeli banks. Zohar and Mazgini need money in a hurry to sort out their lives and certainly could have concocted their alien story, falsely believing people pay lots of pictures of aliens. It all adds up to another pathetic attack on local Ufology. But there is good news. Once this fraud passes, I will report on a genuine abduction case in Ramat Gan and I have the pictures to back it up. I add, David Ronen reported this case as well with great skill and insight.

GETTING WEIRDER

As the Israeli UFO wave progresses along its unexplainable path, the phenomena associated with it have turned weirder and probably eviler. Two incidents among Jews involving the transformation of entities into uglier forms are well known but suppressed. In 1997, a fourteen- year-old Russian immigrant from Rishon Letzion approached what he thought was a little girl in a park who turned into a grey-like alien. The autumn before, two fashionable Tel Aviv women on an equally fashionable Tel Aviv street saw a tall man turn into a monster that clung to their car window and held on even while the terrified women desperately tried to drive away. The story, I am reliably informed, was buried because one of the women was the television news reporter, Ayala Hassan. Since then, almost all similar publicized incidents have involved Arabs. It is possible that the reports of demons have nothing to do with the

UFO wave. That cannot be said of the gruesome animal mutilations, which almost always were accompanied by UFO activity and evidence.

1997 saw a peak in UFO video films, culminating in the filmed capture of an invasion of low flying black "sponges" over downtown Tel Aviv. April 1998 saw Israel's first crop formation. The wave is expanding into areas which seem beyond reason...unless reason is not the point of it at all. I recorded the current state of affairs in a series of reports over the Internet:

ARABS REPORT ENCOUNTERS WITH DEMONS

The Arabs of Israel and its disputed territories have been harassed in recent months by what they believe are demons. The following stories have been reported in the respectable daily newspapers *Yediot Ahronot* and *Maariv*.

On October 14, Dr. Harav Ibn Bari, a physician at Hasharon Hospital in Petach Tikveh, was returning from Beersheva by car with his cousin Dudi Muhmad at the wheel. He relates, "After passing the bridge to Tel Aviv at 3:30 AM, I saw a strange figure on the opposite side of the road. We did a U-turn and stopped the car. The figure came out of the shadows and into the light. He was small and his body color, light. He lifted his right leg and approached us at terrific speed. He had huge, bulging, round black eyes. They contrasted with the white color around them. It was as if he was reading my thoughts and I couldn't take my eyes off his for six seconds. He lifted his right hand and Muhmad pressed on the gas and took off."

On October 19, Khaj Muhmad Jamal Kavah, 45, a Tel Aviv cab driver who lives in the Arab village of Al-Arian, met his cousin Ataf Kavah at 6 PM at Mei-Ami Junction to drive to a dinner party. "I saw him and signaled that he wait a moment while I relieved myself first. I heard him say, 'Okay.' When I was finished, I approached the car and saw that Ataf was wearing a shiny suit. I thought to myself, in his whole life Ataf never wore material like that. I bent down to open the door and saw that Ataf wasn't sitting in the driver's seat. I stared over and over but the driver paid no attention to me. Then I saw the weird creature. He had long hair reaching to his shoulders; his nose was enormous like an eggplant, colored purplish black. I almost had a heart attack. But I regained my senses and began walking backwards towards the highway. My plan was to make a break for the cars if he followed me. But I couldn't run because I felt something holding me in place for fifteen minutes. Then Ataf opened the door and came out looking totally confused. I shouted at him, 'You're not Ataf. What do you want from me?'"

Is there a connection with UFO sightings and reports of demons in Israel?

Ataf recalls sitting in the car and wondering why it was taking Muhmad so long to get in. He got out of the car and asked him what he was waiting for. He remembers Muhmad yelling, "You're not Ataf. Who are you? Where's the shiny suit you were wearing?"

Since the incident, Muhmad took and passed a polygraph test arranged for him by Maariv. His home has become a pilgrimage center as dozens of people a day come to hear his story. Included among them are Muslim religious leaders who have concluded that Muhmad met a demon and irritated him by relieving himself in his territory. They say the demons are rising because so many Arabs are straying from their religion.

The next night, October 20, will never be forgotten by Eli Hawald, 33, of a village near Haifa called Kfar Hawald. The tiny village has no electricity and when Eli Hawald went outside at 11:00 PM, all was too clear for him. "Out of nowhere, I saw a gigantic green light, the color of a traffic light, fall out of the sky. I ran into the house, locked the door and watched from the window. When the craft was about ten meters above the ground, the light was dimmed and three figures were 'shot' to the ground from it. I began to shake. They had human-like bodies, but, because they were 20 meters from my house, I couldn't distinguish their faces, just their color, which was completely black. They acted oddly. They would fan out, quickly return to one formation and fan out again. I remember two things distinctly. They reformed after a siren was sounded that resembled puppies crying. And their speed was fantastic, tens of meters in two seconds. At this point, I alerted my wife and children and we escaped through the back door."

Two days later, Jenin was the site of perhaps the most remarkable incident of all. According to Yediot Ahronot reporter Said Badran, a Jenin resident picked up a hitchhiker on the Jenin-Dotan road. A few moments after he sat in the front seat, the driver looked at him and saw his face had become that of a dog with one eye. The driver stopped his car, got out and fainted after he saw the hitchhiker disappear.

Badran concludes, "The incident has become the talk of Jenin. Some of the religious leaders believe that the passenger was a demon who lives in the area. Others believe he is a devil known as The Blind Liar who has returned to presage the arrival of the messiah. The driver is still in shock and is being treated at Jenin Hospital."

The latest encounter was reported by Maariv on the 29th of December. On December 26, Daoud Ahmad, of the Nur-a-Shamat refugee camp, was taken to hospital with severe bruises and there told doctors he was beaten brutally by two small aliens he had surprised in his house.

According to Ahmad, "I awoke at one in the morning feeling thirsty. I tried to get out of my bed, but two creatures jumped on me and beat me. They were 60 cm. in height; each had only one eye, hand and foot. They were very strong. They wore black leathery clothes and had a line of hair on their heads. After they beat me, I lost consciousness."

Ahmad's wife took him to hospital and he was awaited upon his return home by a journalist from the Palestinian television station who reported that the bruise marks were made by a being with three fingers. Neighbors confirmed that they heard a ruckus in Ahmad's home but did not see anyone leave.

PALESTINIAN POLICE INVESTIGATE ALIEN KIDNAPPING ATTEMPT

On October 19, 1997, the Israeli newsmagazine Yerushalayim reported that the Palestinian police were investigating their first alien kidnapping.

The event occurred three days before when a young girl, Suha A'anam from the village of Dir Al Awasan near Tulkarem, was rescued by fellow villagers from the clutches of an alien. The police report states that Suha, a grade ten pupil, was standing on her 2nd floor balcony when suddenly an alien began pulling her left hand. She screamed hysterically, alerting neighbors to the scene just in time to save her. She was taken to Tulkarem Hospital with scratches to her arm.

A neighbor told the police that she heard a noise like a helicopter, looked out her window and saw "a whirlpool in the air, spreading ash everywhere" opposite Suha's balcony. Two other witnesses saw aliens the same week. Six days before, sixteen-year-old Muhand Faras was walking home from school when he came upon a strange being of a man's size but with a small "root" in the middle of its face.

Its skin was colored "like a frog's," it had two tiny hands with three fingers on each and long fingernails. The alien made a threatening, clawing gesture at Muhand's face, screamed something and "flew to the sky." He does not know where the creature flew because he "was too frightened to look at it anymore and thought it might shoot something dangerous" at him.

Three days later, an engineer, Raid A'anam saw a black creature in the sky just before sundown. He told police investigators that the outline of the flying object was "human, with two arms and two legs."

Palestinian police have since set up ambushes to trap the "intruders" and put an end to the villagers' terror. Needless to say, many villagers believe the Israeli intelligence agency, the Shabak, is behind the sightings.

When asked why the Israelis would stage such an incident, the villagers answered, "To scare us."

Researcher Barry Chamish believed that UFOs and their alien crews visited Israel and the Middle East in ancient times and have now returned.

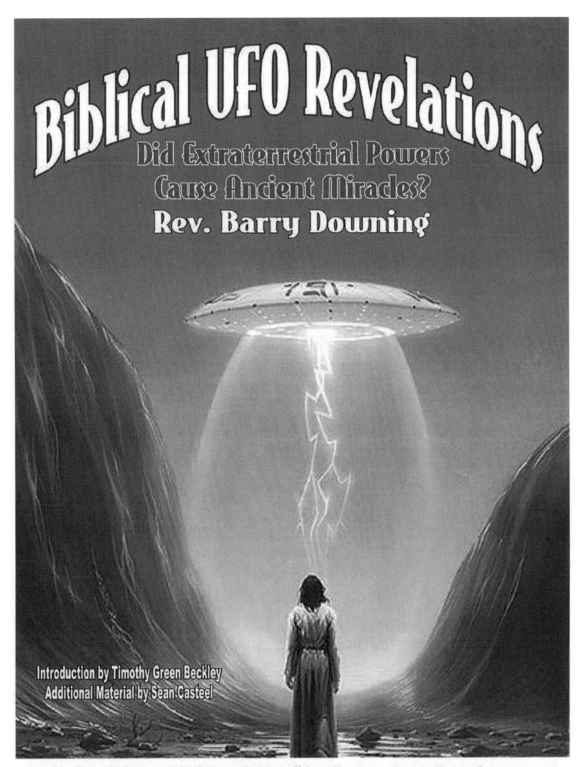

Books like *"Biblical UFO Revelations"* by the Rev. Barry Downing are not afraid to tackle the relationship between UFOs and the Old and New Testaments.

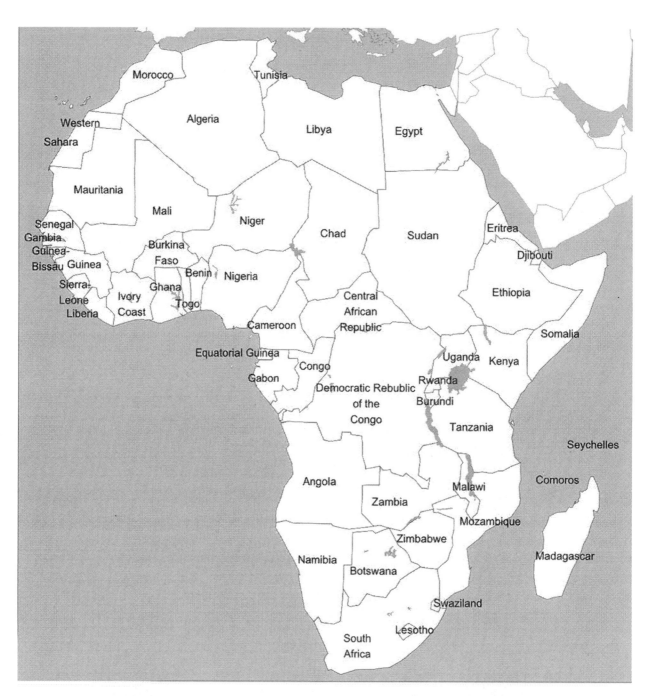

AFRICA

A UFO ABDUCTION ON THE AFRICAN CONTINENT

By Cynthia Hind

PUBLISHER'S NOTE: This is the experience of a mother and daughter being "taken away."

But be forewarned this incident did not take place in Maine where the abduction of Betty and Barney Hill made history, nor in some isolated mountain town in Colorado or Montana, or for that matter in what would be considered to be even a moderately populated area...which is certainly not the case. In fact, Africa is the world's second largest, most-populous continent with an overall population well in excess of one billion. With South Africa at its southernmost tip, Africa is made up of fifty four independent nations with a variety of ecological and political systems. As far as UFOs go, the sightings and encounters on this huge land mass is as diversified as one would expect it to be with its many cultures and historical backdrops. The incident you are about to become enmeshed in takes place in Johannesburg, South Africa, where you might not expect to confront a great deal of UFO activity, but you would be incorrect as this detailed report easily indicates.

I only had some minor correspondence with Cynthia Hind, acknowledged as Africa's most prominent researcher of UFOs. But our limited contact alerted me to the fact that she was totally above board and widely dedicated to the UFOlogical cause.

Cynthia Hind grew up in Namaqualand, South Africa and received her education at Good Hope Seminary and, for a short while, at Cape Town University. After serving in the South African WAAF, she married an RAF pilot and went to live in northern England where her two children were born. It was during this period that she started to write professionally and many of her short stories and articles were published in the UK and on the Continent.

147

Subsequently, the family immigrated to what was then Rhodesia (now Zimbabwe), where she and her husband helped to build up the family furniture business. At this stage, through her writing and investigative reporting, Cynthia became involved with UFOs, and worked as a Field Investigator for MUFON of America when the material for this book was collected. Cynthia was coordinator for Africa in MUFON and covered UFO events in many parts of the world, although concentrating mostly on Africa.

Cynthia Hind was Africa's foremost ufologist and summed up in detail a lifetime of work spent in careful investigation of a host of most unusual cases. Whether she was leading us on the spot through the strange appearance of silver-suited aliens and unique light phenomena at the La Rochelle estate, uncovering the fraudulent crash-scenario of the James van Greunen case, or meticulously working her way through the abduction chronology of two wealthy Johannesburg women, Cynthia Hind always upheld the highest standards for scientific researchers. She remained unflappable, virtually foolproof, but open-minded to the end. Her trademark was the extended and repeated interview where heretofore unretrieved and forgotten facts are often brought to the subject's conscious mind by gentle and persistent prodding. Here, for the first time, is the complete story of the Ariel school UFO landing. We are given first-hand accounts of the ship's descent and landing by over a dozen young students who witnessed, and later illustrated for their teachers and UFO investigators, what they saw that most memorable day.

A resident of Zimbabwe, Cynthia Hind was MUFON's coordinator for Africa. After a stint in the South African WAAF, she married an RAF pilot and lived for a time with her husband and two children in northern England. She edited and published the biannual magazine UFO Afrinews. Her first book: *"UFOs - African Encounters,"* was considered a milestone in African UFOlogy. Cynthia Hind died on August 21st, 2000.

· · · · · · · · · ·

A MOTHER AND DAUGHTER ABDUCTION

This is the story of an abduction which occurred in Johannesburg, South Africa, and involved two women: Phyllis (the mother) and Diane, 34 years old (her daughter).

INCREDIBLE ALIEN ENCOUNTERS

Not everyone in UFOlogy accepts abductions, and my own belief is not the point in question. The real essence of this report is that neither Phyllis nor Diane have had access to UFO literature; that South Africans as a whole are totally ignorant of the developing scenario of UFOs on a world-wide basis; and that the only media support that UFOs have are the occasional interviews on radio and limited coverage in the press. Usually the latter consists of an unidentified object which the reporter and his editor have recognized as being identifiable (even with their limited experience!).

To me, one of the salient factors in this report is that for almost three plus years, the two women did not know to whom they could turn to report their story, however bizarre or ordinary the explanation might be. On the night of the 5th of July, 1988, Diane's husband told her that he had a TV commercial which had to be ready for the following day. He needed her to work through the night with him. Diane then called her mother, Phyllis, asking if she would come to her house and help her. This Phyllis agreed to do and all three of them worked until 3:30 in the morning, when Phyllis said she was tired and wanted to pack up and go home. Diane made a cup of tea and then drove her to her home, only about seven minutes away.

Phyllis told me that it was a strange night; silent and cold, with a pink haze low on the horizon. As they got into the car Phyllis noticed a particularly bright star which seemed to be throwing out rays of light—"just like a Christmas star." As they drove down the hill on a winding road to Phyllis' house, it seemed as .though this star was following them...first on the right and then on the left. Phyllis thought it abnormally large as she could see it clearly while Diane concentrated on driving.

In front of Phyllis' house, there is a jacaranda tree and a street light, but feeling a little nervous, Phyllis asked Diane not to stop in front of her house but to carry on, about two or three houses down. Diane stopped the car in the street and turned to look at the light. She saw it as an elongated shape in orange with the outside edge darker than the centre. Phyllis said that when the object was stationary between the trees, it appeared square to her, with rounded corners. All the windows in the car were open but Phyllis quickly closed her window, when the light appeared to draw closer. They both sat and watched it creep up over the trees, and that was when it had that elongated shape and the edges were definitely hazy. It was completely orange with a light around it which changed from blue to magenta. "You had a funny feeling from it," Phyllis said, "almost as though we were being distracted."

While Diane was parking the car, the light shot towards them at a terrific speed. When it reached them, it turned round and flipped over. Phyllis thought it looked just like a doughnut, a wheel within a wheel. She could see the inside of the whole object, and looking up at it, she realized there were people there. She was counting them to see how many there were: two at the back and two closer to her, and, as it turned round, she could also see two people on the top deck. One of the men on the top deck was standing with one hand on his face and the other on his hip, and he was looking at and pushing some buttons. There was a younger man next to him with long blonde hair. The older man was bald on top.

By now the object had come much lower down. Phyllis was afraid. She thought to herself..."Oh my God, it's going to come down on top of the car." At this time, Diane was leaning across her mother, watching the light, and she too saw it move towards them at a great rate.

On the night of July 5, 1988, two South African women had a bizarre UFO encounter that forever changed their lives.

As Phyllis watched, she compared the object to the size of her lounge: about 6m x 6m (18ft. x 18ft.), and she realized the object was as large as that. Diane was nervous; she was seeing something unbelievable, inexplicable. However, she did not see the figures in- side, which Phyllis had observed so clearly. At first, Phyllis thought there were six people, but when she started to work it out again: two upstairs on the upper deck, and six inside, she knew there had to be eight people in all. When Diane saw the object coming close to them, she gasped, "I don't even want to look," and covered her head with her arms, laying her head on the steering wheel.

FROM A TINY DOT TO A HUGE THING

Phyllis said, "Don't be silly, you'll miss out." But Diane wasn't having any. "It had been so small to start off with," she said, "and then it literally took only a split second from a tiny little lump in the sky to being this huge thing." She noted it was bright orange on the outside and yellow on the inside, but when it was far away, it was a blue-white colour. Phyllis said that when it shot towards them, it looked like a giant star, but when she had first seen it, it was just a small star. At this stage, she could see it was hollow underneath, and it reminded her of a lot of bangles (bracelets) moving, as though being dropped from above. From underneath, Phyllis saw portholes. The top deck also had portholes. These were square with rounded corners.

When Phyllis looked underneath, she could see these, and beyond that, the stars were shining brightly. The man on the top deck, who stood with his face in his hands, had a band across his head and something that came down on either side, "like little flaps over his ears." But this did not apply to the younger man. "Before the ship stopped," Phyllis said, "I saw the man doing something on a panel and beyond him I could see the stars and the sky."

They both turned round to look at the light, and Phyllis said to Diane that she could feel a presence in the car. Diane shivered and said she also felt it. They then heard a "click" sound – it was quite clear." The next thing, they were being led up a ramp into the craft. Diane kept asking, "Where am I, where am I? Am I dreaming?"

There was a woman standing on Diane's left, and she smiled at Diane. She was holding Diane's arm with her other hand on Diane's back, guiding her into the craft.

Phyllis was slightly in front of them, saying, "No, Di, No, Di," and pushing her back, while the woman was guiding her forwards, not aggressively but strongly. Diane didn't know where she was; one minute she was in the car, the next minute on the ramp of a craft. She felt completely confused. Something was very odd indeed.

Diane noticed that the woman guiding her had very fine-textured skin with almond-shaped, almost oriental, eyes (Phyllis thought she was very beautiful). She had no hair, but this was not offensive, nor was she ugly or "bug-eyed." She had a nose and a mouth, and she was overwhelmingly beautiful. The woman had tiny ears and she was small, about 1.60m (5'2"), a little taller than Diane who is 1.58m (5'1").

Her skin was darker than normal, as though deeply suntanned. Strangely enough, they saw that her teeth were in a single band, not separated like ours. They didn't notice it at the time, but later she smiled, and they could see one top band and one bottom band. It actually looked quite ugly. She wore an all-in-one track suit. Initially, it was a dark colour, like navy blue, but much later on, when they were about to leave the craft, they noticed the colour of the suit had changed to pale blue with a purple collar. Diane was intrigued by the way the woman walked: She would put her toes down first, and then lowered the rest of her foot; the men walked the same way. (They knew she was a woman because she looked like a woman and also because she had small breasts.)

When they came into the craft, a mist enveloped them. It was a white mist, as though they were going through steam, except that this had a beautiful fragrance, very mild and relaxing, as though incense was being burned. They were also aware of a lemon scent. When Diane, confused, asked repeatedly, "Where am I? Where am I?" the woman spoke to her in perfect English. She said, "Greetings, I am from the Pleiades and my name is Me-leelah" (or Me-Iila or Me-lah). The two women looked at each other in puzzlement as they didn't quite understand what she said. She repeated it again, and still Di and Phyllis were not too sure. The woman's English was perfect, but her voice was slightly high-pitched and lilting.

Phyllis, on Diane's right, was aware of a little man standing next to her. She noticed that the back of the craft was completely closed. The woman was guiding Di into the craft, and Phyllis was trying to stop her going in as she was concerned about their safety, but then she realized the door had already closed behind them. It was pointless to struggle further.

INSIDE THE CRAFT

Once they were inside, Phyllis looked around with curiosity. Although the man next to her was small, he was taller than she was. He had a nicely tapered waist and a good build even though he was so short. He wore a belt, a broad-based belt which rested on his hips. He really had a beautiful body. She noted that all of them had brown eyes which were very slanted. Phyllis said to Di. "He looks almost Japanese."

The man smiled, as though he was not insulted. But their eyes were bigger than oriental eyes. They had no hair at all; except for the two men on the top deck (whom only Phyllis had seen). The whole ship looked white and clinical; the walls were white with a shine to them. The craft was circular inside with portholes all around. In the centre of the room, there was a high steel table.

A wide variety of UFOs have been reported over the African continent.

The two women were led towards the table, but this was quite high (about one metre), and it was difficult for Phyllis to get on to it. Diane jumped up readily enough when they asked her, but she did aerobics and was fit enough. She felt calm immediately after they had walked through the mist, so she had no fears about doing what she was told.

When the man with Phyllis realized she could not make it, he put his hand in the small of her back, and she felt herself lifted up and laid on the table at the opposite end to Di, with their feet facing to the centre. Unlike her daughter, Phyllis did not feel at all calm. There was something that looked like a light in the ceiling, but afterwards it came down above the two women, like a type of X-ray machine; and that is obviously what it was. It was a baby pink colour and about one metre square, and it looked as though it had a glass cover

At the back, two men were seated at a desk, and another man sat at a table on his own. They seemed totally unperturbed by the appearance of the strangers; they never even looked up. They also had all-in-one suits on, but the colour was a sort of milky, bluish grey. They all had different colored collars, and later on, Me-leelah explained that this denoted their rank or position. Phyllis thought to herself: "Well, there's not much we can do. There are only two of us and so many of them." All at once, she saw an opening; a narrow opening, and turned to it in an attempt to escape, but her escort stood there with his arms crossed over his chest, and he smiled, obviously barring the way. She walked back to the table. On one side, where the two men were working at a desk, one of them turned something over that he was busy with some paper clamped on to a board. The clamp was a really old-fashioned clamp. The man had a lot of white paper on the board and just sat there, doing his own thing.

The two women were surprised: Here they were being confronted with extremely high technology, and yet the clamp was from their own time. Phyllis said, "I tried to get out of there three or four times, but each time I had only to think about how I was going to escape, and almost immediately, as though he could read my mind, there stood the man, barring the way. At one stage, I went up some steps leading to the top deck where I saw two men and a woman. They turned round and the woman indicated to me that I should go down again."

It was at that time that Phyllis also got on to the table. In the meantime, Diane was already lying on the table, fascinated by everything and quite calm, completely trusting in everyone. Me-leelah had said, "I mean you no harm," and Diane believed her implicitly. The pink light machine was right above them. It wasn't fixed tightly to the ceiling; it must have been operated by a cord. They couldn't quite make it out. But Me-leelah stood there, and it came down, and then almost immediately it shot up again. It only took a second or two.

Me-leelah had said when they arrived: "Greetings, I am the commander of this craft." There was some controversy over this as Phyllis thought she had said, "Greetings, I am the captain of this starship," but when questioned, Diane corrected her: "There was no mention of the word "starship," she said "craft." Me-leelah then turned round and picked up a map; a big square map of Earth in full colour. Both women said that it was an ordinary map, like one would find in any bookstore. Me-leelah said "I have something important to tell you."

She asked if they recognized the map, and Phyllis said, "Yes, we only know one world. This is a map of the world and this is Africa,"– and she put her hand on South Africa. Then Me-leelah told them that there would be a world cataclysm "and all this" – she indicated the low-lying land of the Cape – "will be destroyed. The water will rise and the land will be pushed up. Waves of 72 meters will come over the Cape area." She added, "You will have to go farther in and higher up." (At the time, Phyllis did not know what she meant, but later she realized it meant farther inland and higher up in the land.)

A CRY FOR HELP

Me-leelah next pointed to a mountainous part of Spain and said, "This area will remain. But a lot of the land is going to break away. Every few thousand years there are changes and many people will die; and many of us will also lose our lives." She also said she could see a war raging between America and the Middle East (remember, this was in 1988). She added, "You've heard of AIDS. You think it is only a homosexual disease but it is not. It will be widely spread all over the world. Man is destroying himself." In conclusion she said, "You must realize that mankind is very unpredictable," and then she added, "You have some very important work to do. Are you prepared to help us?"

Phyllis said, "Well, I want to know what I have to do first, before I make any promises." Me-leelah replied, "We need you to help us with the children. At any time, anything could happen, and even though the Earth will change, mankind must not die out. We will also get hurt if we help you, but at least we could help you if we had your RNA and DNA." Phyllis asked what that entailed. Me-leelah said they would have to do some tests.

A PAINFUL MEDICAL EXAM

Diane and Phyllis were now lying on the table, opposite one another. When the pink machine came down and went up again, Me-Ieelah said, "The X-ray is finished now." She took something out of the machine and went with it to the back of the room, then returned to them with a clamp in her hands. She clipped something onto it and hung it back on a hook on the wall. Then she bent down, and when she straightened up, she had an instrument in her hands, attached to a needle as thick as a crochet hook. The instrument's edges were rounded; it wasn't square. Speaking to Diane, she said, "We are going to test you for RNA and DNA. Open your top."

UFOs have visited each of the 54 independent nations that make up Africa.

Diane unzipped the top of her track suit. Underneath she was wearing a vest, which she pulled up, leaving her chest area naked. Then Me-leelah inserted the needle just under her right breast, and there was a sharp, but short, burst of pain, and Diane gasped. The other woman in the room had now joined them and was standing behind Diane. Me-leelah was taller than this woman, who seemed to project a tremendous calm. She put her hand on Diane's forehead and the pain immediately went away. Diane had the most wonderful feeling of euphoria with no pain at all. When Me-leelah inserted the needle, Phyllis sat up and cried, "You can't do that to her." She could see it was hurting Diane. "What the hell are you doing to her?" she asked again, angrily.

While Me-leelah was pushing the needle into Diane's chest, it kept clicking as Me-leelah was pushing, turning and pushing. There were little plastic containers fixed all around it, and she turned and pushed, turned and pushed. She said, "We're nearly done," and then withdrew the instrument slowly. She told Diane they had taken samples of her blood and bone marrow. Phyllis asked why they were doing these things. Me-leelah explained that they were also going to take skin and tissue samples; and then she turned the instrument and said, "Now we are taking blood from the vein leading to the heart, where it goes in, in an impure fashion, so if there are any medical faults we can pick them up."

Phyllis asked why they did not put the instrument in from the back, as she felt it would be easier, but Me-leelah did not answer. When she finished, she walked round Diane, and a man picked up the instrument and did something with it that they were unable to see.

The other woman went away and appeared to prepare the instrument. Then she looked at Phyllis and smiled. Phyllis said apprehensively: "You're not doing that to me," remembering Diane's pain. Me-leelah explained, "If there's trouble, then we can't help you unless you allow us to use this instrument. We have your daughter's structure, and we will be able to help her." So Phyllis said, "Oh, what the hell," and they pushed the instrument into her. She gasped but again the other woman put her hand on Phyllis" head and that made her feel good.

When Me-Ieelah had finished with Diane and withdrawn the needle, she put a little yellow plaster on the small hole left in Diane's flesh. Diane cried excitedly: "Oh, now I can show my friends what has happened to me!" But even as she was looking down at it, the plaster dissolved in front of her eyes and the hole underneath healed. There is a small circular scar where the needle was inserted.

Me-leelah took the small containers over to the man at the back of the room and put them on the table. He spoke to her, and they were looking at a chart. They were also looking at each other in a strange way, and Diane felt uncomfortable with that look; she felt as though something was wrong. Then Me-leelah came up to her and said, "What do your medical people call your condition?"

Diane said that she had had haemolytic jaundice when she was 12, and none of the doctors had picked it up. She had been ill since 1966; really ill for years on end. At one time, due to her illness, she only weighed 38 kg (84 lbs.). Since the abduction, her illness has apparently cleared up, and she has never needed medical attention since, as she has been absolutely well. She has not visited a doctor since the abduction. Prior to that, no one had been able to find a cure for her condition. When all this was finished, the two women sat up. Phyllis climbed down and was looking around. She realized that her count of eight people in the craft (besides Diane and herself) had been correct. Diane was very quiet, and the others just carried on with their business, sitting with their backs to the humans. They didn't even look up at them.

Me-leelah said, "I won't be a minute," and then she did something and said something, but they cannot remember what it was. Phyllis suddenly noticed that the jacket Me-leelah wore was now a completely different colour: a bright blue and strikingly attractive. Me-leelah sat down at a table. She told them they were going to descend now, adding, "We will take you back to your car."

Phyllis was excited. "You mean we are up?" Me-leelah said, "Yes." "How high are we?" Phyllis asked. The woman replied, "You are two and one third times higher than your tower."

RETURNING HOME

Diane and Phyllis looked out of one of the portholes, and they could see the Brixton tower. Diane said, "Oh, there is the Brixton tower." But Me-leelah corrected them: "No, the Hillbrow tower," and when they looked again they could both see the

Hillbrow tower. (There are two towers in central Johannesburg, the Brixton tower and the Hillbrow tower, both used for telecommunications.)

Phyllis asked how high the tower was. Me-leelah was sitting with her back to them, and Phyllis thought how lovely her back was with this soft pink head of hers; it was all so beautiful, she wanted to reach out and touch her. She had this terrible, desolate feeling and her heart was thumping. From having been apprehensive at first, she now didn't want to go back home. She felt so sad at the thought of having to leave Me-leelah and the ship. She could not analyze her feelings; it was just an overwhelming feeling of loss. Me-leelah took a pencil and tore a piece of yellow paper from a pad. She said, "You are two and one third times higher than the tower and that is the height of the tower..." She wrote down some figures, "So I'll just multiply that..." and then she gave the paper to Phyllis.

When Me-leelah was writing the figures down for Phyllis, Diane thought to herself, "My God, you're a beautiful woman," and Me-leelah said, "Thank you" out aloud. Diane asked what she was thanking her for, but she knew Me-leelah had read her thoughts. Phyllis was watching Me-leelah write, and she had a funny feeling in the pit of her stomach, because she realized that the woman had no nails on her fingers. She pointed this out to Diane without speaking, and Diane said aloud, "Just like Apie." She had a monkey called Apie when she was a child. Me-leelah turned round to Diane and said, "What is Apie?" Diane did not want to hurt her feelings, so she said, "Oh, a friend of mine."

Me-leelah looked at Diane as though disappointed and annoyed; she brought her face right up close to Diane's and her eyes changed. The pupils narrowed and became vertical, almost reptilian. Diane was frightened. She knew Me-leelah realized she had lied to her. Me-leelah's eyes at that stage were intensely blue – almost turquoise. Now Me-leelah said, "We'll take you back to your car and you'll be calm."

"Do we have to go?" Phyllis asked, reluctant to leave. As they left the craft, Me-leelah told them, "We'll meet soon, in two years" time." Diane asked, "You mean two years of our time? Why so long?" Me-leelah replied, "No, two years of our time, which is four years of your time."

Diane asked again, "Can't you be more specific?" and Me-Ieelah said, "Around May." Well, May 1992 has come and gone and although the two women waited, nothing happened. At a later stage, in 1993, they were joined by Shirley MacLaine on one occasion but again, they were disappointed.

Being an investigator and aware of many similar incidents, I know only too well how many promises of return have been made, yet never consciously fulfilled. The man who had brought Phyllis into the craft, and one of the others, took Diane and Phyllis down the ramp. The women were holding on to the railing, and Diane commented that it was like a molding. They could put their thumbs into it. It was extremely supportive. Phyllis felt a bit wobbly; she didn't know why. She stumbled and nearly fell; but the man with her put his hand on her back and that supported her, as though she was being held upright. Phyllis said, "The funniest thing happened: Di and I went down the ramp and they took us to the car. Di opened her door which we had locked, but now it was unlocked."

When they got to the car, one of the men opened the door for her. Diane laughed. "When we got into the car, I climbed in back to front." "She was sitting with her bottom on the steering wheel," her mother added, "and the little man gently helped her to turn around."

"After I sat correctly," Diane went on, "the man said, "Put your button down," so that I would lock my door. But you know, we do it aggressively, jabbing our finger downwards to show what we want people to do; but he didn't do it like that at all! He pointed at the button and then slowly bent his finger downwards – it was very gently done. And I knew immediately, telepathically, what he was telling me to do. And then he briefly folded his arm across his chest with his palms turned inwards, then raised his hands at shoulder level, with the palms facing me. I think he was saying good-bye and go well. That was the impression I had."

Phyllis then remembered getting out of the car to go into her house. She said, "Listen how quiet it is! Not a bird, not a sound; nothing. It's just like a dead street!" She asked Diane, "What is this piece of lemon-colored paper in my hand?" It was all rolled up, and when she looked, it had numbers on it. She showed it to Diane. "It looks like someone's telephone number," Diane replied.

MENTAL CONFUSION

Phyllis stayed a moment longer saying good night, and then went into her house. Once inside she put the piece of paper in the telephone table drawer in the hall and then walked quietly to the bedroom to get undressed and into bed. As Phyllis was getting undressed, she had difficulty in getting her track suit top over her head; the suit was tight around her neck and uncomfortable. She suddenly realized that it was on back to front, although she knew full well that it had been on normally when she left Diane's house.

At this point the maid came into the room with the early morning tea. Phyllis was startled. What was the maid doing with the tea in the middle of the night? "What time is it'?" she asked the girl brusquely. "Why, 6 o' clock, madam. That's when I usually bring in the tea." Phyllis looked at the bedside clock. Indeed, it showed couple of minutes after six. She knew they had arrived home from Di's house at about 03:45. What in heaven's name had happened to them during the past two and a quarter hours?

Initially, they had no recall of the incident, but little by little they started to recall more of what happened to them. Before their experience they never had any involvement with UFOs and didn't know anyone who could help them. But they did call the Johannesburg Planetarium. Dr. Tom Geary, who is the director, does not believe in UFOs, but the secretary did give them two forms to fill out. Later on, they heard of Elizabeth Klarer (a well-known South African contactee) through a friend of Diane's, and she knew Elizabeth's address, so they went to call on her. When they told Elizabeth Klarer their story, she wanted to include it in her new book The Gravity File. Elizabeth has since passed away, and I cannot think that her book will ever be completed now.

HAD THEY GONE CRAZY?

By this time Phyllis and Diane had spoken to a few people about their experience and inevitably, it became public knowledge. But the general public and their friends and relations thought that the two women were crazy.

Elizabeth Klarer later met the abductees and seemed satisfied that they had undergone a legitimate experience.

"The thing is," said Diane, "when you see someone being murdered, they will believe you when you tell them. Why don't they believe me now?" "I would like to study UFOs," Phyllis added, "so that I can understand more about it all. They told us they came from the Pleiades; they said we were galactic and they said that Diane had a counterpart: One question I am definitely going to ask them is about Diane's counterpart."

Kenny MacKinnon, who accompanied me on the interview, asked if they knew of Billy Meier and pointed out that he had said his space people had come from the Pleiades, but the two women were not aware of Meier, nor of his story. The name meant nothing to them. (JUST AS WELL!).

It was at this time that Diane remembered something strange that had happened to them inside the spaceship. "We saw this hologram. It was like watching a film; it came up on the wall in black and white. It was like being in a hall with seats in rows. One person politely excused himself and walked in front of the people. It was like a panel. I'm sure they did that for our benefit. My mother said, 'My God, did you see that?' We were sitting there, feeling so depressed, as we didn't want to go back to Earth. It looked almost like a person standing there, the hologram was so clear; it came up like a puzzle that one sees on TV"

When they met Elizabeth Klarer, she told Phyllis that she had to move and had nowhere to go, So Phyllis, who is a most generous and kind-hearted person, invited Elizabeth to move into her home, and she stayed with Phyllis and her husband for six months. Through Elizabeth, Phyllis and Diane attended several UFO meetings and met up with Jean Lafitte.

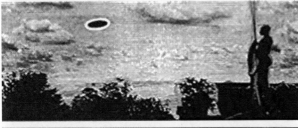

Cynthia Hind's book, *"UFOs Over Africa,"* details a lifetime of work spent in careful investigation of a host of the most unusual cases in Africa.

When the first meeting started, Diane said, "I kept saying to my Mom, why is he looking at us?" Phyllis went on: "Everyone was told to be there early, and then we sat there for about an hour until he came. He maintained that he knew about them because he had been in the craft when they had come aboard."

Jean Lafitte had become quite famous in South Africa for claiming a UFO abduction in which the aliens had allegedly marked his forehead with a green light. He had received a great deal of publicity through the pages of People, a Johannesburg-based magazine, and he subsequently appeared on both radio and television. John Robbie, of Radio 702 in Johannesburg, South Africa, says they tried very hard to see the green light on Lafitte's forehead in the darkness of the studio, but nothing was visible to them.

Lafitte had obviously heard of Phyllis and Diane's story as their experience had become well-known among the UFO club members, and even though the story had not been told in the detail recounted here, there was enough material available for him to know what had happened. He was on the top deck (he alleged) of the craft onto which the two women had been abducted. He also claimed to be Diane's counterpart.

Phyllis told me: "He moved into my house and stayed for two and a half years." When Phyllis was in the craft, she said, during her efforts at escape, she went up the stairs, and there were two people there: an older man and a young boy with thickish-blonde hair. After their experience, Diane met a girl who was talking about starships, and Diane said she and her mother had had an encounter, and this girl said, "Oh, that's interesting, as this man Lafitte is having a meeting and he has been on a starship."

Phyllis remembered meeting him before. "He came up to see Elizabeth Klarer one evening while she was staying with me and when he arrived, I ran up the stairs to leave them alone, so I didn't speak to him or get to know him then."

For a long time now I have felt that the whole UFO phenomenon needs a rethink, something that can only be achieved if there is a total togetherness among UFO investigators and those scientists who have come "out of the closet," not necessarily admitting involvement, but to prove their open-mindedness.

SUGGESTED READING

There is more to this abduction experience along with an in depth history of the UFO phenomena over Africa. Copies of the book "*UFOs Over Africa*" may be published from its American publisher, Horus House Press, Box 55185, Madison WI 53705. Include $20 for the book and shipping.

Now deceased, Cynthia Hind was considered Africa's foremost UFO investigator.

A BRIEF HISTORICAL VIEW - UFOS IN AFRICA

eNCA.com LIST OF SIGHTINGS 1965 - 2015

1965 - After midnight on September 16, two police constables saw a "shiny, copper-coloured craft", which apparently landed at in the middle of Bronkhorstspruit Road in Pretoria. Their patrol vehicle cut out as they watched the craft rapidly ascending, while emitting a sea of flames through two portals, leaving the asphalt ablaze afterwards.

Residents of the East Rand (Ekurhuleni) had earlier reported seeing an "enormous white light" and a "red ball" in their skies.

1991 – In April a "hovering triangular craft with red central lights, and white star-like lights on each extremity", was spotted by a family at Baviaanspoort, Pretoria. Around the same time in Belgium, a similar craft was sighted.

1996 – On August 28 a "glowing disc" was apparently seen by a Sergeant Becker near the Adriaan Vlok police station in Erasmuskloof, Pretoria. The pulsating light contained a "red triangle and emitted bright green tentacles." A radar operator at Johannesburg International Airport (OR Tambo International) confirmed its presence.

About 200 policemen and a police helicopter gave chase, but the helicopter chase was abandoned at 10,000ft near Bronkhorstspruit when the object made a sharp vertical ascent.

1998 – On December 27 a family videotaped a group of "roundish triangular craft" passing over the town of Graaff Reinet.

The "crafts" changed colour and circled each another, before being overtaken by a much larger, shiny, golden craft.

2004 – In June 27 a resident of Durban observed and video-taped a brightly coloured light, which changed shape from oval to circular, suspended in the air near her home for three hours. Family members and neighbours also observed it.

2010 – In July, residents of Booysens, Pretoria, observed a "triangle of bright lights which hung motionless in the sky for two hours".

The objects then slowly descended towards the horizon at 8.30pm. The lights were blue and emerald in colour, with a white light which shone downwards.

2011 – In May, about "20 orange lights" were observed travelling faster than an aeroplane over Tierpoort near Pretoria. On June 15, seven of similar objects were observed and some photographed as they crossed the sky in single file over Tierpoort.

2015 – A UFO was reportedly spotted in Cape Town on November 28. Social media was abuzz with various reports of what seemed to be a green light over the city.

UFO Afrinews was edited by Cynthia Hind for over a decade. Postings can be found on the web for some of the back issues.

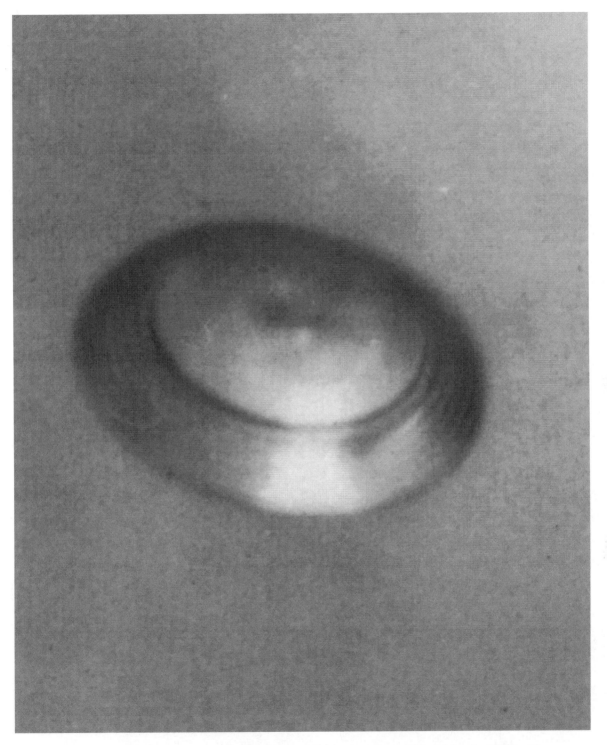

Contactee Elizabeth Klarer took this photo of a UFO over South Africa in 1956. Klarer claimed that this UFO was a spacecraft piloted by an extraterrestrial named Akon from the planet Meton. She said she was taken to Akon's planet where they fell in love and she gave birth to their son before she returned to Earth.

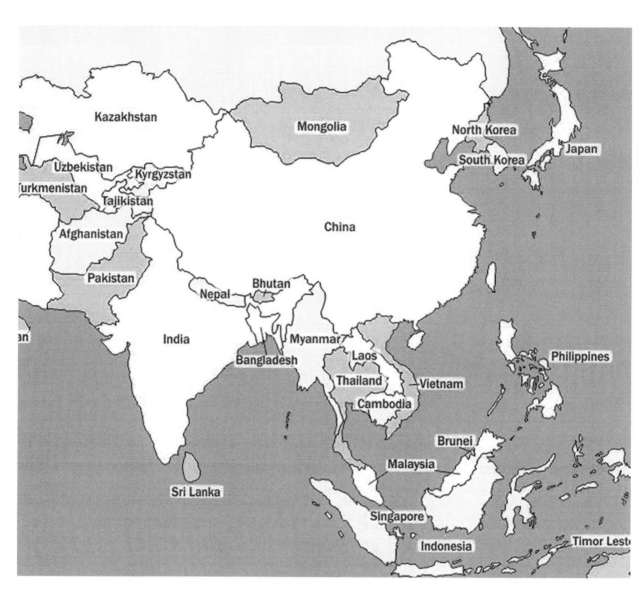

 ASIA

MINIATURE UFO CAPTURED IN JAPAN

The Little Known Kera UFO Incident
By Tim R. Swartz

In late 2019, Tom DeLonge's To The Stars Academy signed a contract with the U.S. Army to collaborate in the study of "exotic metals" – i.e., parts of crashed UFOs. Both parties hope that this agreement will lead to the development of advanced technologies. However, a group of Japanese schoolboys in 1972 did what To the Stars Academy and the military have not yet been able to do (at least to the best of my knowledge): they actually captured a miniature UFO.

But they lost it.

Only to recapture it.

And then they lost it again.'

Several times.

Missed it by that much...

This case is little-known in the West and has been largely forgotten in Japan. Nevertheless, this incident is one of most bizarre and frustrating cases in modern UFO history.

ONCE UPON A TIME ON SHIKOKU ISLAND

Kōchi City is the capital of Kōchi Prefecture on the Shikoku island of Japan. With its subtropical climate and facing the Pacific Ocean, the area is well-known for its seafood and as a popular gathering place for surfers from all over Japan.

Nearby is the Kera area, with a total population of about 20,000. Kera is a quiet, residential area, considered to be one of the best places to live for those who work in the neighboring cities.

This suburb became the focus of attention starting on August 25, 1972; when 13-year-old Michio Seo, who was on his way home from school, spotted a strange, metallic object hovering in the air over a rice field that ran along the side of the road.

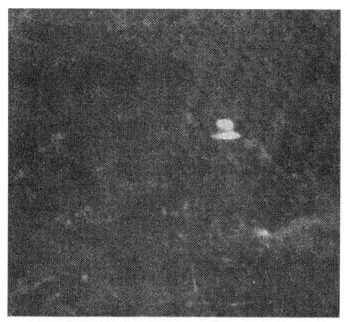

The boys were able to take several photographs of the tiny UFO as it hovered a few feet over the rice field.

Seo watched as the strange, hat-shaped device flew back and forth over the overgrown field. Seo later compared the movements of the object to that of a bat making sharp turns in pursuit of insects.

Intrigued by what he was seeing, Seo tried to get closer to the small craft, only to be repelled when it shot a dazzling beam of light at him. Seo knew that the bright light was a warning for him to keep his distance, so he quickly headed home and told his friends about what had just happened.

Along with his friends – Hiroshi Mori, Yasuo Fujimoto, Katsuoka Kojima and a friend named Yuji, Seo returned to the field around 7:00 PM in hopes of seeing the tiny UFO again. At first the object was nowhere to be seen, but the group decided to wait. After about an hour, the craft returned and to their amazement it flew back and forth over the rice field, pulsating with a bright, rainbow colored light. When one of the boys got brave enough to try and approach it, the small disc began to emit a loud "popping" noise and glow a bright blue. This sudden change was unsettling enough that the frightened boys decided to call it a night and quickly run to their homes.

However, their curiosity got the best of them and the children returned to the spot over the next several days, hoping to once again catch a glimpse of their mysterious visitor. On September 4 the craft returned, but the boys were again too nervous to approach it. They vowed the next time to bring a camera and prove that what they were seeing was real. On September 6 their vigilance paid off when they found the craft sitting once again in the field.

After it fell to the ground, 14-year-old Hiroshi Mori picked up the tiny UFO. He later said that that he felt something "moving" inside.

One of the boys pointed their camera and took a photo. When the flashbulb fired, the UFO began to spin and quickly rose into the air. Another photograph was taken, but this time, when the flashbulb went off, the small object fell to the ground and continued spinning for a short while in the soft ground.

Fourteen-year-old Hiroshi Mori cautiously approached the now dormant object and picked it up. Later, he said that it felt like something was "moving" inside. One of the other boys took a photo of him holding the craft.

The boys took turns holding and examining their prize. Finally, Miro wrapped it in a plastic bag and took it home for a closer examination. It was determined that the silver-colored object weighed about three pounds, was around four-inches across and eight-inches high. The underside had circular grooves...almost like a vinyl record. In the middle was a square with 31 holes surrounded by three unknown symbols.

CAPTURED AND RECAPTURED

At this point, the boys felt that it was important to reveal their find to their parents, who had grown concerned about the boy's unexplained nightly activities. Yasuo Fujimoto's father, Mutsuo, was the director of the Center for Science Education in Kochi. They figured that he would be the best candidate to try and identify the object.

"The frequent nights out of the boys began to worry parents," Mutsuo Fujimoto said. "I told my son if it was true what he said, to bring the object to me. He did, and it was something like an ashtray, cast iron, but too light for this metal. It was impossible to open, and inside were pieces similar to a radio. I did not give it more importance, but now I regret not having studied it more closely."

After Mr. Fujimoto's examination, the craft was again placed into Mori's backpack...only to mysteriously vanish the next day.

Over the next few weeks, the boys would spot the little UFO, or one that looked like the first one, flying over the rice paddy. They noticed that it never appeared on rainy days, which led them to come up with a strategy in hopes of recapturing their prize.

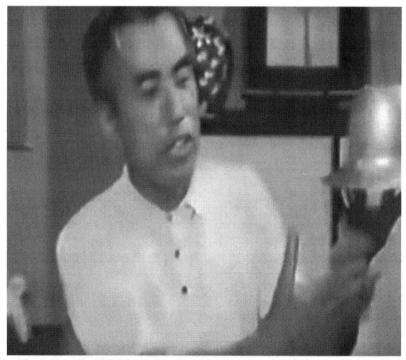

The father of one of the boys, Mutsuo Fujimoto, gave the object a quick examination, thinking it was of little significance.

On September 19, they returned to the field, carrying a bucket of water and some rags. Once again they discovered the device sitting quietly on the ground. Quickly covering the object with the rags, the boys poured water over it, and then turned it over and poured water into the holes underneath. When they did this, the tiny UFO began to brightly glow and a loud buzzing sound burst from the interior. The group retreated, fearing for their safety, and began throwing rocks at it until it quieted down.

Satisfied that it was now inoperative, they took it to Katsuoka Kojima's home for a closer look.

FULL OF ELECTRONICS

Examining their recaptured UFO, they attempted to look into the tiny holes underneath. Inside they saw what appeared to be levers, symbols, and electronics. Next, they forced a wire into one of the holes and hung it upside down. This caused the top of the dome to slightly separate from the lower section. The boys could see "complicated electronic equipment" as well as an unidentified viscous material. They feared that this was the remains of a tiny alien pilot they had accidentally melted when they poured water on it.

Then, with a large hammer, they struck the object several times to test the exterior. Despite the apparent low density of the metal, the hammer bounced off with no damage or even marks left on the craft.

To further test the UFO, the boys wanted to place it in the oven and then the refrigerator, only to be stopped by Kojima's mother, who refused to allow such experiments using her appliances.

Since there was to be no further testing that night, the boys wrapped the disc up for the night in rags and covered it in pillows, thinking that this would help prevent any exposure to "atomic radiation" that could be coming off it. The object was given to Seo and Mori for safekeeping, while the rest returned to their homes for dinner and homework.

When the group returned later that night and checked under the rags and pillows, they were shocked to discover that the disc had once again vanished. At this point they realized that the tiny UFO could be some sort of robotic device that was being operated by someone, or something, using remote control.

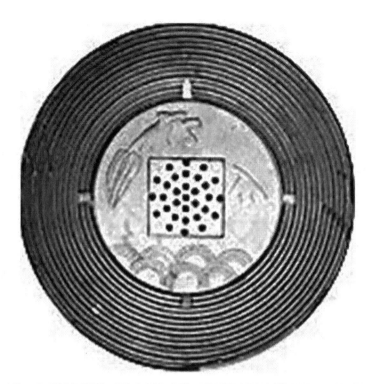

The underside of the craft had 31 holes in a circular configuration surrounded by three unknown symbols.

HIDE AND SEEK

Over the next week the miniature UFO seemed to be playing a game with the six boys. It would appear in places where they frequently played, allow itself to be captured, only to disappear from bags, cupboards or whatever method the boys thought up to try and keep it safe. During this time, the friends decided that they should mark the silver dome with paint to confirm that they were actually finding the same UFO again and again. The boys had lost and found the object so many times at this point they naturally assumed that if it disappeared they would eventually find it again near the paddy field or in one of their backyards.

It seemed, though, that whatever was controlling the UFO was growing tired of the game. The group had taken to sealing the object in plastic and then placing it inside a bag of water. They would then make sure that the bag was physically tied to the wrist of one of the boys.

All of these precautions seemed to be of little avail, as, on the evening of September 22, the team met for a bike ride in the city of Kochi. They decided that all of them would take turns carrying the device, which they no longer left unattended.

On close examination, the boys said they could see "complicated electronic equipment" inside.

The knotted bag containing the UFO was placed in a canvas bag and placed into the bicycle basket of the carrier. The bag went from cyclist to cyclist as they cruised through the city, heading for a local bike shop. Suddenly, the boy holding the bag, so to speak, said that he felt that the rope attached to his wrist was being forcefully pulled.

The boys immediately untied the rope and opened the bag, but when they looked inside, the little UFO had once again mysteriously vanished. This time, however, the disappearance was permanent...the boys would never see their intriguing little disc again.

ALMOST FORGOTTEN

It's not known whether or not any UFO groups in Japan investigated this case afterwards. Word certainly got out, as there is part of a documentary available on YouTube that was obviously filmed some years after the incident. In the film, the boys, who appear to be high school age or even older, recreate the events. Their parents and other witnesses are also interviewed. Unfortunately the YouTube version has a narration that covers the original audio track and it is impossible to tell what the witnesses are saying.

In 2004, *"UFO Comics"* in Japan published an illustrated account of the case. This introduced the encounter to a whole new generation of UFO enthusiasts. In 2007 – Shinichiro Namiki – the director of the Japan Space Phenomena Society (JSPS) – reopened the investigation. The head of the JSPS Osaka chapter, Kazuo Hayashi, was sent to speak with the remaining witnesses. All maintained that everything had happened as they had originally reported.

BATTERIES NOT INCLUDED

The Kera UFO case is certainly unique. Obviously, some skeptics denounce it all as simply a hoax, perpetrated by a bunch of bored schoolboys. It does sound suspiciously like some of the plots of popular Japanese science fiction television shows like Ultraman and Kamen Rider. If it wasn't for the parents, who later confirmed having seen and handled the disc themselves, it would be very easy to dismiss everything as a prank.

Approximately six-months after the Kera, Japan UFO encounter, a similar miniature UFO was photographed at Suonenjoki, Finland.

INCREDIBLE ALIEN ENCOUNTERS

There have been other cases involving miniature UFOs. Starting in March, 1973, Jarmo Nykanen, who was watching over a friend's house and summer cottage in Suonenjoki, Finland, was witness to a series of startling sightings of a small, bell-shaped UFO. The area around the house and cottage had previously been the focal point of other UFO sightings and possible landings. Because of this, Nykanen kept a camera with him every time he ventured outside.

At one point, while Nykanen was walking around the cottage, he heard a humming sound behind him. When he turned around, he spotted a small UFO hovering about six-feet above him. The bell-shaped object, which he estimated to be about 20 inches in diameter, would descend close to the ground as if it was going to land, only to abruptly rise back up again...all the while glowing with an eerie blue light.

Nykanen started taking photos of the UFO and, after about five photos, he decided to try and get closer. As he did, the mini-UFO backed away and shot up into the sky. Later that day, it reappeared, again glowing blue and making a strange humming sound.

Nykanen tried to sneak up and get closer to the craft, all the while taking more photos. However, on his way, he stumbled and the UFO shot a blinding red beam of light at his face.

Nykanen hid himself behind a fir tree and managed to take one last photo of the disc before it shot into the sky with a flash of light and red smoke. In total, he was able to take 12 photographs of the small object.

The photographs taken by Nykanen show a small UFO that does have a close resemblance to the Kera object. Both UFOs produced bizarre humming and buzzing noises as well as shooting out bright beams of light. The dates when these encounters occurred are also close enough to leave one to wonder if there was any kind of connection between these two cases.

It can be surmised that these miniature UFOs are some kind of remote controlled (or even autonomous) "drones," as their size bars having any sort of living pilot inside. OK, I admit that there have been reports of mini-UFOs seen with tiny pilots walking in and out of them. The August 19, 1970, encounter at the Stowell Primary School in Bukit Mertajam, Malaysia comes to mind. Eyewitnesses said that they saw five 3-inch tall humanoids, wearing identical blue uniforms, march down the gangplank of a miniature UFO that had landed in the schoolyard.

The six boys involved with the Kera UFO said that they saw a "viscous" substance inside the disc...which left them wondering if they had accidently melted a tiny extraterrestrial pilot.

Considering that the UFO phenomena has all sorts of mind-bending facets that leave researchers in a permanent state of puzzlement, it is not that outrageous to consider that at least some mini-UFOs that have been spotted over the years might be piloted by tiny creatures whose origins are unknown.

So the next time you are taking a stroll outside, walk lightly, as you might accidently crush a tiny, interplanetary (or interdimensional) craft that has landed to take in the sights of Planet Earth.

Cleaning your shoes off after something like that would certainly not be a pleasant task.

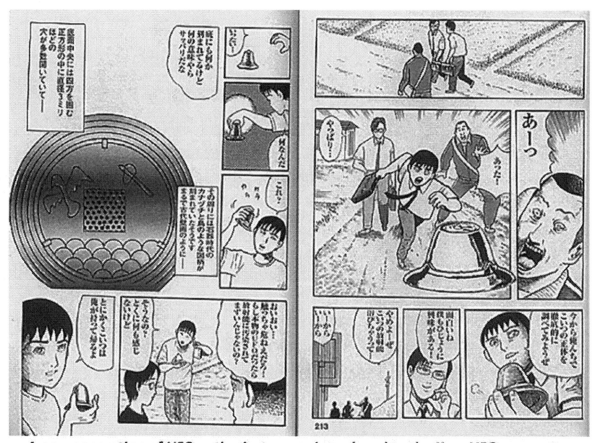

A new generation of UFO enthusiasts were introduced to the Kera UFO encounter when "UFO Comics" published an illustrated account of the case in 2004.

ABOUT THE AUTHOR: Tim R. Swartz is an Indiana native and Emmy-Award winning television producer/videographer, and is the author of a number of popular books including *"The Lost Journals of Nikola Tesla," "America's Strange and Supernatural History," "UFO Repeaters," "Time Travel: Fact Not Fiction!," "Gef The Talking Mongoose,"* and is a contributing writer for the books *"Brad Steiger's Real Monsters," "Gruesome Critters, and Beasts from the Darkside,"* and *"Real Ghosts, Restless Spirits and Haunted Places."*

As a photojournalist, Tim Swartz has traveled extensively and investigated paranormal phenomena and other unusual mysteries from such diverse locations as the Great Pyramid in Egypt to the Great Wall in China. He has worked with major U.S. and international television networks and has also appeared on the History Channels programs "Ancient Aliens," "Evidence," "Ancient Aliens: Declassified," and the History Channel Latin America series "Contacto Extraterrestre."

His articles have been published in magazines such as "Mysteries," "FATE," "Strange," "Atlantis Rising," "UFO Universe," "Unsolved UFO Reports," and "Renaissance." As well, Tim Swartz is the writer and editor of the online newsletter Conspiracy Journal; a free, weekly e-mail newsletter, considered essential reading by paranormal researchers worldwide.

Tim is also the host of the webcast "Exploring the Bizarre" along with Timothy Green Beckley on the KCOR Digital Radio Network. kcorradio.com

His website is: www.conspiracyjournal.com

The Hessdalen Lights appear regularly in the sky above the Hessdalen Valley in Norway. Usually the strange lights are roughly ball shaped. Sometimes they spit out smaller balls that zoom around the sky.

SIGHTING! TLOS IN SEATO

By William Kern

AUTHOR'S NOTE: I am reasonably certain about the date of the sighting because, as I recall, the USS Ajax, AR6, had departed for Japan two or three weeks earlier, around the last week of July or first week of August, 1968. Ajax, having arrived near the end of June, had been in port to repair gun mounts aboard the USS Boston. The repairs, as I recall, took approximately seven to ten days. A former shipmate served in Ajax and he had invited me aboard for an hour or so. If any shall read this, former officers and crewmembers of the Ajax will immediately know where this sighting occurred. (Mum's the word, mates).

THE EVENT

I watched two TLOs (Transient Luminous Objects) sailing over a military base for 1 hour, 45 minutes, while standing the midnight to 0800 security watch. This sighting is detailed as follows: In mid to late August 1968, I was standing the 2400 to 0800 security watch at a top secret intelligence facility in Southeast Asia during the Vietnam conflict. I had just phoned the OOD at 0600 to report all secure and decided to step outside to get a breath of fresh air, something I had never done before that night.

The two-story concrete building was behind me. To my right (south) was a range of low mountains obscuring approximately 20 degrees of the southern sky. To my left (north) was (a bay) and the South China Sea. I was facing east where, about 20 miles away, another range of mountains obscured approximately 5 degrees of the sky.

Immediately upon stepping outside the building, I saw a bright luminous object gliding silently from west to east above the range of mountains on the right.

This is a daytime aerial view of the facility. Sighting occurred from 6 AM until 7:45 AM.

This is a daytime aerial view of the facility. Sighting occurred from 6 AM until 7:45 AM.

This is a daytime aerial view of the facility. Sighting occurred from 6 AM until 7:45 AM.

This is a daytime aerial view of the facility. Sighting occurred from 6 AM until 7:45 AM.

I felt the presence of another object (like the touch of fingers on my neck) and turned toward the bay to see an identical object gliding at the same altitude, direction and speed as the first. The objects were approximately one mile apart.

The second object sighted made a sharp right turn; not a sweeping turn, but a vectored immediate right angle deviation, glided overhead at an altitude calculated to be 1000 to 1500 feet, passed behind the first object and disappeared from view beyond the mountain.

A NOTE: Speed, altitude, separation and sizes of aerial objects, having no spatial references, are extremely difficult to estimate and, so, are subject to great errors. The sizes, speeds, distances and altitudes related here are simply my first impressions and may be completely wrong.

CONTINUE: The first object sighted continued eastward at approximately 10 to 15 miles per hour. Both objects were as bright as a 1,000 watt street light as seen from a distance of 200 feet. Neither object made any noise and neither object displayed any normal aircraft running lights. The objects were the size of a dime as seen at arm's length. I estimate their size to be 40 to 50 feet in diameter and spherical rather than elliptical in shape.

The first object was in sight for approximately 1 hour and 45 minutes. It did not deviate from its eastward course, nor did it pulsate or change colors. Its speed appeared to remain constant throughout the entire sighting.

I stood transfixed and was unaware that an hour and 45 minutes had passed until the morning crew began arriving for duty at approximately 07:45. At the sound of automobiles approaching from my right, I turned abruptly, astonished and frightened, and I rather felt myself explode violently downward into my body while experiencing a strong pressure against my eardrums, something like slamming the door of a Volkswagen with all the windows rolled up.

It seemed only a few minutes and now the sun was rising! At that time (7:45 A.M.) the east-bound object was a pinhead-size bright light still visible on the face of the rising sun! Oddly, I found myself in a small field of grass and weeds where two roads diverged about fifty to sixty feet farther east from the building than where I thought I had been standing on the macadam carpark while I observed the TLOs.

The field was a very poor vantage point from which to observe the eastbound TLO because it (the field) was laced with weeds and knee-high grass, and scrub trees at 5 to 6 feet or more. Some, at that time, were even taller, although not in the line of my sight of the object.

At 7:45 AM, the object was a bright light on the face of the rising sun.

I was disoriented and confused for a brief period until I realized where I was and what had transpired. I calculate that the object was approximately 20 to 25 miles away at the time I returned to the building. Of course, it may have been much farther than that.

I signed over the duty log, relinquished my sidearm and went back outside. The object was still visible on the lower edge of the rising sun, which was approximately 10 to 12 degrees above the horizon.

But the spell was broken. After only moments of observing the tiny dot, I went to my car and drove to my quarters.

I later remembered that the duty crash cameras, a 4x5 Speed Graphic and a 16mm Cine Special camera, were inside on the floor beside my chair and I had not even thought to take a picture!

I had been in the Navy for 12 years, the entire time as a photographer, a portion of that time as an aircrew member. My MOS was Photographer but my job was processing and printing overflight surveillance and intelligence film from U2s, RA3Bs, RF101s, RF4s, and other (at that time) secret reconnaissance aircraft.

I had been around aircraft, both civilian and military, for fourteen years.

I cannot explain what I saw, but I believe they were not fixed wing or rotary wing aircraft, not weather balloons (one turned, the other did not) and they were not celestial bodies or atmospheric phenomena. My original assessment, although the objects appeared to be identical, was that I had seen two different things, one perhaps a weather balloon, the other a slow flying aircraft of some kind. Neither, however, displayed the movements or identification lights one would expect for either object.

I no longer consider this as a possibility. Weather balloons, when blown by the wind (there was none that I recall) wobble and bob through the sky. Instrumentation packages or RAWIN Targets swing below them, causing them to change shape and direction. Additionally, weather balloons are not lighted from within nor do the instrumentation packages carry such bright lights.

Helicopters can certainly fly at 10 to 15 miles per hour; however, none known at that time could fly silently at 1000 to 1500 feet and then to 10,000 feet or more. Neither of the TLOs emitted engine sounds or exhaust trails or displayed navigation lights.

Rotary wing and fixed wing aircraft, particularly military aircraft, have all sorts of lights on them which are on at night to alert personnel on the ground and other aircrews the direction the plane is going. There are colored lights, port wing tip red, starboard wing tip green, strobe lights, tail beacons and formation lights. While some aircraft may have a brilliant light similar to the TLO, it would be a landing light visible only from the front of the aircraft and used when taking off or landing at night. One would not see a landing light when an aircraft was flying away from the observer, and especially not after 20 or 30 miles.

When seen against the sun, even at a distance of approximately 25 to 30 miles, no hull shape or fuselage could be seen.

The glowing orb seen against the sun appeared to have traveled in a straight line; that is, not following the curvature of the Earth. At last sighting, I estimate the altitude of the object to be 10,000 feet or higher above the ground.

Because of my background in photography and my experience as an air crewman, I feel I objectively calculated the altitude, speed and size of the objects; however, as noted above, airborne objects having no spatial references are difficult to measure and, so, are subject to great errors.

The descriptions of the two TLOs do not fit any known aircraft or weather balloon. They do, however, perfectly define the objects known as Transient Luminous Objects, which have been shown to glide silently and slowly for long distances, change directions with apparently intelligent purpose and emit no sounds or exhaust trails.

TLOs do not display any overt signs of hostility or covert curiosity. None that I have observed, that is. They do not damage objects or affect the environment in any apparent manner. They simply appear, move about the skies for a time, then glide away or vanish, leaving stunned and confused witnesses to wonder what they have observed.

Unlike the objects known as UFOs, which seem to have destinations and purpose, and are solid and three-dimensional (or more), TLOs are truly unexplainable, having no observable substance or core, no common size or brightness, no common speed or direction. They may forever remain a mystery to those of us who have been fortunate (or unfortunate) enough to observe them.

CHANGED

This event changed me in ways I cannot easily explain. It has left me uneasy and suspicious; at times, even fearful and anxious. I returned from Southeast Asia with an illness and disease that no one would validate and the sighting of the TLOs was constantly at the back of my thoughts. I could not sleep in the house so I placed a thick piece of plywood across two sawhorses under a mulberry tree in the backyard and slept outside with a loaded .30 caliber M1A- 1 carbine fitted with a 30-round extended clip. I could not shake the dreadful feeling that someone was going to come for me and I didn't want to be trapped inside the house.

I feel certain my reaction to the event contributed significantly to my divorce from my first spouse a few years later. She just thought I was mad, of course (who can deny it?). Sadly, when others think you mad, they usually run away with the house, the car, the kids and the bank account. I harbor no ill feelings although I was homeless for nearly three years, living under a tool cover on the back of my old Chevy pickup truck.

ONLY THE LIGHT

When one is engaged in any activity, whether watching a boat race, a football game, children playing or when raking leaves from the yard, one is aware of many other concurrent events, such as aircraft and helicopters flying over, birds flitting from tree to tree, the smell of fireplace smoke, autos passing on the streets, cats and dogs, people talking and jogging by and many other things, including an awareness of one's self as a participant in the drama of life. But while observing the two TLOs I had absolutely no awareness of myself as a living being. Moments after the second object vanished behind the mountains on my right, I became aware only of the remaining TLO. I do not recall seeing or thinking of the night, the trees, the building behind me, the ships in the bay, my abandoned duty post, heat, cold, wind, comfort or discomfort. I had neither awareness of myself nor the will to look away from the light.

There was only the brilliant globe. I was possessed by it. I was as if entranced and enraptured, so engrossed in the light was I. I simply could not tear my gaze from it and, indeed, did not even think of it. There was only the light.

And it is this very loss of identity and awareness of self, my loss of will and single-minded fixation with the light that has troubled me for so many years. I simply did not exist in this time and space for nearly two hours. I do not recall having gone anywhere or encountered anyone or anything. I do not recall being inside any vehicle and do not recall being questioned or examined or instructed.

I was simply entranced by the TLO. There was only me and only the light, the observance of which for nearly two hours had released me from all physical bonds of will and all memory of earthly existence. It was a sort of empty awake sleeping death.

In my mind's eye, as I recall it now, there was only the unwavering light that I was somehow compelled to watch.

But I am unable to explain how or why I wandered into the field, although I feel there must be a wholly logical explanation for it.

TRY THIS ON FOR SIZE

I ask the reader to try this experiment: Go into your street or into a deserted parking lot at 6 AM in the morning and, standing as still as possible, stare without cease at the nearest street lamp or other bright light for an hour and 45 minutes. Do not speak, do not fidget, do not smoke or drink or adjust your clothing. Do not scratch or cough. Above all, do not turn your gaze elsewhere.

I'll wager you can't do it. But I did, apparently, and that is troubling for, while doing so, I forsook every other thing in this world, including myself.

It is a frightening thought and I am frightened by it.

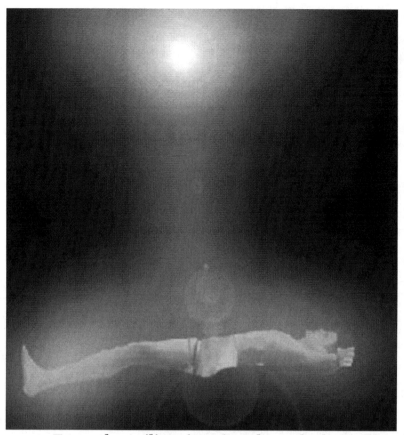

ANOTHER LIGHT

A couple of years later, back in the States and working on the space programs, I one day, while alone, fell into a kind of trance or state of stasis or suspended animation. All sound and feeling and normal senses disappeared. I was awake but could not move. My thoughts were never more clear and attuned. I wasn't morbidly afraid or worried. I was, however, somewhat apprehensive about the descent of a vaguely familiar globe of light.

From the ceiling (passing through the ceiling from outside the building, it seemed to me) a very bright orb of light (the TLO again?) appeared. It was the apparent size of a soccer ball. It floated down to touch me. As it touched me, it spread out to completely cover my entire body, almost like liquid light. I became aware of sounds that might have been voices but were not in a language I could understand. Over all was a sort of opalescent bubble.

I remember a low-pitch music-like tone, very soft and pleasant, and a tinkling sound like glass breaking far away, or glass wind chimes. I was wrapped in the light and sound for what seemed to be 10 or 15 seconds, then the light floated up through the ceiling, leaving me wondering what had happened! Almost two hours had passed while I was in the light. And, again, there was a loss of self-identity, this time for two hours. The being that was me did not exist for two hours. This loss of identity of self only reinforced the feelings of anguish and fear that began with the TLO sighting in Southeast Asia. I began to wonder if I were going mad or if some machine or energy was driving my thoughts, or if I was simply hallucinating.

A FRENZY OF READING

Almost immediately thereafter, I began reading as many books as I could get my hands on. I read some 300 books each year for a period of about three years. Often, I would lay out up to three books at a time, open each to page one and read all the page ones. Then I would turn all the pages to pages 2 and 3 and read all those pages, and so on until the books were finished. Generally, I could read all three books in a single evening and could pigeonhole the information in each so it did not become confused with the information in any of the others.

I think I stopped reading because I had run out of the material I wanted to read.

Unfortunately, my private life was going to hell in a handbasket about that time and that may have contributed to my waning interest in further information.

But here is something I learned: In books having the same or similar content, I would often find the same information, even the same sentences or paragraphs very close to the areas I found the same information in the other books, and occasionally, on the same pages!

I began to refer to these sentences or paragraphs as the inklings of truth. But what import it had then or has now, I have no clue. It seemed so important that I discovered those inklings at the time, but soon it meant little or nothing to me.

AND, SO

These are only two of the many events I have witnessed since I was an infant in 1937 and, with these two, I am simply trying to describe my feelings and why the loss of identity and awareness of self, and the loss of will, have caused me so much anguish for over 40 years. Make of it what you will.

As for me, I hope to explore and dismiss every terrestrial explanation before I turn my eyes heavenward. I feel reasonably certain the answers will not be found in the skies.

The answer will most likely be found in the fact that I worked at NRTSC and Defense Intelligence Agency in Washington, D. C. (Arlington, Virginia) from 1963 until 1965, at which time I was transferred to the facility described in this essay.

These dates may be significant. Or not.

Cautious Believer is Cautiously Skeptical

The two-story secret facility as it appeared in 1968, with the small camera repair shop directly across the carpark and ROICC building at lower left. The cluster of small structures center bottom is the film and classified documents burning furnace.

*I must estimate times in this narrative since I was not aware of the passage of time. I went to the Quarterdeck to look at the clock to learn how much time had passed. But I am not certain when this event began, so the times given here may be wrong by several minutes.

ADDENDUM FOLLOWS...

HMAS Hobart (RAN) during the Vietnam conflict. Without getting too detailed, I would like to point out that the Hobart was not a PBR (river patrol boat) as shown in your HANGAR 1 presentation of UFOs in Wartime.

Hobart was a first class ship of the line built in Bay City, Michigan, as an Adams class Destroyer and was later modified to fire guided missiles, becoming a Guided Missile Destroyer of the RAN. Hobart was hit by air to surface missiles fired from USAF aircraft while on station supporting allied forces in South Vietnam.

I was stationed at Subic Bay (Cubi Point) Republic of the Philippines and was assigned to photograph damage to Hobart after she pulled in to Subic Bay for repairs.

Although I cannot categorically state that Hobart was not struck or attacked by UFOs, the damage I recorded indicated that it was not some alien ray gun or pulse weapon that damaged the ship.

This little vignette is provided to add some corroboration to the preceding report of TLOs that I witnessed while stationed at Cubi during the same period.

I believe Hobart returned to duty in SEATO around the end of July, 1968, and the two TLOs were observed shortly thereafter (August).

But the sighting and this report is some slim evidence that UFOs and TLOs were certainly in the area during that period of time. Whether they had any involvement in the attacks on the two Australian ships (Hobart and Edson) and one US ship (Chicago, a cruiser) on the same night, or not, I cannot address and have no opinion.

I was transferred back to CONUS November, 1968, and was assigned to USS Constellation at North Island, California. I retired from USN in 1975.

At the present time, I am the layout artist for Tim Beckley's Conspiracy Journal.

scriaben@earthlink.net

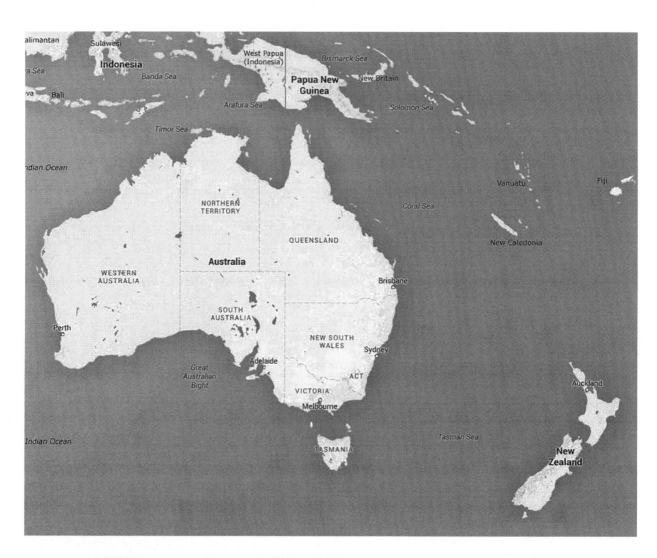

AUSTRALIA
NEW ZEALAND

UFO CRASH AT STIRLING

From *"UFO Encounter Magazine,"* Issue 306, August/September 2019

Many years ago my brother and I witnessed a UFO chase that resulted in one of the craft crashing into a tree which still bears its visible scars today.

This is not a sci-fi story. This is a true account to the best of my ability that describes actual events which occurred during February 1980. I have told this story before to close friends and some UFO groups. These people are likely to be the only ones who are prepared to listen.

I am not a pilot or naval officer, nor do I hold any position of authority. I am an ordinary, moderately "successful" Joe, albeit, slightly off-centre. To some extent this lack of social status also allows me a certain amount of freedom. I believe that most witnesses of such events experience a negative response. This response I am very familiar with. It includes the usual expression of disbelief and a barrage of plausible explanations. One often gets caught up in trying to convince the listener that his judgment and interpretation were accurate. It is fortunate that I'm not overly concerned about being labeled as a kook, and even recognize that I may have travelled quite some distance down this unusual path without looking back to see where it all began.

I have since read many UFO cases and recognise that it is the inclusion of detail which is necessary to create credibility. The social status of a witness is even more influential. I am unable to vary this factor but can offer a detailed description. It is the detail that offers readers an opportunity to experience the event as seen from the eyes of the witness, and allows the reader to respond and judge for themselves as to whether they would have reached the same conclusion. After all, these events are not

UFOs have been seen and photographed on many occasions over Australia. This amazing photo was taken on March 10, 1993 at Maslin Beach, Australia.

like a movie, where the camera seamlessly follows the action through scenes to paint a clear and comprehensible story.

The Stirling event began shortly after my twin brother and I went to bed on an ordinary Thursday night during February 1980. We were 10 years old, and it was the start of a new school year. My brother called out to me from his room. "Phil...come and check this out."

We lived in Aldgate (21 kilometres south-east of Adelaide) on Coromandel Rd, and our house was positioned high on the side of a valley that looked towards the Stirling Township. The house was reasonably modern, with the land recently subdivided into allotments of around 6000 square meters. Few houses were built and the land was sparsely treed, not like it is today. We had a perfect view of the valley.

Toward Stirling, and around one kilometre away, a line of trees followed a gentle ridge forming the end of the valley. The slight rise blocked us from the lights of the township centre which lay one kilometre further on past this ridge. I jumped out of bed and ran into my brother's room to see what had caught his attention. From the window we saw a bright yellow object slightly larger than the apparent size of Venus, bobbing around just above the tree line at the end of the valley. We guessed it must have been in the vicinity of the Stirling woodyard and Gould Rd, which lay just past the ridge. It hovered 50 metres to 100 metres above ground level. Although we didn't discuss distances or other metrics at the time, we considered all of this detail later.

The damaged tree on Daryl Browne's property. Stirling, South Australia. *"Australasian Post"* - March, 1980.

The object appeared to have some purpose. It wobbled slightly as it hovered, then moved with haste back and forth and then resumed its hover. It was a mild summer night and very clear, the air was still and there was no noise. In the past we had watched over our valley many times and had seen helicopters, and listened to cars as they wound their way through the Aldgate s-bends up Mount Barker Road towards Stirling. The sound of the car engines travelled down the valley and we could hear the noise clearly until they passed the ridge and became more muffled. (Later when selling the house a prospective buyer also commented on this effect).

On this night, there was no noise, no car engines, just silence. Not that this was unusual, there were fewer people in the hills back then. But there was no engine noise from this bobbing light at the end of our valley. We watched for several minutes with interest, and recognised that this object was certainly not behaving like conventional aircraft. Shortly a second object appeared emitting a red light. It entered our view from above and approached the yellow object. It also had a slightly larger apparent size and brightness of Venus. The red object zoomed up to the yellow object, stopped and reversed, and then did it again as if to prompt a reaction. And it got one!

The yellow object took off with the red object in close pursuit. They zoomed around, zigzagging across the sky with extreme speed and acceleration, like a couple of blowflies on steroids. They crossed the valley-head back and forth many times in a hectic paired chase. When older I attempted to estimate some of the velocities based on the time it took to move a measurable distance between landmarks and the possible accelerations involved. The results were extraordinary, so it is better that I describe what I saw and let the reader do the calculations.

From a stationary position, the object accelerated, travelled half a kilometre and then instantly reversed within around half a second (give or take). Throughout the chase, the yellow one seemed to get stuck mid-flight and shake back and forth as if caught by some invisible force. Then it freed itself and the chase continued. There seemed to be no apparent inertia. The craft changed direction and reversed without changing speed, like a ping-pong ball does when hit with a bat. The motion almost had a cartoon-like quality to it. This chase went on for several minutes. Eventually the yellow object sped off at extraordinary speed to our right and disappeared behind the hill. Had I blinked, I would have missed it. The red one had also gone. Neither myself nor my brother were certain whether the red one had followed or simply left. We waited for quite some time after the sighting to see if the objects would re-appear, but they did not. I estimate that the total sighting lasted for around 15 minutes or within that proximity. At some point during the sighting, we ran into our parent's room to persuade them to get out of bed, but were told to go back to sleep, so we resumed viewing the spectacle.

Aussie Sure UFO Damaged Trees

MELBOURNE, Australia (AP) — An unidentified flying object may have made an emergency landing in some trees near the small South Australian town of Stirling, a UFO research group said today.

But police are making no comment except to say there are unexplained broken branches and no other physical evidence.

A 21-year-old farmhand claimed to have seen a "speedboat-shaped yellow thing" Thursday night in some trees near the horse farm where he works.

Daryl Browne told police late that night that his dogs began howling while he sat watching TV.

"And then I heard the trees smashing. I locked the kids inside and went outside with a torch," he said.

He said he shone the flashlight up into the trees and saw the object. "It was about 25 to 30 feet long," he said, adding that it had not emitted any sound or light.

Browne said he called the police but the object had disappeared by the time they arrived.

The damage to the trees was about 100 feet from the ground.

C.O. Norris of the Australian International UFO Research Group said the scene revealed many of the classic signs of a UFO landing.

There were very high infra-red readings at the site on today, he said. The dogs' howling probably indicated the UFO's noise was above the human hearing range, as dogs can hear higher-pitched sounds than people can, and the layout of the land and vegetation were typical of other reported UFO landing sites, he said.

UFO is the name given to unidentified objects reported to have been seen flying at various heights and speeds and regarded variously as light phenomena, hallucinations, secret military missiles and spacecraft from other planets. U.S. authorities generally regard them as scientifically explainable.

1980 newspaper article.

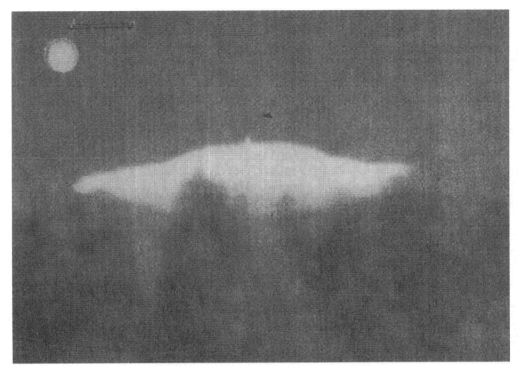

A UFO plays hide and seek in the trees.

A friend suggested that we must have been gobsmacked by this sighting. The reality is that at 10 years old, one is open to experience without overwhelming emotional involvement. We were certainly impressed, and recognised that these objects were not within the human inventory, but the feeling was more like "oh, so this is what a UFO must look like." The lack-lustre response from our parents compounded the "ordinariness" of the event.

The next day was a "school day." After that it was the weekend and we were planning to visit our grandma. I headed back to my room and went back to bed. I believe that we must have talked about the event at school on the following day. But the subject couldn't have gained significant attention as I can't recall a great deal of conversation about it, only that it seemed interesting.

On Saturday we arrived at "Gran's" house. The first thing she did was present us with a cutting from the local paper, the "Advertiser" I think. It reported a UFO crash in Stirling on the same night and time that my brother and I had witnessed the chase. There was a compellingly clear connection. At this point our parents became interested and our credibility had been fully restored with an apology and some level of regret for not joining the witness box when requested. The story was reported by

Daryl Browne, on the 7th or 8th of February 1980. He described hearing a loud crash which had terrified his pet dogs. He went outside to see what had happened.

When he went around to the back of the house where the noise had come from, he could hear a tree creaking and groaning. Upon pointing his torch into its upper branches he saw a yellow craft measuring around 8 meters in length. He described it as a speedboat shape. It was wedged between the broken branches, and causing the tree to groan under its weight. A branch measuring around 30cm in diameter had been knocked from the tree.

Daryl called the authorities, but the craft managed to take flight before they arrived, leaving no wreckage, only damage to the tree as evidence. (http://www.project1947.com/loren/loren_ufo_notes.htm, page 20)

Although this incident was one of the more intriguing events that I have witnessed, at the time it seemed unrelated to ordinary life and I mentally filed it away in to the "camp fire and ghost story" section of my mind. My brother did the same and we both let the event rest in peace for the following 30 years.

The pilot Frederick Valentich vanished after observing a UFO closing in on his aircraft.

Fast forward to the introduction of the Internet. In 2009 I decided to dig up that old story and look for Daryl, the house he had lived in and maybe even the tree if I were lucky. I Googled a map of Stirling, searched my memory for where I had believed the events had taken place and looked for a likely trajectory that would lead me to the crash site. Daryl Browne failed to come up in any search so I had to rely on my own investigation. The clues which I had at my disposal, thanks to various news articles were: Big pine tree out back of house, horses kept at property and the name of the property XXXX.

The chase had been fast and furious, and we had not seen the craft re-appear. I made an assumption that it was likely to have finished immediately after disappearing from view. I marked a line on the map extending along Gould Rd, where the craft had been travelling and then marked a plot area north of the Freeway. This represented my search area. I drove to this location knowing that many larger plots of land existed within this region of Stirling, but there was no sign of "XXXX" and large pines were a common feature. Eventually I picked the property of my best guess and headed down the driveway. At the end was a pretty cottage and marked on the wall was the name XXXX. Not bad hey! And out the back of the house was a stand of large cypress pines. There were around a dozen to choose from.

Despite the really, really poor copy of the photograph showing the tree in question, it did provide significant clues. The branches extended nearly all the way to the ground, ruling out all but one tree. The photo also showed something that was only evident once standing there on site. This was the slightly unusual angle of the ladder. It became clear that the tree grew at the bottom of a now visible embankment and the ladder must have been placed at the top of the embankment, leaning awkwardly against the tree. This tree had to be it. To add a little more certainty, visible damage and a large unusual scar cutting vertically through an upper limb existed on the side facing the likely trajectory. The damage faced the clearing cut by the wide freeway, making a direct path for any fast moving object.

I did eventually find Daryl's family who, although they did not witness the crash, confirmed Daryl's description and certainty of the events. Their belief was that he was telling the truth. They also confirmed some of the smaller details. Daryl had passed away only months before I had begun looking for him. These findings gave me absolute certainty that my interpretation was spot on. The objects that my brother and I had seen were advanced craft of some description, they were physical, and they were at odds with each other.

Following this I began to bring up the UFO topic in conversation when the opportunity arose. I suppose that I am even more pushy now. Soon I found other witnesses. Two contacts even described a chase similar to the one I had witnessed. One of them involved a crash which was cleaned up by the military. The other was described to me before I had exposed any part of my own experience, eliminating the possibility of being a copy-cat. These descriptions and details were incredibly similar to my own.

I then printed my experience within some of the UFO groups and received many returning stories. These stories were varied, but had overlapping details, often describing the similar movement and acceleration of the craft, involving hypersonic speed and more chases. What became clear was that there were many more witnesses than I had previously believed possible, and that these events were not uncommon.

Sheryl Gottschall is Group Director of UFO Research Queensland (UFORQ).

MUFON and NUFORC record between 5,000 and 10,000 sightings per year. It has been estimated that this represents 1/10th to 1/100th of the true scale. Not every second person has such a compelling experience, but the overall numbers are large. If there is any truth to even a fraction of these reports, then humanity truly has to wake up.

I hope this gives the reader a bird's-eye view of how I began investigations into this enormous topic, and how my views have progressed.

I am unable to verify other people's accounts, but I am able to compare similarities between them and my own new understanding of what is possible. Without a personal experience, it would be easy to dismiss something that appeared to rub against our scientific beliefs. But having personally witnessed the extraordinary capabilities of these craft, I am compelled to include these accounts within the realm of possibility, especially when some compare so closely to my own experience. I can confidently say that I know we are not talking about weather balloons or any other human-created machines. Hopefully we will soon be able to have real discussion on this incredibly important topic.

ISSUE 306
AUGUST-SEPTEMBER 2019

INSIDE:

UFO Crash at Stirling, SA
Kaikoura's Last Witness
The Hunt for the Ropen
Astral Travelling to Mars

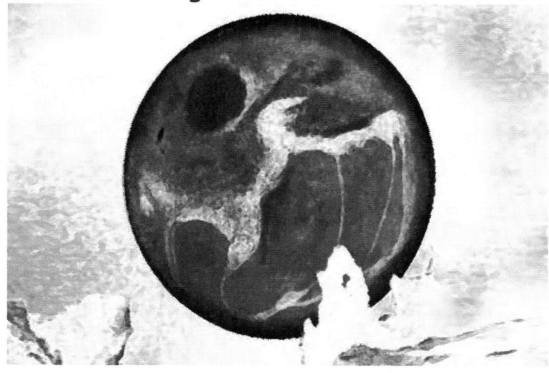

"UFO Encounter Magazine" from Australia has been published for over 60 years.

DISCLOSURE DOWN UNDER:
NEW ZEALAND RELEASES (SOME) UFO FILES
By Sean Casteel

UFOCUS director Susanne Hansen deserves credit for having pushed the NZ government to release its UFO files.

The intent to release formerly classified UFO documents in New Zealand happened largely because of the efforts of Suzanne Hansen, the Director of a civilian UFO group called UFOCUS NZ. In her campaign to make the files public, Hansen negotiated for over a year with the Chief of Defence Force NZ, Lt. General Jerry Mataparae.

Mataparae was initially unwilling to cooperate. He told Ms. Hansen, "It would require a substantial amount of collation, research and consultation to identify whether any of that information could be released." The Lt. General further stated that he was not in a position to deploy staff to undertake that task given their other work priorities.

However, the Chief of Defence also acknowledged his own feelings on the subject, saying, "In the longer term, recognizing the ongoing public interest in this topic, I would like to see a summary of information held about UFO sightings produced, in much the same way as that which was produced by the United Kingdom Ministry of Defence. Given the existing constraints, however, I cannot predict when that objective could be achieved."

Chief of Defence Force, Lt. General Jerry Mataparae assisted in the UFO Disclosure movement in NZ.

Which sounds like Lt. General Mataparae was sympathetic to the cause of Disclosure and even a little apologetic about having to withhold the files from UFOCUS NZ.

Then, in December of 2009, after many months of ongoing communications, the Chief of Defence sent another letter to the New Zealand UFO group.

"I am pleased to be able to inform you," Mataparae wrote, "that two New Zealand Defence Force officers have begun the task of assessing classified files held in relation to this topic with a view to declassification. I would expect that files which are transferred to Archives New Zealand would be subject to extensive embargo periods in terms of access by the general public."

There was also this from a spokesperson for the Lt. General's office: "The declassification of the UFO files is now a 'work in progress' in conjunction with Archives New Zealand. The files must be amended to meet new requirements of the Privacy Act."

Meaning it will be necessary to edit the files so that no personal information on the private citizens who made the sightings reports to begin with, for example, is made open to the public. Many people, given the stigma often attached to the subject, may not appreciate having the fact that they once reported a UFO announced to the world.

The process of removing personal information from the files was to take several months with the expected release date sometime in 2010. The Defence force agreed to notify UFOCUS NZ when the process was complete and to give them the opportunity to actually access the files as soon as they became available.

Meanwhile, Hansen states on the group's website that the archives of UFOFOCUS NZ already contain "credible and detailed UFO sightings reports from

New Zealand pilots, air traffic controllers and military personnel. In addition, the research network holds sightings reports from members of the public who experienced significant UFO sightings dating as far back as 1908. Some of these prominent cases were investigated by NZ Air Force personnel."

A particularly important case that happened in New Zealand is called "The Kaikoura Lights," which made headlines throughout the world in 1978/79. John Cody, currently a member of the NZ UFO group, is a former Chief Air Traffic Controller of Wellington International Airport. Cordy was a witness to the Kaikoura Lights and saw the event transpire on radar there at the control center.

"I hope the files will validate the reality of the sightings," Cody said, "and vindicate key witnesses who observed them and faced 'trial by media.'"

UFO sightings are on the increase in New Zealand, with patterns and characteristics that parallel reported sightings and flaps occurring worldwide, according to Hansen. The increase in sightings reported to UFOFOCUS NZ is a direct result of heightened public awareness and growing interest in the subject in New Zealand.

The main stream non-UFO press in New Zealand also made note of the fact that the military there would be releasing UFO files. An online newspaper called "The Press" based in New Zealand said the release would include hundreds of pages on sightings from 1979 to 1984, and will include files on the aforementioned Kaikoura Lights.

In that incident, lights were seen in the sky over Kaikoura in December 1978 and were filmed by an Australian news crew. Aircraft tracked the lights, which were also seen on radar. A man who was working at Christchurch International airport at the time said he also saw United States Air Force planes with unusual call signs touring the area and believes the full story about the lights has not been disclosed.

"For the U.S. Air Force to come all that way," said the man, who prefers to remain anonymous, "and spend three days here, there must have been something going on."

In any case, the New Zealand Defence Force seems willing to cooperate.

This photograph taken on Oct 27 1979 in Montonau is said to be among the most authentic ever taken in NZ.

"At the moment, we are working on making copies of these files, minus the personal information," a Defence Force spokeswoman said. "Once this work is completed, we are hoping to be able to release a copy of all the UFO files, including some ahead of their release time, within the year."

The publication *"The Press"* also made its own request to the Defence Force for access to the UFO files under the Official Information Act and was given the same answer as UFOCUS NZ, that the public files were available from Archives New Zealand. When "The Press" requested access at the Archives, they were told they were currently unavailable because they had been borrowed by the Defence Force. The article also stated that Suzanne Hansen of UFOCUS NZ was frustrated by the delays but understood the privacy reasons.

"We have been in discussion with the New Zealand Defence Force for many years," Hansen said. "It is frustrating from a research perspective because we would like to collate these sightings with international research."

Some sightings could have been of alien technology, she said.

"There are cases that are certainly not our technology. It has been scientifically proven that this is entirely possible."

If you're interested in visiting the Archives New Zealand, the website address is www.archives.govt.nz. For more information on current and historical activity on NZ activity we highly recommend: www.ufocusnz.org.nz

MORE ON THE KAIKOURA CASE

An Internet survey of New Zealand UFO cases quickly leads to the conclusion that the Kaikoura incident of 1978 is the most controversial in the region to date. Entries on the case abound and there is much interest and anticipation as to what the eventual release of files to the Archives New Zealand will have in the way of comment on the event.

UFO Casebook webmaster Billy Booth provides a capsule history of what happened:

"An extremely rare case of a plane flight for the express purpose of filming a UFO occurred on December 30, 1978, in New Zealand," Booth writes. "For some time, there had been a spate of UFO sightings in the area, and an investigation was called for."

With an Australian television film crew onboard, the plane soared over the Pacific Ocean, northeast of South Island, and a UFO was sighted. One of the television crew members stated that he saw "a row of five bright lights, which were pulsating and grew from the size of a pinpoint to that of a large balloon." The whole sequence was then repeated and the lights then appeared over the town of Kaikoura, between the aircraft and the ground.

Air traffic control at Wellington radioed the pilot that they had a return for an unknown object following the plane. The pilot made a 360 degree turn in an attempt to confront the UFO, which could still not be seen by crew members aboard the plane. Air traffic control again confirmed a target near the plane, which they said had now increased in size. The flight crew then made visual contact with the UFO, but the plane's navigational lights made it impossible to film the object. After the pilot turned the lights off, the crew members could see a large, bright light. The television crew managed to film the object for 30 seconds with a handheld camera.

The pilot turned the plane around and the UFO was no longer visible, although the airport was still seeing the radar target there. Finally, the plane landed at Christchurch with the UFO still visible on radar.

The same plane was sent aloft the very next night, and this time two UFOs were sighted. One of the news crew observed one of the objects through his camera, describing it as a spinning sphere with lateral lines around it. Near the end of the flight, two lights could be seen, and as the plane landed the airport ground control still had both objects on radar.

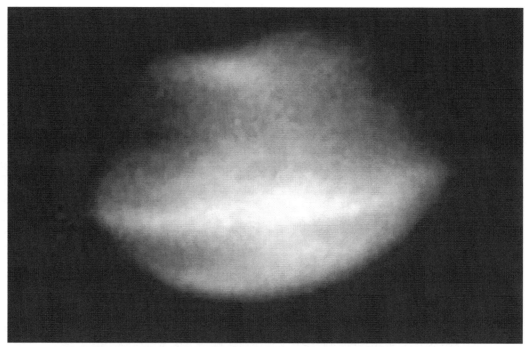

In this frame of the Christchurch footage the UFO looks like a typical "flying saucer."

The film taken by the Australian news crew would be seen around the world, with the BBC even making it their lead story on an evening news show. Although the film was quickly debunked by skeptics, the Royal New Zealand Air Force had planes on full alert to confront the UFOs if it became necessary.

A U.K. newspaper called The Daily Telegraph, noted for businesslike and scientific observations, remarked, "The scientist who suggested that all on the aircraft were seeing Venus on a particularly bright night can be safely consigned to Bedlam (an insane asylum)."

Subsequently, the Royal New Zealand Air Force, the police and the Centre Observatory in Wellington conducted a joint investigation into the sightings. The results were stamped "Top Secret" and archived in the Wellington National Archives. The sightings have never been adequately explained.

· · · · · · · · · ·

Interestingly enough, when the story first broke the initial media coverage in the U.S. came about partly due to the efforts of the editor of this book. Tim Beckley working in association with the late publicist Harold Salkin informed the American Press of the matter by organizing a press conference in Manhattan where Naval optical data expert Dr Bruce Maccabee put forward a strong case that the object photographed was not part of a fishing fleet or any other optical illusion. Mcaccabee has had a long time interest in UFOs dating back to the days of Nicae and is highly educated in his profession having received a B.S. in physics at Worcester Polytechnic Institute in Worcester, Mass., and then at American University, Washington, DC, (M.S. and Ph. D. in physics). In 1972 he began his long career at what is now the Naval Surface Warfare Center Dahlgren Division, in Dahlgren, Virginia, finally retiring from government service in 2008. He has worked on optical data processing, generation of underwater sound with lasers and various aspects of the Strategic Defense Initiative (SDI) and Ballistic Missile Defense (BMD) using high power lasers.

ATMOSPHERE OR UFO?
By Dr Bruce Maccabee

NOTE: This is a greatly abridged version of a paper that was written as a response to the 1997 Review Panel of the Society for Scientific Exploration (sometimes called the "Sturrock Panel" after Dr. Peter Sturrock who convened the panel with support from other SSE members and Laurence Rockefeller.) It was published in the *Journal of Scientific Exploration*, Vol. 13, pg. 421 (1999) The complete text can be found on Dr. Maccabee's Research Web Site http://brumac.8k.com/index.html

HISTORY OF THE SIGHTINGS

In order to fully understand the significance of the radar event (#16 below) to be discussed it is necessary know the events leading up to that event. A history of the various sighting events represented by the numbers in Figure 4 will now be given. At point (1) the aircraft passed over Wellington at about midnight. It reached a non-geographical reporting point just east of Cape Campbell at about 10 minutes past midnight (point 2 on the event map) where the plane made a left turn to avoid any possible turbulence from wind blowing over the mountains of the South Island.

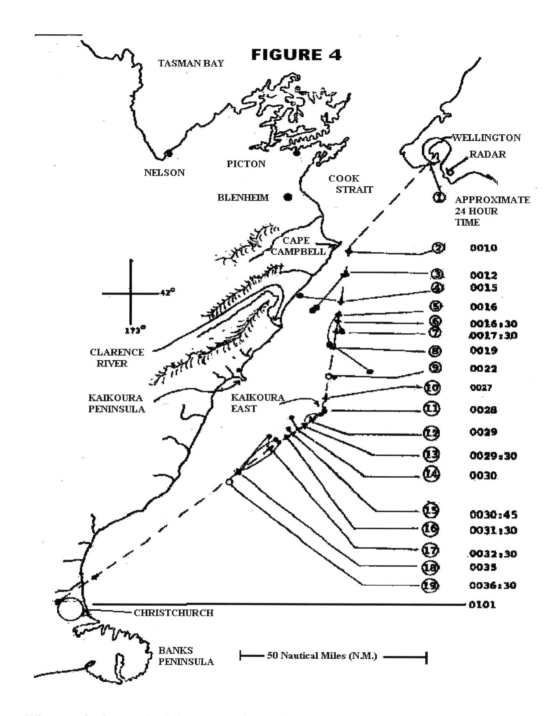

FIGURE 4

This turbulence had been predicted by the flight weather service, but was not detected at all during the trip. The captain reported that the flying weather was excellent and he was able to use the automatic height lock, which would have automatically disengaged had there been turbulence that would change the altitude of the aircraft. The sky condition was "CAVU" (clear and visibility unlimited) with visibility estimated at over 30 miles. (Note: the definition of visibility is based on contrast reduction between a distant dark object and a light sky. Thus a black object could barely be seen against a bright sky at 30 miles. However, a light could be seen in the night sky for a hundred miles or more, depending upon its intrinsic intensity.) The air crew could see the lights along the coast of the South Island, extending southward to Christchurch about 150 miles away.

At about 0005 (12:05 A.M., local time), the captain and copilot first noticed oddly behaving lights ahead of them near the Kaikoura Coast. They had flown this route many times before and were thoroughly familiar with the lights along the coast so they quickly realized that these were not ordinary coastal lights. These lights would appear, project a beam downward toward the sea, and then disappear, only to reappear at some other location. Sometimes there was only one, sometimes none and sometimes several. After several minutes of watching and failing to identify the lights the pilot and copilot began to discuss what they were seeing. They were puzzled over their inability to identify these unusual lights and their odd pattern of activity, which made the captain think of a search operation. (Similar activity of unidentified lights nearer to Cape Campbell had been seen by ground witnesses during a series of UFO events that had occurred about ten days earlier. See Startup and Illingworth, 1980)

Optical expert Bruce Maccabee is frequently interviewed by the media. He proclaimed the Christchurch footage to be authentic.

At about 0012 they decided to contact Wellington Air traffic Control Center radar to find out if there were any aircraft near Kaikoura. At this time, point (3) on the map, the plane was traveling at 215 nm/hr indicated air speed and had reached its 14,000 ft cruising altitude. There was a light wind from the west. The average ground speed was about 180 nm/hr or about 3 nm/minute. Since the copilot was in control of the aircraft on this particular journey, the captain did the communicating with WATCC. "Do you have any targets showing on the Kaikoura Peninsula range?" he asked. The controller at WATCC had been busy with another aircraft landing, but had noticed targets appearing and disappearing in that direction for half an hour or more. He knew it was not uncommon to find spurious radar targets near the coast of the South Island. These would be ground clutter effects of mild atmospheric refraction so he had paid little attention to them. About 20 seconds after the plane called he responded, "There are targets in your one o'clock position at, uh, 13 miles, appearing and disappearing. At the present moment they're not showing but were about 1 minute ago." (Note: directions with respect to the airplane are given as "clock time" with 12:00 - twelve o'clock - being directly ahead of the aircraft, 6:00 being directly behind, 9:00 to the left and 3:00 to the right. The "1:00 position" is 30(+/-)15 degrees to the right.) The pilot responded, "If you've got a chance would you keep an eye on them?" "Certainly," was the reply. Shortly after that the other aircraft landed and from then on the Argosy was the only airplane in the sky south of Wellington.

At about 0015 (point 4) WATCC reported a target at the 3:00 position on the coastline. According to captain (7), at about that time the TV crew, which had been below deck in the cargo hold of the aircraft filming a short discussion of the previous sightings, was coming up onto the flight deck. The air crew pointed out to the TV crew the unusual lights and the ordinary lights visible through the windshield. The crew did not see the target at 3:00.

The TV crew had to adapt to the difficult conditions of working on the cramped and very noisy flight deck. The cameraman had to hold his large Bolex 16 mm electric movie camera with its 100 mm zoom lens and large film magazine on his shoulder while he sat in a small chair between the pilot (captain) on his left and copilot on his right. From this position he could easily film ahead of the aircraft but it was difficult for him to film far to the right or left and, of course, he could not film anything behind the aircraft. He was given earphones so he could hear the communications between the air crew and WATCC. Occasionally he would yell over the noise of the airplane to the reporter, who was standing just behind the copilot, to tell the reporter what the air crew was hearing from the WATCC. The sound recordist was crouched behind the cameraman with her tape recorder on the floor and her earphones. She was not able to see anything. She could, of course, hear the reporter as he recorded his impressions of what he saw through the right side window or through the front windows of the flight deck. She heard some things that were more than just a bit frightening.

At approximately 0016, the first radar-visual sighting occurred. WATCC reported "Target briefly appeared 12:00 to you at 10 miles," to which the captain responded, "Thank you." (The previous target at 3:00 had disappeared.) According to the captain (7), he looked ahead of the Argosy and saw a light where there should have been none (they were looking generally toward open ocean; Antarctica, the closest land in the sighting direction, was about 1,000 miles away; there were no other aircraft in the area).

He described it as follows: "It was white and not very brilliant and it did not change color or flicker. To me it looked like the taillight of an aircraft. I'm not sure how long we saw this for. Probably not very long. I did not get a chance to judge its height relative to the aircraft." This target was not detected during the next sweep of the scope. (Note: each sweep required 12 seconds corresponding to 5 revolutions per minute.)

About 20 seconds later, at about 0016:30, WATCC reported a "...strong target showing at 11:00 at 3 miles." The captain responded "Thank you, no contact yet." Four radar rotations (48 seconds) later (at point 7) WATCC reported a target "just left of 9:00 at 2 miles." The captain looked out his left window but saw nothing in that direction except stars. Eighty-five seconds later, at about 0019, WATCC reported at target at 10:00 at 12 miles. Again there was no visual sighting.

The captain has written (7) that he got the impression from this series of targets that some object that was initially ahead of his plane had traveled past the left side. He decided to make an orbit (360 degree turn) to find out if they could see anything at their left side or behind.

Members of the film crew who took motion picture footage over Christchurch
are from left to right:
Quentin Fogarty, David Crockett and Ngaire Crockett.

At about 0020:30 the captain asked for permission to make a left hand orbit. WATCC responded that it was OK to do that and reported "there is another target that just appeared on your left side about 1 mile....briefly and then disappearing again." Another single sweep target. The captain responded, "We haven't got him in sight as yet, but we do pick up the lights around Kaikoura." In other words, the air crew was still seeing anomalous lights near the coast.

At this time the plane was about 66 miles from the radar station. At this distance the 2.1 degree horizontal beamwidth (at half intensity points) would have been about 2 miles wide (at the half power points on the radiation pattern). The radar screen displays a short arc when receiving reflected radiation from an object, such as an airplane, that is much, much smaller than the distance to the object (a "point" target). The length of the arc corresponds roughly to the angular beamwidth. Hence in this case the lengths of the arcs made by the aircraft and the unknown were each equivalent to about 2 miles. If the controller could actually see a 1 mile spacing between the arcs, then the centers of the arcs, representing the positions of the actual targets (plane and unknown) were about 2 + 1 = 3 miles apart.

As the plane turned left to go around in a circle, which would take about two minutes to complete (point 9), WATCC reported "The target I mentioned a moment ago is still just about 5:00 to you, stationary."

During the turn the air crew and passengers could, of course, see the lights of Wellington and the lights all the way along the coast from the vicinity of Kaikoura to Christhurch and they could see the anomalous lights near Kaikoura, but they saw nothing that seemed to be associated with the radar targets that were near the aircraft.

During this period of time the WATCC controller noticed targets continuing to appear, remain for one or two sweeps of the radar, and then disappear close to the Kaikoura Coast. However, he did not report these to the airplane. He reported only the targets which were appearing near the airplane, now about 25 miles off the coast. The TV reporter, who was able to watch the skies continually, has stated (8) that he continually saw anomalous lights "over Kaikoura," that is, they appeared to be higher than the lights along the coastline at the town of Kaikoura.

By 0027 (point 10) the plane was headed back southward along its original track. WATCC reported "Target is at 12:00 at 3 miles." The captain responded immediately, "Thank you. We pick it up. It's got a flashing light." The captain reported seeing "a couple of very bright blue-white lights, flashing regularly at a rapid rate. They looked like the strobe lights of a Boeing 737..."(Startup and Illingworth, 1980). At this time he was again looking toward the open ocean.

From the time he got seated on the flight deck the cameraman was having difficulty filming. The lights of interest were mostly to the right of the aircraft and, because of the size of his camera, he was not able to film them without sticking his camera lens in front of the copilot who was in command of the aircraft. When a light would appear near Kaikoura he would turn the camera toward it and try to see it through his big lens. Generally by the time he had the camera pointed in the correct direction the light would go out. He was also reluctant to film because the lights were all so dim he could hardly see them through the lens and he didn't believe that he would get any images. Of course, he was not accustomed to filming under these difficult conditions.

Nevertheless, the cameraman did get some film images unidentified lights. He also filmed known lights. He filmed the takeoff from Wellington, thereby providing reference footage. The next image on the film, taken at an unrecorded time after the takeoff from Wellington, is the image of a blue-white light against a black background. In order to document the fact that he was seated in the aircraft at the time of this filming he turned the camera quickly to the left and filmed some of the dim red lights of the meters on the instrument panel. Unfortunately the cameraman did not recall, during the interview many weeks later, exactly when that blue-white light was filmed, nor did he recall exactly where the camera was pointed at the time, although it was clearly somewhat to the right of straight ahead.

The initial image of the light is followed by two others but there are no reference points for these lights. They could have been to the right or straight ahead or to the left. The durations of the three appearances of a blue-white light are 5, 1.3 and 1.9 seconds, which could be interpreted as slow pulsing on and off. After this last blue-white image the film shows about 5 seconds of very dim images that seem to be distant shoreline of Kaikoura with some brighter lights above the shoreline. Unfortunately these images are so dim as to make analysis almost impossible.

Although it is impossible to prove, it may be that the cameraman filmed the flashing light at 0027. Unfortunately the camera was not synchronized with either the WATCC tape recorder or the tape recorder on the plane so the times of the film images must be inferred by matching the verbal descriptions with the film images. The cameraman did not get film of the steady light that appeared ahead of the aircraft at 0016.

Regardless of whether these blue-white images were made by the flashing light at 0027 or by some other appearance of a blue-white light, the fact is, considering where the plane was at the time, that this film was "impossible" to obtain from the conventional science point of view because there was nothing near the airplane that could have produced these bright pulses of light.

The only lights on the flight deck at this time were dim red meter lights because the captain had turned off all the lights except those that were absolutely necessary for monitoring the performance of the aircraft. There were no internal blue-white lights to be reflected from the windshield glass, nor were there any blue-white lights on the exterior of the aircraft. The only other possible light sources, stars, planets and coastal lights were too dim and too far away to have made images as bright as these three flashes on the film. These images remain unexplained.

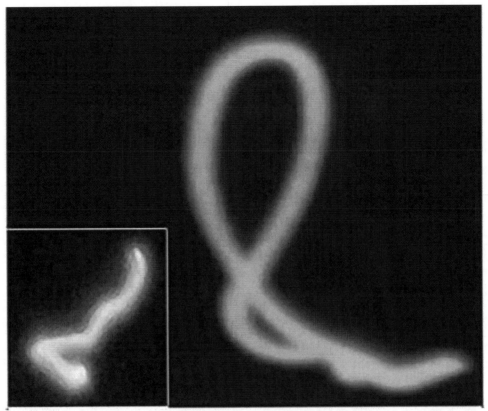

The film footage of the UFO recorded above the town of Kaikoura would soon make international headlines.

There is a similar problem with determining exactly when the reporter's audio tape statements were made since his recorder was not synchronized with the WATCC tape. Therefore the timing of the reporter's statements must be inferred from the sequence of statements on the tape and from the content.

Recorded statements to this point mentioned lights seen in the direction of the Kaikoura Coast, as well as, of course, the normal lights along the coast. But then the reporter recorded the following statement: "Now we have a couple right in front of us, very, very bright. That was more of an orange-reddy light. It flashed on and then off again...... We have a firm convert here at the moment." Apparently he underwent a "battlefield conversion" from being a UFO skeptic to believer.

The probability is high, although one cannot absolutely certain, that the air crew, the reporter and cameraman all saw and recorded on tape and film the appearance of the light at 3 miles in front of the aircraft. If true, then this might have been a radar/visual/photographic sighting. (A radar/visual/photographic sighting did occur about an hour later as the airplane flew northward from Christchurch.)

As impressive as this event was, the radar/visual event of most interest here was still to come. At about 0028 (point 11) the Argosy aircraft made a 30 degree right turn to head directly into Christchurch. WATCC reported that all the radar targets were now 12 to 15 miles behind them.

Then at about 0029 (point 12 on the map) WATCC reported a target 1 mile behind the plane. About 50 seconds later (after 4 sweeps of the radar beam) he reported a target about 4 miles behind the airplane. Then that target disappeared and about 30 seconds later he reported a target at 3:00 at 4 miles. Two sweeps of the radar beam later he saw something really surprising. He reported, "There's a strong target right in formation with you. Could be right or left. Your target has doubled in size."

The extraordinary condition of a "double size target" (DST) persisted for at least 36 seconds. This duration is inferred from the time duration between the controller's statement to the airplane, made only seconds after he first saw the DST, and his statement that the airplane target had reduced to normal size. This time duration was about 51 seconds (four radar detections over a period 36 seconds followed by a fifth revolution with no detection plus 3 seconds) according to the WATCC tape recording of the events. The radar aspects of this DST event will be discussed more fully below.

The pilot and copilot and the cameraman were able to hear the communications from the WATCC. The reporter and sound recordist could not hear the WATCC communications, but the cameraman would occasionally yell (loudly because of the extreme engine noise) to the reporter what he heard from WATCC. The cameraman told the reporter about the target flying in formation and the reporter started looking through the right side window for the target. The copilot was also looking and after some seconds he spotted a light which he described as follows:

"It was like the fixed navigation lights on a small airplane when one passes you at night. It was much smaller than the really big ones we had seen over Kaikoura. At irregular intervals it appeared to flash, but it didn't flash on and off; it brightened or perhaps twinkled around the edges. When it did this I could see color, a slight tinge of green or perhaps red. It's very difficult describing a small light you see at night."

The captain had been looking throughout his field of view directly ahead, to the left, upward and downward to see if there could be any source of light near the aircraft. He saw nothing except normal coastal lights and, far off on the horizon to the left (east), lights from the Japanese squid fishing fleet which uses extremely bright lights to lure squid to the surface to be netted. Neither the captain nor copilot saw any running lights on ships near them or near the coast of the South Island, which implies that there were no ships on the ocean in their vicinity.

When the copilot reported seeing a light at the right the captain turned off the navigation lights, one of which is a steady green light on the right wing, so that the reporter wouldn't confuse that with any other light. There were lights along the coast but the city lights of Kaikoura were no longer visible, hidden behind mountains that run along the Kaikoura Peninsula. Ireland (1979) suggested that the witnesses saw a beacon at the eastern end of the Kaikoura Peninsula. This beacon is visible to ships at a range of 14 miles from the coast. It flashes white twice every 15 seconds (on for 2 seconds, off for 1 second, on for 2 seconds off for 10 seconds). The plane was about 20 miles from the beacon and at an elevation angle of about 7 degrees, which placed it above the axis of the main radiation lobe from the beacon. The combination of the distance and off-axis angle means that it would have been barely visible, if at all. Moreover, the light seen by the copilot and others appeared to be at about "level" with the location of the navigation light at the end of the wing which, in turn was about level with the cockpit, or perhaps a bit above since the plane was carrying a heavy load. Hence the light was at an elevation comparable to that of the aircraft and certainly above ground level. Many months later, at my request, the air crew attempted to see the Kaikoura beacon while flying along the same standard flight path from Kaikoura East into Christchurch. Knowing where to look for the beacon they stared intently. They reported seeing only couple of flashes during the several trips they made past the lighthouse. The copilot has stated very explicitly that the unusual light he saw was not the lighthouse.

During this time the reporter also saw the light and recorded his impression: "I'm looking over towards the right of the aircraft and we have an object confirmed by

Wellington radar. It's been following us for quite a while. It's about 4 miles away and it looks like a very faint star, but then it emits a bright white and green light." Unfortunately the light was too far to the right for the cameraman to be able to film it (he would have had to sit in the copilot's seat to do that). The captain was able to briefly see this light which the copilot had spotted. This event was a radar-visual sighting with several witnesses to the light.

About 82 seconds after Wellington reported that the DST had reduced to normal size, when the plane was approximately at point 17, the captain told WATCC, "Got a target at 3:00 just behind us," to which WATCC responded immediately, "Roger, and going around to 4:00 at 4 miles." This would appear to be a radar confirmation of the light that the crew saw at the right side.

Fifty seconds after reporting the target that was "going around to 4:00 at 4 miles" the WATCC operator was in communication with the Christchurch Air Traffic Control Center. He told the air traffic controller that there was a target at 5:00 at about 10 miles. He said that the target was going off and on but "...not moving, not too much speed..." and then seconds later, "It is moving in an easterly direction now." The Christchurch radar did not show a target at that location. This could have been because the Christchurch radar was not as sensitive as the Wellington radar, because the radar cross-section (reflectivity) in the direction of Christchurch was low (cross-section can change radically with orientation of an object) or because the target may have been below the Christchurch radar beam, which has a lower angular elevation limit of about 4 degrees.

At about 0035, when the plane was about at point 18, WATCC contacted the plane and asked, "The target you mentioned, the last one we mentioned, make it 5:00 at 4 miles previously, did you see anything?" The captain responded, "We saw that one. It came up at 4:00, I think, around 4 miles away, " to which WATCC responded, "Roger, that target is still stationary. It's now 6:00 to you at about 15 miles and it's been joined by two other targets." The reporter heard this information from the cameraman and recorded the following message: "That other target that has been following us has been joined by two other targets so at this stage we have three unidentified flying objects just off our right wing and one of them has been following us now for probably about 10 minutes." Unfortunately, as already mentioned, the reporter could not hear the communications with WATCC so he did not always get the correct information. These targets were behind the plane and one of them had been "following" the plane for 7 - 8 minutes.

Then the WATCC reported that the three targets had been replaced by a single target. The captain, wondering about all this activity at his rear, requested a second two minute orbit. This was carried out at about 0036:30 (point 19). Nothing was seen and the single target disappeared. From then on the plane went straight into Christchurch. The Christchurch controller did report to the aircraft that his radar showed a target over land, west of the aircraft, that seemed to pace the aircraft but turned westward and traveled inland as the aircraft landed. The copilot looked to the right and saw a small light moving rapidly along with the aircraft. However, copilot duties during the landing itself prevented him from watching it continually and he lost sight of it just before the aircraft landed.

· · · · · · · · · ·

LARGE ORANGE BALLS OVER TAUPO

A website called UFOINFO provides a wealth of UFO reports from New Zealand. The organization provides a sightings report form for witnesses to fill out, with the reports then helpfully posted on the Internet.

One report, dated April 24, 2010, comes from Taupo, Waikato.

Time: 10:30 P.M.

Number of witnesses: 3

Number of objects: 5

Shape of objects: Large orange ball leading light with dark saucer-shape attached behind, and large orange ball with dimly lit elliptical shape above.

Weather Conditions: High clouds, moonlit balmy night. Sightings were below the clouds and flying cross-wind.

Description: First appeared as large orange light attached to large saucer-shaped body, followed within a minute by two more similar balls. Two minutes or so later two more followed with the last looking a little more like a dimly-lit hot air balloon above a bright orange light-ball, but flying cross-wind to the north, northeast. The wind was blowing from the west at six mph. There was no sound except for neighborhood dogs howling. We thought we were getting a good film clip, but the camera (or operator) malfunctioned.

Additional information: I realize I can't explain my sighting very clearly, but I feel I must add that the body of the first craft was frighteningly large, and all the sightings I would estimate to be within 2000 feet above us.

A NEW YEAR'S VISITATION

Another New Zealand case happened on January 2, 2009 in McLaren Falls, Bay of Plenty, Tauranga.

Time: 2:23 A.M.

Number of witnesses: 4

Number of objects: 7

Shape of objects: Yellow balls.

Description: Hi. My name is Doug. While celebrating the New Year at McLaren Falls Campground on the 2nd of January, 2009, at 2:23 A.M., four of our group were just gazing at the stars, looking toward 70 degrees east in line with the Milky Way, six yellow balls arose from the horizon in formation. They darted towards the north, then forming in a diamond gem-type shape then descended down in the horizon. They only traveled in a northeasterly direction. After they descended, another yellow ball arose same as the first and with the same motions as the first. It began to descend, only it started to flash. So we, being cheeky, flashed our torches back. It seemed to stop in midair for a while and then carry on its way. I have some videos taken on my cell and a photo which is attached. Would love to get some info back.

A BEWILDERED SKEPTIC

On January 23, 2009, in Ongley Park, Palmerston North, a skeptic had a bewildering UFO experience.

Time: 5 A.M.

Number of witnesses: 2

Number of objects: 2

Shape of objects: Rectangle.

Weather Conditions: Clear, first quarter moon.

Description: First, I would like everyone to know I am not claiming to have seen aliens, merely exactly what UFO stands for, objects I cannot identify. It was a hot night, a friend and I decided to go for a walk as we couldn't sleep. As we walked across Ongley Park, looking into the sky, we both noticed a rectangle shape much larger than any star in the sky, with the source of white light being on the two longer sides, sitting stationary in the sky. After about 30 seconds, it started to move away, darting side to side to the east and getting further away very fast, considering the distance required to travel to have that affect on the eye. After approximately one minute the object faded out of eyesight in the east of the sky. To the best of my knowledge, it was too high and sporadic for a plane, too fast and again sporadic for a satellite and heading away from the earth, so clearly not a typical meteor. We caught the second object in the later phases of exactly what I just described from the northwest to disappear in the north. I am by no reach of the imagination a conspiracy theorist. In fact, I'm rather the opposite, but I cannot explain this. If someone can, please do so, as I have looked at every site I can about balloons, satellites and the International Space Station.

A REAL MYSTERY

On September 26, 2009, in Timaru, South Canterbury, the following event occurred.

Time: 8:15 P.M.

Number of witnesses: 2

Number of objects: About 10 visible.

Shape of objects: Bright orange, glowing like a star.

Description: About 10 bright orange glowing objects like a star shape were moving in the night sky. Three or four across the top and four or five fanning out below on both sides. Two then veered off to the left. This was witnesses by two people for about five minutes, then the objects disappeared into the cloud. We looked many times over the next hour but didn't see them again. What did we see? A real mystery. I rang the Timaru police to report what we'd witnessed.

PULSATING SHAPE-SHIFTERS

Location: Mairangi Bay, Auckland, New Zealand.

Date: February 3, 2006

Time: 8:30 A.M. to 8:55 A.M.

Approach Direction: North, heading east.

Departure Direction: Disappeared straight upwards.

Witness Direction: Northeast.

Description: At 8:30 this A.M., my mother was hanging out the washing when she called me outside to look at some objects in the sky. At first, I suggested that they were a cluster of weather balloons and counted ten altogether. As we continued to watch, some of them started to change colors from the original shining bright silver to reddish orange to luminous violet-blue. They started to make formations. Almost pulsating and changing shapes from round to oval, and some moved into clusters. The clouds were wispy and the objects were moving in the same northerly direction as the clouds but slightly faster. Then they changed direction and moved slowly east and stopped directly above our house. Some of them formed the Southern Cross constellation and the pointers turned red.

I phoned the Auckland Observatory and asked if anyone could see them from that location in Royal Oak. Unfortunately, they could not see them. Eventually, after 25 minutes, they disappeared directly upwards. Perfectly round and silver in colour again.

Color/Shape: Changing shape from round to oval and back to round again. Sometimes pulsating and making formations. Colour shining silver initially then a couple went to red-orange and violet-blue. Then back to silver again.

Height and speed: Difficult to assess.

TV/Radio/Press: I phoned the Observatory while watching them at about 8:40 A.M. Then I phoned TVNZ at approximately 1:45 P.M. and spoke to the newsroom to see if there had been any other reported sightings. None had been reported, and unfortunately we did not have any footage as proof.

• • • • • • • • • •

This has been but a brief, partial sampling of UFO reports from New Zealand in recent years. As Suzanne Hansen of UFOCUS NZ stated earlier in this chapter, sightings are increasing there as awareness of the phenomenon grows.

ABOUT THE AUTHOR: Sean Casteel is a freelance journalist who has been writing about UFOs, alien abduction and many other paranormal subjects since 1989. Sean's writing appeared in many UFO- and paranormal-related magazines, including *"UFO Magazine," Tim Beckley's "UFO Universe," "Fate," "Mysteries Magazine,"* and *"Open Minds Magazine,"* most of which are now defunct but were a major part of a thriving UFO press in their heyday. Magazines in the UK, Italy, Romania and Australia have also published Sean's work.

Sean has written or contributed to over 30 books for Global Communications and Inner Light Publications, all of which are available from Amazon.com. Sean's books include *"The Heretic's UFO Guidebook,"* which analyzes a selection of Gnostic Christian writings and their relationship to the UFO phenomenon, and *"Signs and Symbols of the Second Coming,"* in which he interviews several religious and paranormal experts about how prophecies of the Second Coming of Christ may be fulfilled. To view and purchase books Sean has written or contributed to, visit his Amazon author page at: www.amazon.com/author/seancasteel

SOUTH AMERICA

MAN KIDNAPPED BY GLOBES

AS REPORTED IN THE PAGES OF THE APRO JOURNAL IN 1962

Report by Olavo T. Fontes, M.D.

The tragic case I am going to relate here was investigated to the limits that any investigation can reach when every piece of evidence is analyzed and evaluated, when every clue is exhaustively followed, and when every conventional explanation is explored and dismissed for lack of proof. In a case of this kind, however, we could only establish a definite conclusion if that conclusion could be negative. We could be sure, in other words, if the body of the victim was found; if facts or motivations in the past life and personality of the victim or witness were demonstrated, showing that they couldn't be trusted, were psychotic, or had reasons to simulate the whole thing; or if additional evidence was not uncovered connecting the facts in the case with the sighting of unconventional aerial objects. As the body was not found, facts or motivations of such a kind were lacking and there was definite evidence concerning the sighting of UAOs – the case must be accepted as possible despite the lack of absolute proof. On the other hand, we must recognize the witness obviously cannot present more than was presented: his report about the mysterious disappearance of his father. You can believe it or not. The absolute truth, that only the witness himself can be sure about it.

The readers may not like this report. For one reason, it will show them that such things as UAOs from other planets could be interested in kidnapping humans, in order to become better acquainted with them. In fact, personal experiences such as the one related here will cause you to wonder about missing people – about how many of the individuals who are yearly reported as missing might have chanced to come upon a UAO in some lonely spot and were captured as specimens.

The case was featured in an article for the Italian weekly magazine *"Domenica del Corriere"* for September 30, 1962, including a rather dramatic illustration.

A noise of running steps, a shadow seeming to float into the dark room, two ball-shaped objects emitting light and discharging a strange yellow smoke, a human being disappearing into that yellow mist before the eyes of his terror-stricken son – such is the fantastic story told by a 12-year-old boy, Raimundo de Aleluia Mafra. His father, Rivalino Mafra da Silva, is missing. Raimundo states that he was kidnapped by two strange objects, on the morning of August 20, 1962, just in front of his house, in a place called Duas Pontes, District of Diamantina, State of Minas Gerais.

The sixteen thousand citizens of Diamantina are divided in their opinions about the happening: some believe there was merely a murder with a missing body; others think that Rivalino ran away for some unknown reason and his son is telling a tale to cover him; still others think the whole thing was "the work of the Devil"; many others are certain that the child is telling the truth. On the other hand, the situation is quite different in Biribiri, Mendanha and Rio Vermelho, small villages in the vicinity of the area where the strange events took place. The residents at those places – those who still remain there – are living with panic in their hearts. They do not dare to go outside at night. They do not risk walking alone through the fields.

The colonial style town of Diamantina was the scene of one of the most bizarre UFO "captures" of all time.

Their doors and windows are closed after 8:00PM...their streets are empty and silent at night. Many families are leaving toward Diamantina. You cannot laugh at them – they are too frightened, haunted by the pitiful cries of a child: "They've got my father! I want my father back! Help me!"

They are under the terror of the almost unreal, of something alien and unexplainable, something so different from common sense that your mind is repelled by it. This may sound to you like the science fiction stories you customarily read in science fiction magazines. Perhaps this is best for your sanity – if you don't believe in UAOs from other planets.

RAIMUNDO ALELUIA MAFRA'S REPORT

Rivalino disappeared on August 20. That same day the police were called and the investigation started. Rumors began to spread and reporters were alerted on August 24. The case hit the headlines on August 26. On the evening of August 25, the boy Raimundo was interviewed by the press about the circumstances related with the disappearance of his father.

In spite of his undernourished aspect and obvious anxiety, the youngster was able to give a clear and detailed account of the tragic event. He falters only when forced by direct questions about his father: then he begins to cry. He is only a small boy, who has never attended school and doesn't even know the alphabet. He lives in a small house in a lonely spot, about 28 kilometers from Diamantina. He helps (or helped) his father as the oldest son, taking care of the two small brothers and doing all the house work. His mother died about one year ago. In his ignorance, living in a deserted place outside the civilized world, he has never heard about flying saucers, "space beings" from other planets, comics, or even radio and television.

His report was given in the presence of Lieutenant Wilson Lisboa, police chief at Diamantina. For the twentieth time, according to the information of that authority, he tells about the incredible drama lived by his father before his startled eyes. He says that things started in the night of August 19. The whole family was in bed – himself, his father and his two brothers (Fatimod, 6-years-old, and Dirceu, 2-years-old). He cannot tell the time, because there is no clock in the house, but he was awakened by the sound of steps and got the impression that people were walking hurriedly through the room. He called his father, who lit a small candle. Then, under the flickering light, they saw a strange silhouette, more like a shadow, floating in the room without touching the floor.

"It was a weird shadow, not looking like ours because it was half the size of a man and not shaped like a human being. We remained in the bed, quiet, and the shadow looked at us; then it moved to the place where my brothers were sleeping and looked at them for a long time, without touching their bodies. Afterwards, it left our room, crossed the other room and disappeared near the outer door. Again we heard steps of someone running and a voice said: 'This one looks like Rivalino.' My father then yelled: 'Who goes there?' There was no answer. Father left the bed and went to the other room, when the voice asked again if he really was Rivalino. My father answered it was right, that Rivalino was his name, and there was no answer. We came back to bed and heard clearly their talk outside, saying they were going to kill father. My father started to pray aloud and the voices outside said there was no help for him. They talked no more.

"We passed the night awake. In the morning, still afraid, I had the courage to go outside to get my father's horse in the field. But then I sighted two balls floating in mid-air side by side, about two meters from the ground, one meter from each other and a few meters away from our door. They were big. One of them was all black, had a kind of irregular antenna-like protuberance and a small tail. The other was black and white, with the same outlines, with the antenna and everything. They both emitted a humming sound and appeared to give off fire through an opening that flickered like a fire fly, switching the light on and off rapidly. I was frozen by fear. I called father to see those strange flying objects. He came out of the house, still praying and asking about what those things could be, his eyes locked on them. He warned me to stay away and walked toward the objects. He stopped at a distance of two meters. At that moment the two big balls merged into each other. There was only one now, bigger in size, raising dust from the ground and discharging a yellow smoke which darkened the sky. With strange noises, that big ball crept slowly toward my father. I saw him enveloped by the yellow smoke and he disappeared inside it. I ran after him into the yellow cloud, which had an acrid smell. I saw nothing, only that yellow mist around me. I yelled for my father but there was no answer. Everything was silent again.

Photo taken around the same time that the kidnapped man was taken by a globe-shaped UFO – destination unknown!

"Then the yellow smoke dissolved. The balls were gone. My father was gone. The ground below was clean as if the dust had been removed by a big broom. I was confused and desperate. I walked in circles around the house looking for father, but I found no tracks, footprints or marks. Was this the work of the Devil? My father had disappeared in mid-air. I have searched the plains, fields and thickets with no results. I have watched the flight of vultures, looking for clues to locate his body, but I saw nothing. Five days have passed and nothing was found. Is my father dead, taken by the globes? I want my father back."

(Unquote-Belo Horizonte DIARIO DE MINAS, August 26. Rio de Janeiro CORREIO DA MANHA, September 4. Lieutenant Lisboa's report, transcribed verbatim).

THE POLICE INVESTIGATION

Lieutenant Wilson Lisboa, Police chief at Diamantina, was called the same day of the strange disappearance. He put the Raimundo boy under cross-examination but failed to make him change his incredible story. He then decided to make a complete investigation. Policemen were ordered to look for Rivalino's body, to find him at any cost. The search was started inside Rivalino's house. No clue was found. The surrounding country was covered by trained men. At the spot Rivalino had been kidnapped by the objects, according to the boy's report, the ground was clean of dust in an area about five meters in diameter, but no tracks or marks were visible. About fifty meters away, a few drops of blood were found. Lieutenant Lisboa collected samples and the analysis identified them as human blood. The search for the missing body spread through the whole district of Diamantina. It took ten days. Police dogs were sent from Belo Horizonte, bloodhounds trained by the military police to follow tracks and find missing people. They found nothing. A complete investigation of Rivalino's past life, possible love affairs, enemies, friends, relatives, etc., was undertaken. No clues were found.

Another investigation was made concerning the possible sighting of UAOs over the region by other witnesses. The following reports are of interest: (1) The vicar at Diamantina's cathedral, priest Jose Avila Garcia, contacted Lieutenant Lisboa to inform him that, by a strange coincidence, a friend of his had reported an unusual fact the night before Rivalino's disappearance. That friend, Antonio Rocha, was fishing at the Manso River, close to Duas Pontes, when he sighted two ball-shaped objects hovering over Rivalino's house. Priest Garcia believed that the boy had dreamed and his father had been murdered, but it was his duty to report all facts to the police – even those opposed to his own opinion.

Mr. Antonio Rocha, who worked at the Mail Department in Diamantina, was called and confirmed his story. On the evening of August 19, he was fishing at a place near Rivalino's house. "At 4:00 p.m.," he said to Lieutenant Lisboa, "I sighted two strange ball-shaped objects in the sky. They were flying in circles over Rivalino's house. They came very low and were gone a few minutes later. I don't know anything about Rivalino's disappearance, but from the report given by his son Raimundo, I have the impression he saw the same objects I sighted."

(2) Rivalino Mafra da Silva was a diamond prospector. Lieutenant Lisboa interviewed other prospectors in the district who did their mining work with Rivalino. They told him a startling story. Rivalino had informed them that, on August 17, when going back home, he had seen two strange persons digging a hole in the earth at a spot

near his house. When approached, the creatures ran away into the bushes. They were approximately three feet tall. A few moments later, he sighted a strange object which took off from behind the bushes and disappeared into the sky at high speed. According to Rivalino, this object was shaped like a hat and surrounded by a red glow. They didn't believe him, of course.

(3) Doctor Giovani Pereira, a physician living at Diamantina, went to the police to report the sighting of a disc-shaped object over his own house two months before. He had had a night call from a patient and was driving back in his car. When closing the car's door to go inside his home, he suddenly sighted a brilliant object, shaped like a disc, hovering low over his house. He stopped and watched it for several minutes. Then it moved away at high speed after crossing over the sleeping town. He said he had kept the sighting secret because he knew nobody would believe him.

(4) On the morning of August 24, a UAO crossed over the town of Gouveia, about 42 kilometers to the south of Diamantina. The sighting was witnessed by more than fifty people, including the local police chief, Lieutenant Walter Costa Coelho. According to the observers, the object was white colored, shaped like a soccer ball and encircled by a kind of fluorescent glow – remaining in sight for about two minutes. It was traveling to the north (toward Montes Claros), then changed course to the northwest.

A few minutes later, the same (or similar) object was spotted in the sky by more than one hundred citizens at Brasilia de Minas, a small town about 120 kilometers to the northwest of Montes Claros. Again it looked like a soccer ball and was surrounded by a white glow. According to the local priest, this UAO hovered for a long time over the town's church before disappearing to the west at high speed.

This sighting was printed in the papers on August 28. The news had a deleterious effect on the residents of small towns and villages in the same area of Duas Pontes. The coincidence was too much for them: a ball-shaped object, sighted over the same region, just four days after Rivalino's disappearance. The consequence was panic and hysteria.

The last step in Lieutenant Lisboa's investigation was to check and recheck the sanity of Raimundo and the reliability of his report. Raimundo was intensively questioned by the police and, at police request, a psychiatric examination was made by Dr. Juan Antunes de Oliveira. He was found to be sane. Dr. Oliveira then decided to make a last experiment. It was a cruel test, but justified due to the circumstances in the case. In the presence of witnesses, the boy Raimundo Mafra was taken to a room where there was a human body covered by a cloth. "Raimundo," said Dr. Oliveira, "this is the body of your father. He is dead. You lied when you told us that he had been kidnapped. Tell now the whole truth: what really happened on the morning of August 20?" The boy began to cry, in a state of great emotion, but continued to affirm that his story was not a lie, that his father could be dead but had been taken by the two objects. "Perhaps they brought him back dead." was his conclusion. This ended the experiment. Dr. Oliveira was interviewed by the press. He said: "I don't wish to discuss the facts in the case. They are beyond my competence. But I can tell you that the boy is normal and he is telling what he thinks to be the truth."

An attempt was also made to cross-examine the kid applying the technique known as hypo-analysis. The attempt failed because Raimundo was not receptive to hypnosis.

So Lieutenant Lisboa came to the end of his investigation and found himself in a very peculiar and difficult position. He was certain that Rivalino had been murdered, but the corpse had vanished. He had thought that the boy was lying or out of his mind, but failed to get proof showing he couldn't be trusted, was psychotic, or had reasons for simulation. He didn't belief in flying discs or balls, yet the evidence he had collected pointed in that direction. At this point, he decided to do two things: (1) to continue the search for Rivalino's body; (2) to make a written report to the Secretary of Public Security of the State and send Raimundo Fafra to Belo Horizonte, the State capital.

RAIMUNDO MAFRO GOES TO BELO HORIZONTE

On August 30, the boy arrived at Belo Horizonte. He had a companion, Mr. Antonio de Carvalho Cruz, the Commissioner of the State Child's Department at Diamantina, who had the mission of taking the boy to the proper authorities in the capital. At that moment, general curiosity had been aroused about the kid, and he was interviewed by the whole press and even appeared on a television program. Then Colonel Mauro

Gouveia, Secretary of Public Security in the State of Minas Gerais, took charge of the case. Raimundo was questioned, cross-examined, photographed and again submitted to medical and psychiatric examination. Three days later, he was taken into custody by military authorities. An Air Force plane took him to Rio de Janeiro, where he disappeared behind the protection of a tight security ring. No one knows where he is now.

EPILOGUE

A month after the mysterious disappearance of Rivalino Mafra da Silva, the police at Diamantina decided to stop their investigation and to close the case. The body is still missing and every effort to find new clues has met with complete failure. Lieutenant Lisboa and his policemen are depressed. One of them, policeman Clemente, said to the press: "Nobody expects to find a satisfactory explanation with respect to Mr. Rivalino's disappearance." (Belo Horizonte ULTIMA HORA, September 22, 1962).

At this point, it would be preferable merely to present the evidence and to allow the reader to draw his own conclusion; but I find it necessary to call attention to a very important thing: Reports indicate space creatures have been investigating the Earth closely for many years. They appear to follow a very methodical plan, step by step. Available evidence indicates they have already taken specimens of terrestrial flora, water, rocks and soil. An investigation of the fauna was apparently lacking, as far as the collection of specimens is concerned. However, would it not be logical that they eventually turn their attention to collecting specimens of fauna? It would be surprising, indeed, if they overlooked the most interesting example of terrestrial fauna – man himself.

The case of Rivalino Mafra da Silva appears to be the first one – in the whole UAO history – where vanishing people and UAOs are definitely connected by direct evidence. Therefore, in spite of some incredible details we cannot explain (i.e., the happenings at night inside and outside Rivalino's house), I am forced to conclude he was kidnapped by two ball-shaped UAOs – in the presence of his own son. There is no other alternative. And, as they always repeat their moves, it is reasonable to expect that other similar cases will happen soon.

Goodness gracious, great balls of fire

Was it a bird? Was it a plane?

No, the bright, speeding object which flashed across the sky south of Hamilton yesterday was probably a fireball, says a leading New Zealand astronomer.

Dr Wayne Orchiston, the director of the Carter Observatory, in Wellington, believes Waikato people who spotted yesterday's UFO actually saw a small rock — the size of a thumbnail — from space, disintegrating in the Earth's atmosphere.

Hamilton's chief air traffic controller Graeme Opie was among several Waikato people who saw the UFO.

Mr Opie saw the object, which had a bright head and a long sparkly orange coloured tail, from the Hamilton airport control tower about 1.20pm.

Dr Orchiston, who has a special interest in meteorites, said the phenomenon was probably a fireball. Fireballs ranged in size from thumbnail to fist size and were much smaller than a meteorite which reached the Earth intact.

Fireballs usually disintegrated in a flash of heat and light at between 25km-50km above the Earth.

He said the observatory received a report of a fireball every couple of months.

Mr Opie said the UFO looked like a meteorite, but did not behave like one. It shot across the sky maintaining a level flight path. It travelled from east to west at a height of about 2500m and roughly 16km south of his position.

Initially Mr Opie thought he may have seen a jet aircraft but he rang radar operators in Auckland and they had no targets on their scopes south of Hamilton.

But yesterday Dr Bob Valkenburg, of the Te Kuiti-based Unexplained Phenomenon Research Society, said there had been a lot of UFO activity in the area recently and he expected it to increase.

"We cannot be alone on this tiny piece of dust in an infinite universe."

Several other people rang the *Waikato Times* to report the incident. Te Kawa couple Gail and Keith Stanley also saw the object as they were driving south along SH3. Mrs Stanley said it caught her attention because it was so bright. She said it had a rainbow-coloured tail.

Two Cambridge schoolboys said they saw what looked like a comet flying through the sky.

Brad Hooker and James Gill, both 9, were playing cricket during lunch at St Peter's Catholic Primary School when they spotted the object.

□ Meanwhile, a woman rang the *Times* yesterday to recount an experience at Horotiu on Sunday. She said a triangular shaped craft hovered only about 5m over her vehicle and followed her towards SH1.

She was reluctant to tell her friends in case they thought she was going "nuts".

As this clipping indicates, it's not the first — or only — time that a UFO ball of fire has attacked without warning.

UFOs seem to have a preference for dark, deserted places – quarries, garbage dumps and cemeteries.

STRANGE PLACES: UFOs AND CEMETERIES

By Scott Corrales

In 1979, an unusual film graced screens across America. Billed as a horror/sci-fi flick, *"Phantasm"* presented the story of a small town whose less-than-human funeral director (a character known only as the Tall Man) modifies human corpses into "slave labor" – dwarfish creatures resembling the Jawas from *"Star Wars"* – on a distant planet. When the film's youthful protagonists discover the ultimate fate of their dead relative's mortal remains, they undertake a quest to vanquish the Tall Man and his works. So compelling was this piece of fiction that it spawned an enthusiastic fan base and three sequels.

While the merits of this cinematic event are best left to film reviewers, *"Phantasm"* drew attention to a curious aspect of the UFO phenomenon: its unusual affinity with human burial grounds, ancient and modern.

But before proceeding along this line of inquiry, it is necessary to differentiate between UFOs and the balls of light seen at many graveyards in this country and in others. Known as "cemetery lights" or "graveyard lights," they have been described as having sizes ranging from candle-flames to large azure fireballs. These lights, which can either dart around or remain perfectly motionless, have been attributed to the presence of phorphorated hydrogen, which has luminous properties. Researchers such as Spain's Salvador Freixedo have remarked about the sentient quality exhibited by these objects and dubbed them REPQEN – Residual Psychic Quasi-Intelligent Energy.

A HISTORY OF SIGHTINGS

In the early decades of the UFO phenomenon, investigators would write about the phenomenon's preference for dark, deserted places – quarries, garbage dumps,

241

cemeteries – and suggested that these choices were ideal low-visibility places for alien spaceship crews to land undetected by humans. As the paranormal aspects of the phenomenon began to be acknowledged in the 1970s, researchers admitted that such places had also been favored by shadowy creatures from terrestrial traditions.

One of the most the most remarkable cases involving the presence of unidentified flying objects over an ancient North American burial ground was recorded by investigator John Magor in his article "Strange Sights in Yukon Sky" (Canadian UFO Report, Vol.1. No.1). The incident took place in the environs of Canyon Creek on the Alaska Highway in December 1966 and involved the family of one Bob McKinnon.

According to Mr. McKinnon, he first became aware that something was amiss when a powerful beam of light poured through the windows of the rest area he operated on the highway. Even more surprising was the fact that the light beam had its origin in an ancient Indian burial ground half a mile away.

McKinnon thought at first that the light issued from construction work being done at the site, but soon realized that this could not be the case, since the beam "was hanging absolutely motionless in the air, maybe a hundred feet up, and looked to be about two feet in diameter. It was bluish-orange in color, something like the reflections off a diamond."

UFOs near Jewish cemetary - Pine Bush, NY (taken by unknown individual).
PineBushUFO.com

As his alter ego, horror host Mr. Creepo (aka Tim Beckley) holds meditation in cemetery to call down UFOs. Scene from *"Barely Legal Vampires, The Curse of Ed Wood."*

The rest area operator called his relatives to witness the event and went outside the structure to get a better view. The light initiated a slow descent over the burial ground. The source of light almost touched the ground and lit the four-foot-tall wooden huts, into which the bodies of the dead were deposited. "We definitely had a feeling it was interested in the place," noted the main witness.

Then, as suddenly as it appeared, the light vanished. McKinnon contacted the Royal Canadian Mounted Police and was told that the object must have been a meteor – a suggestion that the witnesses could not agree with.

Magor's report concludes with the rest area operator saying that, despite his lack of interest in flying saucers, "there definitely was something strange happening out there over the cemetery that night."

On the night of July 21, 1977, three members of the Bradford, Pennsylvania, police department were treated to the sight of two luminous objects flying low across the city sky toward Oak Hill Cemetery. That very same evening, a triangular UFO sporting white and red lights was seen over Limestone, N.Y. Adding to the baffling phenomena was the problem of "unidentified radio signals," mostly in a language similar to Spanish, pouring in over area air waves, disrupting police-band communications. While local experts dismissed the radio "skips," as they were known, no official explanation was ever put forth for the anomalous radio activity.

Even rock and roll musicians have experiences to share: Rob Zombie recalled having had a UFO sighting in 1973 while attending a third grade Halloween party. The future rock celebrity was leaving the event when he saw a UFO hovering over the cemetery adjacent to his grade school. "That was pretty freaky," he admitted to journalist Gerri Miller.

EVEN SOUTH OF THE BORDER

A UFO was inadvertently "caught in the act" of showing its interest for human burials on April 28, 1976, when Angel González photographed funeral services being held for Rev. Antonio Roque of the Barrio Navarro Baptist Church in Gurabo, Puerto Rico. At no point were the photographer nor those attending the service ever aware of the unidentified flying object: the dark, oval-shaped object appeared when the color film was developed. Gonzalez's snapshot shows the object suspended at a certain distance over the crowd. The photo appeared in the May 20th edition of the *Caguas La Semana* newspaper and went on to become one of the memorable images of Puerto Rico's mid-70s UFO wave.

On the other side of the Caribbean, residents of the Las Margaritas and Santa Rosa developments in the city of Jalapa allegedly witnessed a collision between two UFOs in mid-flight, directly above the Bosques del Recuerdo cemetery in the early hours of October 27, 1995. Both objects had been flying at high speeds and low above the ground.

It was approximately 4:00 AM when the dispatcher of the Canal 35 Hermandad taxi company, Ms. P.Ch.C, reported from her vantage point at the summit of Lomas Margaritas that a huge light which had been flying over the area had subdivided itself into three smaller lights, two of which had collided in mid-air. This report prompted a large number of cab drivers to rush to the scene of the events. Mrs. Y.F.G., a resident of the aforementioned development, stated that similar events had occurred days earlier and that she herself had seen the objects disappearing in the vicinity of Cofre de Perote, a nearby mountain.

Dr. Rafael A. Lara of the Mexican research organization CEFP, a resident of the state of Veracruz, managed to interview the witnesses for his *Terra Incognita* journal. Ms. P.Ch.C. added that after the objects disappeared, three women were seen in the middle of the cemetery, although the cab drivers who reported to the scene could not find anyone.

Contradictions did not wait long to emerge, as the selfsame Ms. P.Ch.C declared that what she had seen had not necessarily been "alien spaceships," and that an overeager radio journalist, Antonio Trujillo, had reported the "alien spaceships" over Bosques del Recuerdo Cemetery. The media frenzy led to the young woman being besieged at her workplace by reporters interested in learning "if she had undergone any emotional or physical trauma as a result of witnessing the UFOs."

Mexico was not alone on the list: UFOs also staged appearances at cemeteries in Brazil during the April 1996 flap that caused excitement all over the South American giant's northeastern region. On April 5, 1996, a woman named María José and her son were driving along the road linking the cities of Joao Pessoa and Natal in the state of Paraiba when they became aware of a UFO hovering in the vicinity of a local cemetery. The unknown object sped directly toward them, passing over the car's roof at low altitude. Mrs. José was so unnerved by the experience that she was hospitalized in the city of Campinha Grande.

Even more compelling is the case involving a direct link to one of South American ufology's strangest cases: the 1949 death of Joao Prestes due to an alleged "UFO bolt" which roasted him to death. Researcher Pablo Villarubia managed to find fresh leads and witnesses to this case in recent years, delving into the misperceptions between what was reported and what actually happened. One of the most interesting side stories involved the unfortunate Joao's brother Emiliano, who had seen "two fireballs rising and striking each other" and repeating the same action in the vicinity of the Aracariguama cemetery a year after his brother's death. Emiliano Prestes was reportedly encircled by the fireballs and could feel the intense heat arising from the unknown objects. He dropped to his knees in fervent prayer until the lights departed, perhaps sparing him a fate similar to his brother's. According to Hermes da Fonseca, whom Villarubia interviewed, the fireballs remained active to the present: In 1995, Giomar Gouveia, a champion jockey and owner of some stables at Ibaté, saw a light hovering over his animals, giving off orange beams of light.

Aracariguama Cemetery had its own eerie stories to tell. Nelson Oliveira, the local gravedigger, informed the UFO researcher that around 1989, he had seen something strange in the cemetery: an unusual circular flying object which resembled "an upside-down hat" made of aluminum. The object hovered for a while before heading in the direction of the city of Sao Paulo.

TOMB RAIDERS FROM BEYOND INFINITY

Compelling evidence for UFO interest in the discarded mortal coils of human beings comes from West Virginia journalist Bob Teets, who mentioned the following cases in his book "*West Virginia UFOs*" (1994).

Elk Garden, a community of 300 souls in Mineral County, has attracted the disturbing attention of unidentified objects since at least the early 1960s, when local residents began to see them in the vicinity of Nethken Hill, whose cemetery contains a number of the small town's most prominent citizens as well as a Methodist church. The Kalbaugh family, living on a farm located a small distance away from the cemetery, claims having seen "lights" throughout the late 1960s and early 70s, and being clearly aware that they were neither airplanes nor helicopters. Eyewitnesses are in agreement that the lights were invariably white in color and accompanied by a high-pitched sound.

But the most memorable and eerie of the apparitions over Nethken Hill would occur on October 8, 1967, when Reverend Harley DeLeurere and two male members of his congregation, intrigued by the stories of sightings, went up to a promontory from where they could have a panoramic view of Nethken Hill and its cemetery. Their skywatch was rewarded later that evening when one of them saw an object described as "a big turtle with lights on it" appear over the hill and move deliberately toward the church.

The witnesses were stunned by what happened next: the turtle-shaped luminous object descended to approximately six feet off the ground as it shone its lights toward the graveyard. One of the men (identified by author Teets only as "Leonard, Jr.") recalls that the object's lights projected into a day-old grave at the cemetery. Rev. DeLeurere allegedly mentioned that it would be a good idea to exhume the body in the new grave to check for signs of disturbance. "It seems like every time there was a new grave, within the next couple of nights, people would see lights up there."

Seeing the events through the prism of early 90s abduction research, the author suggests the interesting possibility that the UFOs were engaged in the business of retrieving alien implants from the bodies interred on Nethken Hill.

SCIENTIFIC CURIOSITY OR UNHEALTHY INTEREST?

Why are UFOs (whatever their origin) interested in our final resting places? What could they stand to gain from such pursuits? Trying to ascribe reason to an utterly unreasonable phenomenon leads us to consider that "alien scientists" can glean important biological information from the deceased, or as suggested in the West Virginia scenario, we are witnessing a cleanup operation aimed at removing implants left in the bodies of longtime abductees.

There is still a less wholesome possibility to consider, and it is as mind-bending as it is sordid: could UFOs be piloted by "recycled" humans? If it is true that the technology of any advanced alien civilization would be indistinguishable from magic, as Arthur C. Clarke noted in *Report on Planet Three and Other Speculations*," a spacefaring civilization might choose to leave the dangers of space travel to beings created specifically for the purpose, rather than jeopardizing its own citizens.

In November 1974, Luis and Maribel R., a married couple from the city of Huesca, Spain, stopped their car on a deserted highway in the middle of the night to hold a strange conversation with a pointy-faced, all-too-human ufonaut, who asked them a surprising question: Would they be so kind as to lend him a monkey wrench? A semi-spherical UFO with alternating red, yellow and white lights hovered in the background, and the car's driver wondered what good a wrench would do aboard such a vehicle. The ufonaut introduced himself as having been the former "Dr. Flor, from Barcelona."

Producer Ed Wood first revealed the connection between spaceships and cemeteries
in his classic low budget epic, *"Plan Nine From Outer Space."*

Perhaps even more alarming is a case investigated by Spanish researcher Manuel Carballal: According to the testimony of a number of witnesses, a young man who identified himself as Frederick Valentich, the Australian pilot who disappeared mysteriously in 1978, was alive and well in 1990 at Plaza del Charco, a seaport square on the island of Tenerife in the Canary Islands. Displaying an Australian passport to prove his claim, Valentich told those with whom he spoke on several occasions that he now belonged to a group of humans who had been "recruited" by extraterrestrials. It is also worth noting that the supposed Valentich showed no signs of aging, and resembled the photos circulated around the time of his disappearance.

Another case involving a possible "recycled" human occurred in the Dominican Republic on September 22, 1973, as insurance salesman Virgilio Gómez drove to a business appointment. Heading toward his destination, he became aware of someone waving him down. As he slowed down, Gómez became aware that the person was clad in a green uniform and that there were two others standing a few dozen feet away. The insurance salesman could not have been prepared for what happened next: The man in the green uniform told him that his name was Freddy Miller, a man who had "supposedly" drowned thirteen years earlier with other people in a boating accident, but that he had in fact been rescued by a modern device, "a module known to people as a UFO."

Suspecting that someone was playing a prank on him, Gómez asked the stranger which planet he came from. He was stunned when the man soberly answered that he thought he came from Venus, and that he had been rescued "on account of his knowledge of radio technology," adding that there had been no room for the other hapless boaters and that they would not have survived the "adaptation process."

Gómez remarked that "Freddy Miller" had a disgusting grayish-yellow skin tone that he found repulsive, spoke in a thick, deliberate voice and was virtually hairless. The entity's body was covered by a form-fitting green coverall without zippers or pockets. A large wristwatch "similar to the ones worn by scuba divers" adorned the wrist of its left hand.

The insurance agent was shown a half-concealed vehicle in the woods by the roadside – a fact that caused him to realize that the situation was no joke. The oval-shaped craft had a chrome-like sheen to it and largely resembled "an American football" (unlike the traditional soccer ball used throughout Latin America) and was windowless, betraying no external seams or rivets.

Cemeteries are always spooky at night, especially when UFOs are seen hovering over the tombstones. Art by Carol Ann Rodriguez.

Did "recycled" humans resembling burn victims make an appearance in a 1967 UFO case in Western Pennsylvania? In a case researched by the defunct Pittsburgh UFO Research Institute, a man known only as "Mr. Rible" took his daughter to an airstrip near Butler, Pennsylvania, to possibly catch a glimpse of the strange nocturnal phenomena which had plagued the vicinity for some time. Father and daughter soon found themselves staring at the revolutions of two luminous objects which suddenly headed straight for their Volkswagen. Yet, rather than crashing into the hapless car, the lights morphed into a half-circle of five humanoid figures "dressed in sloppy green-gray trousers" with their heads covered by flat-topped caps. The exposed skin of their arms and faces was coarse and gave the appearance of being severely burned. After Mr. Rible coaxed his rear-engine car into starting, he found it necessary to drive around the semicircle of unpleasant figures.

Could the Men-in-Black, who played such a prominent role in the early days of the UFO phenomenon, correspond to this category of nonliving beings, for want of a better term? Descriptions of these entities in their ill-fitting clothes, superannuated vehicles and odd physical characteristics have filled the casebooks of researchers in North America, South America and Europe.

A compelling example can be found in John Keel's "The Mothman Prophecies" (Signet, 1975) as the author turns his attention from the goings-on in West Virginia to the no less strange occurrences on Long Island, New York's Mount Misery. In the late spring of 1967, a young contactee began to have repeated encounters with a personage she at first took to be the local librarian, clad in old-fashioned, 1940's-style clothing (the author notes that this was before any "retro" styles were in fashion). A series of subsequent encounters occurred in which the strange personage – always wearing the same garb – tried to address the contactee. "There was something wrong about her movements. It was as if...she were dead."

Much has been made of the Men-in-Black's choice of clothing: white shirts, black ties and black suits. Perhaps these intriguing characters have been reanimated from the grave, still clad in their burial clothes? A ludicrous proposition, but the MIB who caused a coin to vanish before the startled eyes of Maine physician Herbert Hopkins in 1976 was described as wearing heavy white makeup and lipstick. An effort to hide the disfigurations of a cadaver? The intervening twenty-odd years have not shed any further light on this case.

CONCLUSION

Humanity has developed a series of ritualized behaviors to deal with its dead, a subject that is usually avoided and is considered taboo by primitive societies living in fear that the unappeased dead may return to haunt the living. In his book on Roman history, M.P. Charlesworth mentions the Roman peasant's terror that "vampires would carry off the dead." Aside from the obscurantism of a pre-technological age, could there have been a somewhat rational basis for the ancients' fears? The activity of these strange lights, and the hair-raising testimony of the parties who have witnessed the events described in this article, would seem to confirm this.

ABOUT THE AUTHOR: Scott Corrales became interested in the UFO phenomenon as a result of the heavy UFO activity while he lived in both Mexico and Puerto Rico. He was also influenced by Mexican ufologists, Pedro Ferriz and Salvador Freixedo, a former Jesuit priest who advocated a paranormal, interdimensional interpretation of the phenomenon. In 1990, Scott began translating the works of Freixedo into English, making the literature and research of experts and journalists available to English-reading audiences everywhere. This led to the creation of the SAMIZDAT journal in 1993 and his collaboration with Mexico's CEFP group, Puerto Rico's PRRG, and the foremost researchers of Spain's so-called third generation of UFO researchers.

In 1998, the SAMIZDAT bulletin was replaced by the "Inexplicata: The Journal of Hispanic Ufology," as the official publication of the Nascent Institute of Hispanic Ufology. In addition, Scott has been a guest on numerous radio shows and his articles have been featured in several national publications.

Scott is author of such books as: *"Alien Blood Lust," "UFO Hostilities," "Screwed By the Aliens."*

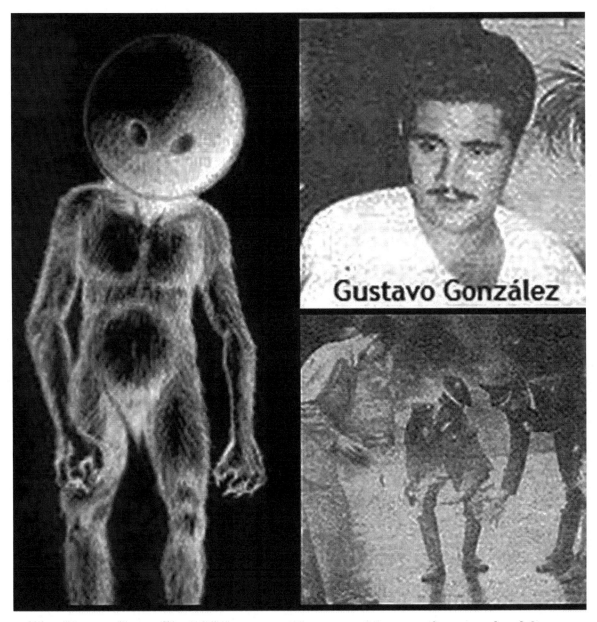

Gustavo González

On November 28, 1954, near Caracas, Venezuela, truck drivers Gustavo Gonzales and Jose Ponce found the road blocked by a luminous sphere over 10-feet in diameter. A small creature with claws and glowing eyes came toward them and Gonzales grabbed it. He observed its body was hard and covered with fur. The creature reportedly clawed at Gonzales in order to escape. At the same time, two other dwarfs emerged from the bushes and all three jumped into the sphere which flew away in a blinding flash of light.

FOR FEAR OF LITTLE MEN: PARANORMAL DWARVES

By Scott Corrales

Since ufology's earliest days, and going even farther back in history, accounts of diminutive intelligent beings have played a crucial role is shaping our perception of the phenomenon. The sizes of these creatures range from a scant twelve inches to a not-so-small four feet in height. They occupy a special position within the study of the unknown, since they straddle the divide that separates folklore from contemporary approaches to enigmatic creatures: every culture on earth has a tradition that involves small beings that can be good or malicious, intelligent or brutish. That accounts of such creatures occur in our highly technological twentieth century, and in relation to the UFO phenomenon, constitutes an enigma in itself.

The European tradition's brownies, pixies, gnomes and dwarves have their equivalents in the Mexican *ikhals, chaneques* and *aluches*. As Salvador Freixedo wisely observed, it is extremely odd to find such a variety of names to describe creatures that supposedly do not exist.

MEXICO'S UNEARTHLY ENTITIES

Do contemporary UFO abduction experiences and bedroom visitations have anything in common with the ages-old tradition of playful dwarves and elves disrupting the nocturnal slumber of humans?

In 1980, Luis Ramírez Reyes, one of Mexico's foremost UFO writers, had an experience of this nature during a stay at his friend Dr. Paco Medina's country house in Moyotepec, Morelos state. He had originally accepted the invitation to the country retreat to investigate a tree on the property that had allegedly been zapped by a passing UFO for no apparent reason. Upon reaching the site, Ramírez was able to confirm the unusual damage to the tree. Since the hour was late, both he and his host turned in for the night. It was to prove one of the most frightening nights in the ufologist's life.

As he drifted off to sleep, a heavy weight dropped beside him in the guest room bed. Ramírez awoke with a start, thinking a snake may have dropped onto the bed from the rafters. Frozen in place, he managed to extend a hand to feel what it was that had fallen into the bed. To his complete astonishment, the bed was empty. The following day, he had the opportunity to speak with the children who performed housekeeping duties for his host, and was startled when they calmly told him that dwarves had visited him. "They are like children, but we call them *chaneques* here," he was informed. "They play with us when we sweep and mop the house."

Unwilling to be the victim of childish pranks, the investigator subjected the youngsters to a cross-examination. They indicated that the entities would chase the children around whenever they arrived; allegedly out of fear of being harmed by adult humans, the entities remained invisible, but could be clearly seen by young humans, who described them as being large-headed, bald, slender, and for modesty's sake, clad in "cloth shorts."

Mexico's Luis Ramírez Reyes had an incredible encounter.

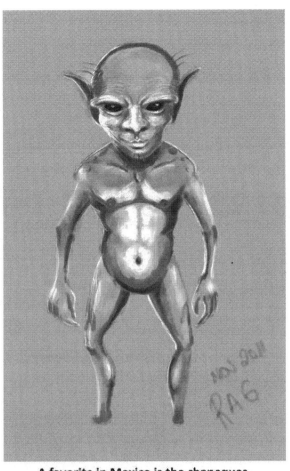

A favorite in Mexico is the chaneques.

Ramírez's host later informed him that both he and his family had been subjected to the nocturnal antics of these *chaneques* more than once, to the extent that his wife refused to return to the country house. The creatures could be persuaded to desist by asking them to do so "using kind words."

This experience convinced Ramírez of the interdimensional origin of these and other similar entities, which in spite of their playfulness can be outright frightening. While the descriptions of the creatures given by the young housekeepers of the Medina estate may be troubling, it must be observed that beings with similar descriptions and wearing similar items of clothing have been reported in a number of cases in Puerto Rico and in the Canary Islands.

Maria Luz Bernal, a Mexican journalist researching her country's magical practices, came across a faith healer known as "cuate Chagala" in the region of Mexico known as Los Tuxtlas. Chagala informed the journalist that he had obtained his healing powers at the age of twelve while fishing for *mojarras* at a lagoon near his village. His deceased grandfather, who had drowned in the lagoon in years past, allegedly appeared before him to grant him special powers that would turn him into a healer. Chagala believed that his grandfather had been turned into a *chaneque*, described in this context as a "water gnome/elemental," having been lured to a watery death by similar creatures. When prompted by the reporter, the faith healer explained that when these water gnomes appear at night, their purpose is to ensnare the intended victim to drown them and turn them into water gnomes. When they appear by day, however, they do so to confer "gifts" upon unsuspecting mortals.

INCREDIBLE ALIEN ENCOUNTERS

While traveling throughout Mexico, paranormal researcher Salvador Freixedo was able to document a similar belief. Interviewing peasant women, he learned that they were terribly afraid of the little creatures – *chaneques* – who played restlessly every night in the water basin located on the rear of their property. The dwarves considered it a great sport to rattle the family's pots and pans, placed in the basin to be washed by the children. The women added that the creatures would appear and disappear through the culvert that fed the water basin.

DWARFISH "PEEPING TOM?"

Perhaps one of the most unusual stories involving the actions of diminutive creatures in our times involves the series of bizarre events taking place in the ever-mysterious Canary Islands, off the western coast of Africa. It was here, on the island of Tenerife, in a town with the ominous name of La Matanza ("the slaying") that diminutive, dark olive-green colored beings were reported on many occasions by visitors to the area, with the added riddle of the seeming complicity among local humans to "keep the lid" on such stories.

Nonetheless, locals and visitors alike agree that the dwarves are very real, and are known as "los diablillos" (the imps). Appearing after dark at a beautiful country retreat known as Finca del Duque, it was at first believed that the short-statured creatures were attracted by the activities of couples using this remote area as a lovers' lane. Further cases have shown that any human presence after sundown produces the appearance of the "diablillos."

In November 1992, an anonymous resident of Tenerife drove to the lovers' lane one evening with his girlfriend. From within the car they were able to hear the sound of branches rustling as if being parted by someone. The driver looked out the window and allegedly saw a creature some three feet tall and covered in grayish or black fur all over. The entity carried a staff or rod of some sort in its hand, and was described as having "cat-like eyes." The couple left the area in a hurry, refusing to return even by daylight.

Alberto Dieppa, a young man from the island of Gran Canaria, discussed his 1993 encounter with the beings during an interview with journalist Carmen Machado.

According to the story, Dieppa and his friends drove to the remote Finca del Duque simply to enjoy the ride. The group remained within the car with the dome light on, chatting late into the evening, when they suddenly became aware of six or seven presences outside their vehicle, staring at them intently. Dieppa turned on the headlights, and was in for the surprise of his life. "They were like little children with adult faces," he explained. "They appeared to be naked, at least from the waist up. What I did notice was their dark, olive green skin color and their intense red eyes."

The car's occupants remained in stunned, paralyzed silence until one of them began screaming hysterically, causing the driver to set the car in motion and abandon the area as quickly as possible. Dieppa added that at no point did the "diablillos" try to block their way – in fact, they seemed to vanish as soon as he touched the ignition key.

Badly shaken, the friends agreed not to discuss what had occurred at Finca del Duque, not even among themselves. Intrigued by the incredible experience, Dieppa returned alone two weeks later. Although he was unable to see anything on this occasion, he claims to have felt the presence of the creatures surrounding him. The experiencer told the journalist that he believes the imps to be an integral part of the island rather than creatures from another planet, suggesting that there may well be a "portal" of some sort to a dimension producing these creatures.

ABDUCTED BY FAIRIES?

Dr. Raul Rios Centeno is a UFO investigator based in Lima, Peru. His investigative efforts take him to the remote areas of his Andean homeland, where impoverished peasants still speak Quechua rather than Spanish and believe in a hodgepodge of pagan and Christian beliefs. In late 1997, while part of relief efforts aimed at providing assistance to victims of landslides and calamities triggered by "El Niño," Dr. Rios visited the department of Piura in northern Perú, and returned with the most recent case profiled in this article – the summer 1997 disappearance of a young girl, allegedly at the hands of "fairies."

"I myself never believed in such things, doctor. Even now, I don't know what to think." These were the words with which don Modesto Salas, a Piuran farmer in the town of Catacaos, began telling his story to Dr. Rios. His small farm is located some 2 km SE of Catacaos. He lives off his crops and a few animals he raises. The region's heat and its proximity to the Equator — only some 220 kilometers away – causes the well-known algarroba trees, mangroves and banana plants to grow.

Modesto has lived for almost ten years with Ms. Olga Vandilla, with whom he has three children: Manuel José, 9, Olga Luzmila, 7, and the missing Evelyn Rosario, who would have been five years old next April. Despite the strong customs that reign in the Peruvian localities in which the Catholic Church still preserves its predominance, Modesto and Olga never married.

The approximately ten-acre farm has at its center the small house in which the family resides. The two eldest children were baptized as soon as they were born, in step with Catholic tradition, but when it came to Evelyn's term, something unexpected happened: the local priest died. For this reason, a priest from the region of Flores, some 25 kms away, would come to Catacaos every Sunday for the Eucharist and confession.

"I went to talk to him, doctor. I asked, I begged, but the *padrecito* didn't want to. He told me that all ceremonies had to be done in Flores. He even pointed out to me that a few couples wished to marry, and he had turned them down, saying he'd only been entrusted with the Sunday masses. A new *padrecito* would soon arrive, and he would be able [to do these things]."

"I wanted to baptize my Evelyn where she was born, because to baptize her in another place where I don't know anyone, and where I have no friends, doesn't seem right to me."

Time went by and the priest never showed up. Evelyn remained unbaptized. "My daughter grew up pretty. She was tall and had grey eyes. At first my friends laughed at me, saying that she wasn't my daughter, and that Olga had certainly deceived me, because how could my daughter have grey eyes, when both me and my wife have brown eyes?"

According to Olga, Evelyn was the most rambunctious of all her children, although she was also the strangest.

You have to be kidding? No, you're not. Aluches, the Mayan elf.

"There were times when she would sit on the ground and start talking, even shouting and laughing. Other times she'd climb up the tree and would begin talking alone. My wife told me this wasn't normal and told me to take her to a doctor, because the girl was suddenly going insane!

"The doctor referred me to a young lady who asked Evelyn to draw pictures – she showed her little figures. The young lady told me Evelyn was at the age in which kids have imaginary friends, and that it would stop once she went to school. Last June, Evelyn climbed onto one of the carob trees; Olga had seen her climbing up and down the carob tree for a number of days. The girl would stay up there for three hours at a time, talking alone.

"Evelyn told her mother that she had little friends her own size and that she was the only one that could see them. They would show her their toys and even offered her their food."

When Modesto went to speak to the psychologist, he showed her Evelyn's drawings. He told her that some children might see things, but that his girl had counted the three little figures and given them names. "She would tell me about her little friends, and told me that the food they fed her was transparent and sweet, like gelatin. There were times when she would stop playing with her brothers to climb up the blessed tree."

Unlike Olga, Modesto is a strong believer in the occult. On occasion he has consulted seers, sorcerers and shamans. The town shaman told him that when a child remains unbaptized it can communicate with beings from other dimensions, which we commonly know as fairies. Westerners speak of fairy treasures, but in this case Evelyn never discussed treasures, only the food and games and pranks they played. The shaman told Modesto the child must be baptized before they "conquered her."

"He told me that he could baptize her, because otherwise she would be with the demons. God did not make fairies; they are envoys of the Evil One, and can often cause problems for the families to whom they appear."

When Olga learned that her husband wanted the shaman to baptize Evelyn, she retorted that the shaman wasn't a priest, and that their daughter would only be baptized by a man of the cloth.

"I made an agreement with the shaman to come to my house. I would send my wife to visit her mother, and since Evelyn was always up on the tree, I would make her stay."

The shaman reached Modesto's home where, according to him, he could feel the devil's presence. He prayed and chased the enemy off. Everything took place as planned: the shaman baptized Evelyn with a special oil he kept in a bottle.

"He told me he carried holy oil blessed in the Huaringas, and that it not only served to have God bless her, but it would also bring my little angel joy and happiness."

Evelyn was baptized in strict privacy as per the ritual imposed by the shaman, her father being the only witness. The shaman asked Modesto not to wash the girl's head for two days. He agreed and the shaman departed.

"After the baptism, Evelyn returned to the tree and cried disconsolately. It seemed as if someone was chastising her and she cried as if when her mother reproved her."

Olga returned that afternoon, and on that very same day, what they call the "kidnapping" took place.

"I was on my hammock enjoying the air when I saw little Evelyn climb the tree after my wife got home. Now she was talking and laughing, as if drunk. I thought she was playing as usual and didn't pay much attention.

"At a given moment, everything went quiet and the sky grew cloudy all of a sudden. It seemed as if a massive rainstorm was about to fall. So since there's usually lightning when it rains that way, I went to the tree where I'd last seen Evelyn, but she was no longer there."

Modesto thought that Evelyn had gone into the house, but he was surprised that he hadn't seen her come down. Upon entering the home, which was some 30 meters away from the tree, he asked his wife about the child.

"Olga told me she'd seen her go up the tree and that she should still be on the blessed tree because she hadn't seen her come down."

Modesto returned to the tree, checked the adjacent ones, but could see nothing. Olga ran out, shouting desperately, but it was all in vain. At that moment Olga approached the tree and climbed up to find some trace of her daughter, but only found "something like a cobweb on the trunk, which was slightly burned. It appeared freshly burned due to the smell that emanated from the trunk."

At that moment, they thought they heard a howl coming from the doorway to the house. For one moment they thought it was Evelyn, but upon getting closer and opening the door, they found nothing at all. "It was a sound like that of a *pututo* [Andean flute], but it came from the sky."

Modesto and Olga never found their youngest daughter again. The police were notified, word was sent to radio stations and to a television channel in Piura, but the whereabouts of their daughter were never discovered. "Doctor, I feel the fairies took my little angel. Otherwise, how can I explain her disappearance? Not even the dogs barked. Nothing."

El Duende, from Latin America, are said to hide out in the shadows and are especially fond of watching children play.

CONCLUSION

The mystery of the dwarves or imps that appear to inhabit every single region of our world remains one of the many enigmas that may someday be unraveled by investigators. While the UFO context helps place the mystery in a more modern light, its antiquity must not be forgotten.

Gervase of Canterbury, a medieval monk writing in the year 1138 A.D., left a detailed description of one such dwarfish creature that suddenly materialized in the German abbey of Prüm. According to Gervase's account, the abbey had been in an uproar due to the fact that something was tampering with the large barrels of wine in the building's cellars and spilling the intoxicant all over the floor. The abbot initially reprimanded the cellarer for his ineptitude, until the actual culprit was found: a friar had caught a small black imp, like the ones described in Argentina, drawing wine from the casks.

The creature dwelled in the abbey for a brief spell, but would neither eat nor drink, nor even speak. Its presence must have irked the abbot after a while, who summarily decided that the imp "was a devil in human form" who had refrained from harming the monks "by the mercy of God and the merits of the saints," whose relics were kept within the abbey. Gervase reports that the creature "vanished from their hands like smoke."

©**Scott Corrales**

SUGGESTED READING - CONTRIBUTIONS BY SCOTT CORRALES

ALIEN BLOOD LUST

UFO HOSTILITIES

SCREWED BY THE ALIENS

CHUPACABRA DIARIES

Inexplicata-The Journal of Hispanic Ufology
inexplicata.blogspot.com

A supposed gnome caught on a cell phone.

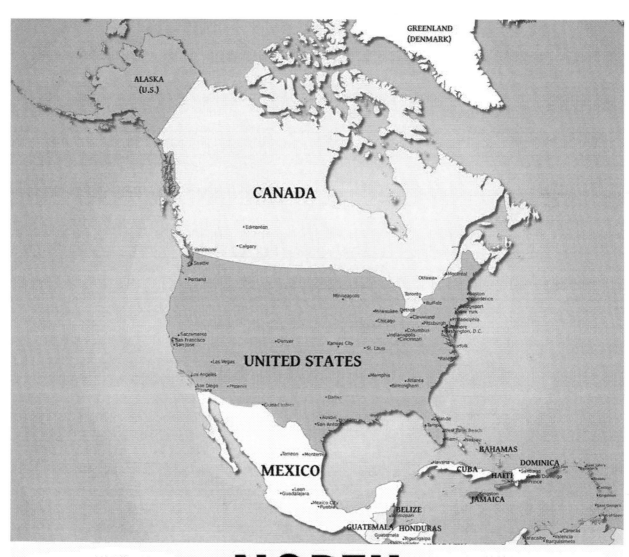

NORTH AMERICA

SEDONA: UFO GATEWAY TO ANOTHER DIMENSION

By Brad and Sherry Steiger

PUBLISHER'S NOTE: One of the hottest UFO hot spots is, in my opinion, snuggled away in the red rocks of Sedona, AZ. There are even guided tours to take you around to the places where UFOs have been seen and photographed. Longtime resident and UFO repeater Tom Dongo knows the places to go. He has an entire scrapbook that must weigh five pounds containing a huge dossier of UFO pictures taken around this community. Though the majority has been taken by other witnesses, Tom has, upon occasion, been able to point his camera toward the sky and some pretty amazing, far out, phenomena will appear for all to marvel at. But why Tom Dongo, you ask? "A hundred times I have said – why me?" Tom said in an interview with Beckley. "This stuff has been going on for over 25 years now, and I have written six popular books regarding many of these inexplicable occurrences. Why is it that I have such strange paranormal happenings around me, sometimes on a continuous basis? I don't understand it. I don't have a clue. I have had many borderline-psychotic explanations from, usually, well-meaning people as to the reason behind this activity. Maybe I will never know why." If you can't get to Sedona in person there are any number of travelogues on Amazon Prime and YouTube, some with quite a bit of UFO content. Brad and Sherry Steiger and I spent the day in Sedona and picked up on the area's full throttle New Age vibes. Here is their report.

• • • • • • • • • •

Perhaps one of the most beautiful and mystical locations on Earth exists in the breath-taking red rock country of Arizona. The fabled vortexes are credited with accomplishing everything from dramatic past life recalls to miraculous healings. Sedona, Arizona, is a place with a history strong in Native American Medicine traditions - and it is an area with an active past record of UFO sightings.

Dr. Patricia Rochelle Diegel, an internationally famous mystic, re-incarnationist, and UFOolgist, told us that there seemed to be four main categories of sightings in Sedona. The first category, she explained, occurs when groups go out to sit on or near the vortexes and meditate, chant, and "call down" the UFOs. "Usually three-fourths of the group will say that they have seen the UFOs, and each percipient will give nearly identical descriptions of what he has seen," Dr. Diegel told us. "Some teachers have had those who spotted the UFOs write their reports separately and the accounts are consistent."

Dr. Diegel noted that this first category of UFO sighters was composed of men and women who had been interested in metaphysics and UFOlogy for quite some time.

"The type of craft that they most often spot are the roundish, disc-shaped, so-called 'Pleiadean' space vehicles," she continued. "The people in this first category are usually from out of town and have come with teachers or leaders who have their own methods of getting the individuals in the group in 'sync' and in an altered-state-of-consciousness so they will be able to see the spacecraft."

Brad and Sherry Steiger.

The second category, according to Dr. Diegel, also seems primarily to be out-of-towners who have come to Sedona with a leader, such as our friend Virgil "Posty" Armstrong, who takes the group out into an open field on particular nights in a concerted effort to see the UFOs. "From what I've understood from people who attended such gatherings, about half of them say they've seen UFOs," she stated. "Remember, though, that a lot of the folks in the second category are beginners at this sort of thing.

"Of those who report UFOs in this category, there appear to be two different types of craft sighted. Again, one is the disc-shaped Pleiadean ship, the other is the Close Encounters-type of 'mother ship' UFO. They report both of these types in slightly different sizes.

"Some have also filed reports of an elongated 'cigar'- shaped ship that darts about, making square corners and that sort of thing," Dr. Diegel continued. "The disc-shaped craft seem more often to hover and are less lively than the cigar-shaped vehicles." Dr. Diegel observed that an individual's openness toward the UFO experience would undoubtedly have a great deal to do with his success in sighting a craft. Such an observation led her into the third category of "Sedona Saucer Sightings," the private encounters, "where a person has made a sighting by himself while driving on one of our backroads."

Psychic Patricia Diegel believed Sedona to be a gateway to another dimension.

Dr. Diegel related the experience of a woman named "Doriel," who was driving home when she spotted a UFO flying low along the road, several yards in front of her. Her husband, "Gary," was following behind her in another automobile, and she desperately yearned to see his headlights in her rearview mirror. As Doriel went around a curve, the UFO moved around the curve just ahead of her. When, she decided to slow down, the craft decreased its speed. She slowed further, hoping Gary would catch up with her. She felt eerily alone, for there happened to be no other cars on the road. Besides, she wanted Gary to witness the UFO.

When she neared the village of Oak Creek where they lived, she at last saw Gary's headlights behind her. But almost simultaneously with his arrival, the UFO suddenly took off straight up and zoomed out of sight.

"Gary said that he saw 'something,'" Dr. Diegel stated, "and he knew it wasn't a falling star because it was going in the wrong direction. Doriel was able to describe the craft as being one of the disc-shaped Pleiadean-type vehicles."

Dr. Diegel told us that she had given readings for as many as thirty-six individuals in the Sedona area who testified that they had encountered a UFO while driving in their car at night with one or two people. "Their descriptions of the encounter are remarkably similar to Doriel's," she commented. "The flying saucers follow them, hover over them, move on ahead of them - and the minute another car appears, the objects zoom almost straight up and then disappear." Dr. Diegel pointed out that none of the percipients who described such encounters to her knew one another, thus making their reports all the more evidential and convincing.

We learned that the mysterious "Black Helicopters" reported by so many UFOlogists have also made their appearance in the Sedona area.

A young man reported to Dr. Diegel that while he was climbing up monumental Bell Rock late one afternoon just before sunset, a black helicopter with smoked glass windows hovered over him and blasted its loudspeakers at him with a warning: "Get down from this rock. You don't belong here. Stay away from here!." In the six months since the young man filed his report with Dr. Diegel and her husband, Jon Terrance Diegel, they have received complaints from several other people who have had black helicopters chase them away from the Chapman area near Boyton Canyon, Bell Rock, and Cathedral Rock.

"The black helicopters appear to be patrolling the area," Dr. Diegel remarked. "A rumor has started that there is some kind of UFO base back in the mountains near Sedona. At least 16 people have claimed that those are C.I.A. helicopters monitoring the UFO base and keeping people away."

We wanted to know Dr. Diegel's opinion as to the validity of the alleged UFO base. "As a UFOlogist, I cannot prove its existence," she replied thoughtfully. "But as a psychic, I feel that there is some kind of a base, probably a bit farther back in the hills. There has just been too much of this 'black helicopter' activity around here. I do not feel, however, that the UFO energy in the so-called 'base' is at all negative."

There is a powerful spiritual maxim that may also apply to UFO encounters: What you bring to an experience in a large part determines what you will receive. In other words, it is the level of your own consciousness that determined whether an encounter is negative or positive. For the most part, people interpret their Sedona UFO experiences as positive and this may be due to the high spiritual energy that has permeated the area during countless Native American Medicine ceremonies.

Since both of the authors of this article are deeply interested in Medicine Power as well as UFO research, our experiences in the vortexes have been empowering and enriching.

In July of 1987, we were visiting the vortexes as part of a seminar that was sponsored by Dr. Patricia Rochelle Diegel and her husband Jon Terrance. As we visited a Medicine Wheel that had been constructed at one of the vortexes, the editor of this publication was able to capture photographically a remarkable occurrence.

Sherry has practiced extremely deep meditation for many years, and she often attracts powerful energy fields about her. As she sat apart meditating at the vortex, Tim Beckley was able to photograph electromagnetic energies moving toward her. The energy grew stronger and stronger, until, to the camera's lens, her body had all but completely disappeared. Sherry seemed totally at-one with incredible vibrations of light. Many metaphysicians have maintained that there is a spiritual city which exists directly above Sedona. What is more, this city focuses energy down on the area.

Sherry and Tim celebrate Tim's birthday in Sedona, albeit quite a few years ago.

Tim Beckley stands tall before Bell Rock - UFO hotspot. Photo by Charla Gene.

Sedona has become a kind of pilgrimage region for at least the last twelve years. Metaphysical leaders such as Dick Sutphen regularly hold major seminars near the vortexes. Top psychics such as Page Bryant and Dr. Diegel have established their homes in Sedona. Hollywood stars with metaphysical leanings are also beginning to move there or to establish second homes in the area. Talented psychic artists such as Luis Romero abound in the village.

Among the reasons members of the metaphysical community mention for coming to Sedona in particular – and the entire state of Arizona in general – are the following: The desert sand and climate of southern Arizona are conducive to mysticism and psychism. The powerful energies remaining from the ancient Amerindian and pre-Amerindian civilizations continue to exert a great influence on contemporary psychic sensitives. There is a strong "Egyptian" vibration and influence that contributes toward making a number of Arizona regions sacred "power places."

It has been said that large portions of the state of Arizona will provide "safe" places during what many metaphysicians see as a fast-approaching period of cataclysms and Earth changes. Sedona is seen as a virtual citadel of safety during these troubled times. The late Helen Frye told Brad and Sri Darwin Gross, who was at that time the spiritual leader of Eckankar, that the waters which run through Oak Creek Canyon have even greater healing properties than the Ganges River of India.

Helen was convinced that Sedona was "a place of miracles." Continuing her comments, "Even the animals sense the wonder of the area. My Hopi grandfather told me of seeing the lights of guardian spirits in the area. In Eckankar, we are in attunement with the 'Blue Light' of our masters and teachers. These lights have also been seen near the spiritual city."

According to longtime Sedona resident Alon MacCarthy, lights of a very peculiar nature came down on the city one Fourth of July evening in what he recalls would have been 1983.

The community was having a small fireworks display from a supermarket parking lot when a boy in the audience suddenly called out: "Oh, oh. You'd better not send up the next rockets, because there's something else going to happen."

People turned to look at the boy, wondering what had caused him to say such a thing, and then, MacCarthy reports, four or five huge balls of light were seen to appear to come down over Capital Butte. The glowing objects moved erratically, within a discernable pattern, but in a strange kind of harmony, until they came to hover over the area from which the skyrockets were being launched.

MacCarthy made the point that several hundred Sedona residents were witnesses to this occurrence, for many people had gathered in the supermarket parking lot and many more were observing the fireworks from other areas.

The lights were of no particular color, appearing very much like huge "lightbulbs," though a few witnesses claimed to have seen a pulsing blue light beneath the objects.

Just before the huge glowing lights shot off and disappeared, MacCarthy said that he somehow received the impression: "They're scanning us."

Remarkably, Dr. Diegel told us, even with dozens of witnesses observing the maneuvers of the mystery lights, there were some people in the Fourth of July crowd who claimed not to have seen anything. "I personally feel that an individual has to be in some kind of altered-state-of-consciousness to see the great majority of what we call the 'UFO phenomenon,'" she commented.

"Many of the UFOs may be multidimensional in nature, but even if they are physically solid, extraterrestrial craft, they would probably be moving in 'hyper-speed,' and we would have to be in fourth or fifth dimensional consciousness in order to see them." Alon MacCarthy said that, in about 1976, when he first arrived in Sedona, he was with a group of people meditating at the airport road vortex who sighted three gigantic incandescent balls of light rising up out of the ground. On this occasion, he claimed, everyone in attendance witnessed the event.

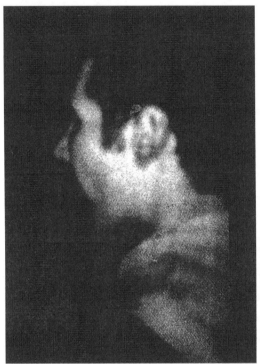

UFOs are no strangers to Sedona. But it is rare that their occupants are hotographed, as in the case of this "blue man" from the Tom Dongo collection. The being was not visible when the picture was taken.

According to MacCarthy, such occurrences at the airport road vortex continued intermittently for about seven years before they ceased to manifest. "Many people in town saw them," he told Dr. Diegel. "There have been lively discussions as to whether the huge lights are coming out of the mountain or up out of the ground in the valley. There are also differences of opinion as to whether the objects make themselves visible so that they can be seen – or if witnesses with psychic abilities somehow pierce the shield that normally keeps them invisible."

Dr. Patricia Rochelle Diegel told us that she participated in a group sighting during a 1989 Labor Day seminar that she and her husband were hosting at the Sunset Inn.

She recalled that the well-known metaphysical artist Luis Romero had come into the conference area and motioned to her to accompany him.

"When we were outside," she continued, "Luis pointed up to where Mars is. There I saw a bright object that appeared to have little 'shooting stars' coming out of it. It was making big curves in the sky and moving out in different directions."

Romero and Dr. Diegel went back inside and summoned the seminar participants to come out to observe the manifestation. "Ninety per cent of the people saw what we were seeing," she said. "It was as if 'someone' were putting on a light show for us.

"Next, the object with the 'shooting stars' moved away from Mars and soared to a portion of the sky with no easily discernible stars. Here, it repeated the looping motions."

At the same time Romero had walked to the other side of the inn and observed that a similar "light show" was occurring in that section of the night sky.

The object was making the same kind of zig-zagging maneuvers and replicating the "shooting star" effects. "It was as if," Dr. Diegel speculated, "they were saying, 'Okay, you people have been conducting spiritual exercises. You are now in a nice altered-state-of-consciousness. Now we'll let you see us!'"

Dr. Diegel told us that everyone who had observed the objects had received a very good, very positive, "benevolent" feeling from them. When the seminar participants returned inside and entered into the Diegels' "Trinity Process," they felt that they received such messages as the following: "We are your friends." "You're not ready for us to come to talk to you yet." "We just wanted you to know that we're out here." "You're not evolved enough yet."

Dr. Diegel has given over 47,000 past-life readings, and she told us that the Soul-essences of most of the people for whom she had done readings were from other constellations. She said that she had made a scientific determination of their place of origin, the kind of dimensional energy that they had when they arrived here on Earth, and a description of their original physical appearance.

"I believe that I'm being used to let people know that we didn't all look like 'humans' when we came here, that we were all different body types and skin types and so on, so that people will cease being afraid of alien life forms and extraterrestrial visitors," Dr. Diegel states. "I also believe that the movie 'E. T.' was given to us so that we would realize that 'they' don't always look like us."

On the other hand, Dr. Diegel expressed her opinion that some extraterrestrial or multidimensional entities may appear very human. She further speculates that many science fiction writers are "plugging into" past life memories when they produce such works as "Star Trek," "Battle Star Galactica," and the "Star Wars" series.

"I believe that we are being prepared to be able to accept outer space visitors into our population," she went on. "I don't look upon this from the negative aspects that some UFOlogists do.

"Perhaps there are entities that are not as friendly and as loving to us as other types may be. Perhaps there have been so-called 'hostile' acts on the part of some beings. Perhaps there has been a government cover-up. But I feel the negative entities will be held in check by the benevolent ones.

"As a past-life reader with my track record of accuracy in the things that I have told people, I believe that the many sightings in the Sedona area, and elsewhere, are designed to prepare us for the time when our outer space visitors are ready to make themselves known to the world on a mass scale," Dr. Diegel said firmly, emphasizing her position.

Then she added with a soft chuckle: "Most of the people who come to me are of extraterrestrial origin, 'cuz I are one, too."

In her concluding remarks, Dr. Diegel also expressed her opinion that there are some aliens "walking among us" in very human-like bodies.

"Some of them are walking around in their first incarnation in a human body. They have a memory of where they are from and what their mission is to be on Earth.

"I really do believe that 90 percent of the aliens among us, as well as the extraterrestrial visitors, are friendly," she stated. "While some entities may be negative, I think the benevolent ones will curtail their activities."

The late Brad Steiger was the author, along with his wife Sherry, of over 400 books on the paranormal.

INCREDIBLE ALIEN ENCOUNTERS

SUGGESTED READING

REAL ENCOUNTERS AND OTHER WORLDLY BEINGS By Brad and Sherry Steiger

MYSTERIES OF TIME AND SPACE By Brad Steiger

UFO REPEATERS – THE CAMERA DOESN'T LIE

MERGING DIMENSIONS and UNSEEN BEINGS, UNSEEN WORLDS

WANT TO KNOW MORE

"Mr UFOs Secret Files - Tom Dongo"

INVISIBLE ALIENS "INVADE" TOWN – UNDERGROUND BASES EXPOSED!

www.youtube.com/watch?v=HFgvjjjrClM&t=1664s

Captured in a spiritual mood, Sherry Steiger receives the healing rays coming from what may be the opening of one of Sedona, Arizona's famous vortexes. (Photo by Tim Beckley)

EXPLORING THE BIZARRE

ERICA LUKES

Readers will enjoy a conversation on "Utah's Strange Legacy: Skinwalker Ranch, Shapeshifters, Men In Black and UFO Bases" with Erica Lukes on "Exploring The Bizarre" (KCORradio.com) which is archived on our Mr. UFO's Secret Files, on our YouTube channel, at: www.youtube.com/watch?v=ROiXE9uDdjU&t=308s

THE PILOT, THE HAM RADIO OPERATOR AND THE UFO

By Erica Lukes

PUBLISHER'S NOTE: I always look forward to having Erica Lukes on "Exploring The Bizarre." She is so well informed, and most importantly of all, levelheaded. Within her close proximity in the state of Utah, Erica has had a persistent interest in the Skinwalker Ranch, a location of regularly reported paranormal activity. She has assembled several decades worth of case reports of mass UFO sightings, alien abduction reports and animal mutilations from her years of field research in and around the ranch.

In more recent years, due to the massive amount of information she has accumulated, she has chosen to specialize in archiving the UFO topic, finding rare and out-of-print books, periodicals, audio, and video recordings and other ephemera in an effort to create a regional library for use by researchers in the western US. She has recently visited area universities to study their holdings of early UFO researchers and "phenomenologists," like those of the late Dr. Frank Salisbury of the Department of Plant Science at Utah State University. Salisbury contributed important work on UFO reports in Utah with the help of "Junior" Hicks, a well-known UFO investigator.

Erica Lukes also has an undying passion for the mysteries of the universe, particularly UFO reports and other strange aerial phenomena. Since childhood, she has been fascinated with imagery of how vehicles and beings from space might appear, and she pursued this interest quietly but with determination. Due to her already established abilities with singing and some voice over production work, she was approached to perform media broadcasting work. This, coupled with her long-term interest in strange phenomena of nature, led her to take her first steps into radio in 2014 by developing her own programming and interview techniques with known figures in this topic. UFO reports became her specialty and she joined the Mutual UFO Network (MUFON) in 2014 as a field investigator. She eventually became its State Director for Utah.

Erica is working on a forthcoming book with co-author Gordon Lore about her experiences with paranormal matters and investigations. The archives of her UFO Unclassified program can be found at: *https://kcorradio.com/KCOR/UFO-Classified-Hosted-by-Erica-Lukes-KCOR-Digital-Radio-Network-Podcast.php*

• • • • • • • • • •

"Most researchers would trade their homes for a UFO case like Nephi, Utah: A clearly-seen object, qualified pilot witnesses, radar and audio tapes – even a ham radio listener! Lukes, Puckett, and Cox do their competent best investigating a thoroughly inexplicable sighting. Their verdict: **Unknown!**" – Rob Swiatek, Board of Directors/MUFON.

AMERICAN AIRLINES FLIGHT #434

On 14 JANUARY 2016, between 1208hrs and 1215hrs MST, radio show host and amateur HAM radio operator Pat Daniels was intercepting a chance radio transmission between an American Airlines flight #434 (Airbus 321) Pilot and Salt Lake City Air Traffic Control (SLATC). The flight route was from San Francisco to Philadelphia, wind speeds between 5 mph and 14 mph (ESE), with a maximum gust speed of 16 mph. The visibility was reported to be 7 miles.

According to Mr. Daniels, he often scans first responders and air traffic control frequencies, but this one in particular stood out and appeared unique.

Daniels described the pilot as being "excited" when asking SLATC "if they see the object on radar." Shortly thereafter, the pilot identified himself as AA flight #434.

SLATC/FAA denied seeing anything out of the ordinary on radar, which led to the following transmission between the pilot and air traffic control (transcribed):

Pilot: "Would you happen to know what this bright orange square is that we are flying over, would you?"

SLATC: "Uh, nah, that's a good question. I am not sure what it is... Is it off to your right side?"

Pilot: "It's like directly off our nose right now, it's like right below us, we have been watching it for a while now. It's like – I don't know what it is. It's a perfect, uh, square, bright and orange. What town are we next to, this town that's off our 2 o'clock low?"

SLATC: "Uh, American #434, that's Nephi, huh, Nephi, Utah."

Pilot: "Nephi, OK, cool. I'll see what I can find... Thank you!"

SLATC: "You bet!"

Following my initial conversation with Daniels, I realized that time was of the essence in retrieving all pertinent information, as the FAA routinely recycled all long range radar tapes every 2 weeks, and it had already been several days since the event had taken place.

An American Airlines pilot sees a UFO from the cockpit of Flight #434.

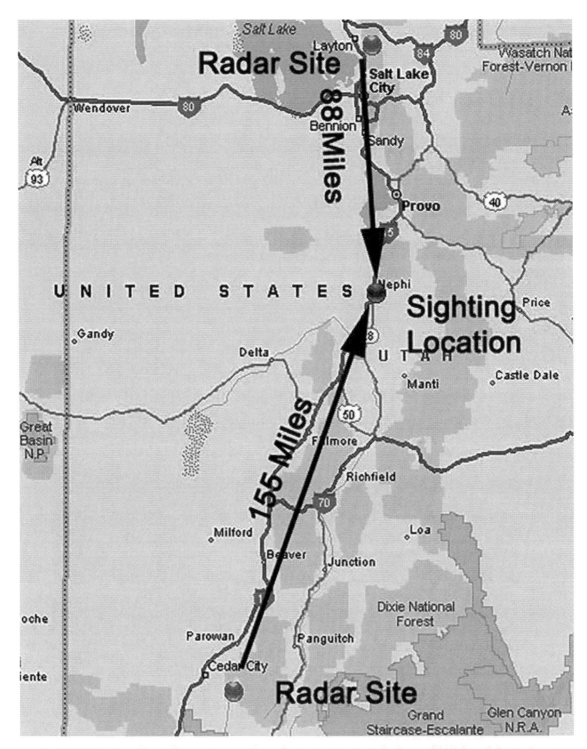

RADAR MAP: The pilot reported seeing an extremely large bright object that he estimated to be a mile wide to his right. The air traffic controller told him that he was looking in the direction of Nephi, Utah. Apparently the air traffic controller told the pilot that the object was not detected on radar. The object appeared to keep pace with the aircraft.

With the assistance of fellow investigators Geoff Cox and William Puckett, we were successful in determining all essential flight data along with portions of the radio transmission off the Air Traffic Control (ATC) website. The initial information obtained was sufficient to solicit a Freedom of Information request (FOIA) from the FAA.

Within six weeks, we were supplied with radar and transmission data, as well as (partially redacted) tower logs.

Scouring the flight path corridor throughout Salt Lake City and Nephi areas for eye witness or security camera accounts did not prove successful. Inquiries with local law enforcement agencies and the Salt Lake City International Airport media relations department were equally without result.

Despite posting ads, flyers and conducting a month-long media campaign, no credible data could be documented.

Radar Analyses: Investigator William Puckett analyzed a total of 106 radar returns between 1200hrs and 1230hrs MST, spanning an approximate nine square mile area. In addition, we also consulted with third party air traffic controllers due to the unusually high amount of radar return data within this usually quiet and remote geographic setting.

An animation of the radar data, flight corridor and surrounding areas can be seen at www.ufosnw.com

A NEW REPORT FROM UFOS NORTHWEST

SIGHTING FROM AIRLINER

Description: "My 17 year old son and I were on a SW Airlines flight from Denver to Albuquerque last night. The 9:50 flight left closer to 10 PM. About 10 minutes into the flight he started seeing bursts of light below us and called me to the window to watch them. I would guess that would put us over Colorado Springs. The lights burst larger and smaller, sometimes a good 300 feet across (guessing), and sometimes smaller. Sometimes they happened in a pattern of three bursts, then stopped for a bit. Sometimes the burst was between a low cloud and the ground. The lights kept pace with us for 13 minutes. Then we didn't see them again for 15 minutes. Lastly we saw them one more time, moving in a zigzag pattern near a river. They didn't flash over densely populated areas, but did over slightly populated areas. The light was always white, and solid (not sparkling like a firework). A few times it was two bursts at once. We asked our flight attendant our speed, which she pulled up online at 472 miles per hour. I wouldn't think anything flying that fast should be that low to the ground. We tried to record it and may have gotten the last bit of burst of what we saw."

Note to Commenters: If you are reporting a sighting, be sure to include the location (city, state, country), date and time of your sighting. Be detailed in your description. You may also use our **report form to report your sighting.** Comments will only be published if they are in "good taste" and not inflammatory. Also the name that you list in the comment will be posted. Use abbreviations or aliases if you don't want your name listed. **www.ufosnw.com/newsite/report-a-ufo-sighting-form-2**

Erica Lukes is host of "UFO Classified," heard live Fridays at
4:00 PM Pacific (7:00 PM EST) on KCOR Radio. kcorradio.com

THREE IN A CRAFT – THE REAL STORY BEHIND THE KENTUCKY ABDUCTION

From the Files of Timothy Green Beckley

This is what I would consider to be a very strong case. I spent several hours on the one with one of the witnesses. Mona was being, as far as I am concerned, very truthful about her experience. It seemed to me that she was not "gilding the lily," but was being honest and aboveboard. This case received a degree of publicity when the incident first broke, but I think it has been forgotten in the passing shadows of time.

STILL IN TOUCH

"They are still with us, all of the time."

Elaine Thomas' words echo the feelings of all three Liberty, Kentucky, women who were abducted by UFOnauts on the night of January 9, 1976.

"I think they want me to be quiet," Elaine says. The "they" she is referring to are the creatures who held her and her girlfriends, Mona Stafford and Louise Smith, captive on a UFO for approximately an hour and a half. "I think they are beaming that thought to me," she continues. "And I'm sure they are communicating with us."

Elaine Thomas revealed this to *UFO Review* in an exclusive interview. We asked her to elaborate.

"One night after it happened, I told the girls that I had a feeling I could communicate with them, and that I was going to do just that," Elaine says. "They laughed at me. Still, they agreed to go along with what I wanted to do.

"And what I wanted to do was to go back to the Redwood Restaurant in Sanford where it had all started. Nothing happened there or on the way back," Elaine reports, "but when I was standing alone outside Louise's home, I felt this trembling come over me. I went inside and I noticed that I had all these golden cobwebs on me. I told the girls to look. I felt that this was their way of symbolizing that they had communicated with me that night.

"I grabbed a strand of this mysterious substance and it squeaked between my fingers. Louise came over to look at it under the light, and as soon as she touched it, it vanished. There were little golden strands all over me, like hair. But they all disappeared quickly." According to Elaine Thomas, everyone in Louise's home saw the strange web-like material. She described it as being "stiff to the touch, like metal or plastic, and very shiny."

The woman was convinced that the beings which had held her captive were trying to make their presence known. Louise and Mona share that feeling. Louise Smith declared, "I feel that they know everything I do. It's a bad feeling, because there are so many things I remember about the incident that have never been told. I remember making a promise to them that I would never tell. .. and if I did tell, I felt that I would not know what would happen to me."

The witnesses in the Kentucky case seemed to be honest and sincere.

THE STRANGE CRAFT

It was Mona Stafford's 35th birthday, and to celebrate, the trio had decided to dine at the Redwood Restaurant. Finishing their dinner, they left for home at 11: 15 P.M. The restaurant is located 29 miles from Liberty in Stanford, Kentucky. Normally, it takes Louise roughly 40 minutes to complete the drive from the restaurant to her home - this evening it took much longer!

The route she takes is Kentucky # 78, a small country road which runs between Sanford and Hustonville. It's a winding road, cutting through the hilly countryside dotted with farms and wooded areas. All three were sitting in the front seat of Louise's green 1957 Chevy Nova. They were laughing and chatting when Mona suddenly gasped, "Look, its coming down! It's going to crash!"

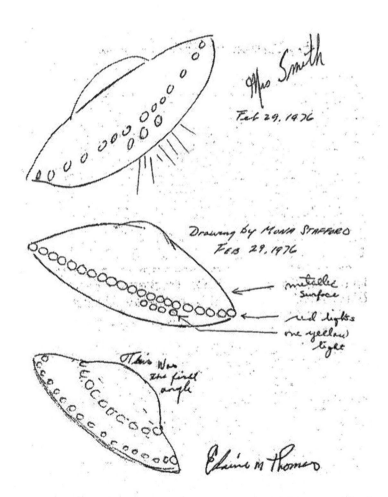

**Drawings by Louise Smith, Elaine Thomas and Mona Stafford
of the UFO they encountered on January 6, 1976.**

Their immediate thought was that a jet plane was on fire and that it was screaming toward the Earth right ahead of them. The object was a brilliant red light, and it was coming down very fast and at a sharp angle. The "thing" suddenly stopped at tree-top level and then paced the car. Elaine Thomas was able to tell that the object was disc-shaped and domed, with its leading edge tilted down toward the car. She estimated that it was less than 100 feet away.

The lights on the object were red and yellow and appeared to rotate around the bottom of the craft. It rocked back and forth, moving from one side of the car to the other. The object was huge! It was what researchers might term a "mothership."

Mona Stafford's illustration of the UFO lifting their car off the ground.

At this point, Elaine appeared to fall into a trance-like state. She opened the car door to get out. Mona, in the middle, screamed at her, reached across and shut the door. The vehicle suddenly picked up speed until it was moving at about 85 miles an hour - of its own accord. Mona shifted her attention to Louise, who struggled desperately to keep the car on the road.

"Mona yelled, 'Slow down!'" Louise says, "but a split-second later we were in Hustonville, about eight or nine miles from where we had the sighting, and we were thinking, 'How the hell did we get here so fast?' Yet that split second had been an hour and a half later!"

Louise gasped, "Mona, look! My foot's not on the gas pedal!" Louise Smith said later, "We were so frightened. I'm not ashamed to admit I was really scared. The light from the spacecraft came into the car. It's hard to describe. It was like a fog, a bluish light, and our heads began to hurt something terrible.

"And my car went out of control," Louise recalls. "I yelled to Mona to help me handle the wheel. The two of us struggled, but we couldn't control the car. It was very hot inside and it was difficult to breathe. The car felt like it was being drawn toward what looked like a rock wall with an opening where a gate should be.

"Then all at once we had the feeling that the car was being pulled backwards," Louise says. "It went over a speed breaker in the road, but we learned later it was a cable crossing through a gate, and we were drawn right through the opening."

Louise told us that she felt the car was being drawn to the craft by way of the light or beam emanating from the ship. She was aware of the car being lifted off the ground, but after that her memory is blank. Nor can Mona or Elaine remember what happened after the Chevy Nova began its ascent.

MEMORY LOSS AND A NECK BURN

In Liberty, Louise drove to her mobile home. Inside, she complained about her neck hurting her. Mona and Elaine looked at it and saw that she had an ugly red mark, like a burn, which ran from her hairline down to her back. Mona and Elaine had similar marks on their necks. Mona took off her ring and saw that the skin under it was very red. She also noted that her eyes burned her.

Louise said, "I had taken a bath before going out to eat, but now, for some reason, I felt very dirty. I don't know why." The mystery of the women's wristwatches was never solved. According to a report in "The Ohio Sky Watcher," Elaine's watch had stopped. Louise's watch showed 6:00, and the minute hand was moving as fast as the second hand. She was so frightened by her watch's behavior that she jerked it off her wrist and threw it down. She then went into the kitchen to look at the stove clock. It read: 1:25.

The three of them were amazed. They should have been home at midnight. Where had they been for the last hour and 25 minutes?

BLISTERED PAINT

After an almost sleepless night, the three decided to drive back to the road they had been on the night before. That was when they saw the blistered paint on Louise's car, which looked as though it had been subjected to terrific heat. They drove to the area, but found nothing of interest.

The most puzzling aspect for them was why it had taken them so long to get home. Mona Stafford felt that she couldn't keep quiet about it any longer − she had to tell someone. She called the Kentucky State Police. The officer listened politely, but said he could do nothing for her. Mona then called the naval recruiting office in Danville. The individual there got in touch with the Lexington television station, Channel 27. Mona, Louise and Elaine found themselves in front of TV cameras. The last thing they wanted was publicity. All they really wanted to know was what had happened to an hour and a half of their lives.

Subsequent interviews appeared in local newspapers and the stories then found their way to OUFOIL (Ohio UFO a Investigators League, Inc.) Jim Miller, an investigator for the organization, offered to help the women, However, because of previous commitments, he and a team of researchers from the group were unable to get to Liberty, Kentucky, until the latter part of February.

Drawing of humanoid UFO occupant recalled by Louise Smith
after hypnosis, dated October 1, 1976.

By that time, the women had suffered great changes. Each had dropped 15 pounds of weight. They had lost their appetite. Sleep was almost out of the question; they would not go anywhere alone and did not dare venture out after dark. Writing in *"The Ohio Sky Watcher,"* Jim Miller states: "We talked with the women, saw the remains of the burn marks on their necks, checked the blistered areas on the car, talked to the local police and had a good idea about what had happened to the women."

One odd "after-effect" was that when Mona came near her pet parakeet, which was normally very friendly, he would now fly toward the back of the cage like he was trying to keep away from her.

"We called the weather office in Lexington and found visibility was fifteen miles on January 6, with a cloud cover at 10,000 feet and the temperature was 38 degrees. We also had other reports that same night from people in the county of strange lights in the sky that were not from airplanes."

HYPNOTIC REGRESSION

It was agreed that hypnosis might be the answer, the feeling being that the women might recall under hypnosis what their conscious minds had kept blocked from them. The women also agreed to undergo polygraph tests.

It must be pointed out here that these interviews with The Ohio UFO group were made over a period of months.

By July, the women were no better off physically than they had been shortly after the sighting. They continued to lose weight. They found themselves running to doctors more than ever. They had nightmares. Mona Stafford's eyes still bothered her.

In fact, Mona's nightmares were probably scarier than the others. She reported that every time she closed her eyes to go to sleep, a strange vision of an eye would appear to her. It frightened her so much that she quickly opened her eyes.

On July 7, while she was trying to doze off, two "eyes" appeared. They looked like rather normal eyes, but they did jolt her nonetheless.

On July 19, Mona had been watching television. As the last program went off the air, a snowy pattern appeared. She stared at it and suddenly she felt someone was staring at her. Turning away from the TV, she caught sight of a man's face. He seemed to be about five feet away from her He had red hair and a red curly beard. When she jumped up, the entity vanished.

This was indicative of the kind of hell the women were going through during this period.

Finally, Dr. Leo Sprinkle was called in to hypnotize the women. Dr. Sprinkle, an associate professor of psychology at the University of Wyoming, has been involved in many UFO missing time cases, and felt that this was a good one.

The hypnosis and the polygraph testing were conducted at the Brown Motel in Liberty. The women passed the polygraph tests with no difficulty, and after two days of hypnosis, some startling results came to light.

THE HUMANOIDS

Louise related, "Under hypnosis, we were able to recall quite a bit about our time in 'captivity.' One of the things in particular was that I was alone on the craft, separated from Mona and Elaine. In fact, we were all separated from each other. At no time were two of us together.

"It was very hot," Louise continued. "They kept my face covered most of the time. But at one point I begged so hard, crying that I wanted to see, that they removed whatever they had over my face, and I did see. I guess they were humanoid, that's the only way I can describe them. They were about four and a half feet tall. Their hands were very different from ours, like a wingtip with jagged feathers instead of fingertips."

We might add that Louise is also the most daring of the three women. She often drives along Kentucky #78, sometimes alone and late at night, to prove to herself that there is nothing to fear.

NOT THE SAME PERSON

"I feel I have a knowledge now, a knowledge that's hard to explain. You know, I never really thought much about UFOs before. It's the kind of thing you have to experience before you can tell what it's like.

"I don't feel that, whatever they are," says Louise, "that they want to harm or destroy me. I believe there could be life on other planets, and if we can go to the moon, why can't they come here? I think that, eventually, everyone will see them. Maybe not in the same way we did, but at least everyone will be aware that they are here.

"Looking back, that was a beautiful thing. I'd like to study it. Maybe try to communicate. I crave knowledge about anything and everything. Before, things like that didn't bother me."

Elaine Thomas also feels that she is not the same person she had been before the abduction. The tall, large-featured woman told us that she is no longer interested in painting. She feels that her intuitions about things have become much stronger. "And, you know, sometimes I feel kind of like a little child. I just want to get out and play."

UFOlogists insist that this case is bona fide. They all believe the women are telling the truth. Their polygraph tests prove that they were not lying

This remains one of the most intriguing abduction cases we have yet investigated. The individuals involved were all very sincere and did not give off a hint of deception.

The case is possibly closed as I do believe all three ladies have passed away or have not been heard from in years.

Witnesses claim to have encountered living creatures that look almost exactly like traditional garden variety gnomes.

UFO VISITATIONS AND ROGUE OCCUPANTS

By Susan Demeter-St. Clair

PUBLISHER'S NOTE: Elsewhere in this book, Scott Corrales brings up encounters with dwarf-like beings and the craft they arrive in. Imminent researcher Jacques Vallee long ago pointed out in his trend setting *"Passport To Magonia"* that the UFO occupants of today may have been the elementals of yesterday. Susan Demeter Saint Clair has found her research going in this direction, bringing her into very strange avenues of discovery.

Author Susan Demeter-St. Clair

The author is a Canadian born writer, storyteller, painter, and costumed historical interpreter.

"The themes of my writing, research and art incorporate my lifelong interest in exceptional human experiences, nature, social history, mysteries, and cosmic magic," Susan proclaims and rightly so.

"Currently," she explains, "I am conducting a series of experiments based in part on the work of the late mathematician, Dr A.R.G Owen and psychotherapist Dr. Joel Whitton that will be the focus of my book on UFOs, social PSI, and Magic with the working title 'Conjuring UFOs.' I have co-collaborated with renowned Spanish artist Dora Garcia on a major contemporary art exhibition on the theme of exceptional human experience, anomalies, and marginalization, at the Harbourfront Centre, in Toronto Canada.

"A pagan of Celtic origin, I am exploring my central European roots and magical traditions in Bologna Italy. My studio's window faces a mountain peak that was in ancient times considered to be a holy place by both the pagans and early Christians. And it is here that the Otherworld Ones inspire my art. For further information, including my work on UFOs for the Canadian Department of National Defence, please check out my website. Or you can find me through social media: https://susanstclair.com

"In early July 2016 I created a personal blog post entitled "Fairies: A Canadian Research Project" and I asked my readers to share or submit personal encounters with me. The post was shared numerous times and I received a good number of responses, including ones from outside Canada. The following report in the witness' own words is one of those, and, despite being outside of Canada and having occurred approximately 20 years ago, I thought it definitely worthy of sharing with the PSICAN readership.

THE EXPERIENCER WRITES:

"Hello – Although I am American and this did not happen in Canada, it happened close to the New York State-Canadian border. I'll be happy to answer any questions you may have about my experience, which changed my life considerably. I still think of it all the time, almost daily.

I live in New York City, but in October of 1996 was visiting my mother and extended family, who then lived in Williamsville, which is outside of Buffalo, New York. It was the middle of October and my mother, my aunt and I had taken a drive out into the country to see the foliage. It was a very beautiful, cool, clear autumn day.

Towards late afternoon, we stopped in the small town of Great Valley to have dinner. My mother and aunt wanted to shop afterwards, and I wanted to take a walk in the countryside which surrounds the town. I walked to the edge of the town and then out into the rolling land around it – open fields in the center with woods on either side. I was in a relaxed, happy and contemplative mood.

I had been walking about ten minutes when, suddenly, I 'heard' a kind of sing-song 'chanting' in my mind, which 'sounded' like a multitude of very sweet, pleasing voices that were all speaking the same words almost simultaneously, in a kind of cascading aural waterfall effect. I had never experienced anything like this before at any time, and the words were, '*Don't you see us? We're all around you. We're all around you, don't you see us? Look—don't you see us?*' Stunned, I stopped walking and took the experience in. There was a smallish tree near me, but otherwise I saw only the open fields, woods at a distance to my right, and a two-lane road beyond on either side. I did look around me, certainly not expecting to see anything unusual, and saw nothing except the autumnal landscape I had come to see. I 'heard' the voices for about 90 seconds, and then the voices abruptly stopped.

I walked on for another 20 minutes, and then returned to the town, where I met my family. I said nothing to them about my experience, and reflected upon it on the long drive back to Williamsville.

The next morning I was preparing to take the afternoon train back to New York City, and, having packed, went for a walk on a familiar wooded path behind my mother's housing development, a path which ran adjacent to Ayer Road, a residential street of traditional old American homes. I had been walking for about 10 minutes when, suddenly, I 'heard' the voices again in exactly the same manner I had the day before.

The voices said, '*We're here—come this way, walk this way. We're here,*' and I looked to my left and saw another path through the woods that led to Ayer Road, which I could plainly see at the end of it. I turned left and walked down the path, still 'hearing' the voices, which, as I approached Ayer Road, came to a stop. Ayer is a fairly quiet street but does get some car traffic, and, somewhat stunned and dazed by this new experience, which seemed to validate my experience of the day before, I walked north past the homes using the lip of the road, as there were no sidewalks. Ayer Road curves slightly at various points, and rounding one of these curves, my eyes fell upon a grouping of four garden gnome statues on the front lawn of one of the homes. The statues were traditionally sculpted and done in what I would call a tasteful and 'realistic' manner; they weren't the kind of mass-produced cartoonish garden gnomes so prevalent today.

The four gnomes were in sitting positions and arranged so that they were facing one another. When I saw them, it was like receiving a blow to the chest, though I realized instantaneously that they were statues. But seeing them at that moment seemed to 'identify' the source of the voices to me in a manner which I can only call profound, as if the statues were what I was meant to see when I turned off the initial path and walked down the other towards Ayer.

Several hours later, on the Amtrak train, just as dusk was falling and the last of the day's light was disappearing from the surrounding farmland, I turned to look behind me at the setting sun, and just as I did so, I heard the voices again in the same manner I had before, and again, the voices were '*sing-songy,*' but less so than on the previous two occasions. The voices, which I have to paraphrase in this case, said, 'You're leaving us now, and the autumn door is closing. You will forget about us for a long, long while, but we have a date with you in the distant future. *You will meet us again,*' then, at that moment, the sun disappeared behind the horizon. I found this third experience exhilarating and emotionally powerful.

So I never 'saw' anything visually (other than the garden gnome statues), but I have, for some years now, come to the tentative conclusion that the 'voices' were 'fairy' voices. What struck me most, and still strikes me now, is that 'they' thought I would 'forget' them and the experience, which I certainly never have, nor have I ever come to think of it as unimportant.

I also want to state that, before the three experiences, which all took place within just over a 24 hour period, I did not believe in fairies or elves by any means. I had never had an experience of 'hearing' voices mentally, nor have I since. The experience did profoundly change the way I think about reality and my own life. Due to the nature of these experiences, they're very difficult to put accurately into words as I experienced them."

Researcher notes:

The photo at the beginning of this chapter was sent along with a couple of other examples of garden gnomes that the experiencer felt gave a good example of what they looked like. In our correspondence he indicated he was very confident they were actual statues nothing more, but was perhaps guided towards seeing them. Again I will share in the witness' own words:

In 2016, Susan created a blog called "Fairies: A Canadian Research Project." She asked her readers to share their encounters with elementals.

"I am absolutely sure the gnome figures I saw were stone statues. I was very close to them when I walked down the wooded path – they had been placed so that they were facing one another in a loose circular formation and there was a large red mushroom, also stone or cement, in the middle of their 'circle.' The gnomes were similar to those in the attached photos (though they were all in the same sitting position), which I would consider 'realistic' looking. These kind are rarely seen any more.

But I was walking down the path out of the woods towards Ayer Road, having just heard the 'voices' again, saying, 'Come this way.....we're here!' very enthusiastically, in the same sing-songy voice, and as I approached Ayer Road, certainly not expecting to see anything, I was astounded, stunned, to see the gnome statues grouped there. It took my breath away for a moment. For a moment, it was frightening, and I am not easily frightened.

They were large for garden gnome statues – about 2 feet or more – and beautifully constructed and painted. It was as if the statues were what I was meant to see to identify the 'voices.' But I'm sure they were statues.

T.S. Eliot talks about the 'objective correlative' – "the artistic and literary technique of representing or evoking a particular emotion by means of symbols that objectify that emotion and are associated with it," and that's what I think the statues were and were intended to be or represent. That they were only stone statues took nothing away from the experience for me, ultimately, because I was led out of the woods and down that particular path by the 'voices' – and right to where those statues were. Today, of course, I would have taken out my iPhone and taken a photo of them, to retain a record."

The voice of Susan Demeter St. Clair resumes here:

I have had several strange encounters of my own since I was a child, and I have been researching primarily UFOs since 1997. One of the reasons I had decided to take on this fairy project is that I am very much in agreement with Dr Jacques Vallee's ideas that were expressed in "***Passport To Magonia***" and within his later works. There is an undeniable connection or parallel between modern UFO lore and experience and faery encounters spanning centuries, if not farther. In my queries of the witness I asked if he had any prior encounters or events with what he believed may be paranormal and he shared with me the following UFO encounter:

"I did have one other paranormal experience, which was, in its own way, almost equally profound. It took place on the early morning of June 23rd, 1994, just after 1:00 AM.

I had been sitting up watching the NBA finals with my roommate (John*), in which the New York Knicks were playing the Houston Rockets. I was very excited about the game and very disappointed when the Knicks lost. John had gone to bed, and I was reading in my room. At the time, I had lost my job and often stayed up late reading, but at no point had I been asleep.

Our apartment was a 'penthouse' apartment (7th floor) in an old brownstone in Williamsburg, Brooklyn, quite close to the East River, so that we had a spectacular view of the then-World Trade Center buildings in Manhattan.

I got out of bed to get a drink from the refrigerator, and as I was standing in the kitchen in the dark, I remembered there was supposed to be a moon that night, and looked out the large, tall kitchen window, which faced west, to see if I could see it.

Just as I did, a huge, bright greenish figure, shaped like a 'minnow' or an elongated teardrop turned sideways with the larger end forward, 'flew' into view in the open air and space over Williamsburg.

I was not a believer in 'unidentified flying objects' of any kind; my initial reaction was, 'The nerve of that thing, to be flying right over the rooftops of houses and buildings!' Below on the corner there was an Orthodox Jewish School, and I could see two school buses parked outside, so it gave me a good comparison of its size – it was about the size of the two standard school buses placed back to back.

It flew with what I call a 'trundling' motion – it flew forward, hovering at some points, but moved slightly up and down as it did so, as if shaking. It flew into my range of vision, but at an upward angle, then 'flew' sideways and backwards so that it moved between two very tall housing projects, still 'trundling,' and then, in an incredible burst of speed, zoomed straight out of sight into the clouds over the World Trade Center, where, as it entered the cloud bank, the clouds briefly turned green with its light. And then it was gone.

I woke up John, I called the police to report it and ask if anyone else had. The next night, I walked down to the waterfront bars along the East River on the Williamsburg side to see if any of the 'hipsters' who drank there had seen or reported it. No one else had reported it, and though the police were polite, they really didn't have much of a response. Afterward, I told my friends, my family, everyone.

It did not look like 'a craft from another planet' or any kind of craft at all. It looked like a clear blown-glass teardrop, as I said, with bright green smoke or liquid swirling inside it, almost the color of antifreeze. There were no other lights on it, no 'doors' or panels or windows. Nothing at all to make it look like a 'craft.' I know this sounds eccentric, but it almost looked like a bright green 'cartoon,' or 'animated' image, superimposed over 'reality,' like the cartoon characters in 'Who Framed Roger Rabbit?'

Nothing about it physically suggested it was 'manned' or created by man – though it certainly behaved like it was or was guided by intelligence. I grew up along a canal system in North Miami Beach, Florida, and it reminded me of a scene I had witnessed hundreds of times as a teenager: a little fish swimming briefly into view along the shallow waters of the shore and then quickly darting out of sight again.

The thing that struck me, and strikes me still, is how low over the city it was flying. I was on the 7th floor, so it was flying at, I would say, about a 9th or 10th floor level. When it moved backward and sideways between the two housing projects, there were many floors of those buildings above it. So if someone living in one had been awake like I was, they would have seen it at eye level.

Subsequently, I have read a lot about 'green fireballs' seen throughout the 20th and 21st centuries in America and elsewhere, and I wonder if what I saw was what those people also reported, though what I experienced looked nothing like a meteor, a rocket, or anything else. It moved carefully and decisively, as if alive or intelligently guided. But I do not believe it was an 'alien craft,' and today do not believe in the 'alien spacecraft' explanation for unidentified flying objects."

* The name has been changed to John in order to protect privacy

More notes: It is interesting to note that the auditory fairy experience followed after a seemingly unrelated visual UFO event. In further correspondence, he has told me that, while profound, even life-altering, these experiences were in no way perceived as negative. He also shares the following:

"I want to share with you that, prior to the experience with the 'unidentified flying object,' I had no belief in UFOs as such or almost any other kind of paranormal subject. I was very much an 'earthy realist' and lover of hard science. At most, I enjoyed reading about various forms of American and world folklore, but the folklore I had read had never touched on UFOs.

"As a boy, I did love monster and science fiction films, and faithfully read *'Famous Monsters of Filmland'* magazine every month, as well as Ray Bradbury, Edgar Rice Burroughs, Ian Fleming and H.P. Lovecraft, but never confused those forms of entertainment with reality, and gave all of that up in my late teens regardless."

My personal thanks goes out to the witness for sharing these extraordinary experiences and other information with me. I greatly appreciate and value the courage and trust it takes to do so. If you have had a similar encounter in Canada please email me at sue@psican.org

Your privacy will be protected.

Perhaps we have not been able to find the answers about UFOs because we haven't been asking the right questions. In fact, our brains may be unable to even conceive of the questions that are needed to understand the UFO mystery. We view our world, our reality, as a mirror image of ourselves . . . and why not? We have no other references other than our own experiences. Yet we expect to find answers to something that may be far beyond human conception. We are looking at UFOs from the cracked mirror of human experience and conditioning, growing frustrated when no answers are forthcoming, yet continuously tantalized by the brass ring that seems to be forever just out of reach.

SUGGESTED READING

Six-book children's series entitled "***Haunted or Hoax***." The books present ghost stories and encourage the reader to use their reasoning and critical thinking skills to decide if they are true or not. The books are intended for Grades 4-5, Ages 9-10. Published by Crabtree Publishing. Expert review, including fact checking, and proof reading. Completed January 2018.

LOOKING AT UFOS THROUGH A CRACKED MIRROR

MR. UFO'S SECRET FILES ON YOUTUBE

www.youtube.com/watch?v=RoqcmjAbors&t=101s

At the museum with creator and curator, Italian scholar Morena Poltronieri at Museo dei Tarocchi/Museum of Tarot.

Some examinations are done for the purpose of curing humans of all sorts of diseases and ailments.

FRIENDS IN HIGH PLACES - STRANGEST OF THE STRANGE

By Preston Dennett

PUBLISHER'S NOTE: I can say with utmost certainly that Preston never let me down. While editing *"UFO Universe"* I knew I could depend upon this top notch west coast researcher to supply us with some of the best thought out and researched material around. He has always had a knack for digging around and finding some of the most appropriate material. And while Preston has written over a dozen books, I think of him as the go to man for USO reports as well as those involving cases of UFO healings. In this presentation, with material adapted from his "Healing Powers of UFOs," and "UFO Healings," we balance out the primarily negative aspects of those Ultra-terrestrial foes with a twist of a much more positive nature, indicating that at least some UFOs are here to help us along, even on a personal, individual, basis.

Preston Dennett began investigating UFOs and the paranormal in 1986, when he discovered that his family, friends and co-workers were having dramatic unexplained encounters. Since then, he has interviewed hundreds of witnesses and investigated a wide variety of paranormal phenomena. He is a field investigator for the Mutual UFO Network (MUFON), a ghost hunter, a paranormal researcher, and the author of 24 books and more than 100 articles on UFOs and the paranormal. His articles have appeared in numerous magazines, including *Fate, Atlantis Rising*, MUFON *UFO Journal, Nexus, Paranormal Magazine, UFO Magazine, Mysteries Magazine, Ufologist* and others. His writing has been translated into several different languages including German, French, Portuguese, Russian, and Icelandic. He has appeared on numerous radio and television programs, including *Midnight in the Desert with Art Bell, Coast-to-Coast* and also the History Channel's *Deep Sea UFOs* and *UFO Hunters*. His research has been presented in the *LA Times,* the *LA Daily News,* the *Dallas Morning News* and other newspapers. He has taught classes on various paranormal subjects and lectures across the United States. He currently resides in southern California.

www.prestondennett.weebly.com

Illustrations for this chapter by Christine Kesara Dennett (www.kesara.org) - Kesara grew up and pursued a formal artistic education. Early on, she displayed an unusual ability to perform "psychic drawings". She discovered she could intuitively see and illustrate unseen or future events.

• • • • • • • • • •

Preston continues to bring forth incredible stories involving the healing powers of UFOs.

Why are ETs here? Many people believe they have been healed, helped, rescued or saved from tragedy by ETs. This help comes in a surprising variety of forms. My book, *"The Healing Power of UFOs,"* documents more than 300 cases of this kind. What follows is a collection of fifteen of the strangest and most incredible cases. These cases are the strangest of the strange.

INCREDIBLE ALIEN ENCOUNTERS

UFOS RESCUE SOVIET SOLDIER

In 1987, an anonymous Soviet soldier was fighting with local partisans in Afghanistan, when he lost his machine gun and became severely wounded, most severely on his leg. Rather than surrender to the enemy and risk possible torture from the "Mujahideen," he decided to commit suicide with a grenade.

At that moment he saw a shiny disc-shaped object hover above him. It came lower and projected a beam of light, pulling him inside the craft.

The soldier found himself inside a bright circular room. He was no longer in any pain. Strange "people" appeared and communicated with him telepathically. They placed the soldier on a table surrounded by medical devices. Using these devices, they showed images of his organs on large screens above him.

"We can cure all your wounds," said one of the aliens, "but we cannot save your leg, so we must amputate your leg."

The soldier asked them why, with all their advanced technology, they couldn't save his leg. They told him it was beyond their capabilities, and that if they did not amputate, he would not survive. The soldier blacked out.

When he awoke, he was still in the battlefield. When a medical team arrived, they were shocked to find the soldier's leg not only amputated, but almost completely healed. It appeared to them that surgery to amputate the leg must have occurred a year earlier.

The soldier said that he had been taken and healed by extraterrestrials. The medical team accused him of delirium and transported him by helicopter to a field hospital. Senior doctors there were amazed and asked the soldier what happened. The soldier repeated his story and was again not believed. Still, the doctors remained baffled. The soldier was discharged. He told his story to a friend, who reported it to investigators, Natalia and Leonid Tereteyev.

HEALING OF A SHARK BITE

In January 1991, store owner, Amador Piazza Velez saw a UFO hovering over a mountain in Las Cuchara in Ponce, Puerto Rico. Unknown to Velez, there was another witness. Jose Maria Fernandez Martinez (a fisherman and the father of seven children) also saw the UFO earlier the same week as Velez. When the object remained in place for more than ten minutes, Fernandez grabbed his camera and tried to record it. At that moment, his camera malfunctioned.

Following the incident, something very strange happened. Some days earlier Fernandez had been bitten by a shark. His family and those around him saw Fernandez's wound on his lower leg, which was severe enough that everyone knew it would take a long time to heal. The morning after trying to film the UFO, Fernandez woke up to find his leg and foot healed, showing only a scar on his heel. "I cannot tell that the beings who came in the ship cured me," says Fernandez, "but something strange happened to me because my wound closed since that night."

On the same evening, Fernandez's wife, Gloria Santiago saw strange lights coming up out of the water.

FOUR PEOPLE HEALED OF COLDS

On the afternoon of July 12, 1975, four friends (Richard, Pat, Nancy and Ross), were having lunch in a crowded coffee bar in Dunedin, New Zealand. The weather was cold and damp, and all of them were suffering from various degrees of the flu. One of them suffered from a migraine headache. There were, they estimated, about eighty people sitting at various tables around them.

As they ate together, something very strange happened. Time stopped. Everyone around them became perfectly still and unmoving, however, the four friends could still move. Richard was struck by the sight of unmoving steam above the espresso machine, and by the sight of a waitress frozen in place as she bent over an oven pulling out hotcakes.

Staring around in shock, the four of them saw a strange figure appear at the top of the stairs on the opposite side of the room, which was the only public entrance and exit to the restaurant. He appeared to be a young man about six feet tall, slender, with black wavy hair, and olive skin. He was tastefully dressed in normal clothes and seemed to have a whitish aura of light glowing around him. They watched him float down the staircase, levitate across the room to the end of the line, where customers waited for their food.

The moment the man got into the line, time began to flow normally again. The four friends watched as the people around them moved normally without any indication or awareness that something strange had just happened.

The four friends watched in amazement as the man ordered a glass of juice, sat at a nearby table, then acknowledged their attention with a smile.

The group decided to confront the man. Rather than do it at the man's table, which was difficult to access from where they were, they left the restaurant and waited by the exit for him to come out.

When he failed to appear, Richard ventured back inside only to find that he was gone. Even more surprising, the group discovered that their various flu-like symptoms, and a migraine headache, were gone.

Six weeks later, the same group of friends spotted the man at the same restaurant. He appeared at the entrance, walked lightly (and unnoticed by others) down the stairs, ordered another glass of juice, sat at a table and again smiled back at them. He was dressed the same as before, only now, his aura appeared more green than white.

This time the group was determined to confront him. When they tried, they found themselves unable to move. As if against their will, they found themselves getting up and leaving. Pat reports that she tried desperately to turn around but was unable to do so. When she finally could, she returned back shortly later, but the strange man was gone.

CURED OF SPIDER VEINS

On December 29, 1999, Natalie (pseudonym) was driving down 13th Street in Denver, Colorado on her way home, when she saw a strange-looking object hovering very low in the sky ahead of her. It was rock-still, with two blue lights on either side, and a red light in the center. It couldn't be a plane, because the lights were too still. It must be a helicopter, she thought. Then she drove under it, and changed her mind.

Some witnesses maintain the aliens have a tremendous glowing aura surrounding them.

"As I passed under the object, I saw a grayish-black, boomerang-shaped object. My mouth hung open, and I said aloud to myself, 'What in the #@*!% is that?'"

She wanted to slam on the brakes and jump out of her car, but seeing other vehicles behind her, she turned off at the next street, pulled over and got out. Only thirty seconds had passed, but the object was now gone. She pulled a U-turn and kept looking. She turned around a third time, but the object was nowhere to be found.

Convinced she had seen a genuine UFO, she reported her sighting to NUFORC and to a MUFON investigator. Not long after the sighting, Natalie began to exhibit a number of remarkable medical symptoms. Says Natalie, "About two months after my encounter, all of the moles on my body began to fade, then to completely disappear. To date, five moles have completely disappeared and nine more are in different states of fading. About five months after the event occurred, all of the hair on my arms and legs began to change to light blonde."

Normally Natalie had brown hair. She thought perhaps she was turning prematurely gray, but she's only twenty-nine years old. The hair changed color from the root upward, turning from brown, to reddish to blond over a period of about five days. The hair also became much finer.

Natalie had suffered from spider veins in her legs for several years. "About two months ago," she says, "my spider veins in my legs began to fade. Now one that I have had for about five years is completely gone, and another is fading rapidly."

Then came the "dreams." Says Natalie, "Since this has occurred, I have had 'dreams' almost nightly of entities who talk to me and claim to be an intelligent species from somewhere else. They keep trying to give me strange information I don't understand. I have woken up a few times and caught myself uttering some language that I have never heard before. But I have ruled out speaking in tongues, because this 'language' seems to have structure and form."

Natalie has also noticed other changes. "Throughout the day I have feelings of hot and cold in different parts of my body. I get pulsating feelings on the bottom of my feet and up my legs and down my arms, and on the palms of my hands. Sometimes this pulsating becomes so intense, it is painful. I have also felt this heat/pulsating feeling right below my eyes, between my eyes, and in the front of my brain. I am very upset and confused as to what is going on with me."

Natalie is hoping to work with more investigators to deal with the after-effects of her encounter.

HEALED OF KIDNEY FAILURE

It was July 2006, and Ms. E.A. Sabean (from Canada) was having a very bad year. Her father had just passed away, and now she was feeling very sick herself. She was exhausted and sad. Then her feet started to swell. As the weeks passed, her feet remained swollen, and the inflammation spread up her legs and her lower back. She felt nauseous, weak and had stopped eating, drinking and was unable to urinate. She went to the doctor and was diagnosed with hypertension and chronic renal failure. Her kidneys were failing, causing edema and toxins to spread throughout her body.

Her doctor gave her two options, dialysis or kidney transplant. Sabean was devastated. Neither option was good. The doctor said she had to be immediately hospitalized. By this point, Sabean also had a fever.

Still, she refused. She wanted to go home and pray first, which she did. She called up everyone in her family and asked them to pray for her. She emailed her friends, told her employer. As she lay in bed that evening, she found herself surrounded by "brown creatures with hooded robes on."

Sabean was amazed at what happened next. "...[The] strange creatures massaged my kidneys all night, and by Saturday morning, my kidneys were working again."

Says Sabean, "Even before I felt totally safe that I was alone in my room, I had to go use the bathroom. This was a strange feeling since I had been unable to use the bathroom for days. I was amazed that my kidneys were apparently working again...When I went back to the hospital on Tuesday for another blood test, I was feeling much better...the tests showed that my kidneys were indeed working now and my doctor was amazed. When I asked him how this was possible when he [already] told me that it was impossible for kidney function to be restored, he just shook his head and said it was possibly a misdiagnosis on his part. I didn't tell him about the creatures. I didn't tell anybody for a long time...My sisters and friends were amazed at my recovery. And I simply told them that the angels came in the night and healed me. I left it at that. I didn't want to tell them the scary details, and at that time I was so frustrated if people didn't believe me."

While the beings cured her renal failure, Sabean still feels some sensitivity there. Nevertheless, she is thankful. "I decided these creatures must be angels or something.

If not, then why—on a night that every person was praying for me—did they show up? They did not harm me. In fact, they healed me, apparently. They were obviously not of this dimension. And I heard them speak in a manner that was obviously not of this Earth...Regardless, I was left distressed and traumatized by the events of that night, although always thankful that my kidney function had been restored."

Sabean's UFO healing wasn't over yet. One year later, she had what appears to be a checkup. "I dreamed I was in this circular white room that was a strange type of medical examination room." She sat on a stool, while an unseen doctor held a tool against her kidneys. In front of her Sabean could see a full-color, three-dimensional, living model of her kidney, displayed on a table in front of her. "I was amazed at this technology...then I saw my liver...It was all black. The doctor told me this is what was happening to my liver from drinking diet coke, and I needed to quit drinking it because it was damaging my stomach and liver."

ALIEN PREVENTS HEART ATTACK

In the middle of the night on June 9, 2013, Steven (pseudonym) of Manchester, New Jersey, suddenly woke up. This wasn't unusual, as he was a light sleeper and often woke up in the middle of the night. On this particular occasion, however, he was startled to see a tall, thin, glowing white humanoid. "With no sound, the being reached into my left chest area," Steven says. "I didn't feel any pain, pressure or discomfort. That lasted about five minutes. The being removed its hand from my left chest and stood there for about two minutes and then vanished."

Steven was baffled and amazed. He never saw a UFO, just the one humanoid. He felt physically fine, and wondered why the being had behaved the way it did. He had no chest pains, but "a strong intuitive urge" overwhelmed him; he had to visit a cardiologist. A few months following the experience, he finally went and got an EKG and stress test. The doctors told him that his health condition was dire and he was lucky to still be alive. He had arrived at the hospital just in time. They told him that he had been born with a bicuspid aorta valve; it should have been tricuspid. In addition, he was suffering from severe congestive heart failure. "So," says Steven, "I was rushed to the hospital to prep me for a triple bypass and a replacement aorta valve."

The doctors joked that Steven was getting a two-for-one operation, a bypass and a valve replacement. "My take and feelings on this incident," Steven says, "was the white, light being made temporary repairs for me to not have a heart attack or stroke ahead of time...It was a miracle...The white, light being made adjustments to give me the time and the strong intuition to get into a hospital to save my life."

GRAYS STOP MAN FROM COMMITTING SUICIDE

In 1992, John (pseudonym) was living in southern California and battling suicidal depression. On April 10 of that year, he made a fateful decision. "I drove to a location in the mountains to commit suicide."

Around noon, John found an isolated area outside of Lake Isabella. "When I got there, I got out of the vehicle and walked around it, looking around my surroundings to make sure nobody was watching...After about fifteen minutes of making peace with it and saying goodbye, I was now ready."

John held a 357 magnum, loaded, with the trigger pulled back and ready to fire. "I was no more than ten seconds from pulling the trigger," John writes. "I noticed something moving out of the corner of my eye."

John became upset because he thought people were watching. He turned his head and saw two figures. "Both stood facing me," writes John, "one motionless and the other one leaning...leaning just enough into my peripheral vision that I would see them. They were exactly like the small grays you see, like in the Roswell accident."

John could barely believe his eyes. "I saw them, twenty feet away from me. I even had a loaded gun and could've shot at them and probably hit them...[but] when I noticed that I was not alone, it simply voided the suicide, and I left, which I thank them for really."

As John drove away, he realized it was now 11:30 p.m., and there was a full moon. It was as if the moment the ETs appeared, darkness had already fallen. He had seen them only in the nighttime, which meant that there were about ten hours which he could not remember.

While the experience prevented him from committing suicide, it had other repercussions. "It took years for me to actually accept what I saw with my own eyes."

Now, however, John has accepted what he saw. "There is no doubt whatsoever, 100 percent absolutely positive beyond any doubt that I saw them, twenty feet away from me."

UPGRADED!

Martin (pseudonym) has a form of autism called Asperger's Syndrome. He grew up in South Dakota and as a result of his condition, was given heavy cocktails of prescription drugs. By age sixteen, he was still under five feet tall, suffering from depression, and in a drug haze. Believing the drugs were stunting his growth, he decided to go cold turkey, and he took himself off the Ritalin, the Paxil, the Abilify and the Zoloft. That year, he grew to six feet two inches in height, and gained 120 pounds. His Asperger symptoms and depression became much more manageable and "hardly noticeable."

There were other beneficial effects. "My creative levels jumped through the roof. I was suddenly able to draw, paint, work with ceramic. I could look at patterns and discern things that nobody else could see was there. My intelligence level jumped from near genius to well above."

What happened to cause this sudden boost? Martin wonders if it was more than just getting off prescription drugs. The reason was, Martin thinks, a secret that he's kept from almost everyone. "I have had close encounters of the fourth kind, for many years, several times a year...For nearly as long as I can remember--the first instance being at the age of four—I will have a visit from what I refer to as a gentleman, three to five times a year, every three months or so, sometimes with an extra one thrown in. I wake up in the middle of the night in a panic for no apparent reason, very similar to what some might call night terrors--instantly, fully awake, terrified, panicking, unable to move...The only thing I can control are my eyes and my breathing. And near me, maybe two or three feet away, is a small gray."

Martin describes the "gentleman" in familiar terms: "Small, smooth grey skin, almond-shaped, jet-black eyes, tiny nostrils, thin-lipped mouthed, usually hairless. They scare the daylight out of me."

He has no memories of being poked, prodded, anally probed or implanted. The figure just stands there and observes him. "He is older, I can tell that much, how, I'm not sure. He doesn't do much. He observes me, passes a hand over me now and then, but he never touches. He doesn't poke or prod or anything of the sort. He simply observes. And occasionally he will wave a hand about in the air, almost as though touching a computer screen...My waking state goes from petrification to irritation. There is no threat except for the fact that I am restricted."

Martin has tried to send the being thoughts. When he does, the being "usually stops and stares, cocks his head to the side and makes another note." Martin isn't sure if the being understands him, but occasionally Martin picks up "images" and "snippets" of the alien's thoughts and emotions. He believes the ET has no desire for world domination and is merely curious.

"...I personally think that they may have injected nothing more than a few cells into my body that they take readings, and they can read when they are in close proximity to me. It would certainly explain why they run their hands through the air above me, reading something magnetic perhaps."

When they first appeared at age four, there were multiple grays. After that, it was always just one. It would appear once or twice a year. However, at age sixteen, when he took himself off the prescription drugs, the visitations increased to three, four or five times a year. Usually, the gray would remain for a half hour, maybe an hour. Now, when it arrived, it stayed for three or four hours at a time.

It was then that Martin began to notice that there were some very unusual things about him physiologically. First, he has two unexplained scars on his abdomen, which have been there as long as he can remember. Even more strange, however, is his unusually hardy physical constitution. "I have never broken a bone in a serious way, even though I have been in a serious accident--my knuckles a few times in a fight [and] my knee cap in what should have been a fatal ninety-MPH accident while not wearing a seat belt. My wounds heal at a rate about twice as fast as predicted by professionals...I hardly ever get sick. Family members around me will be sick for three weeks at a time, while I will be sick for two to three days with the same symptoms."

Not all Ultra-terrestrials are land based. Some of them make their homes in the sea.

Are the ETs responsible for what he calls his "medical oddities?" Martin believes they might be. "I'm convinced there's a connection between the increase in visits and length and my unusual physiology, that for some reason or another, they took an interest in keeping me alive for observation."

Martin isn't sure why he was chosen to be studied by extraterrestrials, but he has his theories. "Perhaps they are interested in autistic individuals; perhaps Asperger's individuals specifically. I've always been a little off, a little different...I just wish they'd talk to me instead of restraining me. I hope one day that my curiosity to converse with them will overpower the fear I have while they are in my presence..."

On February 25, 2015, Martin's wish came true. He was dozing in bed when he became fully awake, suddenly consumed with a petrifying fear of an approaching presence. His bedroom door opened, and in walked a gray-type ET unlike any he had seen before. "He was tall," Martin explains, "above eight feet. He had to stoop to avoid hitting the ceiling with his head. His body was thin, very thin...his face was comparable to the beings which I have seen before, but it was ancient beyond anything I can describe—withered and hard, but with an emotion I can only describe as softness in the corner of his massive, black eyes."

A long telepathic conversation followed. The being said his name was Prou (pronounced Prow), and that he was pleased to meet Martin. Says Martin, "I, in a moment of incredulity, extended my hand and he shook it with his. It felt strange, wooden in texture, but warm and soft. It enveloped my entire hand, and he held it for a moment before telling me it brought him joy to experience friendship with someone he had studied closely for so many years."

Strange images filled Martin's mind. "Flashes of colors, scenes from distant worlds I can't describe in any way other than fantastical, soaring skyscrapers, flashes of movement, bizarre creatures with too many eyes and limbs that moved like fluid, glass domes and red and gold skies over green oceans."

Further conversations followed. "He apologized for the many years of fright and assured me there was no reason to be afraid. He told me there was a purpose behind their visits, and the visits of millions of other people around the world have, but are completely unaware of."

What is the purpose of their visits? According to Martin, "They harvest memories. They observe our world, our culture and our society through our eyes...In harvesting this information; they have been able to greatly advance their own culture. His explanation was that humanity and humans as individuals are vastly more creative than their own. They are a logical people, and as such, have limitations. Humans, he said, are basically insane, and as a result, think so far out of the box that we end up inventing things far beyond our time. And we are so diverse that we devote massive amounts of time to thousands of projects...They seek out unique individuals, those with genius intellect, the mentally unstable but still functional, the creative thinkers, and they observe their minds for the spark of motivation. They take our mundane, day-to-day ideas and they create each and every one of them. If you are one of their subjects, every crappy daydream invention you've come up with, they have made it, utilized it, improved it, tested it, and incorporated it into their lives."

The being told Martin that he was surprised that Martin was able to consciously recall the visitations, and that the vast majority of people they visit have no memory of it, not because of them, but because of the human mind's tendency to repress memories. "The ETs have no hand in making us forget," says Martin. "Our mind does not want to remember, so it does not. My accurate memories of visits and contemplation of them makes me very unique in their books, it would seem."

He told Martin many other things, that the human race is unique in how it has technologically progressed so quickly, that many other races fear our aggression, which is delaying the progress of our society, that their civilization is nearly 20,000 years old and that we may be related to their ancestors, that they implant humans with a biological-type implant which records all the information they need from us and much more.

Says Martin, "That's my crazy tale. Think of it what you will."

PROTECTED FROM THE STORM

On the east coast of the Yucatan Peninsula is a small Mayan village outside Tulum. In 2004, the village was being battered by hurricane force winds and rain. A resident of the village, Geraldo and his family, were worried about the village being flooded and like many others, were preparing to evacuate. At this point, a brilliant light appeared and the rain stopped. "Overhead, just at treetop level," says Geraldo, "there was a UFO. It was round, and it lit up the whole village. The rain stopped. The wind stopped. The UFO was like an umbrella. It was protecting us. For several hours the UFO stayed over our village. When the wind and rains lessened, it moved on."

Geraldo says that everyone in the village saw the craft and a few reported abductions. Geraldo asked the Mayan Elders what they believed the explanation was. "They said the Sky Gods came back to protect us," says Geraldo. "They said our village survived because it was a reminder of the injustice visited upon the Maya people by the Mexican government."

UFO PREVENTS AUTOMOBILE ACCIDENT

"In 1977/1978," writes the anonymous witness, "I was living in Forest Hill, Texas...I was about twenty-one years old and had BS'd my way into a job in which I had no skills. One skill I needed was typing so I had immediately enrolled in a night typing course which was in Fort Worth, Texas. I was traveling home on I-20 east. There was not much traffic that time of night. In fact, I do not remember any traffic at all, which now seems rather strange to me. All of a sudden, there was a huge light -- the brightest light I have ever seen before or since...I slowed down to see what it was but could only see the light. I then realized what the light was showing me. There was a mattress in the lane ahead of me that I would never have seen, which would have caused me to have an accident.

"I pulled to the side of the road," the witness says, "forgetting about the mattress, and rolled down the window. My first thought was that it was a helicopter, but there was absolutely no sound. When I say no sound, I mean no sound—as in any normal sounds of night or traffic, much less a helicopter sound. I wasn't scared. As a matter of fact, I felt a feeling of peace like I have never felt. All of a sudden, the light was gone."

Some witnesses' lives have been saved by their close encounter with a UFO.

The witness went home and called nearby Carswell AFB, who denied any knowledge of unknown aircraft, but still seemed interested and questioned the witness about the sighting.

The witness finally reported the sighting to MUFON, after viewing a television program about UFOs. The witness writes, "What I experienced back then was the most awesome and peaceful event that anyone could experience. I do not know what it was, but I do know that it was real, very real. Whatever or whoever it was saved me from what could have been a horrible accident. It could not have been something from this Earth."

UFO RESCUES STRANDED MOTORISTS

In the fall of 1959, three friends (all teenagers) left their homes in Hollywood, California and ended up in Goldfield, south of Tonopah, Nevada. One of the witnesses, fourteen-year-old Bradley (not his real name) had also brought along his girlfriend.

Bradley writes that they had pulled off the highway and their pickup became stuck in the sand. Attempts to extricate themselves only ended up burying the truck more deeply, until it was buried up to its hubcaps. The teenagers spent the next few hours trying to dig themselves out, but the sand was too deep. They decided that one of them would have to walk out in the morning and they resigned themselves to spending the night in the desert.

The four of them sat in the truck star-gazing and talking when the conversation eventually turned to flying saucers. Bradley's girlfriend said, "Let's see if we can contact a saucer to help us."

Only half-serious and not expecting anything to happen, Bradley and his girlfriend "started trying to telepathically contact a saucer."

Writes Bradley, "Not long afterward we all saw a light approaching. I don't know the direction it came from. It looked just like a bright star, except it was moving toward us. It got much brighter as it drew overhead...At that moment we felt the truck move. It rose straight up in the air about a foot or two off the ground, floated to the middle of the road, and gently set down. Then the light moved back in the direction it came from and blinked out."

At the time, Bradley recalls that they all screamed in fear and left the area. However, forty years later he was able to contact his former girlfriend. Writes Bradley, "The first thing she said was, 'What do you remember about that night?' We agreed on all the details except I remembered screaming and she remembered laughing."

While the case does admittedly have fantastic features, the witnesses have sought no publicity and insisted upon remaining anonymous. Nor did they report the sighting until many years later.

ET EMPLOYMENT AGENCY

In his book, *"Abducted by Aliens,"* Chuck Weiss describes his lifelong contact with gray ETs, including numerous healings. While he has had many interactions with the grays, one particular incident stands out above the others.

At the time, Weiss had been unemployed for a prolonged period. One evening, he had one of his alien "dreams." Writes Weiss, "I was given a sheet of paper by my supervising Gray and told to look at it very carefully."

As usual, Weiss felt complete deference to the gray and believed that his cooperation with the ET was extremely important. He studied the paper carefully. It showed columns of letters grouped together, along with slashes. "It didn't make any sense to me," says Weiss, "and that's where the dream ended."

A few months later, Weiss's employment agency sent him to a company that specialized in copying and dubbing radio and television commercials. Weiss was given the job of reviewer. His duties were to review work orders to make sure they were coded correctly.

"After a round of introductions in my new office, I was shown the paperwork that I was expected to proofread. My jaw dropped to the floor when I saw a column of station call letters running down the left side of the paper...It was exactly what I had been shown months earlier by my supervising Gray!"

Weiss was shocked. Had the grays set up this job opportunity for him? Writes Weiss, "It was suddenly obvious to me that it had been determined long before I went to work there that I would find employment at that particular company and in that particular office of the company. I was blown away. Aside from a couple of spontaneous healings that I couldn't be sure weren't to just keep their rat running the maze, this was my first real indication that, for whatever reason, I was somehow special to them. I had never heard before of the ETs going out of their way to find a job for an experiencer, nor have I since. After five months of working at the company as a temp, I was made a permanent hire with vacations and full benefits."

ALIENS LEAD MAN TO GOLD

Late one evening in July 1939, gold prospector Joao Lucindo was camping in an isolated area near Serra Do Gordo, Brazil when he was woken up by a loud whistling sound. Lucindo grabbed a lantern and a rifle and went to investigate. He found a light in the forest where he saw two tall humanoid figures almost six feet in height, each wearing metallic body-suits.

The men told Lucindo to look up. When he did, he saw a large metallic disc-shaped object. Suddenly the two men grabbed him and all of them went up into the craft. Inside, Lucindo was examined and told that his experience would benefit his family.

The night after being released, Lucindo had a strange dream during which the humanoids he had seen told him precisely where to dig for gold in the mountains. He eventually went to prospect where the humanoids had instructed. At this location, he found a rich vein of gold, which improved his family fortunes.

Lucindo died in 1970, shortly after sharing his experience with Brazilian UFO researcher, Jackson Luiz Camargo.

REPTILIAN SAVES MAN FROM DROWNING

In January of 1977, twenty-year-old Jose Alvarez was hiking in the high basin area of Amazonia, east of Lima, Peru. He was seeking a water source, when he fell into a marsh and became trapped. "In spite of my efforts," he said, "I could not get out of it, and I had lost all hope to survive when, suddenly, four small beings appeared...They were less than one meter tall, their bodies covered with green scales, and their hands had three fingers with claw. Uttering growls and gesticulating, they held branches to me that allowed me to pull myself back on firm ground."

Once freed from the swamp by the strange creatures, Alvarez fainted. When he woke up, the beings were gone.

UFO PREVENTS RAPE

One evening in August 1986, Carolyn (pseudonym) found herself in a dangerous situation. She was at the Waweep Campground near Page, walking along the shore of Lake Powell, Arizona. She was alone when, without warning, a bald-headed man attacked and tried to rape her. He forcefully threw Carolyn down so that she was half-in and half-out of the lake. Then he climbed on top of her and pinned her to the ground. Looking up, Carolyn saw a pair of what she first thought were shooting stars. One disappeared, but the other suddenly dropped down and "seemed to land at the end of the lake."

Carolyn assumed at first that it must be an airplane, but then suddenly it moved toward them. At the same time, the winds began to pick up. The "plane" now took on the appearance of a "big ball of fog." It approached closer and the wind became so strong it was lifting up small stones which struck both of them.

At this point, Carolyn's attacker stood up and looked at the object. He became frightened and ran away, yelling to Carolyn, "We better get out of here!"

Says Carolyn, "I looked at him and the ball of fog and decided I would rather go with the ball of fog. So I started walking out into the water toward the ball of fog. Then it just vanished. The water and wind calmed down and it was quiet again. I did not know what to make of this. I have not heard of many reports like this, but it seemed like it made a special trip down from the sky just to rescue me from this man."

Carolyn reported her account to NUFORC in the hopes of finding more information about her experience.

INCREDIBLE ALIEN ENCOUNTERS

These types of UFO rescue cases are not well-known, even within the UFO community. And yet, as can be seen, many different types of rescues have occurred. Once again, we are left with the question, why are ETs saving people? What does this say about their relationship to us, and their agenda on our planet? Could it be that some aliens are altruistic? As my book, The Healing Power of UFOs shows, one of the primary ET agendas is to help humanity in a number of startling ways.

SUGGESTED READING

SCHOOL YARD UFO ENCOUNTERS

UNDERSEA UFO BASE

INSIDE UFOS

NOT FROM HERE!

UFOS OVER CALIFORNIA

SUPERNATURAL CALIFORNIA

ONE IN FORTY- UFO EPIDEMIC

Many witnesses recall face to face encounters with "extraterrestrials" without the use of hypnosis.

"IN YOUR FACE" ALIEN ENCOUNTERS

By Linda Zimmermann

"It was those eyes! Those large, black, piercing eyes that struck me the most."

So began the interview with Nancy, one of two witnesses to a chilling alien close encounter in the middle of a dark, empty road.

Skeptics always point to the unreliability of hazy recollections of bizarre extraterrestrials elicited through hypnosis. But what about those encounters where witnesses literally come face to face with terrifying entities and have perfectly clear, conscious memories of what they saw and experienced, without any hypnosis or therapy?

The following cases from the Hudson Valley of New York (each of which I personally interviewed the witnesses) have credible men and women describing frightening and disturbing "in your face" encounters with creatures whose appearances and actions can only be described as alien.

In the fall of 1984, Joe, a local political figure and school administrator, was renting a house in the town of Putnam Valley, New York. One night his dog, a golden retriever, began to whine. Joe assumed the dog wanted to go out, but when he opened the door to the backyard, the dog began to tremble and whine even more. Joe couldn't understand his dog's unusual behavior, and when he finally pushed the frightened dog out the door, it immediately curled up into a tight ball and whined even louder.

Joe then suddenly had a very "weird" feeling, and at that instant, the sky went dark.

There, right above him, at an altitude of no more than 250 feet, was a solid black triangle at least the *size of two football fields*. Greenish-yellow lights lined the edges of the enormous craft, and the most disturbing part was that it was totally silent and completely motionless. Joe yelled for his wife, who came running out and was stunned by a sight that was beyond anything she ever imagined. The massive triangle just sat above the house for at least five minutes, and they were both almost in a panic because of the incredible size of this unknown object so low in the sky. When the massive craft finally began to move, it was so slow that it took at least ten minutes for it to travel out of sight.

This remarkable sighting, alone, would have left a lasting impression on Joe, but unfortunately, that was only the beginning. Soon after, the "nightmares" started.

About a week or so later, Joe was asleep in his first floor bedroom, when he suddenly awoke and felt a strong presence. He looked at the window and there, staring back at him, was something with big eyes. It had to have been about four feet tall, and its head was about the size of a child's, but much narrower. The most disturbing feature was its huge eyes, which Joe described as being as large as those of a squirrel, a very large squirrel. He woke up his wife, but by the time she looked it was gone.

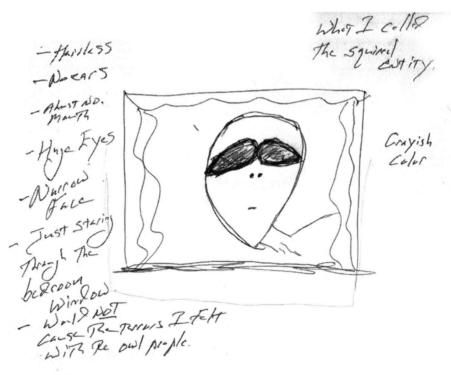

Joe's sketch of the "squirrel people" in his window.

The following week, he awoke again with a start, and found that something else was staring at him, only this time it was *at the foot of his bed!* He wanted to scream, but was so paralyzed with fear that he couldn't make a sound. This figure was also short, but unlike the "squirrel person" with the narrow face, this one looked more like an owl, with a large, very round head that "kind of melded into the shoulders." Once again, the most frightening feature was the eyes – "oriental or like almonds" – and, again, incredibly huge. Unlike the face at the window, however, this "owl person" terrified him. It just stared at him with those frighteningly big eyes, and then the next thing he knew it was morning.

These encounters went on month after month, sometimes only once a week, sometimes two nights in a row, but always in the same manner – the squirrel-like face looking in the bedroom window, and the terrifying owl eyes that stared at him from the foot of the bed. Then five or six hours would pass as if it was only a second, and he would wake up and it would be morning. He knew that these were not dreams, but how could this be reality?

There was one other strange thing that began happening with the onset of these bizarre encounters – Joe started to have terrible nosebleeds. For months, his doctors were unable to find any cause, and then they finally found strange abrasions and scrape marks way up in his sinuses, as if someone had used surgical instruments. They had no explanation for the odd tissue damage.

The awful stress of these encounters wore Joe down to the point that he thought he was beginning to lose his mind. He soon refused to go to bed alone. He told his wife about the horrifying things he saw, and as she never saw any squirrel or owl people, she told him they were only bad dreams. As time passed, however, she saw the effect these nightmares were having on her husband, and she, too, thought he would have a nervous breakdown.

Finally, in August of 1985, Joe couldn't stand the terror any longer and they moved out of that house. The nosebleeds stopped right away. In the new house he did have one dream about the owl person, and he woke up thinking, "Oh please, don't let this start happening again," but fortunately, that was the last he ever saw of the squirrel and owl people.

When I asked him about any experiences he might have had as a child, not surprisingly he used to dream that he would float out of his bedroom window and fly very quickly above the houses in his neighborhood. That was the fun part. Unfortunately, these dreams would always end with him standing in a room surrounded by figures in white robes, and hoods that had small slits for the eyes. These figures absolutely terrified him, with a distinct type of fear he was later to experience again in 1984. Fortunately, nothing further has happened to Joe since then, although it is doubtful he will ever be able to have a peaceful night of sleep again.

Another case of aliens in the bedroom occurred in the 1950s in the small town of Congers, New York. I had been conducting intense interviews with Gary, who had abduction experiences since he was a child. What also came to light was that both of his parents had encounters and missing time going back to when they were children in the 1930s!

When I interviewed Gary's mother, she told me that at a very young age she saw two, three-foot-tall "people" with "very white heads and huge oval eyes" in her backyard. She would continue to be regularly visited by these creatures for almost 70 years. A particularly close encounter occurred in the family home in the 1950s, where Gary also had many experiences.

Gary's mother was coming home from a PTA meeting one evening when she saw these two short, large-eyed beings standing on the edge of her lawn. She ran inside and pulled down all the shades and hoped they would not bother her husband and children, but it wasn't until years later that she found out what happened that night, or at least part of what happened, from her husband.

"He didn't tell me until after we moved from there," she told me, "because he didn't want me to get upset, being that sometimes I would be alone with the children because he worked until twelve at night. He told me one night there were two of them with the oval eyes on the side of the bed, his side of the bed. And he said he quick turned over and covered up his head and put his arm around me."

She then asked her husband, "Weren't you afraid?" And he said, "No. What were they going to do to me, take me away?"

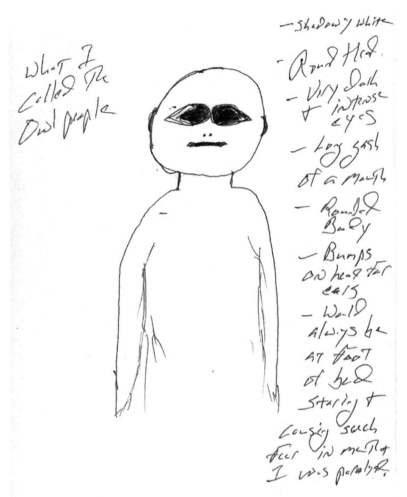

Joe's sketch of the "owl people" in his bedroom.

Given the fact that there are now at least three generations of this family with abduction experiences, I would have to say that, yes, they were in his bedroom to take him away!

Sometimes ETs don't come to us, we try to go to them. Such was the case in Saugerties, New York, around 1991, when two friends, Mike and Patrick, were sitting around a campfire in the woods. They were waiting for their friends who never showed up, so they put out the fire and headed back on the path through the woods. A large tree had fallen in the path, so they went off to the left to get around it. As they did, they both stopped dead in their tracks, overwhelmed with an intense, seemingly "irrational fear." However, the "fear had a direction," and they both turned to look at the same place.

"Holy shit!" Patrick exclaimed. "Do you see that?"

There in the woods, about 30 feet away, were two small, "greenish, illuminated figures. One was standing up, the other hunched over, pushing back branches" to get a better look at them. Mike remained relatively calm and didn't move, but Patrick was very excited and started to rush towards them.

"For a spilt second I thought this was the greatest thing in the world!" Patrick said. "I wanted to run right over to them and welcome them. I started to move toward them and stopped when I got the feeling they were *not* happy I was coming toward them.

"It was like they were in my head and I got this fight or flight response, and my first thought was fight. I actually thought that because they were so small I could run right into them and tackle them both.

"But then it was like they hit my fear button and I had the most overwhelming, irrational fear and I couldn't move a muscle. I don't know if it was for 30 seconds or 4 minutes. And I got the strongest feeling that I wasn't at all relevant to them, that they looked at me like a bug, or a lab rat. It was a very, very negative feeling. Then suddenly I felt like I could move again, and I took off running down the hill.

"Mike was really fast and ran track, and I figured he was right behind me. When I got back to the street and realized he wasn't coming, I thought, 'Oh crap! Now I have to go back and get him,' which I *really* didn't want to do. I had a cigarette and waited, and then, just as I decided to go back for him, he came down."

Patrick actually had the time to smoke several cigarettes before Mike arrived, although Mike could have sworn he took off running right behind Patrick. In addition to Mike's missing time, both men later discovered that almost two hours were unaccounted for that night. As close as this encounter was for Mike and Patrick, it should serve as a warning to those who think it's a great idea to run toward our alien visitors!

There are also uncomfortably close encounters that occur to people in cars. Around 1980, near Mohegan Lake, New York, Don was in the car with his father and grandparents on their way to their summer home. Don's father and grandfather were in the front seat, and he was in the backseat with his grandmother, whom he described as a Marxist intellectual – in other words, she was a woman who didn't believe anything that couldn't be supported with cold, hard facts.

"She was so rooted in intellectual thought," Don explained during our phone interview. "Anything mystical or any type of fantasy was so far from who she was."

And this Marxist intellectual's grandson followed in his grandmother's rational footsteps.

"I don't believe in anything without proof," he stated with conviction.

However, what these two witnessed that night would shake the very foundations of what they believed – and, more importantly – what they didn't believe up to that point.

During the ride, Don turned his head to look out his window, and he was shocked to see a circular craft, about 20 feet in diameter and not more than 15 feet from the car. The craft was flying at the same speed as the car, and it had "jeweled lights" around the perimeter. The vehicle was also "totally lit up inside," which afforded an excellent view of the pilot.

"It had a long neck and the facial features were human-like, but it wasn't like anything I've ever seen in this world," Don explained.

He described the figure as being seated in front of some sort of control panel, and the skin of this figure was greenish. Don's "jaw dropped" as he stared at this bizarre pilot, who was staring right back at him!

I asked how close he was to this figure, and I got a chill up my spine when he responded, "eyeball to eyeball."

After a second or two, Don turned toward the front seat to get his father and grandfather's attention, but when he turned back, the craft and its green pilot were gone. He tried to explain what he just saw, but the two men didn't believe a word. Fortunately, though, his grandmother chimed in that she had just seen the same thing. For the rest of her life, she regularly told Don how thankful she was that he had witnessed the alien craft and pilot, too. Both skeptical, rational people became instant believers that there was other life in the universe.

"It's beyond a reasonable doubt," Don stated without hesitation. "They convict people of murder for less!"

Don never had any other sightings before or since, but that one was enough. For him, that "eyeball to eyeball" encounter was all the proof he'll ever need.

Finally, we circle back to Nancy, the woman on that dark road that encountered a figure with "those large, black, piercing eyes." Aliens were the last thing on her mind that night in 1982 as she and her best friend, Lisa, were driving on Route 9D near Cold Spring along the Hudson River. They were on their way to go shopping in White Plains, and the two women were just laughing and talking about nothing in particular when they saw something up ahead.

"There was something in the middle of the road, so I slowed down," Nancy said. "It was over six feet tall and very skinny, with really thin limbs. It didn't have any clothes on, and its skin was very gray."

The most startling feature, however, was its "huge head," and the big eyes, which were completely black.

"What the hell is that!?" Lisa yelled.

Nancy had no idea what she was looking at, or, more importantly, what was *looking at them*.

"I had to slow way down and move over into the other lane to avoid it," Nancy explained. "It just stood there and stared at us with those black eyes. It was looking right at us, and followed us with those piercing eyes. We passed it by *no more than one or two feet*. I could have hit it, it was so close. Right after we went by it, I looked in the rearview mirror and it was gone."

Lisa was "freaking out," claiming that this was definitely "something not of this world." Nancy didn't know what to think, as she had absolutely no interest in UFOs and never heard of gray aliens. It wasn't until she moved to California about a decade later and saw a book about them that she realized what she had been eye to eye with on that dark stretch of road.

"When I saw pictures of the grays in the book I said, 'Oh my god! That's what we saw!' For years, Lisa and I joked that we must have seen the Elephant Man, because we had no idea at the time."

Nancy has since had other sightings and paranormal experiences, and developed a keen sixth sense with numerous premonitions which came true. While she can't say the abilities began, or were heightened, that day she locked eyes with the tall gray, she considers the experience "a big part" of her life.

What do all of these "in your face" close encounters mean? What does any of this mean?

The universe is much stranger than we can ever imagine...

• • • • • • • • •

ABOUT THE AUTHOR: Linda Zimmermann is a research chemist turned award-winning author of 30 books on science, history, the paranormal, and fiction. She has lectured across the country, and has appeared on numerous TV and radio shows. Linda starred in the documentary, "In the Night Sky: I Recall a UFO," which was based on her research into sightings in the Hudson Valley of New York. The film won the 2013 People's Choice Award at the International UFO Congress. Her two UFO books are: "*In the Night Sky*," and "*Hudson Valley UFOs*," and she is currently working on a third book on the subject.

Timothy Green Beckley with Paul and Ben Eno at the WOON studio.

IT ALL STARTED WITH SASQUATCH – MYSTERY OF THE PENNSYLVANIA TRIANGLE

By Ben Eno

PUBLISHER'S NOTE: I have probably been on Paul and Ben Eno's "Behind The Paranormal" more than any other program. In fact I am no new comer to the radio station that broadcasts the show at noon on Sundays. Back half a century ago, give or take a few years, I made my first appearance on the Boston area station, when I was interviewed by drive time host Joseph Ferriere (he was by no means a shock jock as there was no such animal, or wild beast, in those days). Joe did not host a UFO or paranormal show, but I was on the road promoting an article I had just penned for Saga magazine on UFO sightings of our astronauts. Joe later did admit to being a "silent contactee." He was actually what I would call a "UFO repeater," in that he could venture out, aim his camera skyward and all manner of weird and unexplainable objects would show themselves. But that's another story. Those interested can find the one and only interview ever done with Joseph which is archived on Paul Eno's website.

I have been to his house in Woonsocket, petted the family feline, gone out to dinner with him and his son and wandered about his vast library in the basement of his home. Whatever Paul Eno says I go along with. Some of his theories may be a bit "exotic," and I am sure there are those in the field who can't understand why he mixes and mingles Bigfoot, UFOs, poltergeist and even electronic voice phenomena.

Celebrating approximately 50 years in paranormal research, Paul Eno was one of the first investigators of the early 1970s, beginning while he was studying for the priesthood. His early mentors included parapsychology pioneer Dr. Louisa Rhine, Fr. John J. Nicola S.J. (technical advisor for the film *The Exorcist*) and legendary, first-generation "ghost hunters" Ed & Lorraine Warren. Paul graduated from two seminaries but was expelled from the graduate-level theology program at a third, because of his paranormal work, with less than two years to go before ordination. He ended up as an award-winning New England journalist and the author or co-author of 10 books on the paranormal and two on history.

Paul has appeared on the History, Discovery and Travel Channels, and he and his son and "partner in the paranormal," Ben Eno, have lectured all over America and in Europe. The two host a weekly radio show, now in its 11th year on the air, "Behind the Paranormal with Paul & Ben Eno," on WOON 1240 in the Boston/Worcester/Providence market. The show aired on CBS Radio in four U.S. cities from 2009-2014.

• • • • • • • • • •

THE SABULA SIGHTING

We came all the way from New England to look for Sasquatch. After all, two of us had seen the Big Guy in separate encounters here in 2016. In fact, so had just about everyone who lived in the area, with 30 to 40 people attending the annual neighborhood meetings we organized and reporting not only Bigfoot but strange lights, both in the sky and near the ground.

We'd seen the lights, too, and photographed some of them. But it would be nothing compared with what we witnessed just after midnight on Friday, May 24, 2019.

The location of all these adventures was the heart of what we had come to call the "Pennsylvania Triangle." The "we" on this expedition, the sixth since the investigation opened three years earlier, included my colleague Shane Sirois (of Trueghost.com and our favorite guest co-host on "Behind the Paranormal with Paul & Ben Eno," our Boston-area radio show), along with filmmaker and researcher Aleksandar Petakov of Petakov Media and Charles Creteau of Seacoast Saucers of New England (creator of the "Galileo Interviews" on YouTube). My son and "partner in the paranormal," Ben Eno, wasn't with us this trip. He was back at our radio station, WOON 1240 AM and 99.5 FM in Rhode Island, to produce and host the two-hour, on-location special we planned on the 26th.

As it turned out, we would have plenty to talk about on the show.

With our investigation plan in place after weeks of Skype conferences, we arrived in the Dubois, Pa., area, in the section known as Sabula, late in the afternoon of May 23rd in two separate vehicles. We received the typical warm welcome from the couple who always hosted us at their trim, rural home, which had served as our base camp from the beginning of the case.

We settled in with our usual first-night plans: Scatter over the area in our trucks and our hosts' RV to monitor locations where major phenomena had been recorded on previous expeditions. This monitoring always involved a battery of cameras, including infrared, trail cams, body cams and drones. We also used audio recording devices.

It all started with a grainy photo of a possible Bigfoot inside the
Pennsylvania Triangle.

Du Bois UFO Original

Video by Paul Eno, Copyright 2019 by WOON Radio & Woonsocket Wireless Co.

Above: still 01: The objects as I caught them on video 12:17 am 5/24/19. Object above "mist" came out of it, moved along with it and appeared to be solid. Object at upper right is a star.

Below: Drone shot: Shae Sirois drone went up the next day for a shot of the spot from which the sighting took place (the trees at left center). Interestingly, there are three separate Bigfoot encounters sites in this photo.

What was supposed to be my post for the night was my favorite spot in the area at the highest point in the hilltop field above base camp. That was where I encountered Bigfoot on the brilliantly moonlit night of September 16, 2016. It was a peaceful and almost holy experience. So, before sunset on the evening of May 23rd, I put my trusty Ford F-150 Lariat in four-wheel drive, climbed the hill and settled in.

Meanwhile, Shane was on station in the RV, a few hundred yards downhill, at what's known locally as "the campground" − the heart of the Pennsylvania Triangle in our opinion. You name it and it's happened there. Staying the night there is always an interesting experience.

Dusk was settling over the field, and I decided to try an idea I'd been toying with but had never employed in nearly 50 years in the paranormal trenches. I had recently discovered the beautiful, haunting music of Morten Lauridsen, an American composer who writes music in several languages, some of it liturgical. He has the rare knack of using dissonance (notes that usually clash) in very beautiful ways.

PAUL ENO   SHANE SIROIS   ANDREW VRANES

ALEKSANDAR PETAKOV   LORI GREER   CHARLES CRETEAU   BEN ENO

SABULA WITNESSES: clockwise from upper left − Paul Eno (who captured the video on his Bestguarder NV-300 IR binoculars), Shane Sirois (investigator and 'Behind the Paranormal with Paul & Ben Eno' guest co-host), Andrew Vranes ('Behind the Paranormal' show research assistant − witnessed 'the tone' only), Aleksandar Petakov of Petakov Media (researcher and filmmaker), Lori Greer ('Behind the Paranormal' casting producer − witnessed 'the tone' only), Charles Creteau of Seacoast Saucers of New England, and Ben Eno (who was back at the WOON studios in Rhode Island to host the two-hour radio special on May 26.

As far as Bigfoot was concerned, I thought Lauridsen's origins were most appropriate. He's a native of the Pacific Northwest, where there's supposed to be a Bigfoot behind every tree, and he was once a U.S. Forest Service firefighter.

So, I set the speakers at a level to gently but fully carry Lauridsen's "Soneto de la Noche" (Sonnet of the Night) across the hilltop. I opened the truck's moon roof, sticking my head out to watch and listen.

The high temperature that day had been above average, about 76F. There were a few brief showers, but the evening was cool and clear above, and to the west. As the sun set, however, I was facing directly south. In the distance, far beyond Dubois, was a distant display of heat lightning, probably on the far edge of a warm front. There was another such display far to the east. Over Dubois, however, the sky was crystal clear.

As the "Soneto" played over the field, sudden flashes of white light began to flare around my truck, just above the ground. There were fireflies out that night, and we all commented on how early in the season they were. But what I saw around the truck had nothing to do with any insect I'd ever heard of. They were like silent explosions, about the size of basketballs, with white light radiating from the center for a split second. This went on for about 10 minutes, and I was able to get a few on video.

Meanwhile, Shane was having an uneventful time in the campground. It was a moonless night, and the treetops there obscured the stars. He suddenly was hit by a strong conviction that, instead of doing stakeouts, we needed to "skywatch" that night. I reluctantly agreed.

So, at about 10:30, Shane, Alek, Chuck and I gathered with the homeowners on their lovely, open-air patio, down the hill and within sight of my stakeout post. We lit a blaze in the firepit and talked about my strange lights.

Since the 1970s, I have had some very different ideas about the paranormal: What the phenomena actually are, how they really work, and what they mean when studied in depth. Ben and I had to invent entirely new terms just to talk about some of these ideas: elsewhen, overwash, the Leinster Effect, the flashing nexus, superlife and more.

Where the tone was heard – starting in garage, then led five investigators out to this driveway.

One of these terms is "flap areas" – regions of intense paranormal activity of different kinds that have not traditionally been associated with each other. The Pennsylvania Triangle is a flap area for the record books, and that night we were sitting at its heart. The entire area was the scene of nearly constant UFOs, Bigfoot, ghostly activity, time slips and phenomena that don't even have names yet, and it went back generations.

It was about 15 minutes past midnight.

"What's that?"

At about the same moment, Alek and Shane saw the object coming in from the north, partially obscured by some scattered pine trees. My first sight of the UFO brought to mind my experience with private aviation and small aircraft. It looked like bright landing lights shining through a haze or fog. But there was no haze. The night remained crystal clear, and the moon wouldn't rise until about 2:15 AM.

I ran across the lawn to get a better view, fumbling all the while with my brand new Bestguarder® NV-300 night vision binoculars, which I had never used before. The device more than paid for itself that night, since I caught the whole sighting on video.

Once it came out of the north, the cloud-like object, a bit larger than a half-dollar coin to the naked eye from where we watched, seemed to turn, sliding down the sky, from west to east. It was completely silent. It was accompanied by what seemed to be a solid, circular object that emerged from it, followed it across the sky, then merged with it once again as the whole thing seemed to turn north again and disappear.

One characteristic, visible in both the video and still photos, is a "darker than dark" beam or energy that seems to emanate from the bottom of the object as it proceeds across the sky.

The entire sighting lasted about three minutes.

The rest of the night was quiet, but there was a sequel in the wee hours of May 25th.

A geographical feature known as the eastern continental divide passes right through the land at the center of the Triangle, just where we had seen the UFO. Intrigued by the possibility of a connection, our group headed for a little, hilltop park nearby. This park commemorated the presence of the eastern continental divide, and it commanded a broad view of the area.

Shane, Alek, Chuck and I had been joined by Lori Greer from New York City, one of our show's producers, and Andrew Vranes, our show's research assistant. Atop the hill, just after midnight, I once again played "Soneto de la Noche," and Shane played some tones he had obtained from an activity at Mount Shasta in California, the famous New Age Mecca.

In a distinct departure from our usual feet-on-the-ground research methods, Chuck, a social worker for the State of Maine for many years, led us in a UFO visualization that he had developed in working with alleged alien abduction victims.

We left the hilltop at about 12:45 AM and arrived at base camp soon afterward. There, in our hosts' garage, we began to say our good nights. Chuck had already climbed into bed in the basement apartment that was separated from the garage by a thin door that was ajar. Despite his proximity, he didn't hear what happened next.

A tone – a perfect "C" – suddenly appeared over Lori's head. Those in the garage immediately grabbed for their cell phones, then we looked around for a possible cause.

"Paul, what did you step on?" Alek joked.

But the tone began to move. It left the garage through the closed door, leading us outside. The sound then ascended into the air to our right, faded, powered up again, moved to our left, then disappeared into the sky. Two of us were able to grab quick recordings with our phones.

As mentioned, Chuck, in an adjoining room, didn't hear the tone. Nor did our hosts, who were in a room above the garage, with their windows open.

On our May 26th two-hour "Behind the Paranormal" on-location special from our hosts' kitchen, we played the UFO video and the tone recording. Our show does have a TV feed that accompanies the radio broadcast, and this show may be seen at http://www.onworldwide.com/index.php/o-n-tv-on-demand. The would-be viewer will have to do some scrolling. One trick: On the main ON TV ON DEMAND page, switch the filter to "Most Viewed" and you will find our May 26, 2019, show more quickly.

The question arises: What did we actually see in the Pennsylvania sky just after midnight on May 24, 2019?

The classic assumption is that it was a craft. Not so fast, I say. There are many other possibilities. I suggest that we might have seen a multiversal intersect point, a point of contact, or portal, if you prefer, between parallel worlds – perhaps many parallel worlds. In fact, the smaller, more solid object that came from and returned to the hazy object could have been a craft – or even a living creature – traveling between parallel realities.

In an area of open country like west-central Pennsylvania, where would a population of large primates like Bigfoot live with official discovery? I think they, and many of the strange lights, beings and other whatsits that characterize this area, come and go through holes in space and time, and I think that's exactly what we saw and recorded on video. That's my opinion, anyway.

Sure enough, residents of the area report a number of previous sightings of just what we saw. The tone, however, remains a complete mystery to me.

• • • • • • • • • •

SUGGESTED READING

DANCING PAST THE GRAVEYARD

FACES AT THE WINDOW

FOOTSTEPS IN THE ATTIC

WEIRD WINGED WONDERS (contributor)

KNIFE WIELDING DEMONS (contributor)

BELL WITCH PROJECT (contributor)

BEHIND THE PARANORMAL WITH PAUL & BEN ENO

WOON 1240 & 99.5 FM Providence/Worcester/Boston.

Streaming live on ONWorldwide.com, TUNEIN.com, and the Paranormal Radio App from Talkstream Live Sunday Destination Radio, Noon-1 pm Eastern, 9-10 am Pacific, 5-6 pm UK. www.BehindTheParanormal.com

Send questions or comments before or during every show:
paul@behindtheparanormal.co

Seems Bigfoot has acquired a taste for chicken -- "Popeye's" no doubt.
Spicy art by Carol Ann Rodriguez.

UFO SIGHTINGS OVER DUBOIS – MORE ON THE PHILADELPHIA TRIANGLE

By Aleksandar Petakov

PUBLISHER'S NOTE: I won't beat around the bush. I don't really know Aleksandar, but when I found out from Paul Eno that he had a backup team to coordinate their investigation into the Bermuda Triangle, I figured it was time to tie the knot and see what the team of investigators had managed to pull together in an effort to coordinate their research efforts. Glad I did, as this additional information certainly solidifies the strange comings and goings in and around the town of DuBois, Pennsylvania

Aleksandar Petakov was born in 1993 during the last year of Apartheid in South Africa to parents that fled civil war in the former Yugoslavia. He grew up in the United States and has always been interested in global events, history, the outdoors and adventuring. Aleksandar is a 2015 Quinnipiac University graduate with a BA in Communications with minors in History & Political Science. He currently resides in New England. Traveling across the United States and the world, Aleksandar has looked into various Cryptozoological creatures such as Sasquatch, the Loch Ness Monster, the Lake Champlain monster, Mystery big cats as well as other phenomenon and mysterious places ranging from the paranormal Bridgewater Triangle of Massachusetts to the hermit kingdom of North Korea. He has created short documentary films and series on these subjects, among others. Aleksandar has been a guest on various radio programs & podcasts, as well as spoken at various paranormal/cryptozoological events, public libraries & other venues in New England and across the United States. To book for a speaking engagement, film screening or radio/podcast appearance please contact him at: aleksandarpetakov@yahoo.com

Aleksandar Petakov is an investigator of all things paranormal and Fortean.

Just after midnight on May 24th, 2019, four colleagues and I witnessed what can only be described as an Unidentified Flying Object (UFO) gliding through the night sky over a field in rural DuBois, Pennsylvania. It was truly the strangest thing I have seen to date, and we were lucky to have captured video of the object via night vision goggles, as well as some of the audio of us conversing during the sighting. I'll provide more details on this sighting shortly, but first a little background on the area we had our encounter, an area we've come to refer to as the "Pennsylvania Triangle."

To make a long story short, the "Pennsylvania Triangle" is the name given to an area of Western-Central Pennsylvania around the town of DuBois. The area has a history of anomalous activity such as UFO sightings, Bigfoot activity, black helicopters, and much more. My involvement with this area was the result of being asked to join on a sort of case study of a particular property in the area that was being conducted for several years by my dear friends and paranormal investigators **Paul Eno and Shane Sirois.** This top-notch group of researchers was invited onto the property a few years ago by a reader of theirs, familiar with their work on a similar case in Connecticut.

In recent years there has been general interest in areas of "high strangeness" across North America where seemingly different types of paranormal phenomenon are taking place in some sort of congruence. Areas that have captivated researchers and the public alike are those such as Skinwalker Ranch in Utah and perhaps most notably the "Bridgewater Triangle" of Massachusetts. Pennsylvania itself has another very famous anomalous area known as the "Chestnut Ridge," which is southwest of

Pittsburgh, Pennsylvania. The area is a hotbed of Bigfoot activity, UFO sighting flaps and encounters such as the 1965 Kecksburg UFO incident, as well as other strange phenomena. Researchers like Stan Gordon and Eric Altman have studied this area and others like it in Pennsylvania for years.

In 2018 Paul invited me and another friend and colleague, Charles Creteau, to join their annual expedition to the DuBois area. In previous years Paul, Shane and occasionally Ben Eno (Paul's son), , would spend their time there searching the property, researching the local area, as well as hosting town hall style meetings where locals could share their anomalous experiences in the area. Both Paul and Shane claimed to have had what they believed were Sasquatch related experiences in this area. What piqued my interest was more on the side of the Sasquatch sightings in the area, as that part of Pennsylvania is seen as an active area, in terms of sightings. For the rest of the claims, I'll admit I was a bit skeptical.

Announcement of UFO/Bigfoot community meeting courtesy Out Of The Shadows.

Subsequently I learned that this property had a very storied history, to say the least. It is believed that thousands of years ago a meteor crashed on what is now part of the property. Excavations by the University of Pennsylvania in the area also established Native American burial grounds, finding 160 skeletons and a specialized style of pottery. The family we were staying with had been living on the property for decades with a variety of strange encounters taking place. People were seeing UFO's, strange orbs and black helicopters in the skies. Other family members were seeing "shadow people" in their own homes or reporting "missing time," as well as encounters with Sasquatch type creatures near the woods of the more secluded areas of the property.

Last year Charles Creteau and I conducted a fascinating interview with three generations that claimed to have Sasquatch encounters on the property, which can be viewed here. The town hall we hosted last year turned up a lot of interesting leads regarding what people had experienced in the area, with nearly all of the dozen or so attendees at least having experienced some sort of UFO activity. While we didn't have too much happen while in the area in 2018, it was certainly a great primer into the area and gave us some ideas for the following year.

For the 2019 expedition we again planned to host a town hall event at a restaurant in nearby Rockton, PA, called Over the Mountain. This location was perfect as it was decorated with various Bigfoot statues and artwork, given that there had been various sightings in the immediate area. We planned on doing a presentation about why we were there and some of our theories about the "Pennsylvania Triangle," such as Paul's theory about "flap areas" around the world, multidimensionality and other topics. I chose to present briefly on the recent news that **Pennsylvania was ranked #3** in the United States for Bigfoot sightings and perhaps why that might be the case. However prior to the town hall none of us would have expected that part of our presentation would include a segment on what we would witness two nights prior...

SEQUENCE OF EVENTS

The following is the sequence of events that led up to our UFO sighting and my recollection of what transpired. On the night of Thursday May 23rd, 2019, we spent the evening split up solo on different parts of the property. I stationed myself in a pickup truck down by a wooded ravine, near the home of the folks I had interviewed last year about Sasquatch activity. Thunderstorms and rain began to settle down producing a beautifully clear and starry sky. After a few hours of just hanging around in our separate spots, a few of the other guys made the decision to head back up to the main house to sit in the field and stargaze, with the sky being so clear. Shortly after, I drove up there and joined them.

Shane, Charles, Paul, one of the homeowners and I sat by a fire pit just observing the sky for some time. There were still some lightning storms going on in the distance, but aside from that we observed various airplanes flying overhead, as well as, several shooting stars. It was exceptionally clear, with no clouds visible in the night sky.

About 15-20 minutes after midnight, I noticed what appeared to be a cloud, illuminated by what I believed was either a star or the moon behind it. Looking back that didn't really make sense, but that's the way my mind rationalized what I was seeing. We all then began to observe this "cloud" as it began drifting through the sky, left to right, very slowly. The motion reminded me of a leaf swaying in the breeze in slow motion. It became clear to us then that whatever this thing was, it moved in ways unlike a cloud.

At this point, a few minutes after initially seeing it, we are all walking around in the clearing and trying to get a better look at this object. As we were doing this, a smaller, brighter light seemingly flew off of the "cloud" and then flew back into it a few seconds later. The excitement was tangible and we are all basically shouting in awe at this point as we continued watching this thing fly away slowly. Paul returned to the house to get his night vision goggles, while Shane and I both attempted to record the object with our cell phones, which we didn't have much luck doing. It was this way that Shane inadvertently captured audio of us seeing this object and commenting on it in real time, helping preserve the record of the encounter better.

Paul returned with his Bestguarder night vision goggles and was attempting to capture the object on video, but was having trouble spotting it with the limited field of view and focus on the goggles. I helped him out by pointing in the sky with a powerful laser pointer and circling the object with the green beam. He was able to locate it with the goggles and we all continued to watch this object as it flew over the trees in the distance and was lost behind the horizon. All flabbergasted and blown away with what we had just seen, we began heading back to the fire pit area and proceeded to continue observing the sky and going over what we had just witnessed.

The best description I can give for the larger object is an illuminated fog or haze that appeared quite large and not too far from us in the sky. The behavior of this object was unlike anything we had observed that entire evening. airplanes, shooting stars, lightning bugs and lightning storms. Even after the sighting we watched numerous airplanes in the night sky, none of them flanked by a cloud, haze, or fog. They were clearly airplanes and it was easy to identify them as such based on how they behaved and their characteristics, such as flashing lights.

Before we headed to bed we reviewed the footage we had captured on the night vision goggles. At first there didn't appear to be much as we reviewed the various clips on my laptop. There was plenty of shaky footage of trees and the ground, but not much else. Right before calling it a night, one of the last clips we reviewed turned out to contain the 3 or so minutes that Paul managed to capture of the craft. We were ecstatic to see the footage and how great it turned out. In the video you could clearly see the fuzzy almost peanut shaped object slowly moving through the sky, with a smaller, round object flying beside it the entire time. Towards the end of the video, the larger object itself completely changed its shape, shifting more into a ball shape. See for yourself in the full video below.

The following day I began to attempt some basic video enhancements to the video, to see if we could get a better look at the object. I seemed to have the most luck when inverting it into the negative, as it "popped" that way and became more visually striking. The still image below shows the objects in question in the video.

We have called upon our talented friend and colleague, well-respected astronomer to examine the video. Marc Dantonio is the chief video and photo analyst for the Mutual UFO Network (MUFON) and has spent years analyzing supposed UFO video and photo evidence submitted to the group from around the world. There have been very few UFO submissions that Marc hasn't been able to explain as misidentifications, common aerial objects in unusual conditions, camera artifacts or outright hoaxes. Hopefully Marc will be able to comment further on what it might or might not be.

I'm not going to claim or speculate to know what the object was, but my colleagues and I agree that it was far from ordinary. It doesn't exactly lend itself to being easily explained, so until then it truly fits the description of an Unidentified Flying Object.

All images and videos featured in this article are copyrighted and may not be posted without permission. For videos and postings visit http://petakovmedia.com/blog/

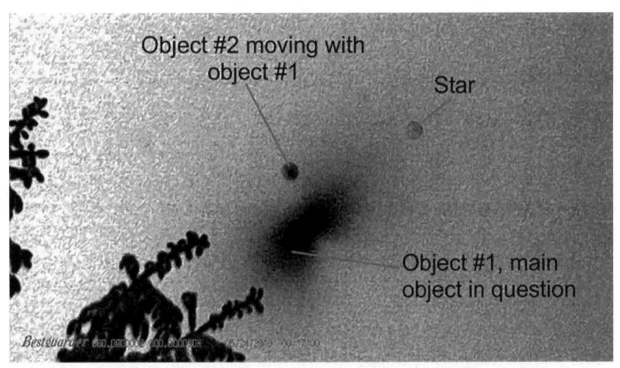

Position of UFOs in the sky. Photo courtesy Aleksandar Petakov and Paul Eno.

For the most part, UFO occupants reportedly come in all sorts of different shapes and sizes.

THE CREDIBLE CONTACT CASE OF COUNTRY WESTERN SINGER JOHNNY SANDS

By Timothy Green Beckley

I must confess I know Johnny Sands pretty well. We did an episode of the History Channel's "UFO Hunters" - hosted by Bill Birnes - together, and then we wandered over to my hotel room and chatted for a couple of hours. You can find the interview on Mr. UFO's Secret Files by typing in Johnny Sands. Or, if you are getting the ebook version, you can just follow this link: www.youtube.com/watch?v=Ls89j8oaZco&t=34s

In several of my previous works, I have discussed Johnny's encounter at length and told how he later on was surrounded by black automobiles and weird hairy creatures (like Bigfoot?) in the desert and went to an office that really didn't exist, as it turns out. It's one of the strangest encounters I have ever gotten involved with. It was even verified by the once prestigious Aerial Phenomena Research Organization. APRO set Johnny up with a lie detector test, which he passed. Anyway, the group is now defunct; both directors, Coral and Jim Lorenzen, have transitioned. I recently came across their original summation of this case and since I consider it one of the best close encounters of all time, I thought I would publish their independent findings.

Date: January 29, 1976

Location: Las Vegas, Nevada, United States

Johnny Sands, a country-western singer living in Las Vegas, saw a 60-foot craft at about 1000 feet altitude, shaped like the Goodyear blimp, with portholes around the circumference. The object appeared to land, and Sands then saw two figures approaching. Then, he "froze" -- he wanted to move, but he couldn't. The figures came near him, to about three feet away.

The last extended, intensive period of UFO activity took place in the fall months of 1973 and at this time, it appears that the fall months of 1975 and the early months of 1976 duplicated the "flap" of 1973 with one major difference - whatever the UFOs are - "they" seem to be getting bolder, and in the "abduction" cases under study at APRO, there are emerging threads of continuity in relation to descriptions of occupants as well as the objects themselves. We are also encountering "warnings" to the victims concerning what they will remember or what they can talk about if they do recall their experiences.

**Sketch of occupant done by a professional artist to
Mr. Sands' specifications.**
Source: APRO Bulletin, Vol. 24 No. 9 (Mar 1976)
"The Johnny Sands Case" (published in March, 1976)

Johnny Sands.

A case in point is that of Johnny Sands, 30, a country-western singer who, at the time of his alleged close encounter, was living in Las Vegas, Nevada where he was trying to promote his first recording and was appearing in a show. A polygraph test administered by Robert L. Nolen of Robert H. Nolen Associates of Las Vegas indicates no deception.

Again, as in the past, the occupants are a new type, as can be seen by the accompanying sketch, which was done by a professional artist to Mr. Sands' specifications. Mr. Sands' account is as follows:

He had been out driving to the surrounding towns to check on how well his record was faring at the radio stations and on jukeboxes. He had left Pahrump at 10 p.m. and was driving on the Blue Diamond road, and at about 10:30 p.m., about 22 miles out of Las Vegas, he saw an unusual aircraft. He didn't pay much attention to it, he said, although it seemed to follow him for about 3 miles. At this point, the car's engine began sputtering so he pulled off the road and got out of the car. He walked around the car, removed the gas tank lid and shook the rear end of the car to determine whether he had any gas. He could hear the gas splashing around in the tank, so he replaced the cover and went around to the front of the car and lifted the hood. It was at this time, looking up, he said, that he saw the craft above him at what he estimated to be about 1,000 feet altitude. Sands said it was about 60 feet long and shaped like the Goodyear blimp, with a large, round ring at the midsection. He also said it had windows or portholes (round) about 10 feet in diameter and about 5 feet apart around the circumference of the ring or "doughnut" section, with a light between each. The object was "rusty orange" in color with flashing red and white lights on the ends. It moved slowly over the mountain to the south of him, lighting up the mountain as it did so, and appearing to land.

Then, Sands said, he turned his attention back to his car, and started to take the air filter off. For some unknown reason, he turned and looked down the road in the direction his headlights (which were on low beam) were shining and saw two figures approaching. He could not make out any details, and at first, thought they might have been muggers. Then, he said, he "froze" - he doesn't know why - he wanted to move, but he couldn't.

The two figures came toward him, one stopping about three feet away while the other stayed about five feet beyond. Sands described them as perfectly bald with no eyelashes or brows and with gill-like protrusions on either side of their faces which moved rapidly all the while that they stood there. The eyes were small, black and the centers (or pupils) were white. Sands said the mouths were very small and never opened, and that their noses were "pug" or "flattened".

Sands estimates that the whole episode, from the time he spotted the two figures until they walked away into the desert, took about 10 minutes. When they left, they walked about 150-200 feet away, then, Sands said, a flash of light "came up" and they were gone.

The road on which Sands was traveling is paved, but he says he only encountered four cars during the trip, and that the last one passed by, going toward Pahrump just after he pulled off the road. He had jumped out of his car and tried to wave it down but although the car slowed, it sped up again and continued along its way. After the encounter with the "figures", Sands tried to re-start his car, and it started with no trouble at all and he drove on into Las Vegas.

When Sands initially reported his experience, he went to the police who referred him to the Office of Special Investigations at Nellis Air Force Base. The spokesman for that office said that the Air Force had stopped probing the UFO problem in 1969 and that office only handles internal criminal matters. He also said the base's radar "picked up nothing" unusual that night, but only the base's runway headings were being monitored. A spokesman at the McCarran Airport tower said nothing unusual was noted on their surveillance radar which covers a 55-mile radius from the surface "to infinity". However, he did note that the radar is "line of sight" and would not register craft beyond the mountains.

The 10-minute episode is the fascinating part of Sands' story, in addition to his description of the humanoids who, although one asked him a number of questions, requested that he not reveal anything of the encounter. Sands has only revealed a part of what happened, saying that if he revealed the rest, it would be a breach of trust.

The questions the humanoid (who was standing closest to him) asked of Sands were:

1. What was he (Sands) doing there? Sands responded that he was an entertainer and was in Las Vegas to do a show.

2. Why were so many people in Las Vegas? Sands said that it was a tourist type town and that people came to Las Vegas from all over.

3. What is your means of communication? Sands was confused and replied that he didn't understand the question, because there are several different means of communication. The humanoid seemed to become irritated and said: "Answer the question!" Sands repeated that he didn't understand, whereupon the humanoid turned to the other, and the two just stood facing one another for 2 or 3 minutes, then his questioner turned to Sands, reached out his left hand and brushed Sands' left hand and told him: "Don't say anything about this meeting. We know where you are and will see you again." The two then trooped off and disappeared in a flash of light.

Sands said that the voice of his questioner was deep, and the words came out slowly and almost mechanically with noticeable spacing between each and an echo-like quality. However, although he could tell that the voice came from the man's "body," the mouth did not move at all.

Sands described the humanoid clothing thusly: A black, silverish all-encompassing overall (the artist got his shades reversed in the painting) with no visible seams. When the questioner brushed Sands' hand, it felt like "rough, heavy duty sandpaper." Besides the white strap which ran diagonally from right shoulder to the left waist, there was a wide white "patent-leather-like" belt on which there hung capsule-shaped objects which were silver colored and about 1 inch long. They appeared to be hanging on hooks and the "man" twisted one of them all the while that he talked to Sands until he brushed Sands' hand and turned and left.

The "men" were about 5'7" or 5'8", about 140 pounds, Sands said, and their gloved hands had a thumb and four fingers like normal humans. He also noted what appeared to be padding over the top of the feet, as well as across the back of the foot.

The feet were covered by the same type of material as the rest of their bodies. They seemed to be very light on their feet and made no sound as they walked, as if they were off the ground, although Sands said they were definitely touching it.

Also very interesting is Sands' description of the face of the one who "talked" to him: "The face was wrinkled. Now, body wise, he looked as fit as a 21-year-old but in his face, facial structure - I don't know, something gave me the idea this guy was 300 or 400 years old. It's a very powerful face, a very powerful set of eyes. He's not so ugly as he is powerful looking," Sands told investigators.

The machinations of a film crew calling themselves Dave Dunn Productions who were beginning work on a TV series dealing with the strange, unusual and unknown, served to muddy the waters considerably. On the evening of February 10, they took Sands out to the site of his experience where he was instructed to stay in the car. Meanwhile, an argument apparently started among the film personnel and, hearing snatches of the conversation, including "what will we do with him (gesturing toward Sands in the car) - he's already heard too much," he started to get out of the car, whereupon two "fuzzy things" ran at the door and kept him inside. He said that every time he tried to get out of the car they would repeat the performance.

Timothy Green Beckley and Johnny Sands.

Mr. Sands called Mr. Lorenzen after they had taken him back to Las Vegas and related these events and was very agitated about the incident. He said that the Dunn people had taken him to dinner and they'd had a few drinks and he wondered if he'd been drugged because he couldn't remember the entire evening.

Piecing the whole thing together, the Lorenzens have hypothesized that the film crew may have had two men dressed in animal-like disguises (the "things" were man-shaped, Sands said) for the purpose of frightening Sands so that they could film him in an actual terrified state.

In a report to John Romero, APRO Field Investigator in Las Vegas, Mr. Nolen, the polygraph operator, states:

"Following are listed the relevant questions and the subject's vocal responses.

"1. On January 29th, did you see two strange figures in the desert? Answer: Yes

"2. Did you communicate with these strange figures? Answer: Yes.

"3. Did these strange figures tell you that they would see you again? Answer: Yes.

"4. Were you under the influence of. anything at the time of this meeting? Answer: No.

"5. Regarding what happened on Thursday, January 29, have you told the truth about what you saw that night? Answer: Yes.

"A total of three charts were obtained using the above relevant questions. During these three charts, Mr. Sands indicated an ability to respond automatically to vocal stimuli. His responses in the critical areas were not consistent with deception criteria."

"After careful examination of this subject's polygrams, it is my opinion that Mr. Johnny Sands was truthful in his answers to the above relevant questions. I am not attesting to the truthfulness of the whole story that Mr. Sands has told, only to the veracity of his answers to the above relevant questions." Unquote.

It has been suggested to Mr. Sands that he undergo hypnotic regression in order to attempt to retrieve further information but he is afraid of hypnosis. APRO consultants feel, however, that some progress may be made in that direction in the future.

In view of Sands' apparent sincerity and the polygraph tests, this case cannot be entirely discounted. Also, there is the verification of the initial sighting of the object by others who called the p6lice department that evening and reported seeing an object in the area, the description of which closely matches that of Johnny Sands'. Obviously, there is considerable follow-up work to be done on this case which is one of the more puzzling ones to come out of the 1975-76"flap."

Johnny Sands was a guest on Exploring the Bizarre, along with Bill Birnes. This episode and others can be heard at kcorradio.com.

HUGE UFO SPHERES OVER TAMPA BAY, AND THEN THE BRIDGE COLLAPSED!

By Diane Tessman

The Silver Bridge.

The Silver Bridge collapsed on December 15, 1967. It was a suspension bridge over the Ohio River built in 1928, and connecting Point Pleasant, West Virginia, and Gallipolis, Ohio.

The Silver Bridge collapsed while crowded with rush-hour traffic at Christmas season. Forty-six people died and two of their bodies were never found. It was discovered that the bridge failed due to one eye-bar, a defect of 0.1 inch in size. Analysis also showed that the bridge had been carrying heavier loads than it was ever designed to hold.

A creature which people called Mothman had been sighted in the area from November 15th until the collapse on December 15th. Supernatural happenings combined with UFO sightings also abounded near Silver Bridge in that year before the collapse. The calamity unfolded like a disaster movie, with cars which, seconds before, had been crawling along in Christmas rush hour traffic now hung on fragments of the bridge before plunging, filled with passengers, into the frigid Ohio River.

Point Pleasant's Mothman cryptoid was introduced to those in the UFO field by John Keel in his 1975 book *"The Mothman Prophecies."* Keel related a number of supernatural events in that area before the bridge disaster, which were topped off by the mysterious Mothman sightings. In fact, Mothman was so prevalent in the year before the Silver Bridge collapsed that the creature established his identity at that point to the paranormal investigative world. Silver Bridge was for Mothman like the first mega-hit for a celebrity singer.

Mothman himself (could he actually be Mothwoman?) was reported to be a huge, semi-human, winged creature with glowing red eyes, sighted in and around Point Pleasant in 1966 and 1967. Between 6.5 and 7 feet tall, with a wingspan of nearly 10 feet, this shadowy creature was said to fly great distances at speeds up to 100 miles per hour.

Even though I respect John Keel's work and consider him one of my favorite Fortean writers, I might be a bit skeptical if I had not had paranormal events in and around my house, a spectacular UFO sighting near my house, and, yes, a Mothman sighting, right before one span of the Sunshine Skyway Bridge plunged into Tampa Bay on May 9, 1980, as I got ready for another day of teaching school. Strange events had been happening at and near my house, since 1979.

The most spectacular UFO sighting of my life thus far, at least which I remember consciously, was over a small park at the end of the street on which I lived. I lived in St. Petersburg, Florida, one block from Tampa Bay; the dual-span Sunshine Skyway could be seen from this park. It was a summer night in 1979 when my daughter and I walked our dog Bailey to the park. I was a field investigator for MUFON and APRO at the time, and so the two huge glowing white spheres which were hanging in the dark sky over Tampa Bay were absolutely thrilling!

We took the dog home, and raced back to the park with a camera. A small group of people had gathered to watch the huge orbs, which had not moved. Unlike weather balloons, there was absolutely no drifting in the breeze. Perhaps this was rocket fuel from a military test at MacDill Air Force Base, Tampa? Then this phenomenon should have slowly dissipated.

These objects were as white and solid-looking as a full moon before it becomes smaller at the zenith of the sky (there was no hint of color as the full moon often has when rising). They were not as large as the moon at the moment it comes up, but they were similar to perhaps 30 minutes later as the full moon rises. They were not directly overhead but seemed high over Tampa Bay, midway between horizon and sky zenith.

Finally, after several hours, as I looked down for just a second, one of the two dazzling white spheres just disappeared. Not a trace of it was left. Strangely, it was the orb with which I felt I was in communication, or trying to establish communication. It was there and then, in the blink of an eye, gone.

The other enormous sphere stayed there, not budging an inch, until I gave up and went home at 2:30 a.m. I had to teach school in the morning, but I have kicked myself ever since for leaving. No weather balloon, rocket fuel debris, helicopter, or Chinese lantern hoax would have stayed stationery for all those hours. I took photos and none turned out. What a "coincidence," a bad roll of film? There were one or two daytime photos at the beginning of the roll and they were also gone.

In 1979, which was the year before 35 people in cars and a Greyhound Bus plunged off one span of the Skyway Bridge to their deaths when the Summit Venture barge hit the bridge, my small house one block from Tampa Bay, which I shared with my parents and daughter, was full of paranormal activity. The walls beeped. The television beeped, at first at set intervals, and then randomly. As time progressed, lamps beeped, the clothes drier beeped, a hair blow drier beeped. Ok, maybe the house was on the path of some kind of waves from MacDill Air Force Base. So I took a cassette recorder on batteries about half a block away from the house, and it beeped too. My daughter and I recorded "the beeps" but when we replayed the tapes, the beeps were either gone or very faint. We never heard them far away from the house, however.

1979 was also my time of awakening as a UFO experiencer. In 1981, I underwent regression with Dr. R. Leo Sprinkle and remembered one of two UFO encounters when I was a child in Iowa.

After the Skyway fell and after I embraced my own UFO connection, the beeps eased off and then soon stopped entirely. Back to the morning of the Skyway disaster:

Wreckage of Greyhound Bus which plunged off the Skyway Bridge.

May 9, 1980, at 7:33 in the morning, I was hurriedly getting myself and my daughter ready for school when our smoke alarm started to beep. Of course I raced around to check for fire, and then realized it was not the fire warning, but also not the "battery low" signal. It sounded exactly like Morse Code, but I don't know Morse Code. My dad was trying to remember what he knew of Morse Code when we heard on the television news that a barge had just rammed into the Skyway Bridge at approximately 7:35 a.m.

The smoke alarm had stopped. And it never did that again.

Was this a desperate call for help from the energy-bodies of those who had just left their physical form? The Skyway Bridge was/is a tall structure and, to plunge off it, there would be a few seconds of falling, falling, and falling in sheer panic through the air in your vehicle.

Or, did whatever had been beeping at us all those months finally arrive at the awaited hour and madly send its message of death on the Skyway Bridge?

It was several months after the Skyway disaster that a memory struck me: I had been outdoors by myself in the summer of 1979, and the stars had suddenly been blotted out by something very large, opaque, and dark, but outlined in blood red. It had whooshed over, giving me the impression of a giant wingspan or a giant spread cape. It swooped low overhead, going faster than a large bird would fly and too big for a large bird, and then the stars re-emerged! *Mothman, I presume?*

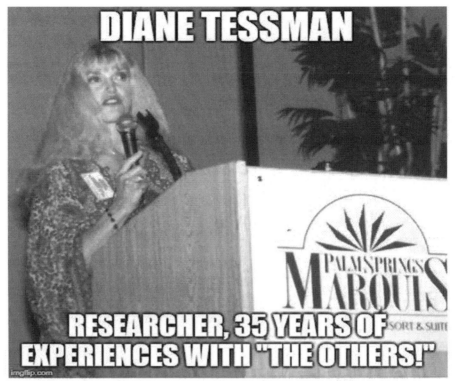

Diane's website: www.earthchangeprecitions.com
Please contact me for a free, online, current issue of my
Change Times Quarterly!

Above: Diane is seen here with Gabriel Green who ran for President in 1960 and again in 1972 as the "Space-Age Candidate."

Below: Diane with one of her many furry friends.

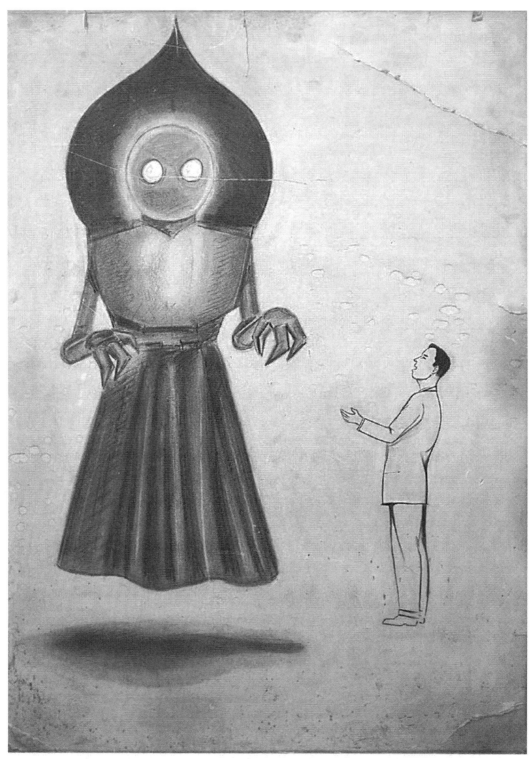

The Flatwoods Monster became a local legend, a Southern spook story that defined the tiny village of less than 300 people for decades afterwards.

THE ROARING FIFTIES – THE ERA OF ALIEN "MONSTERS"

PUBLISHER'S NOTE: I hate to call any living thing a "monster," but sometimes you have to avoid being politically – or cosmically – correct.

If you're a UFO historian – I consider myself to be one of the premier archivists in the field, with my 40 file cabinet drawers and shelves of books on the subject – you will surely realize that the 1950s in many respects was the heyday for flying saucer humanoids, as well as, the somewhat murky claims of those who professed to have encountered the strange crew members who brought their craft to a farm or open field near where they lived.

It is not bad enough that your typical eye witness to some type of puzzling aerial phenomena has to confront the unknown, but then you have those who find themselves face to face with a being, or beings, decidedly not of this earth.

Throughout these pages you will read of flaps and singular incidents that took place during the early days of flying saucer hoopla. This was in the days when the subject was still fresh in the minds of most, if, indeed they were even familiar with the topic at all. There was no podcasting, no 24-hour TV news, or even talk shows to share the weirdness that seemed to be going on all around us, under the cloak of darkness, and lack of media attention. I would assume it was harder to "make up" a story or mimic someone else's tale as there wasn't much information adrift in the cosmic airwaves to invent a scenario that would attract any sort of attention from the "outside" world.

There was the 1954 flap in France where "little men" were escalating assaults on humans, which we cover elsewhere. Let us also not forget the escalating mono e mono "battles" between earthlings and members of our global "creature feature" in Italy, Mexico and South America along this same time line.

The two incidents we would like to cover here and now took place in rural America just a few years apart and could be titled "Rednecks Battle The Aliens." And don't be offended. My daddy and uncle were rednecks from Shelbyville, Kentucky, where one of these spectacular cases took place.

Those deep into the UFO culture would have heard of these incidents, though we have some new information to add, and there are newbie's among us who are still virgins in the area of UFO encounters of the very personal and terrifying kind. Let them be warned: something about this case smells to high hell and back.

· · · · · · · · · ·

IT WAS GREEN AND TALL AND BREATHING FIRE!

By Sean Casteel

According to RoadsideAmerica.com, the Flatwoods Monster (also known as the Green Monster of Braxton County) was officially ignored by the town for over 60 years until the director of the Braxton County Visitors Bureau found an empty glass showcase in the back room and decided to dust it off and put in some local memorabilia.

"One display showcases the famous image of the Monster drawn only days after its appearance by a New York sketch artist, made from descriptions provided and vouched for by two of the witnesses. Another exhibit chronicles the history of the ceramic Braxton County Monster Lamps, first made in the 1960s. One of the original 'Welcome to Flatwoods, Home of the Green Monster' signs is preserved in the museum, as is a rare vinyl copy of the Flatwoods Monster single, 'The Being,' donated by its singer/songwriter, Argyle Goolsby. The museum has what is probably the world's most comprehensive library of Flatwoods Monster newspaper clippings and journal articles. It also has some genuinely bizarre DIY Flatwoods Monster costumes on display, including one made by a local high school theater group. 'I think the face is a pizza pan and the body is a couple of graduation gowns sewed together,'" says Andrew Smith the curator. For those who take their Flatwoods memorabilia quite seriously.

Flatwoods has embraced its monster legacy.

Perhaps the most evocative item in the museum is a section of the tree that stood next to the Monster during its brief visit to Flatwoods in 1952. "Right after the incident, the tree fell over and died," said Andrew. Having a piece of it is "incredibly rare." In gratitude for their contributions, Brandon and Goolsby were each given a toothpick-size sliver of the tree. "Argyle Goolsby just about pooped his pants," said Andrew.

But let us tell the story properly and from the very beginning.

It was a cool and windy night . . . well, I don't know if it was or not, so let's give up on our bad Stephen King opening and get right to the "hard and simple" facts.

The incident that gives the Flatwoods Monster its name took place around 7:15 P.M. on September 12, 1952, in Flatwoods, West Virginia. It began with the appearance of a bright object crossing the night sky near the tiny town of only 300 residents.

Two brothers, Edward and Fred May, along with their friend, Tommy Hyer, said they saw the bright object land on the property of a local farmer named G. Bailey

Fisher. The May brothers went to tell their mother, Kathleen May, what had happened. Mrs. May, accompanied by her sons, Hyer, two more local children and a West Virginia National Guardsman named Eugene Lemon, went to the Fisher farm in an attempt to locate whatever it was the boys had seen.

When the group reached the top of a hill, they saw a pulsing red light. Lemon aimed a flashlight in the direction of the light and momentarily they all saw a tall, "man-like figure with a round, red face surrounded by a pointed, hood-like shape." The creature moved toward them, seeming to be gliding rather than walking. A dog that had accompanied the group, frightened and with his tail between his legs, ran from the creature.

Descriptions have varied. And while some folks believe it was a living, breathing thingamajig, according to a website called Cryptids.Fandom.com, "The entity was initially reported as being about ten feet tall and four feet wide. It appeared to be some sort of robotic suit or spacecraft rather than an organic being. It had a 'cowl' in the shape of an ace of spades behind a round head."

Mrs. May appeared on television in New York, all the way from Braxton County, West Virginia,

The witnesses were reportedly scared out of their wits by their encounter with a ten-foot-tall "something or other" from out of this world.

The ace-of-spades description was reported by different witnesses independent of one another.

"Set in the head were two eyes," our reference continues, "described as 'portholes,' glowing green and the size of half-dollars. The 'body' was a metallic armored structure lined with thick vertical pipes. Discrepancies exist in the actual color of the armor, some claiming it to be black while others say it was green. The existence of arms is a similar matter. Most state the monster was armless, while others claim it possessed small, 'toy-like' arms." Meanwhile, Kathleen May, the mother of Edward and Fred, said the figure had "small, claw-like hands."

The group also saw and smelled a mist that made their eyes and noses burn. When the humanoid figure made a hissing sound and "glided toward the group," Lemon screamed and dropped his flashlight. All of this took place in a very few minutes, during which time Lemon fainted. The others dragged him with them as they fled from the scene.

Another website, thinkaboutitdocs.com, writes that Mrs. May contacted the local newspaper, "The Braxton Democrat," and a reporter named A. Lee Stewart, Jr., was dispatched to investigate her claims. The witnesses were barely able to speak, and Stewart felt there was no question that something had badly frightened them.

Soon afterwards, after Lemon had recovered, he and Stewart went to the spot where the creature and his strange craft were seen. The journalist noted that there was an acrid odor in the air that irritated his nose and throat. He returned alone the next morning and found "skid marks" going down the hill towards a large area of recently matted grass, which seemed to indicate that a large object had rested there. Stewart also discovered two tracks in the mud as well as traces of a thick black liquid. He immediately reported them as being possible signs of a saucer landing, though a local said later he had driven his Chevy pickup to the site to look for the creature himself, which may have partially accounted for what Stewart found.

In any case, the newspapers of the time quickly dubbed the incident "The Flatwoods Monster Sighting." It took place during a flurry of UFOs sightings in the same general region. Bailey Frame, a resident of nearby Birch River, reported seeing a bright orange ball circling over the area where the monster was spotted. It was visible for around fifteen minutes before it veered off towards the airport at Sutton, where the object was also reported.

According to another account, one week before the Flatwoods event, a Weston woman and her mother encountered the same or a similar creature. The younger woman was so terrified that she required hospitalization after the incident. Both mother and daughter also reported the noxious odor.

Years later, well-known researcher and writer John Keel interviewed a couple who claimed that on the evening following the September 12 sighting, and ten to fifteen miles to the southwest of it, they encountered a ten-foot-tall creature emitting a foul odor. It approached their stalled car then returned to the woods, Moments later, a luminous, pulsating sphere arose from the trees and ascended into the sky.

To give the skeptics their due, it was claimed that the bright light in the sky that preceded the sighting of the Flatwoods Monster was more likely a meteor, and the pulsating red light was probably an aircraft navigation/hazard beacon. The creature itself closely resembled an owl. It is suggested that the witnesses' perceptions were distorted by their heightened state of anxiety. The nausea the group experienced is also associated with hysteria and over-exertion.

In spite of any debunking by the Air Force and the various skeptics, the legend of the Flatwoods Monster has endured for decades and has even spawned a tourist industry in that tiny patch of West Virginia. Day trippers and vacationers travel to see the hillside where the monster appeared and to buy touristy trinkets. Local officials have erected a "Welcome to Flatwoods/Home of the Green Monster" sign on the route leading into the town.

Can we suggest you bring your gas mask? Only kidding – the odor cast off by the monster has long since dissipated!

This topnotch case has even become the subject of a film available on Amazon and YouTube produced by Small Town Monsters.

DON'T BLAME IT ON THE MOONSHINE
Roundup by Timothy Green Beckley

My grandfather on my dad's side of the family (whom I never met) had a creepy experience himself that no one in the family liked to talk about. He only mentioned it once to my father, and my dad, being a Southern Baptist, didn't feel it would bring the family closer to the Lord by relating this almost Halloween-like spooky encounter with a headless horseman.

I've only told the story twice, once for one of Brad Steiger's books (hey, "Brother Brad" flattered me several times by recounting paranormal stories from his life experiences) and the second time on Coast to Coast AM when George Noory was hosting.

It was apparently a fall evening and my granddaddy was closing up shop for the night by doing whatever you have to do to shut down a small farm for the night. I guess the dogs were barking up a storm and there seemed to be an amber glow coming from back of the barn. Fearing a fire, Randolph Beckley ventured off to see what the commotion was all about.

There was an illuminated figure seated on a horse dressed in military regalia, which would have been out of place by itself, but you have to add on – or take off, more appropriately – the fact that the figure was headless. Now Shelbyville is nowhere near Tarrytown, NY, and my grandfather was no Ichabod Crain.

I'm told the witness held his ground, though shaking in his boots, no doubt, and eventually the headless figure galloped away. What are we to make of this hereditary supernatural tale? A bit of historical research indicates that Kentucky declared its neutrality at the beginning of the battle between the North and South, but after a failed attempt by Confederate General Leonidas Polk to take the state for the Confederacy, the legislature petitioned the Union Army for assistance. That being the case, we assumed that the headless figure was a Confederate soldier trying to make his escape, only to have his head removed by cannon fire. An ugly situation regardless of the scenario.

Now the account we are about to relate also includes a bit of gunfire, but of a slightly more subtle nature – unless you happen to be the aliens, those little grey goblins, as they have become known – who were on the receiving end of some mighty powerful buckshot.

I feel particularly "close" to this historic UFOlogical event, not only because it remains one of my all-time favorite encounters with a gaggle of UFOnauts, but because I recently, along with co-host Tim Swartz, had the opportunity to interview the daughter of one of the main percipients in this case, which has to remain as one of the top ten humanoid sightings of all time.

But before introducing Geraldine let us unfold the evening's events.

In order to do so, I did a slow crawl through my files and found one of the first printed accounts, which came from an early issue of Gray – "*They Knew Too Much About Flying Saucers*" – Barker's "*Saucerian Review,*" which, for its day, was a rather polished, digest-sized magazine published out of his home town of Clarksburg, West Virginia. Gray was one of my mentors and my first major publisher. The report was written for him by Jacqueline Sanders, one of Barker's freelance stringers, who seemed to have her feet to the fire, being at the right place at the right time to investigate some of the stranger cases of the era. Her account may vary in places from what might have actually happened, but let us give her the benefit of the doubt.

A FULL REPORT FROM JACQUELINE SANDERS ON THE HOPKINSVILLE CREATURE ENCOUNTER

"Here we go again," I told myself. "A spaceship landing and little men."

But this report was different. This was interplanetary war, if the reports had been correct. For a farm family had defended itself against presumed spacemen with guns during a terrifying nightmare that recalled the horror of the Flatwoods, West Virginia monster incident.

When I walked into the Hopkinsville Police Station, it was jammed with people, most of them reporters, some of them law enforcement officials. When I asked about the little men, they became immediately interested in what I had to say, especially after I pulled out a copy of a UFO magazine and told them I was gathering information for a flying saucer publication.

The not-so-serious Timothy Green Beckley and Tim R. Swartz shapeshift into the Kelly "Green Men" at this sideshow display.

Chief of Police Russell Greenwell elbowed his way to the front immediately, took the magazine in his hand, and told me he was quite busy at the moment, but if I would step across the hall into his private office, he would take time to talk with me. I'm sure he used the excuse of being busy to enable him to talk saucers with me alone in his office. He was quite interested in the saucer mystery, but apparently others on the police force were talking, and he had been given "a rough time," he said, "over this deal." Police would yell at him, "Hey, Chief! Caught any little men lately? How many little men have you got in jail?"

I suspect that some of his men had their minds made up before they answered that strange call from the farmhouse, that there was no such thing as little men, spaceships or other planets – nothing, perhaps, but Hopkinsville and the surrounding country of their small little world. But after talking with the people who had witnessed what may have been an attack from outer space, they stopped to think twice about the reality of the saucermen.

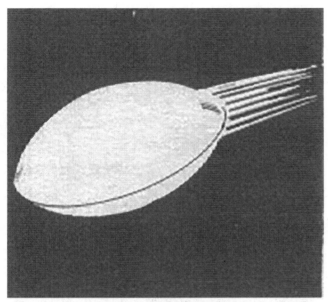

The object appeared as a fireball streaking across the sky in rural Hopkinsville, Kentucky.

The night of August 21, 1955, was the same as almost any other August 21 in Hopkinsville, Kentucky. That is, until shortly before midnight. Chief Greenwell was awakened by the telephone, a call from police headquarters, and thereby was plunged into the most bizarre investigations of his career. Two automobiles with terrified and excited people in them screamed around corners on two wheels, rushing to the station from nearby Kelly to report a strange battle. The spokesman for the group told police how an object resembling a flying saucer had landed in the field behind his home and 12 or 15 little men had emerged from the ship. The little men advanced on a farmhouse in which the residents were living. "We need help," one of the men said. "We've been fighting them for nearly four hours."

At the appeal for help, more than a dozen state, county and city police officers rushed to the scene, including four military policemen who happened to be in the area. They arrived at the farmhouse about 12:30 AM, but found no trace of the spacemen. Slowly the witnesses told their frightened, faltering story. The farmhouse was occupied by Cecil "Lucky" Sutton and his family, along with his mother, Mrs. Glennie Lankford. Some relatives were visiting the Suttons, I learned, along with a visitor from Pennsylvania, Billy Ray Taylor. I could not definitely establish just how many people were in the house at the time of the weird visitation.

SHOT AT THE SPACEMEN

The farmhouse is on Gather McGehe's property, about eight miles from Hopkinsville, and is rented from McGehe. It is an old tenant-type structure that sets about a mile back off the highway. A long hall runs through the center of the house, with screen doors at either end. It was in this hallway that one of the men, about 7:00 PM, saw the beginning of this outré adventure that would travel on news wires across the country. The man was standing at the end of the hallway, looking out the back screen door. Suddenly there was a hissing sound and he saw a brilliant light. Some bright object seemed to have landed in a field about a city block in distance away from the house.

Puzzled, he called to the others. When they came to look they saw three or four little men coming toward the house! But they were not ordinary men, they would soon discern. According to some of the witnesses, they were not walking, but "seemed to float" toward them. The creatures were about three-and-a-half to four feet tall, with huge eyes and hands, large pointed ears, and arms that hung almost to the ground. When asked about the clothing, the witnesses said the little men appeared to be "nickel plated." They didn't wait to see what the little men were up to. Extremely frightened by that time, they ran for their guns. Sutton grabbed a shotgun, Taylor a .22 caliber target pistol.

While they waited apprehensively inside the house for the creatures to attack, Mrs. Lankford begged them not to shoot. The creatures had not harmed them nor made any hostile moves. The man was standing at the end of the hallway, looking out the back screen door. Suddenly there was another hissing sound and he saw a brilliant light. Then a face appeared at the window, and Sutton let go with his shotgun. The face disappeared, seemingly unharmed. Thinking they had wounded the creature, the men decided to creep cautiously outside and investigate. Taylor walked down the hall and out the door. As he stepped under the low hanging roof, Sutton yelled "Look out! He's trying to get you!" – and a huge hand reached down and grabbed a fistful of Taylor's hair!

Taylor managed to pull loose and dashed out into the back with Sutton right behind him. After that, nobody seemed to know just what did happen. Evidently the men opened fire on the weird little creatures that were perched in the trees and on the house. They made direct hits on the "invaders." But bullets seemed to have no effect. When knocked down by a blast of Sutton's shotgun, the uninvited guests would pop right up again and disappear into the darkness.

Taylor told of knocking one of them off a barrel with his .22. He said he heard the bullet strike the creature, then whine as it ricocheted off! The little man tumbled to the ground, rolled like a ball, then floated off in the direction of the spaceship.

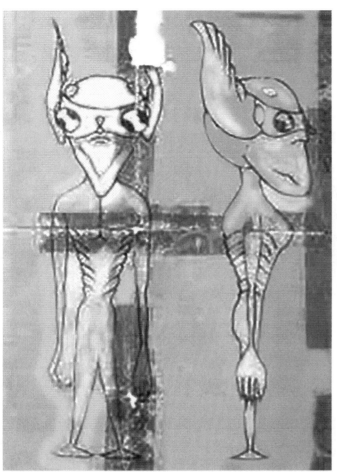

Left and Below...
Original sketches of the Kelly "Green Men" and UFO that were based on the witnesses' descriptions.

Taylor reportedly fired about four boxes of .22 shells. The battle went on for some time before the terrified occupants of the house saw their chance to escape to the cars and go for help.

POLICE INVESTIGATE

Rushing to the farm, Chief Greenwell and the other officers could find no trace of the little men. If they had been there, then they obviously had fled.

There was a hole in the screen covering the window all right, as evidence to show it had been made from the inside. There was only one thing strange about the opening made by the shotgun blast, a square hole, about an inch to an inch- and-a-half wide. When asked to account for the shape of the hole, none of the family could explain it. A shotgun had been fired through the window screen, they insisted, and that's all they knew. Taylor took Chief Greenwell around to the back of the house to show him where the little man had fallen off the barrel. One thing was certain: the man was still frightened. He stood at the low fence, which separated the back yard from the field, and pointed to the barrel – but refused to set foot into the field.

Chief Greenwell, along with the county sheriff and state troopers, searched the area thoroughly, but drew a blank. They found no evidence in the field to indicate that anything had landed in the spot described. Even though the ground was excessively dry and dusty, no footprints, tracks, or unusual markings were found. The painted roof showed no evidence of scratches. Most of the officers were reluctant to express any opinions about the reported invasion, but all seemed impressed with the evident fright and sincerity of the highly excited family. A check with neighbors disclosed that they "were not a drinking family," and no evidence of drinking was found around the place. All the witnesses told practically the same story, with only minor variations, depending on what part of the house they were in at the time of the happening.

"Something frightened those people," Chief Greenwell told me, even though nothing was found to either prove or disprove their stories. "There were a couple of things," he said, "you can take for what they are worth." An officer in his department, a Sergeant Salter, reported seeing a glowing light in the woods. He investigated but found nothing. A state trooper and his wife said they heard a loud "swishing" noise that "sounded like a motor," as they drove up to the farmhouse, yet they saw nothing.

Chief Greenwell impressed me as being an intelligent man. He is a veteran police officer, and in his line of duty has faced many dangerous situations. But never under any circumstances, he told me, had he ever experienced the sense of uneasiness he could feel that night around the Sutton farmhouse. He said the sensation was indescribable and he couldn't explain just how he had felt. "It was mighty uncomfortable," he said. Later he learned the other officers, despite all the people, the lights and confusion, had also felt this strangeness in the air, which one of them had described as "like being alone in a haunted house."

The goblin-like creature appeared at the window and was shot at. Illustration from the Pennyroyal Museum, Hopkinsville, Kentucky.

The investigators got quite a start, however, as one of the MPs was wandering around in the darkness. He happened to step on a cat's tail and it let out a yell that could be heard all over the place. The MP leaped into the air, and for a few seconds there was considerable activity and scurrying around by the more than 25 people present. Finding nothing, the officers returned to town. The next morning, Chief Greenwell went back to the farm to complete his investigation.

THE LITTLE MEN RETURN

Upon his return, the family told Chief Greenwell the little men had paid them a return visit around 3:30 AM. Another shot had been fired through the window. Upon examination the screen proved to show another hole beside the first one. This, too, was made from the inside, but it was a jagged round hole. He questioned Mrs. Lankford about the night's events. She upheld the story the menfolk had told.

"I only know what I saw. I saw two of the men, or maybe the same one twice. I saw one about 10:30, and the other one around 3:30 AM. That time I watched the little man for more than a minute. I had gone to bed and saw him through the window." She went on to say, "Seven out of the eight adults saw one or more of the little men. When seven people see something there must be something there." Mrs. Lankford, according to Chief Greenwell, was "almost petrified with fright." She told him her husband had worked the small tract of ground on which the house stood before his death, and that she had contemplated buying the house. "But after last night, I don't know," she stated.

Reportedly Air Force investigators from two nearby fields thoroughly covered the incident; however, this was denied in one of the follow-up stories in the local paper, ""*The New Era*."" Newswire stories mentioned "glowing green men" and even "a terrible stench." These descriptive phrases were either borrowed from other "little men" stories and added by imaginative reporters, or the Sutton family had told the reporters more than they had told the investigating officers.

Yes, there were indeed strange goings on in Hopkinsville that night. But what did Mrs. Lankford, Cecil Sutton, Billy Ray Taylor and the others have to tell me?

Nothing.

FAMILY DISAPPEARS

PUBLISHER'S NOTE: The author's reporting now gets a bit convoluted as she relates how the witnesses vanished and could not be located. This is in contradiction to the many revelations of "Lucky's" daughter, who appeared on our show recently. But we will get to these recollections in a bit, which will update our decades old encounter, and which is still as enticing as it was the night this incredible saga transpired.

By the time I arrived at Hopkinsville, they had disappeared. Gone, bag and baggage – less than 48 hours after the "invasion." Why? Their disappearance could have been due to a number of reasons. For one thing, people came from miles around to the farmhouse, tramped over the grounds, took pictures of the house, inside and out, and collected souvenirs.

Someone suggested the situation might be alleviated by posting a "50¢ admission" sign. But the people still came, and they made it a dollar. Before they were through, they had the price of taking pictures of the family up to $10.00. Some people may jump to the conclusion that this was the whole idea of the thing, and that perhaps the family had only made up the story. Chief Greenwell didn't think so, however. Especially since they had moved out so soon, while people were still visiting the farm. I thought the story might be a hoax that had just gotten out of hand; or maybe they just couldn't stand to stay around the place any longer after the terrifying night.

There is always Conclusion Number 4: The Air Force spirited them away to keep them from talking, or, Number 5: I guess it is always possible, though perhaps unlikely, the little men might have come back and taken them along with them that time.

I should have gone into their disappearance more deeply, for after thinking it over there is a distinct possibility that the police were protecting the family from curiosity seekers. They told me the farmhouse was empty, they posted "No trespassing, road closed" or something like that. At the time I didn't question it at all. After I was too far away to go back and check for myself at the farm, I began to wonder about the alleged disappearance.

· · · · · · · · · ·

So there you have the complete report from Barker's *"Saucerian Review."* It's a chilling account. Obviously the family and their guests were frightened. There can be no doubt about that. But the family did not really disappear, though they may have played a game of "cat and mouse" with the pubic and the press. How many times can you tell the same story? Hey, we couldn't have them on our show at the time, but years, and we mean years, later we hit the nail on the "alien's" head by having a Sutton sharing our podcast/YouTube microphones in order to give addition details and to make some clarifications.

The following is the press release and posting we put out a few days before the show which we titled: "Terror In Kentucky, With Guest Geraldine Sutton Stith."

"Sixty-four years ago, a rural family in Kentucky found themselves face to face with the unknown. This bizarre encounter brought the Sutton family into the bright spotlight of unwelcome media attention, from which they never truly were able to escape. The Sunday of August 21, 1955, has gone down in UFO history as the night of the Kelly-Hopkinsville encounter. That night, after a UFO was seen to land behind a nearby barn, a number of strange humanoid creatures spent the night tormenting 11 people cowering in the farmhouse.

This week on Exploring the Bizarre, our guest, Geraldine Sutton Stith, will relate what it was like to grow up with the specter of the unknown hanging over her family and how, despite assertions from the skeptics, she knows that something truly frightening happened on that dark night in 1955."

"Exploring the Bizarre," Thursday nights at 10:00 PM EST on the KCOR Digital Radio Network. kcorradio.com."

GERALDINE SUTTON STITH

Geraldine Sutton Stith knows what it is like to grow up with something strange hanging over you. Being the daughter of Elmer "Lucky" Sutton and finding out at a very young age that your family had an alien encounter can be quite alarming! Nine family members and two family friends witnessed something amazing on August 21st,

1955, in the small community of Kelly, Kentucky, that changed their lives forever. Was it extraterrestrial or possibly paranormal? Growing up with the story and knowing what happened that night according to family, she knew someone had to keep it going. Even though there is a great fear, even for her, the story must continue and the community of Kelly must keep their little goblins alive.

Geraldine is the author of the books *"The Kelly Green Men"* and *"Alien Legacy."*

Ok, to put it simply we obviously can't print the entire transcript of the show — but we can take bits and pieces and suggest that those sincerely interested in this all important, historic case may listen to the hour interview on Stitcher, iTunes, Google Plays, or for the visuals get yourself right over to "Mr. UFO's Secret Files" and go directly to the link – www.youtube.com/watch?v=090Nuo8BT1M

TIM: It's fabulous we were able to get Geraldine Sutton Stith on with us tonight. Now Geraldine is the daughter of Elmer Sutton and finding out at a very young age that eleven family members and family friends had an alien encounter could be quite alarming. So why don't you give us the details – the gist – of the story . . .

Highly condensed.

GERALDINE: It was August, 1955. At the time my grandmother was a widow who lived on this little farm in Kelly with her three small children who were twelve, ten, and seven, along with my uncle JC, who was in his early 20s, and his wife, Eileen. Also there was Opie Baker. Opie would stay there during the week to catch a ride to work and along that weekend also was my dad, Elmer Sutton, and his wife Veera and their friends Billy Ray and June Taylor (9 people in all). They'd come in as they worked in the carnival which was stationed in Evansville. My dad had worked with the carnival ever since he was like 14 years old. They came primarily to enjoy some good home cooking and relax a bit, as it was a Sunday evening, which would have been the 21st. That would be their last evening to enjoy some time together.

It was a hot, dry, August evening, really hot and dry, and they didn't have indoor plumbing . . . they had electricity, but no plumbing. And so around 7:30 Billy Ray decided to go around back to the well.

Geraldine Sutton Stith describes the night of terror for "Exploring the Bizarre" listeners.

As he was out there getting some water, he heard something and looked up toward the sky and there was a silver, oval object, which he described as having the colors of the rainbow flowing behind it He didn't know what it was and ran in the house telling everybody what he saw. Their reaction was that they thought, okay, Billy Ray, who was in his early 20s –his wife was only like 18 or 19 – and surely while out back he thought up some cockamamie story just to scare the girls.

Well, he kept on with his sighting, so my dad says "Show me," and Billy Ray took him outside and told him again all about what he had seen. Daddy told him, "It had to be a shooting star!" To which Billy replied that he was familiar with meteorites, as there had been meteor showers all month. Acknowledging that there was nothing to see, they both headed back to the house to enjoy what little time they had left to spend together, when, suddenly, coming from the woods, was this little three-and-a-half-foot being floating atop the ground with huge glowing eyes, huge ears, big head and arms almost touching the ground. They get to the front door and open it and slam it behind them. They excitedly tell the family what they have seen and everyone thinks they are crazy or got together out back and conspired to tell the same story to scare everyone in the house.

At this point, my grandmother tells them they need to just stop it as the kids have to get to bed and they're not helping. But they keep insisting there is something out there and they both take a rifle and a shotgun down and one goes to the front door and the other goes to the back. My grandmother has had enough and so she goes joins Billy Ray out back and he's squatting down there and she wants to know once and for all what did he see, at which point he tells her, in no uncertain terms, "Miss Glenny, I don't know what it was, but I hope it's something that you never have to see.

They sit out there in silence for a little while and then, lo and behold, around the corner of the house right where they were sitting was this little being. Grandma screams and everyone comes running to find out what is going on and she tells them there definitely is something going on, that she just them one of these things. Then a shot rings out. Uncle JC has shot one through the window and the same time a clawed hand reaches down to grab Billy Ray's hair and Aunt Eileen (coming to the rescue) pulls Billy Ray back indoors. A skirmish is going on and my dad runs back out and points toward the roof and shoots at the being, who in turn floats to the ground and rolls away.

They're shooting them off the back fence and the very same thing is happening. They are not dying, even though the men are hitting them over and over. I mean, these are country boys and they know how to shoot a rifle. They can hear where they are hitting them, but the darn things just wouldn't die. They just keep getting back up!

These are just country folks and they have no clue what is happening – not that anyone would today. My dad tries to settle everybody down. The kids are crying, the women are crying, and everyone is just absolutely losing it. They get into their trucks and head toward Hopkinsville to get some help. Hopkinsville is about seven miles down the road. So they try to get themselves together, and, about this time, they hear one of them things go across the tin roof, as you can hear the little nails scratching across it. There is more screaming and crying and when things settle down again Billy Ray says, "Let's go!"

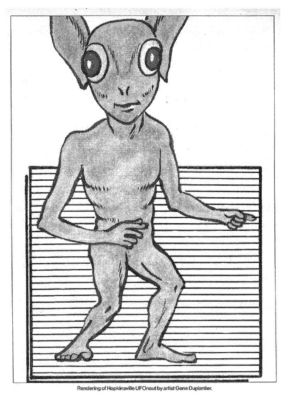

Rendering of Hopkinsville UFOnaut by artist Gene Duplantier.

Saucer, Space and Science editor Gene Duplantier rendered this drawing for a UFO calendar published by Beckley's firm years ago.

They get to the police station and here you have all these people from the age of seven to fifty running in there and they don't know what to do and they're all trying to tell the officer on duty what has just happened to them, how these little men have attacked their farm, and the officer is joined by other members of the police force and they are all trying to understand what is being said and what kind of situation they are having to deal with.

They call over to Fort Campbell Army Base, which is just down the road, to get some help. So there is this caravan of vehicles leaving Kelly in the middle of the night headed back to the house. Of course it is pitch black back then in 55, as they don't have streetlights anywhere.

Well, they pull up to the house and (later they admitted) that there was this eerie feeling in the air and there is evidence that something had happened because there were holes in the screens and the woodwork was shot up. There were even shotgun and rifle shells all over the place and the family was so scared they wouldn't even get out of their vehicles until the officials that had arrived with them had searched the house and buildings and gave the all-clear. There were no body parts, and no blood, so there wasn't anything the police could do and so eventually they left.

• • • • • • • • •

The transcript of the show with Geraldine goes on for another thirty five minutes or so, going into more detail about what happened next. For the full drama, we want you to go over to the KCORradio.com archives or watch our YouTube producer Peter Bernard's visual presentation at Mr. UFO's Secret Files. Geraldine is a great storyteller and she has kept the family's legacy alive. And if you are Kentucky-bound, you have to stop in at the annual Kelly "Little Green Men Days Festival." www.kellyky.com/

And, by the way, the creatures, the goblins, the little men, the aliens − whatever in God's name you want to call them − DID return, and it wasn't until the sun finally came up that they went away and the scratching and all the commotion came to an abrupt end. This is doubtless one of the most incredible encounters that we have been confronted with and certainly belongs in a book that looks into such cases quite seriously.

Glad you survived the journey, but there are more boldly told case studies to come!

One of Geraldine's book covers, available from Amazon.

SUGGESTED READING

ALIEN LEGACY & THE KELLY GREEN MEN
By Geraldine Sutton Stith

TIM BECKLEY'S UFO SAGA

AMERICA'S STRANGE AND SUPERNATURAL
HISTORY by Tim Swartz

UFO HOSTILITIES by Beckley, Casteel, Swartz
and others

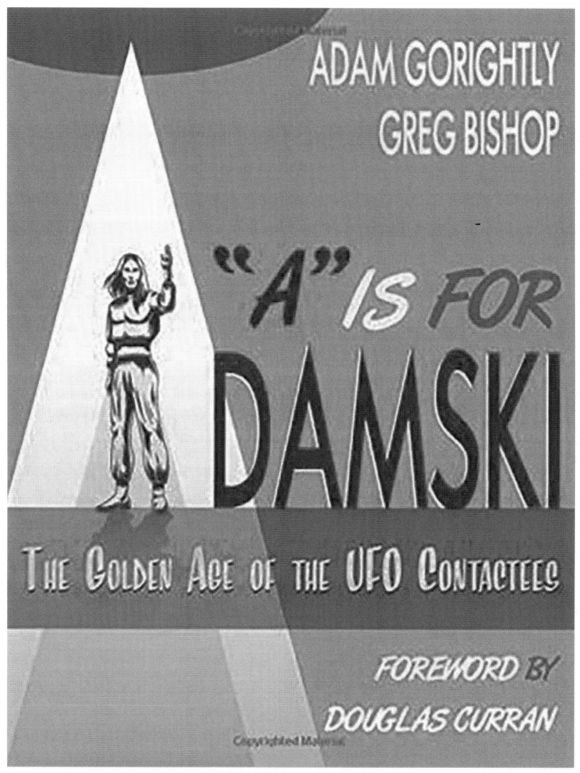

Adam's latest book on personalities in the UFO contactee movement is
"'A' Is For Adamski."

THE INCREDIBLY SEXY SAUCER PEOPLE

By Adam Gorightly

PUBLISHER'S NOTE: One of the things UFO outsiders seem critical of is the "fact" that UFOlogy seems to be an all-male field. Actually, that's hardly true, at least now as opposed to "the way things were" back in the Fifties, Sixties and Seventies. And while the audience at UFO conferences may be "mixed" these days, those delivering the talks are still mainly of the male persuasion.

As for the percipients – i.e., witnesses, contactees and abductees – no survey has been done that I know of. So the number of men vs. the women in this category is difficult for me to determine. It might be that there are a few more gals being subjected to the whims of our ultra-terrestrials "friends." Those that rape, pillage and plunder are excluded!

Adam Gorightly is a treat. The kind of guy you could smoke a blunt and have a brew with. I would consider him to be more of a pop culture icon than a UFOlogist, though he does, I am sure, have any number of solid cases he has looked into under his belt. He lives out near Giant Rock and Joshua Tree, California, which is ground zero for some of the most outlandish UFO tales of all time. But in particular from the early days of flying saucerdom, when a group of humans claimed they were meeting non-earthlings and taking off to Mars, or some other nearby world in space.

On his web site https://chasingufosblog.com Adam gives us two example of the feminine persuasion's personal involvement with the boys from topside. One of the ladies is very much an Earth person, a very attractive one at that, while the other might be a beauty queen on her home planet far, far away.

I knew Barbara Hudson, the "Earth woman," rather well. We hung out in Manhattan and I was so mesmerized by her contact experiences that I was going to write a book based upon her encounters with a band of Nordic-looking Space Brothers she called, "The Group." What was most unusual, or at least everybody seemed to think so, was that Barbara was an Afro-American lady − I would say in her late twenties, though I do not remember ever asking her age. She lived up in Harlem during a period when most of us "whiteys" were afraid to get off the train at 125 Street, which was actually very close to the Apollo Theater. But I was never afraid to go anywhere and would visit her around say 10:00 PM and stay to maybe 2 or 3 and never had any problem getting home. Actually, it may be worse in the subway these days than it was then late at night because of all the homeless and mentally ill individuals who populate the underground.

I do recall traveling to Point Pleasant, West Virginia, with Barbara and Jim Moseley to hook up with Saucerian Press publisher Gray Barker in order to visit the TNT area where Mothman had been seen numerous times, flapping its wings and shooting up into the sky like a rocket.. Though segregation was officially a thing of the past, I do remember getting eyeballed dancing with Ms. Hudson in the Holiday Inn lounge.

Too damn bad for them!

But this is not my story, it is Adam's.

• • • • • • • • •

At the Giant Rock Conventions of the 1960s (and other ufological outings), Barbara Hudson became a running mate of sorts with Gray Barker and Jim Moseley, forming a trio that average middle America probably viewed with a certain degree of curiosity: Two hard drinking white male Ufologist-Pranksters—one gay and one straight—in the company of a young, attractive African-American woman who claimed she belonged to a secret organization called "The Group." According to Gray Barker, Hudson "radiated both a dainty femininity and certain sexiness" amid an "aura of mystery." Barker no doubt helped foster this mysterious aura with his claim that he observed Hudson's doppelgänger at the 1970 Giant Rock Interplanetary Spacecraft Convention, although one could attribute such tales to Barker's penchant to stretch the truth or, conversely, from seeing double after a few too many nips of demon alcohol.

Hudson's entrée into the '60s saucer scene began when three mysterious men (presumably in black) showed up at her apartment in New York City one evening and informed her that she'd been chosen to become a member of a secretive outfit involved with UFOs. The three mystery men drove Hudson to a remote stretch of Long Island, along the way treating her to a demonstration of exotic ET gadgets. When they arrived at the secluded Long Island compound, Hudson was introduced to other members of "The Group," a secret alliance of humans and ETs who had joined forces to reveal the startling truth of the flying saucer mystery! (Publishers Note: Kind of like UMMO or the Friendship groups, which we have "documented" in other works).

"The Group" was responsible for Hudson's involvement with the UFO conference scene, and in fact directed her to attend one of Jim Moseley's conventions so they could "keep an eye on things." According to Tim Beckley, Moseley's interest in Hudson was not only UFO-related, but the two enjoyed a romantic relationship. Hudson—along with Barker, Moseley and Beckley—traveled to Point Pleasant during the Mothman craze, and some of her activities there are chronicled in Gray Barker's *The Silver Bridge* (1970).

Tim Beckley heard many of Hudson's stories firsthand and felt that she related them with conviction, although—as Beckley informed your humble author—there was no way to verify her claims, all of which added to Hudson's "aura of mystery."

At one time or another—according to Beckley—Hudson was writing a UFO themed book, which—it appears—was never completed, although an excerpt from Hudson's book-in-the-works appeared in Beckley' newsletter from 1968 entitled "A Visitor From Saturn?" by Barbara J. Hudson. (Make note of the "J" in her name.)

As I was recently perusing the Jim Moseley memorial site, I came upon a page dedicated to a 2014 "Internet Roast" of Moseley that included this post by long time ufologist Tom Benson, who recalled:

The monster and the lady – Barbara Hudson examines
the creature from Flatwoods, West Virginia
(a model, we hasten to say).

"*I initially observed your activities at the National UFO Conference (NUFOC) located in a semi-rundown motel in King of Prussia, Pennsylvania, in 1974, long after you began your chasing saucers career in 1953. At this Con, you were mainly introducing speakers including Jan Barbara Hudson, author of 'Those Sexy Saucer People' (Greenleaf, 1967, Saucerian ?), and hawking back issues of Saucer News...*

"*Among the most rare of old school UFO books is the aforementioned and wondrously titled 'Those Sexy Saucer People' (1967) authored by a fellow named George H. Smith under the pseudonym of Jan Hudson, copies of which nowadays are nearly impossible to find and go for in excess of the super-ridiculous price of $300 smackeroos. George H. Smith, according to this link, authored a number of saucy adult-themed titles for Greenleaf Press, such as 'Orgy Buyer' and 'The Sex and Savagery of the Hells Angels,' all of them under a variety of pen names, one of which was Jan Hudson.*

INCREDIBLE ALIEN ENCOUNTERS

"Tom Benson's remarks might lead some to suspect that it was actually Barbara Jan Hudson who authored 'Those Sexy Saucer People'—or that Hudson may have supplied content for the book—which seems entirely possible because, as noted, she was working on her own book at the time. Taking my working theory one step further, Hudson then provided a rough manuscript to George H. Smith, who worked his literary magic on it, as demonstrated in the passage below:

"Tom Benson also noted that Gray Barker's Saucerian (?) Press may have also been involved in some way, which got me to thinking that maybe 'Those Sexy Saucer People' was a project that Barbara Hudson was working on for Saucerian, and then the book was later picked up by Greenleaf Press for mass distribution. (Maybe.)

When I ran my working theory by Tim Beckley—that Barbara Hudson had played some sort of role in authoring "Those Sexy Saucer People"—he pretty much pooh-poohed the idea, and seemed confident that neither Barbara Hudson nor Gray Barker had anything to do with the book, and in fact he vaguely recalled having known George H. Smith, as well as the publisher for Greenleaf, William Hamling, who also published a number of pulp magazines of the period, many of which were not only adult themed but also included science fiction and flying saucers, and that Ray Palmer—who some regard as the father of the flying saucer pulps—had been associated with Hamling as an editor, author and co-conspirator.

Anyway—after Beckley let the air out of my "Barbara Hudson Sexy Saucer People" balloon—I thought I'd take one more stab at chasing down this mystery and contacted David Houchin of the Gray Barker Collection at the Clarksburg Library to see if he had any knowledge of a possible book that Barbara Hudson had been working on for *Saucerian Press* at one time or another—or if he was aware of any material in the Gray Barker Collection related to "Those Sexy Saucer People." As it turned out, Houchin did indeed possess a copy of "Those Sexy Saucer People" in all its lurid glory, which is on proud display at the Clarksburg Library, but unfortunately Houchin could find nothing in the files related to Barbara Hudson writing a book on the sexy saucer theme.

Worth the price? This sleazy paperback is going for $100 on e-bay. The author is NO relation to Barbara Hudson.

But—as fickle fate would have it—there was a 20 page document in the Gray Barker Collection entitled—you guessed it! — "*Sexy Saucer People*" that had nothing to do with the book by the same/similar name—or with Barbara Hudson, for that matter. Go figure.

Thanks to Erickson, a fellow seeker with the Scheme Gene Research Community, who shared the images in this post from the ultra-rare "*Those Sexy Saucer People*." Erickson, it should be noted, has willed to me his copy of the book if he happens to get run over by a flying saucer anytime soon.

For more amazing stories featuring *real* UFO contactees, pick up your very own copy of *"A" is for Adamski: The Golden Age of the UFO Contactees* while supplies last!

PUBLISHER'S AFTERTHOUGHT – Poppycock. Greenleaf Classics published extreme, hard core paperbacks, the titles of which I would not even press upon our humble readership, no prude being I, but we should leave works like "SM Mother" alone. Interestingly enough, several well-known conspiracy and UFO authors made extra income by grinding out these pornographic novels at $400 a clip with cash on the barrel head. Somehow Ray Palmer and Richard Shaver got sucked into this porno ring and the FBI even raided Palmer's printing plant in Amherst, Wisconsin, because he had his name on some corporate papers without realizing the nature of the material that was being distributed (though he claimed that he never even printed any of the material). Today, with Pornhub and other web sites with millions of steady viewers, these little trash novels would go unnoticed, though, I repeat, neither Barbara Hudson nor Gray Barker had anything to do with "The Sexy Saucer People." Greenleaf did publish one legitimate UFO book, it was by – yup, you might have guessed it – Ray Palmer.

And while Barbara and I never finished the book – actually we only did two or three short chapters, one dealing with a UFO crash she witnessed in Central Park has been published in my *UFO Crash Legends* book – I did print one or two of her sensational accounts in various publications I was responsible for publishing. The following originally appeared in my "*UFO Review*" tabloid in June of 1979.

· · · · · · · · ·

INSIDE THE SHIP
By Barbara Hudson

In the summer of 1955, I found myself leading a rather typical life for a girl who had just turned fifteen. I had occasional dates and was just beginning to think about my upcoming year in high school. One rather humid night I was tossing and turning in bed, even though the luminous hands of the clock showed the time to be 3:00 AM. Suddenly my attention was turned to the adjoining room where my mother was sleeping. Approaching seemed to be the footsteps of a very heavy person. I could clearly hear the sound of the floorboards creaking beneath the weight of someone walking. Thinking perhaps that it was my father or mother, I neglected to turn to see who it was. But after the footsteps stopped I then became aware of eyes watching me. It was then that I turned over in bed and noticed a man standing in the doorway.

Thinking that he may be a prowler I became alarmed and paralyzed with fear. Through the darkness of the room I could make out a figure of a very tall "human being." My attention was almost immediately drawn to his eyes. They were piercing shafts of light which seemed to have an almost hypnotic effect on me. Then, crossing the room, he stopped at the foot of my bed. I felt slight movement as if I were in an elevator. It seemed like a matter of only seconds before the door reopened, and when it did I found myself in a long corridor with rounded sides and occasional doors down both sides.

By the light from the hallway I could tell that the man who had led me here was way over six feet tall, perhaps closer to seven. He had dark hair, dark complexion and was very broad. Staring closely at his eyes, one could tell that the iris was much larger than those of a normal person. In fact, the black of the eyeball seemed to cover almost the entire part of the eye, replacing the white in a normal earth person's eye. The center of the pupil was more of a dark brown; it had been from here that I had first seen the shafts of light extending toward my bed. Only while in the dark was this glow visible. His facial features, other than his eyes, seemed to be quite normal. Helping me in and out of the "mist" I managed to touch him several times. His flesh felt very soft, almost as if he had no bones in his body. He was warm to the touch and was definitely a physical being. In short, by earthly standards, he wasn't handsome – but he wasn't monstrous either.

This being then asked me to step out into the corridor and to walk to the far end of the passageway. At the end of the passage there was another man. The spokesman for the group told me that I was the first woman since Biblical times to have been taken aboard one of their craft. It was explained to me that I was aboard one of their mother ships, which was used as a laboratory, and that the occupants of this ship were in the process of taking samples of the Earth's atmosphere.

They told me that their main purpose in bringing me aboard was that they wanted to show me what the planet Earth looked like from outside our atmosphere. Then I was escorted to another room where a meal was in the process of being served. It consisted chiefly of fruits and wines. Placed before me was a piece of fruit which resembled an apple or something which looked like a melon. Bowls and bowls of fruit of various kinds were laid out on crystal top tables that were of smoky glass color. After I had completed the meal, I was told that it was time for me to return to my apartment. Before departing I was told that their race was visiting Earth in an attempt to contact "their own."

I was puzzled by this remark and was told that I would understand more about this in the future. At no time was I told from which planet they came— and believe it or not I never thought to ask. It's almost as if this thought had been extracted from my mind so that this question could not be posed. I was led back down the hallway by the one who brought me there. I entered through a sliding door and found myself in an identical cubicle to the one that I had arrived in. I felt a downward motion and could feel myself becoming slightly nauseous as one would feel descending rapidly in an elevator.

A being materialized in Barbara Hudson's bedroom, shooting beams of light out of its eyes

When the door opened, we were surrounded by the same fog-type mist in the center of my dining room. The entity stepped out first and reached for me, grabbing me at the waist and pulling me down after him. Before leaving, he told me that there would be further contacts but he did not give a specific time. Stepping back inside the mist, he raised his hand in a gesture of farewell. I went immediately and turned on the light but saw nothing— even the "mist" had vanished. My dog Sheene came over, greeted me, and went at once to the center of the floor, where the strange capsule from outer space had been only brief seconds before.

Walking back into the front, my mother was sitting up in bed and, as I passed her on the way back to my room, she questioned me as to why I was doing so much walking. Puzzled, I asked her if she had seen anyone else besides me, to which she remarked that the only thing she heard had been footsteps. I went back into my room and sat on the bed, once again unable to sleep. This time the problem stemmed from my brief experience inside a ship from another world.

· · · · · · · · · ·

DID THE SPACEWOMAN AURA RHANES VISIT GIANT ROCK?
By Adam Gorightly

PUBLISHER'S NOTE: Some alien women are sharp cookies. I've heard it batted around that they could be considered "space goddesses." Hey, you must have read the reports of these fully blossomed gals from some far off star teasing Earth men in their tight-fitting jump suits fashioned by Frederick's of Hollywood? Most of these interplanetary vixens are from the realm of a man's imagination, such as Samjasi, who Swiss contactee Billie Meier claims to have hung out with on a regular basis, but who in reality is a dancer from the old Dean Martin TV show, part of his Gold-Digger troop. Billie just blurred her face a bit for his flying saucer fake picture book, but there is no mistaking the image.

The same can't be said for Clarion visitor Aura Rhanes, who has greeted several individuals walking out of her scrow (i.e., space ship for the uninformed). On Greg Bishop's podcast, "Radio Misterioso," "serious researcher" Ray Stanford tells listeners an incredible story, giving details as to why he is pretty certain that Ms. Rhanes is the real thing. Says Bishop: "One personality for whom he still holds a little respect, surprisingly, is Truman Bethurum, who claimed contact with a beautiful space maiden named Aura Rhanes."

http://radiomisterioso.com/2009/01/20/ray-stanford-contactees-psychic-and-scientific-ufology/

In *"Aboard A Flying Saucer"* (1954), Truman Bethurum recounted his amazing interactions with a beret-wearing flying saucer captain named Aura Rhanes, who he described as "tops in shapeliness and beauty." Over a three month period starting in July of 1952, Aura visited Truman on eleven occasions, sometimes materializing in his bedroom, much to the chagrin of Bethurum's wife, Mary, who later cited the comely space captain in her divorce petition.

Carol Ann Rodriguez was inspired to do this portrait of Aura Rhanes, the space gal from Clarion.

Bethurum enjoyed another shot at marital bliss in 1960, although, unfortunately, it wasn't with shapely Aura, but a weathered old gal named Alvira Roberts, their nuptials taking place on the podium of that year's Giant Rock Interplanetary Spacecraft Convention.

A couple months back, my pal, Tim Beckley, asked my thoughts about a purported photo circulating on social media that certain people were claiming was an honest-to-Orthon photo of Aura Rhanes herself at Giant Rock! All of this was news to me, and when I finally got a gander of said photo I recognized it immediately as one among a series of photos that originated from the Bob Beck Collection, many of which appear exclusively in *"'A' is for Adamski: The Golden Age of the UFO Contactees,"* available now from an internet bookseller near you. (Supplies limited!)

On the following page is the photo in question purported to be Aura Rhanes wearing smoking hot black tights (sans beret) in the company of Long John Nebel and another fellow who I suppose could be Valiant Thor of *Stranger at the Pentagon* fame.

Not to rain on anyone's Facebook parade, but no, folks, the photo isn't of Aura Rhanes, although I commend the creativity of whoever floated this social media meme-rumor. Those humans actually pictured in said photo are (left to right) Cortland Hastings, Evelyn E. Smith and Long John Nebel.

I have no idea who Cortland Hastings was, and, of course, we all should know who Long John Nebel was. As for the lady purported to be Aura Rhanes, that was actually Evelyn E. Smith, the author of a number of science fiction and mystery novels, whose work occasionally appeared in the science fiction pulps of the period, as shown.

Below is further documentation that Evelyn Smith was who I said she was, courtesy of the May 27, 1957, edition of *Life Magazine* with a feature on the Giant Rock Interplanetary Spaceship Convention and a photo of Smith (not Aura!), described as "The Queen of Space"!

Now you know the rest of the story!

Mystery photo of "Aura Rhanes" with talk show host Long John Nebel (far right) taken at Giant Rock Airport.

A self-described "crackpot historian," Adam Gorightly's articles have appeared for two decades in nearly every 'zine, underground magazine, counter-cultural publication and conspiratorial website imaginable. Bringing a mischievous sense of Prankster-Discordianism to the zany world of fringe culture, once Gorightly connects his dots, readers are plunged into alternative universes that forever alter their view of "reality." Adam is pictured here seated next to Robert Anton Wilson.

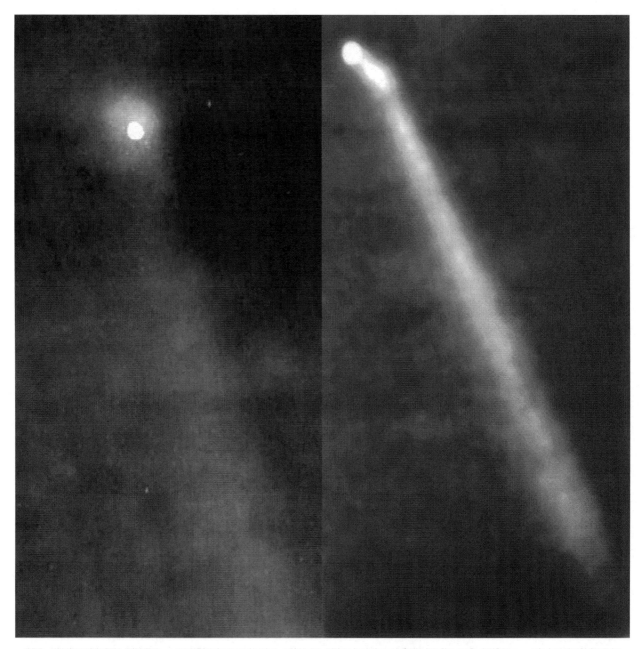

On August 19, 1949, a UFO was seen above the town of Norwood, Ohio. A searchlight operator, Army Sgt. Donald R. Berger, was sweeping the light across the sky during a local carnival when it flashed across a stationary circular object hanging in the sky. The Norwood case involves 10 visual sightings by multiple civilian, clergy, police and military witnesses over a 7-month duration. This case is especially unusual because photos show that while the searchlight beam was projecting several degrees away from the object, it was seen to bend or be "pulled" directly into the UFO.

UFO ENCOUNTERS - OHIO AND THE MIDWEST

PUBLISHER'S NOTE: The state of Ohio has maintained its high ranking as far as the number of sightings go in the Buckeye State. As far as my memory goes back, there has always been an enthusiastic group of believers in the area, especially around Cleveland. I remember tuning in on my powerful radio receiver with a directional antenna on the roof every Tuesday night to catch the latest Cleveland UFOlogy Round Table hosted by that pioneer, Earl Neff, who was the top gun (UFO-wise anyway) in and around the state at that time. The acronym for the group is CUP and the organization is still around and active to this day, holding regular meetings and collecting reports.

But the most active figure as far as I have always been concerned is Rick Hilberg. The publisher of "UFO Digest" has been hitting the UFO trail since we were both teenagers. I met "Ricky" through the "Flying Saucer News" column in the magazine "Flying Saucers From Outer Space," published by the legendary Raymond A. Palmer. Hilberg and I became fast friends. We exchanged newsletters (he was putting out "UFO Digest," while I had "The Interplanetary News Service Report"). He was one of the original founders of the Congress of Scientific UFOlogists which I later joined as a board member, winning one year their coveted UFOlogist of the Year Award. We have stayed in touch for four decades and Rick now appears as a regular on Exploring The Bizarre.

Until I started gathering information for this book, I never realized Rick had had a hard core UFO experience of his own, which fits right in as we begin our investigation into unexplained phenomena in Ohio.

All the early meetings of the Congress of Scientific UFOlogists were held in Cleveland and sponsored by Hilberg and his group.

1999 – MY PERSONAL UFO SIGHTING

By Rick Hilberg

Not too many people in the UFO field know it, but I am an active railroad historian and rail fan. Consequently, I spend quite a bit of my spare time down at the tracks watching and photographing trains. I'm usually there in company with my train-loving grandson, Jeremie. A Thursday in June was one such example. We were down at the Norfolk Southern and CSX tracks on Depot Street in Berea, Ohio, just about a mile or so from our home. It was a beautiful day, 65°F with scattered clouds, light and variable winds and a gorgeous "Carolina Blue" sky.

We were parked facing northwest, not far from the now-abandoned Berea Tower (my uncle retired from there after many years of service as the first trick operator), a real hot spot for train watching action.

At approximately 9:35 a.m., during a lull in the action, I happened to glance up and, observed what I at first thought was an aircraft about 50° up in the northern sky, traveling generally east to west. Our location was less than a mile due south of the outer boundaries of Cleveland Hopkins Airport, so aircraft at all altitudes are the norm for this location.

After first thinking that it was a passing aircraft at a moderate altitude of perhaps 25 to 30 thousand feet, I was struck by the fact that I couldn't make out control surfaces of any kind on it. The almost perfect viewing conditions that day made this fact seem very odd. I can always make out some sort of control surfaces on normal aircraft. The more I thought about this, the more excited I became. After about a minute of observing, I got a small pair of opera glasses that I keep in my car's glove box along with a small 110 camera that I keep for recording "grab shots" of trains when I don't have my 35mm camera with me (I wish I had it that day!).

Anyway, through the opera glasses I observed an intense white lenticular-shaped object, like a disk seen on edge. With the glasses I also observed a medium reddish color, a sort of glowing effect, although steady, at the rear of the object.

John Timmerman (left) from the Center for UFO Studies. Rick Hilberg in the center, and Prof J. Allen Hynek on the right.

At this point I grabbed the 110 camera and exited the car to get a shot. However, by this time the object was beginning to be lost to sight, possibly having made a course change toward the WNW. I managed to take two photos, but since the object only appeared to be 5mm long at arm's length, the small format of the 110 camera makes me doubt if a useful image will show up on the negative. If it does I'll update you in our next issue. (The images never registered on the film.)

The "whatzit" was lost to sight at approximately 9:38 a.m. It was completely silent at all times, and passed behind several puffy cumulus clouds I estimated at being 5,000 plus feet in altitude. If only I had the better camera with me!

· · · · · · · · · ·

THE NIGHT CLEVELAND WAS BUZZED BY UFOS

By Rick Hilberg

Back in the 1960s, I was an active member and elected officer of the Cleveland UFOlogy Project, then-headed by my dear friend and mentor, the late Allan J. Manak. Al was a very energetic guy who was able to breathe new life into the organization by securing a suburban location that was convenient to the membership. One of Al's many projects was the establishment of a 24- hour telephone UFO report center than rang into his home (I would do the same for another local organization back in the 1970s and 1980s, and, believe me, sometimes it's no fun answering calls all hours of the day and night!). The report center had contacts with the two major Cleveland newspapers and just about all of the radio and television stations in the immediate area, so they channeled many calls to us that we could investigate.

The following is a brief overview of one of the most important cases that we would ever receive and investigate: At 8:50 p.m. on the Saturday evening of October 9, 1965, Miss Pat Gresiwald of Cloud Avenue on Cleveland's near west side called the report center to report a large disc-shaped object with white lights around its center. The object's body was silvery in appearance and had a dome or a ball-like superstructure on top. The witness reported that a total of six people witnessed this unusual object at approximately 8:45 p.m. Five minutes later, a call came in from Wade Avenue. This time, twelve people spotted a rather large round object with lights all around it. The object itself was spinning or either the lights were. These first two calls indicated that the object was headed in a northerly direction.

At this point, Manak contacted the Cleveland Press as well as the Plain Dealer. The Press told Manak that they had four calls so far and the Plain Dealer had received none so far. Manak also called Case Tech and was told that the university observatory had had a change of personnel within the last half hour and didn't have any information on any UFO sightings being called in to them. Cleveland Hopkins Airport was also contacted and they told Manak to inform the Air Force. The Air Force Special Investigations Center didn't answer their phone.

After these calls were made another report came in. This time three people on Vega Avenue reported seeing a very large elongated object with lights that seemed to be sequential in order. At the same time the object was spinning, and seemed to be as large as a pencil at arm's length.

Right after this call came in Al called me and asked me to get on my CB radio and inform any interested radio operators to try to spot the object if they could. As soon as I did this, I ran into my backyard on West 119th Street just south of Lorain Avenue and saw the object to the north of me heading slowly west. It appeared to be a disc with lights around its outer edge flashing in a sequential clockwise pattern. The thing was as large as a dime held at arm's length. I then immediately called Al and informed him of what I had just seen. He got back on the radio to find that others were also seeing it heading in a westerly direction.

Shortly after I called Manak he received a call from a party of three male witnesses who told of a large, low object with an underside larger than its top. They reported amber-colored lights circling its entire body, which seemed to be spinning and appeared to be about four inches in diameter at arm's length, a truly fantastic size! The witnesses said they spotted it several minutes before from West 61st Street just south of Lorain Avenue, several miles from where I spotted the thing.

Most of the total of 92 calls received that night mentioned seeing a rather large object with sequentially flashing lights. Most witnesses were from the western part of Cleveland and its suburbs, and most reported having it in sight from two to five minutes. I learned that probably ten CB operators also had the thing in sight. The object was generally silent, only one witness reporting a high pitched whine coming from it. Calls were received by Manak until about 10:15 PM.

The weather that night was typical for October, temperatures in the 50s with a light drizzle and a cloud ceiling at 2200 feet with visibility of nine miles being reported by Hopkins Airport. In February of 2005 I received a letter from a person who had read one of my previous articles regarding this sighting and reported the following incident that happened the same night back in 1965: "We lived above Roosevelt Post 58 on Professor Avenue... The incident happened around 8:00 p.m. that evening.

"We were all together in one huge bedroom (she was the oldest of three children and was 10 when this happened). Our three beds lined up next to each other; the bedroom was at the back of the Post on the second floor. Our bedroom was in front of the solarium heading toward the front of the building. There was a hall, the kitchen, bathroom to the left, and the dining room and living room areas.

A UFO trio hovers over Cleveland, circa unknown.

"It was our bedtime and, according to Ma, we were just about asleep. She was just sitting with us to be sure we were sleeping and suddenly a bright large round disc appeared over us. She was startled and said she was unable to move. There were like 7 smaller discs with the larger disc. Then she heard the large disc speaking to her. It said not to try to move, they were just observing. Mom asked what they were observing and the larger disc told her they were very interested in us, Charley, Chris and me. They were showing the smaller discs what we were like? The larger disc was very calming and told her not to be concerned. They were observing children of our age, and that was it.

"Ma told me it was the strangest feeling not to be able to move and yet being able to converse with these beings. She said as suddenly as they appeared in the room they were gone. She never spoke about this until many years later when I was a young adult. That's the story. They told her they would be back and would keep track of the children's progress."

This "contact" report obviously adds another dimension to the other important sightings in history from the Cleveland area!

The Hilberg clan – Jason, Carol and Rick.

Through her fantasy art, Carol Ann Rodriguez imagines what the Ohio skies would look like were they to be filled with weird flying creatures – and maybe it's not such a fantasy, according to this researcher!

OHIO – CREATURE CAPITAL OF AMERICA

By Charles J. Wilhelm

Scotland has its Loch Ness monster, while the Himalayas serve as home for the abominable snowman. But just between you and me, Ohio is definitely the creature capital of the United States. And with more and more serious UFOlogists attempting to establish a connection between the appearance of such bizarre beasties and UFOs, it's not surprising to discover that this Midwestern state is also a continual hotbed of flying saucer activity.

The following types of creatures have been sighted wandering about Ohio on pretty much a regular basis:

** Bigfoot.

** Saber-toothed tigers.

** Winged men.

** Phantom cats, as well as an assortment of

** Huge birds.

Looking back into history, the earliest recorded sightings of any type of unknown creature in Ohio occurred in 1912. In one event, Mr. J.M. and his mother were picking berries on a farm in Galita County, approximately ten miles from Galliopolis, when suddenly they heard a loud cry. A few steps further on they saw a creature with a bulky head moving parallel to them over a roll in the land which made it impossible to see him from the knees down. But what they were able to observe of the "what was it?" was enough to literally frighten them out of their wits.

MOTHMAN

BIGFOOT

LOVELAND MONSTER

Ohio is home to all manner of bizarre cryptid creatures.

The shoulders of the creature were very wide (probably twice the width of a normal man's), but he didn't have a neck, and, from what Mr. J.M. could remember, the coloring of the creature's hair was very dark. When J.M.'s mother turned towards him, and screamed, "Let's go!," the creature started walking to their left, stopped, and seemed to turn its body around and look at them. It made some sort of sound, like a growling or barking. Suddenly the creature disappeared, and so did the mysterious dark cloud that had also been present. From this incident, one can only speculate that the duo witnessed a large hairy creature, but was it of the Bigfoot type? One might also speculate that the mysterious dark cloud was a UFO.

In 1949, there was a sighting of a five and a half-foot, brown colored creature with a pointed head. This observation was made by Mr. L.S. while passing through Grove City on Ohio S.R. 3 in a Greyhound bus, of which he was the driver. Mr. L.S. claimed it leaped a barb wire fence and disappeared after showing itself to him. He said that it resembled a kangaroo, but it appeared to jump on all fours. Could this report have been a small Bigfoot/Sasquatch? But a kangaroo seems most logical, as nonindigenous animals are always being reported by solid citizens. Kangaroos have been reported in many areas not known to be their natural habitat. L.S. tagged this creature the "Greasy Bearded Varmint."

There have been only two reports of mystery kangaroos in Ohio to my knowledge. In addition to the one I've just related, there was another report in 1968 in Monroe, Ohio, by a patrolman. The states that have had the most kangaroo sightings are Indiana and Illinois. Ron Schaffner interviewed a local game warden near Wilmington, Ohio, whose family had an encounter with a hairy humanoid creature in the summer of 1961. This man's position in the community makes him an excellent witness. The case took place in a small town near Wilmington. "My niece excused herself to the bathroom to brush her hair. Upon hearing an unusual growling sound, she turned to look out the open window. To her amazement, there stood a nine-foot-tall hairy creature. After screaming till she turned blue in the face, she shouted for my grandfather, who grabbed his shotgun off the fireplace mantle."

The group proceeded outside and observed the silhouette of a biped half-running and half-hopping into the nearby woods. The intruder delivered a horrible cry as the grandpa blasted away, and then it disappeared. This is a good case. Not only do we have more than one witness, but other pieces of the puzzle come into full view. The creature just simply vanished after being fired upon. This happens in a large percentage of Yeti-type experiences. The witness manages to load the gun and fire, but the creature disappears with a loud moaning noise, sometimes leaving blood all over the place, but is nowhere to be found.

In this case, a strong stench, like sulfur, lingered for several hours after the encounter. No footprints were found, but this was probably due to the hard ground and heavy foliage that was present at the time of the sighting. Also a blood sample was sent to a local zoo for analysis. When a report on their findings was requested, they refused to give one.

Now, I ask you, isn't this a strange way to react? A similar case occurred on May 18, 1977, around 8:30 P.M., when two boys were chased by a huge hairy creature through a field in Preble County, just south of Eaton, Ohio. The boys were out walking their dog, when she got excited over something. The dog started running away from the boys and they ran after her, finally catching her and picking her up. Suddenly they smelled this awful odor, like rotten eggs. When they turned around, they saw this creature standing about nine feet tall, weighing about 500 pounds, with dirty brown fur and white eyes. Its arms were real long, hanging almost to the ground. The creature started chasing the boys down Old Camden Pike and through a field. As the boys neared their house, the creature stopped and seemed to vanish.

Hairy Bigfoot-like creatures have been sighted at the helm of UFOs in Ohio and elsewhere.

The boys' mother said she was convinced of her sons' story. They were so scared, in fact, that they didn't want any windows or doors open. Even when the Sherriff arrived, they were still shaking and could hardly get the words out of their mouths to tell what had happened.

A small team of investigators arrived upon the scene and started searching the area where the incident took place, looking for any physical evidence. Down a small creek bed, and up a hill, researchers Ron Schaffner and Bill Johns found two prints. One was in good shape, while the other was all but ruined. They estimated the footprint to have been made about one week before the boys' sighting. The print measured fourteen inches long, seven inches wide, and the distance between the two prints was about six feet. It's most interesting to note that this Bigfoot had white eyes. Most witnesses usually observe red or green eyes that glow, or reflect light. Ron questioned the boys on this point in detail, attempting to make them change their story, but they stuck to their original account.

During the summer of 1967, near Middletown, Ohio, a huge bird was seen flying over several farm houses. Mr. James Morgan said the creature had a wingspan of between fifteen and twenty feet, and was dark in color. He couldn't describe the exact color, as it was already past dusk. His description was that of a pterodactyl, a kind of prehistoric denizen that flies. In addition to Mr. Morgan, his wife and four others saw the strange creature as it glided over their porch.

In May of 1977, a small beagle puppy was snatched from a farm and dropped in a pond 600 feet away. The owner, Mrs. Greg Schmitt, said she didn't witness the event, but a neighbor claimed he saw the puppy picked up by a huge bird. This happened in Rabbit Hash, Kentucky, a small town along the Ohio River.

Also in May of 1977, in Middletown, Ohio, a couple saw a huge bird with a wingspan of seventeen to twenty feet. They stated the bird glided and had a huge breast. This creature had no feathers; the skin looked like leather and seemed to be boney. It also made a gruesome sound and moved more like a bat doing loops in the air. The huge bird continued flying south towards Columbus, Ohio. This incident is similar to other "big bird" sightings in Texas and West Virginia. UFO investigator John Keel covered the "Mothman" sightings in his bestselling ***"The Mothman Prophecies***," book which was ultimately made into a motion picture starring Richard Gere.

The "Loveland Frog" is perhaps one of the strangest cases involving unknown creatures seen either in Ohio or elsewhere for that matter. This amphibian was observed by two Loveland policemen at different times during 1972. The first incident took place on the cold night of March 3, 1972. Officer Williams (pseudonym) was driving towards Loveland on Riverside Road. He was driving slowly, due to the icy road conditions, when he saw what looked like a dog by the side of the road. He stopped the car, and this animal stood up immediately when the headlights fell on its body. Officer Williams suddenly realized it wasn't a dog! With its eyes illuminated from the lights on the car, it looked at the officer for a few seconds, then turned and leaped over the guard rail, sliding down the embankment into the Little Miami River. Officer Williams described the creature as three to four feet tall, weighing roughly fifty to seventy-five pounds. His body looked like leathery textured skin, and he had a face that resembled a frog or lizard.

The "Loveland Frog" – up close and personal.

After the creature disappeared from view, Officer Williams called his dispatcher, reported what had happened and then proceeded to the police station. Later that night, he and Officer Johnson returned to the scene and searched the area for any clues. They did find evidence that something had scraped the embankment while heading into the river.

Two weeks later, while driving on Riverside Road, Officer Johnson had a similar experience. Driving out of Loveland from the police station, he saw something lying in the middle of the road. Officer Johnson stopped his cruiser, and, as he opened his door, he saw three strange-looking creatures kneeling at the side of the road. At first he thought that someone was hurt, so he stopped his car to offer help. He quickly discovered that the figures were not human, but stood approximately three feet tall and were grayish in color. Their clothing was also gray and seemed to be tight-fitting as it stretched over a "lop-sided" chest, which appeared abnormally large on the right side, bulging from the shoulder to the armpit.

Over this bulbous area hung a slender arm which appeared much longer than the opposite member. Legs and feet were not visible because they were obscured by the vegetation in which the creatures stood. He got the impression of "something baggy." The heads of these creatures reminded him of a frog's face, mostly because of the appearance of the mouth; it was a thin line cutting across the smooth gray face. The eyes, which lacked eyebrows, looked normal, the nose was indistinct, and the top of the head had a painted-on-like-hair effect, like a plastic doll with corrugated or rolls of fat running horizontally over a bald head.

The middle biped, and the one closest to him, was first seen with his arms raised about a foot above his head, and appeared to be holding a dark-colored chain on a stick, which gave off blue-white sparks jumping from one hand to the other. The confused witness wanted to get closer. However, by the time he reached the front fender of his car, the creatures made a slight "un-natural" move towards him, as if to warn him not to come any closer. Heeding the warning, the witness just stood there for several minutes, simply watching in amazement. The next thing he remembered was being alone in his car.

There have been repeated landings coupled with the sightings of little men in Ohio. Again in the Loveland area, a prominent businessman saw four "strange looking creatures" about three feet tall standing under a bridge. He reported the incident to the police and an armed guard was placed there. A similar event supposedly had taken place near Batavia, Ohio, along the Little Miami River, where a resident observed four "little men," about three feet tall. They were huddled in a group and were described as having features and making gestures not at all human.

All of these cases happened within a short distance of each other, near the Little Miami River. An underground river and caverns exist in this same area, an important finding as we shall see when we draw our conclusions. Fairfield, Ohio, was the place where a three to four-foot-tall hairy creature was sighted in October of 1973. Four people witnessed this event around 9:10 P.M. They all agreed that the creature had very long arms, glowing eyes, moved very fast and its hands seemed to have claws. This creature ran across River Road heading towards the river. Again, this area has legends of underground rivers and an entrance to the so-called "Hollow Earth."

The last case I'll mention took place on a winter night in 1972, in Branch Hill, again on Epworth Road. A Mrs. C.J. was returning home from a late engagement when she saw the outline of a great black feline crouched on an abandoned garage. The creature's eyes were glowing green and it gave out a cry something like a woman screaming. Animals like black panthers are thought to be extinct in Ohio, being more native to foreign lands.

Naturally, the question still remains: Why does Ohio attract so many different types of creatures? Let's look at a few of the possibilities and evaluate the various theories. The Ohio River Valley has continually been the focal point of both creature and UFO flaps in recent years. Along these same river banks are located many caves, where these creatures could possibly be living. Ohio also has a magnetic fault line situated near Ravenna — a lot of UFO sightings occur near such fault lines all over the world.

Besides Ohio, the bordering states of Kentucky, Indiana, Michigan and West Virginia have also had their share of such bizarre reports. Personally, I feel that these states somehow form a huge window area that links them with the past and/or the future. Currently our organization is doing a great deal of research to see if we can't plot a specific route.

Ron Schaffner, who is director of the Para-Anthropoid Research branch of the Ohio UFO Investigators League, of which I am one of the directors, is heading up a team to look into this matter more closely. And, meanwhile, Jim Miller of OUFOIL may eventually give us an answer as to how some of these creatures are able to travel unnoticed from area to area. There is strong evidence on hand to indicate that there exists a huge subterranean passageway that connects Ohio with several of the other above-mentioned states.

ABDUCTION: THE SCREAMS OF A THOUSAND OAKS

By Paul Dale Roberts

PUBLISHER'S NOTE: The author is Johnny on the spot. I know for the fact that he has the ability to get to the "scene of the crime," in a fast and diligent manner. While hauntings and the paranormal are his forte he is adapt at getting his hands dirty with a good ole UFO flap or even an abduction experience as in the case that he has gone about investigating here. Paul heads the HPI (Hegelianism Paranormal Intelligence) and as director of this international organization has done extensive research on the Skin Walker Ranch the case of the missing girl Natalie Holloway, and has even looked for Bigfoot on Mount Shasta. Roberts has an Associate Degree in Criminology and held a Top Secret S.B.I. (Special Background Investigation) clearance as an Intelligence Analyst, later receiving an H-Identifier with OPFOR (Opposing Forces), where Roberts wore a Soviet uniform, ski mask and trained elite troops.

Paul has an active FaceBook page: www.facebook.com/paul.d.roberts.545

• • • • • • • • • •

I meet most of my clients in a public place, usually in Starbucks, or outside if the weather is half way decent. So its not so strange that I am getting some fresh air sipping on a caramel frappachino, and wondering what I will learn this day. The air is gray, with the Northern California fires plummeting smoke into our atmosphere, but yet, I still want to sit outside and prepare for my interview. I am also waiting for another HPI Investigator/Ufologist named Holly DeLaughter, who will assist me in the interview. Today is June 26, 2008, Thursday. Our client Steve Campbell approaches me and shakes my hand. Holly gets comfortable and will interject questions during the interview if there is something that peaks her curiosity. I asked Steve to create a time line of events and he begins with how everything initially got started.

Year: 1960 Location: New Mexico

Steve and his brother are living in New Mexico with their parents. He remembers becoming paralyzed and seeing something that is materializing next to his brother, however, he is unable to describe what he saw.

Year: 1964 Location: Arlington, Texas

Steve experiences what Ufologists consider to be the "Oz Factor." He is in a forest and everything around him is surreal. When this occurred he was either in the third or fourth grade. He describes being sick as a dog a few days afterward.

Year: 1971 Location: Thousand Oaks, California

He remembers walking up the hill at the end of his family's dead end street smoking a cigarette. He felt an evil presence. After this happened he was sick for two months. The sickness felt like pneumonia. It affected his lungs. After the sickness was gone, he felt an obsession to play the guitar for 8-10 hours a day.

Month and Year: November 1975 Location: Thousand Oaks, California

Steve and his brother were playing guitar with a friend at their house overlooking Thousand Oaks, with three other individuals. They witnessed a blue fireball come down into a horse field. When the impact took place, there were blue tentacles of electricity that covered the whole field. Later a pine tree burst into flames. The next day was normal, but when evening came things started getting strange.

At some point, Steve and his brother heard an ungodly terrifying scream which seemed to get increasingly closer. Steve describes it as a woman getting her throat ripped out. Steve and his brother went and got their father. While they were getting their father, they found it unusual that their two German Shepherds remained silent. They also witnessed two fireballs shooting into the neighboring hills. It appeared that the fireballs were traveling at tremendous speed. The screaming continued. Their father called the cops, and told them that they thought a woman was being assaulted in the neighboring hills. The cops came but heard nothing. But, when the cops left, the blood curdling screams started up all over again. The time was 8:30 PM or 9:00PM. Then the screaming stopped for a while only to start back up at 11pm. At this point the brothers heard a strange electronic beeping sound. Steven was worried about his wife who was five months pregnant. Suddenly, a blinding light filled the entire house and then everything went dark. The time of this incident was midnight. When the screaming stopped, the clock read 4:30 AM. The brothers could not understand how 4:30am came so quickly. They felt they were missing four and a half hours of time! This missing time phenomena, is very common, as readers will know among a high percentage of UFO abductees.

The very next day, the brothers discovered what appeared to them to be a UFO landing area. Neighbors made claim of seeing a huge white light. Among the people that were experiencing this UFO phenomenon were Steve, his brother, his ex-wife, as well as his mother and father. Then the next day Steven found himself in and out of the hospital for six months, learning he had developed some sort of blood disorder.

Month and Year: January 1976 Location: Thousand Oaks, California

One of Steve's two German Shepherds, that was no more than two years old, had trouble walking, appearing as if his nervous system had shut down. Soon after his other Shepherd started having problems, and both dogs had to be put to sleep.

Steve's whole life changed. He became proficient in playing the guitar (where he had displayed no talent before), as well as becoming fluent in twenty three computer programs. It was like he was awakened, something turned on in his mind. Everything excelled! In the early years of his possible abduction; he became the fastest runner in his class. Before the abductions, hardly anyone would pay attention to him.

At their beck and call, these are some of the entities Paul Dale Rodgers finds himself having to manage.

As Holly and I, continued our interview with Steve, he tells us that he has a vague memory of being in an oval room with orange lights that were shining from the floor. Through a bright light, a little girl appeared. A telepathic message told him to approach the young girl. He approached the young girl, she screamed, everything went black. Steve feels he is somehow connected to this little girl.

Year: 1991 Location: Sacramento. – The Implant

Steve is out performing when his bass player's, mother-in-law, shows him a picture of her daughter when she was five years old. He is shocked and puzzled as it is the same little girl he saw in the oval room!

As this interview closed, I probed for some type of tangible evidence. Steve reluctantly shows me what he says is an implant on his left leg. The implant actually is over his leg bone and it moves and shifts. Holly and I, were actually moving the implant with our index finger. The implant, after being touched, would reposition itself at the same spot over his leg bone. There were no tell tale scars of a possible projectile entering his leg. The implant reminded me of the kind of implant I saw in a woman abductee's arm at a UFO conference.

Warning! Better not attempt to abduct this guy. Paul has a background in criminology.

As I went over my notes, I had a flashback of when I was sitting in a coffee shop and a beautiful young lady sat close to me. She was wearing shorts and I couldn't help notice that she had beautiful tanned legs. Then I noticed something else, she had a hole in her leg; a hole that looked like a scoop mark. I gathered my courage and asked her the following: "Excuse me, I know this is going to sound weird, but have you ever felt like you were visited by something you can't explain and taken against your will?"

The woman looked at me with a stunned look on her face and said..."Oh my god, how did you know?" Before I knew it she was explaining that she was an abductee. The scoop marks were placed there by Grays. They were taking skin samples from her. I asked Steve if he had any scoop marks and I learned that his ex-wife has a scoop mark below her naval and his mom has a scoop mark on the back of her leg.

I tried to understand why aliens would turn on something in Steve's mind. The only thing I could think that would motivate the Grays to give Steve certain gifts are the following: 1. Musical abilities. Music is a way to influence a culture.

2. Computer programming. Steven programs various government agencies' computers. Would this be a secret agenda of the grays to manipulate our own government computers through Steve and others?

This is only an idea of what could be motivating aliens to allow certain individuals to have 'gifts'. This is a theory only.

Steve has an interesting background. His father, a sergeant in the Air Force, took Steve and his brother to White Sands Missile Range in New Mexico. Their father escorted them to a small building located inside the base. Inside the building was an elevator shaft that took them beneath the ground, Far below, they entered a huge computer complex with many computers and machines throughout the room. The complex was the size of five football fields. I can't help but wondering if there wasn't some sort of a UFO connection with his father?

White Sands Missile Range, New Mexico.

Could aliens have been monitoring the work activities of his father? And was this perhaps the reason why Steve has been targeted?

Steve tells me that in Iowa, a UFO was tracked by radar. The military base was close to Sioux City. His father was involved in the radar tracking of the UFO. When his father retired from the Air Force, he joined the Burroughs's Corporation, which is heavily involved with technology.

Holly DeLaughter, a Certified Hypnotist, trained and certified by psychic Sylvia Browne has offered Steve a session of regressive hypnosis to take him to the periods of his life that he was abducted. Steve is contemplating this idea and has promised to keep in touch with Holly.

During this interview, I discovered it's a small world, because Steve knew Holly's uncle John Sheehan who was the lead singer of the rock band called Ian Shelter back in the 80s. Ian Shelter was a legendary local band that played with Huey Lewis and the News and Nightranger.

Holly was also personally connected to Steve's experiences, they both knew about the "buzzing effect." Where you feel like you are being downloaded with information. The "buzzing effect" affects your nervous system; where you feel an interior vibrating that normally lasts only a minute.

The sensation is exhilarating, in that you feel you are being given something that every day people in society don't receive. Holly can elaborate more about this in her section "Holly's View."

Steve also wants to know more about the "White Thing" or the "Critter" that people who have experienced an abducted often report seeing. Some witnesses describe it as a large white dog that stands taller than a man. Steven wants to know what this creature is. He believes the screams he heard in Thousand Oaks could have possibly been made by such a creature.

Steve says he has more to tell and will do a second interview with Holly and me. For right now, this is where I will end the interview process. I will now allow Holly to give her thoughts about this interview.

HOLLY'S VIEW:

What a great interview and thank you so much for including me. Steve and I do have a lot in common. Indeed we have both experienced the Oz Factor and internal "buzzing effect," but could this be the same sensation one gets with spiritual enlightenment, Reiki Attunements, etc? Or, is this something far different? Further investigation is definitely in order, and I am truly excited about the prospects of meeting Steve's family for a second interview and possibly even hypnotic regressions.

The fact that Steve contracted a blood disorder after losing so much time and has what appears to be an implant in his left leg leaves plenty of room for scientific data. It would be great if he and his family could get copies of their medical records to aid in their investigation and what's more, new tests. I am certain there are doctors out there who would love to know if that peculiar little lump carries a radio frequency. I'll bet Steve and his family would like to know as well.

Here are a few other things we learned we have in common: I also lost time in the company of another and although we lost much less time (20-25 minutes), it was still a very freaky experience and we "came back" with newfound talents and abilities. Steve and I are both able to channel writings we don't recall and don't initially understand. I too have seen UFOs and "fireballs" and probably a few alien beings. But enough about me! This is Steve's story.

Do I think Steve is telling the truth? I absolutely do, and I bet most of you will too!

SUGGESTED READING

HPI STRANGE THINGS

SPOOKY TREASURE TROVE

SECRETS OF MOUNT SHASTA AND A DWELLER ON TWO PLANETS

REAL ZOMBIES

SCREWED BY THE ALIENS

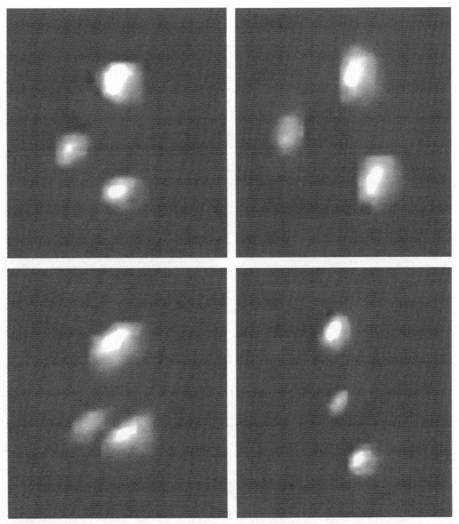

Date of sighting: June 29, 2014 - Location of sighting: Sherman Oaks, California. Eyewitness states: Saw some amazing orbs in the sky yesterday. I was perched on a high ground when I noticed these orbs rise up together in the distance and then even out and float together, which I know balloons don't do! They had a brilliant glow to them like watching a star in the sky only this was day time. As I was video taping them I noticed another orb materialize as it got closer to the orbs then faded out as it moved away. After zooming in i noticed that there were actually three objects, the two yellow orbs and a sky blue diamond shaped object in the middle. They floated till they were straight up on top of me then stopped which made it very hard for me to video tape without straining my already strained neck. I observed them for almost an hour laying on the ground as they slowly faded away.

It seems the sky is full of them but no one bothers to look up for too long.

The "Three M's" – Maria D'Andrea at Oddities Fair in Jersey City along with Marc and Marc, editors of the popular "Weird New Jersey" magazine.

COMMUNICATING WITH UFO / INTERDIMENSIONAL BEINGS

By Maria D' Andrea

PUBLISHER'S NOTE: Maria has been aligned with our way of thinking for many years. Our association goes back to when I ran the New York School of Occult Arts and Sciences in Greenwich Village along Manhattan's bustling 14th Street. I have always found her to be a skilled psychic and knowledgeable on all aspects of the occult and shamanism. She has written over a dozen books for Inner Light – Global Communications, and even though not normally thought of as a student of UFOs, she has, through her understanding of the paranormal, formed her own ideas as to what the phenomena consists of and how we as humans interact with it. As she craftily puts it, "There are an untold number of interdimensional beings in various realms and various stages of progress, and a lot of them feel it is necessary to come close in order to rub elbows with us, regardless of their intentions."

• • • • • • • • • •

Throughout the centuries, shamans, occultists, avatars and various other spiritual leaders have communicated with various non-earthly beings, some of whom are physical, while others are of a non-physical nature. Either way, these beings, these entities, are just as real.

When you think of a shaman or a Native American medicine man, as an example, you might think of pictures of them standing on a mountain top with their heads raised toward the sky and both arms lifted above their heads. This seems like they are praying or asking for spiritual assistance.

Surprisingly, this is not usually the case. There are tools that we can make that carry a frequency level that helps us to communicate telepathically, either to pass on information or to ask for guidance from the other realms.

To the uninitiated, sometimes it looks like jewelry or a decorative object. We still, to this day, do some of our work underground. You will notice on those pictures of occultists, as an example, how they are standing usually on a mountain top. It doesn't matter if it's a mountain top or at the top of a high rise building in a city. The point is to get to the highest ground to have less interference with the energy transfer.

BEINGS WHO HEAL

There is a well-known case. At one time, I remember meeting in another dimension two beings. They looked as though they had electric green wire "outlining" their bodies. It didn't look like they had mouths, but, in that area of their faces, there were round spots that I felt were the same as noses. They both looked stocky and had a very serious attitude. They reminded me of looking at the statues on Easter Island.

I wasn't feeling physically well at the time.

The passing of time means nothing to Maria, as she travels back and forth on the waves of eternity.

I could feel them working on healing me. In the background, there were brown "wires" – with no pattern to them. They were the thickness of something between a wire and a cable.

I realized that there was a tan-looking hand that I could only see up to the wrist above my stomach area, forming a swirling cone of energy that was moving counterclockwise.

I could see the hand pulling what looked like the brown wire out through the top of the swirling cone.

The brown wire seemed to be what was wrong with my body. The being was healing me. It would pull up one wire at a time and kept throwing it away into thin air as it came up.

As I lay there, I could feel heat and a sense of them being focused on a purpose, which was to do healing. I was curious, but felt calm, safe and loved.

To this day, I don't know why they helped, but I do know that there are beings out there in space and in other dimensions who want to help us in that healing way whenever they can.

THE POLICE OFFICER AND THE BABY ALLIGATOR BITE

Tim Beckley says this is one of his favorite cases, as it involves two credible witnesses and there are records from the hospital the deputy visited that will verify that he was healed by a UFO. Tim wrote the incident up for *"Beyond Magazine."* You can still find a copy for sale on e-bay if you want to read his original report. The following is a verbatim report from the files of the National Investigations Committee on Aerial Phenomena, now defunct.

About 11:00 PM on September 3, 1965, a Friday night, Deputy Sheriff Bob Goode, 50, was driving southbound from Damon toward West Columbia, Texas on Highway 36, and because he had suffered a bite on his left index finger earlier that day from a baby alligator, Chief Deputy Billy McCoy, 38, accompanied him in case the pain interfered with his driving. It was a clear moonlit night with Goode resting his arm in the open window when McCoy spotted a bright purple light on the horizon to the southwest which appeared to be about five to six miles away. At first they thought it might be something in the nearby oil fields, such as a drilling rig, but then a blue light, smaller than the purple light, emerged from it and moved to the right before stopping. Both lights remained in this orientation for a while then began to drift upward. This upward floating motion continued until the objects reached an elevation of about 5-10 degrees above the horizon.

Goode watched through binoculars but couldn't discern more detail. They took back-roads to get closer until they stopped and the lights then suddenly dove towards them, covering the distance in 1-2 seconds, then it abruptly stopped practically overhead. Their car and surroundings were brightly lit in purple and they could see purple and blue lights were attached to opposite ends of a massive object hovering about 150 feet from them at about a 100-foot altitude.

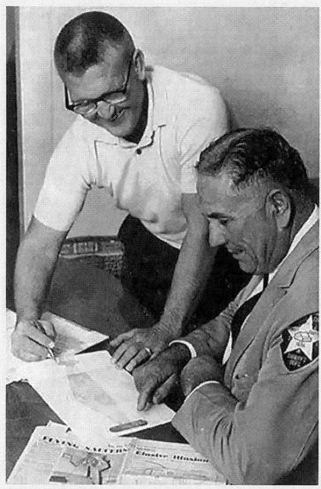

Deputy Sheriff Bob Goode was bitten by a baby alligator, but on September, 3, 1965, a passing UFO that emitted a purple light healed his wounded hand.

Deputy sheriffs Bob Goode and Billy McCoy make sketches of the UFO they saw while on patrol ('Look' UFO Special 1967).

In his statement to the Air Force, McCoy described that, "The bulk of the object was plainly visible at this time and appeared to be triangular shaped with a bright purple light on the left end and the smaller, less bright, blue light on the right end. The bulk of the object appeared to be dark gray in color with no other distinguishing features. It appeared to be about 200 feet wide and 40-50 feet thick in the middle, tapering off toward both ends. There was no noise or any trail.

The bright purple light illuminated the ground directly underneath it and the area in front of it, including the highway and the interior of our patrol car. The tall grass under the object did not appear to be disturbed. There was a bright moon out and it cast a shadow of the object on the ground immediately below it in the grass." To both men, the object seemed "as big as a football field." Goode felt strong heat from the object on his left arm through his sleeve. After a few seconds, with the object hovering almost directly above, they fled and headed toward Damon, making speeds of up to 110 miles per hour, while McCoy observed the object from the rear window. For 10 to 15 seconds, the UFO continued to hover above then abruptly shot back in the direction from which it had come. "After arriving at approximately its original position," McCoy reported, "it went straight up in the air and disappeared at 25-30 degrees above the horizon."

At Damon the officers calmed themselves before deciding to return to investigate again. This time they took an alternate route, but saw nothing, so they returned to the area where they had first seen the lights, and once again observed the purple light on the horizon and a smaller blue light emerge with a strange two-step motion and float upward. Fearing another close encounter, they fled again. Goode and McCoy continued on their shift until 3-4am, then stopped for breakfast at a cafe. Goode noted that his wound was no longer sore, and when he unwrapped the bandage he discovered that the swelling had gone down and that the wound was nearly healed. On the following day, the wound was practically healed with no scarring.

Eventually, the deputies reported the sighting to Ellington Air Force Base, and Major Laurence Leach, Jr., arrived on September 8, 1965, to interview McCoy and Goode and take a statement. Leach's report to Project Blue Book headquarters at Wright-Patterson Air Force Base reflected his puzzlement, stating, "There is no doubt in my mind that they definitely saw some unusual object or phenomenon. Both officers appeared to be intelligent, mature, level-headed persons capable of sound judgment and reasoning."

Here is a brief news report about this very impressive incident –

www.youtube.com/watch?v=oLsDFhxyYgY

THEY COME IN ALL SHAPES AND SIZES

When we speak about UFO's and their occupants, we are actually speaking of more than one type of craft and crew.

As I've said in the past, there are some aliens that are interdimensional and some that are physical. Mainly they are just on another plane of existence. We look at spaceships and sometimes the way they're spinning vibrationally, you might see part of the ship because it will be in synch vibrationally with our realm for a few seconds or for a little while. Sometimes they're simply physical ships. In any case, they have the ability to shift their energy between time and space.

I find from my experiences, when I've run into the aliens, it happened more often when I was going out-of-body rather than seeing them physically. If you look at olden times, people used to think of aliens that could travel between dimensions and through time as gods. They believed in "sky gods," who could have come to this planet in airplanes, rocket ships or flying saucers. But because they "came from the sky," the ancients saw them as gods. I have had contact with one being whom I call Chronos, who is "the angel of time."

A VANGUARD OF UFO OCCUPANTS

In one situation, I saw UFO occupants that looked just like us. UFOlogists call them "Nordics." Let me tell you, it was a very strange experience. I'm not good with heights and things, but they were a little bit taller than me and their skin was a very dark brown color. But the skin looked leathery. When I met them, they seemed very, very friendly.

They primarily wanted to pass on information to me. This really means to "us," or whoever might have shown up. I don't think they were only reaching out to me specifically. (That somehow kills any ego I might have had, right?)

Now, I was getting this telepathically. It wasn't as though I was getting a language or hearing it clairaudiently, which sometimes I do. This was more that you just "know" what they're saying. There's a clairsentience ability where you just know. There's no other way to describe it.

The dark leathery aliens communicated that they wanted to help the world become more "awake." The word I kept getting was "awaken." I would have thought they would say "enlightened" or "to do better," but I kept getting the word "awaken" over and over. They were trying to awaken the planet and they were sending what looked like energy light waves. Think of a laser beam coming from them. It looked like it was coming from what we call our Third Eye and the center of the palms of their hands. They were just sending white light with a little blue around the edges. I don't know why. They didn't explain the light; they just shined it on the planet to help people awaken.

Eventually, this just left, vanished, disappeared. I kind of got the impression they wanted me to incorporate this mantra in the talks and seminars that I give to various groups.

UFOs AND THE CHIEF

Years ago, my friend, Chief Wise Owl, called me on the phone very upset. Of course, I am thinking there's an emergency. And to him there was – he considered it a disaster in the making.

He was a great chief. He was always looking out for his people. He found all sorts of ways to raise money for the reservation, always in a positive way. He truly lived by the thought that what you do always comes back. I've always had great respect for him. We spoke frequently about our shamanic ways and I would do readings for him to help when he needed it. He truly had a big heart.

This is his short story:

He said he was riding in a van (because he was 600 lbs. or more at the time) with some young braves. They were driving home, and on the reservation land already, when they heard a distant sound and, at a short distance, saw a UFO in the process of landing.

As this was going on, the chief told the young men to drive closer and pull over so he could get out of the van.

He was very upset because the young men took off in the truck and didn't listen to him (and he's a Chief). He said he was going to do their "normal welcoming ritual for the occupants of the ship" and now he didn't get to do so, which probably insulted the occupants. Chief Wise Owl said they've been doing this for hundreds of years and he was very upset by the young "braves" brazen attitude.

When Native Americans, being more in tune than the rest of the population when dealing with Light Beings, have a close encounter, it should not be a shocking experience. The chief felt such a meeting should have been taken for granted. It just goes to show how various cultures handle UFO's differently.

INVISIBLE BEINGS

Those that think of themselves as "nuts and bolts" UFO researchers fail to see the flip side of the coin. There are, among the reports, a classification of what we call "Invisible Walkers," entities who occupy the space beside us but that we cannot see under normal circumstances. Some individuals like Marc Brinkerhoff of New York City are what we call "UFO Repeaters," in that they have ongoing experiences all their life with the minions behind the craft. Marc can aim a camera at the clouds and oddly-shaped and -designed objects will appear in the finished photos. Shadows of beings have even appeared on his prints when blown up.

The man who gave flying saucers their name, Kenneth Arnold, before his passing testified of the unseen kingdom he felt we are all a part of. He had experiences where a rocking chair would sway back and forth as if someone were seated in it, occupying space, but unseen to the human eye. Tim Beckley talks about the tall ultra-terrestrials that walked around Starr Hill in Warminster, where he had not only a sighting but a communications experience.

Look with your eyes, but also feel with your heart.

UFOs are all around us, and you don't have to be a psychic or a shaman to come to such a conclusion!

This world keeps moving, hopefully, upward and gains knowledge to connect better with other realms. Everything, after all, is made up of energy. Just the vibrational frequencies vary. As they say, knowledge is the key. So pick up the key, open your spirit, heart and mind and move forward to your abundance and greatness. YES, YOU CAN.

SUGGESTED READING

SECRET MAGICAL ELIXIRS OF LIFE

HOW TO ELIMINATE STRESS AND ANXIETY THROUGH THE OCCULT

ANGEL SPELLS

OCCULT GRIMOIRE AND MAGICAL FORMULARY

TIME TRAVEL TO CONTACT BENEFICIAL BEINGS

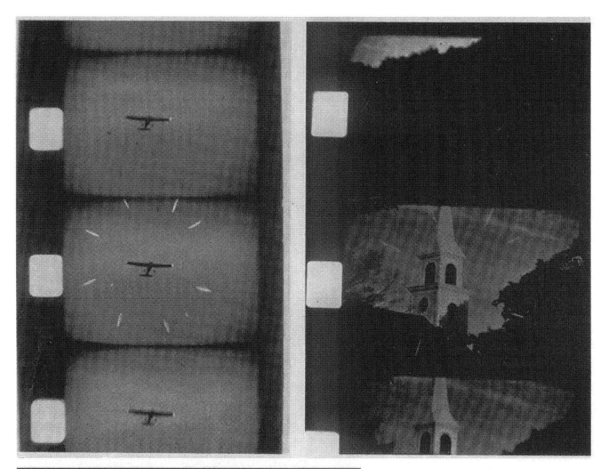

Top: By 1970, Stella Lansing had already been taking photographs that contained strange lights or structures superimposed on them. A mysterious clock-like pattern also began to appear on her films and photographs. Strangely enough, the geometric patterns appear on the film itself, overlapping the frames of the footage.

Left: One of the unexplainable ghostly images that showed up in Stella Lansing's film while she was shooting high tension wires

THE REMARKABLE PARANORMAL ENCOUNTERS OF STELLA LANSING AND UFO REPEATERS

By Brent Raynes

PUBLISHER'S NOTE: Certain people have "special" gifts. They have uncanny abilities which most of us do not have – especially when it comes to UFOs and the Ultra-terrestrials behind their activities. Outsiders, hardcore skeptics and apologists for the enigma at hand, put these "rare" individuals, these percipients, in a league all their own – unjustifiably labeling them kooks, crackpots, screwballs, nut cases and cranks. Yet when they have been scrutinized by psychiatrists and psychologists they have, for the most part, come away with a clean bill of health.

I call them "UFO Repeaters," while noted researcher/author/editor Brent Raynes of the online "Alternate Realities" site phrases it in a more polished manner: "Para-psychiatric study of the contactees and abductees—those who claim contact with the UFO entities—might be especially valuable since, in great measure, these persons have many similarities to gifted mediums. They are readily entranced, and experiments can be devised that seem to incite new UFO contacts and psychic phenomena, and, what is more important, conditions that lead to objective data—possible paranormal films of UFOs, paranormal audiotapes."

One such individual was the late Stella Lansing, and, while I am not one to take bows for my achievements in the field (well that's a bit of a white lie I say with fingers crossed), I take credit where credit is due for breaking her into the field.

Max's Paranormal Blog best recaps the way it started: "Stella Lansing was a middle-aged housewife from Massachusetts who in 1961 began experiencing strange and otherworldly events that over time led her down a bizarre path of UFOs, strange humanoid creatures, Men In Black, and visions of other worlds. Most of which she managed to capture on different types of film. It all began on a cool September day in 1961 when Stella noticed a bright hovering orb outside her home in Northampton, Massachusetts. The object hovered at tree line level off in the distant sky before zooming closely to her, stopping in mid-air between her house and her neighbor's garage. The object appeared to be observing her before it suddenly zoomed towards where she stood. It hovered only yards away from her, before shooting away and disappearing. Although another four years would pass before another encounter, she would soon start to see these mysterious objects more and more regularly. That terrifying incident, although short, marked the beginning of Stella's journey.

I was working with Jim Moseley, who was the publisher of "*Saucer News,*" which was without a doubt the most popular UFO publication of the mid to late 1960s. Jim was a frequent guest on the Long John Nebel Party Line show, broadcast nightly over WOR, a 50,000-watt, Manhattan-based radio station. Jim was also a regular on Chuck McCann's "Let's Have Fun" kiddie program, which was immensely popular at the time and aired on WPIX TV. Chuck, for some peculiar reason best known to himself, brought Jim on several times to hype his semi-glossy UFO publication, although the show was aimed at a ten to fourteen-year-old audience that Chuck kept entertained by using a Charlie McCarthy-like dummy as well as other child-appropriate routines.

As far as New York City went, Jim was most definitely "king of the flying saucer hill." For several years he organized monthly UFO meetings at a number of mid-town hotels, presenting lectures by some of the top names in the UFOlogical field. The average audience grew from a mere 50 people, culminating in 1967 with a crowd of over ten thousand who attended the largest indoor UFO convention ever held. I had worked with Jim helping coordinate both his giant expos as well as the meetings he held in the Times Square area.

Since Jim was always rather busy running around like a mad man giving interviews or even just putting out folding chairs for SRO crowds that might materialize from time to time, I sort of became his eyes and ears. People would approach me when they couldn't get his attention, often wanting some sort of "favor" or even trying to get booked to speak at one of these programs.

One such individual came up to me one evening and introduced herself as Stella Lansing. She had driven down from New England and wanted Jim to view a series of home movies she had taken which showed, or so she said, some really weird things – from UFOs in the sky to spooky figures and faces which were not visible to the naked eye but would show up when the 8mm film strips were developed. Frankly, Jim was a more nuts-and-bolts sort of guy and had expressed his opinion – at least at first – that Stella was "a bit of a flake" or something to that effect. He didn't think that anyone would be interested in hearing what she had to say. He more or less put her in the crackpot category. Which is not to say that some of his regular speakers couldn't also be relegated to this classification, including the Mystic Barber, who walked around with an antenna on his head to ward off mental bombardment from aliens.

But, to me, Stella Lansing seemed pretty sane, and so I offered to step in for Jimbo and view her presentation. Though skeptical about the things she had caught with her home camera, I was also impressed and thought she deserved to have her findings viewed. So, after a bit of arm twisting, I managed to get Stella a booking at one of Moseley's Friday night soirees.

Stella talked about her experiences and showed her home movies, and those in attendance craned their necks forward to get a better view of what was being projected on the screen in front of the hall. After the meeting, I remember Jim saying he, too, was puzzled by what this nice enough lady had managed to photograph. At this point, I think we both realized that the camera doesn't lie, though we weren't willing to offer any suggestions as to what was causing all these eerie, phantom-like phenomena to appear on Stella's film.

To this day I believe, there must have been a number of important researchers in the field present as she gave her talk because soon Stella Lansing was getting asked to speak elsewhere and to share her photographic data with some important investigators, including Jim and Coral Lorenzen, who headed up the Aerial Phenomena Research Organization. In fact, APRO was putting on a public symposium in Baltimore and had asked Stella to make an appearance with her photographic material at a private meeting – Invitation Only, VIP – held in a suite somewhere in the hotel.

Jim Moseley, Gray Barker (who had written the first book on the UFO terrorists known as the Men-In-Black) as well as myself had attempted to crash the event and were quickly escorted to the door . . . sort of funny, since we had, for all intents and purposes, "discovered" Stella Lansing and presented her findings to the world before APRO and anyone else.

Now I will take a bow before handing this sensational report over to Brent Raynes.

• • • • • • • • • • •

A psychiatrist and UFO researcher named Berthold Eric Schwarz was helping the woman and investigating her case. At first he was quite skeptical, but eventually he himself witnessed a paranormal event alongside Stella.

Dr. Bethold Eric Schwarz, M.D., was a distinguished psychiatrist who held both a deep interest in the paranormal and the UFO phenomenon. Unlike the vast majority of his profession, Dr. Schwarz didn't take a mere armchair approach to this subject matter, spinning wholly speculative psychological theories. Instead, he ventured out into the field, interviewing eyewitnesses personally— even skywatching, actively seeking a firsthand experience himself. Dr. Schwarz was in search of hard evidence to substantiate the incredible claims of UFO eyewitnesses.

One case that he looked into quite extensively for a number of years was that of Massachusetts contactee Stella Lansing. It all began at a UFO conference in Baltimore, Maryland, in January 1971, where Dr. Schwarz had given a lecture. After his talk he was planning to have dinner with noted researchers Coral Lorenzen and Dr. J. Allen Hynek, but he had gotten word that this middle-aged New England housewife named Stella Lansing wished to speak with him. He later wrote, "I spent the time in the auditorium listening to one of the most unusual accounts of alleged repeated close UFO contacts that I have ever heard. On the surface, the data was extraordinary, if not preposterous: Experiences involving strange little men, voices appearing out of nowhere, creatures, loss of consciousness, 'electric shock' from a shimmering figure, a gaping round hole in the ice, a craft possibly surfacing from under water, miniscule footprints, religious symbols, bizarre harassments, etc. Fortunately, as I later learned, Mrs. Lansing kept meticulous records of her many experiences."

In the following weeks and months, Dr. Schwarz visited Mrs. Lansing at her home in Massachusetts, and she as well visited his office in Montclair, New Jersey. He reviewed many super 8 mm motion picture films she had made of alleged UFOs, interviewed her and other witnesses in the area, and conducted "physical, neurological, and electroencephalographic examinations" of her, concluding that she was in good health and had "no impairments of vision, hearing, or intellectual functions."

Stella Lansing.

During his visits to Massachusetts, Dr. Schwarz's went skywatching with Mrs. Lansing, an activity that paid off. "On February 12, 1971, after an evening of intensive interviewing of Mrs. Lansing and her lady and gentleman friends, I went with her, at 4:00 a.m., to one of her favorite UFO sites, overlooking a hilltop that was cleared for high-tension wires," Dr. Schwarz wrote. "At that time the dark sky was suddenly lit up and we saw a round, pulsating, bright yellow-orange, noiselessly gliding light, which expanded and contracted, went out and relighted. Mrs. Lansing intermittently photographed this over several minutes, while I tape-recorded the event. Stars and the moon were also seen and photographed as controls."

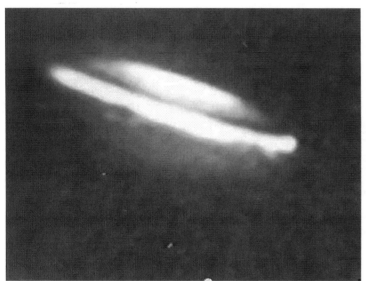
A perfect disc – though nothing was seen in the sky.

Dr. Schwarz was unable to identify what they had seen and photographed with anything conventional. Then he had another skywatch with Mrs. Lansing with even more surprising results. He wrote, "During my second trip to Massachusetts, on the night of April 15, 1971, Mrs. Lansing, her middle-aged lady friend, and I drove to a very isolated rural area at 10:45 p.m. The engine and lights of the car were switched off, we got out of the car, and within minutes the sky over the nearby hill across the field was illuminated by a sudden appearance of one, then two, white-yellowish-orange discs, which pulsated, changed size and color, and merged into one, and then separated into two discs; then they noiselessly glided away at varying speeds. This was simultaneously photographed by Mrs. Lansing on her battery-driven motion picture camera and by me on a spring-wound camera. Unfortunately, my Sony Cassette-Corder (TC 40) suddenly failed to operate at the time.

"While Mrs. Lansing and I were filming these strange lights, an automobile suddenly seemed to appear out of nowhere. It stopped approximately one to two hundred feet ahead of our car. We were shocked to see its headlights illuminate our dark area and flicker alternately left and right (and vice versa) in a manner reminiscent of semaphore signals, and then dim out to a pink, and come on again. At the height of the excitement, the lady friend panicked, and screamed to us to get back in the car, which we did. Fortunately I photographed most of this bizarre incident, and for several film frames the flaming disc can be seen gliding in the background, above and then just over the glaring headlights. The latter part of the event was filmed from the interior of Mrs. Lansing's car, and showed reflections from her windshield. The mystery car then suddenly turned up its lights, started its engine, and barreled past us at great speed. Because of the blinding headlights we could not make out the license plate, but the auto seemed to be a rather large, nondescript General Motors model of several years ago."

The lady witnesses said that they had never had an experience like this before. The location that had been selected that night was selected in a spontaneous spur-of-the-moment manner. It was not an advanced and planned visit to this particular site, and so it seemed unlikely that anyone knowing of their activities would have been present to have staged this strange signaling car event. (To view a brief video of Stella Lansing, Dr. Schwarz, and others describing these and similar events, as filmed by a crew from the former television show Sightings, go to:

www.youtube.com/watch?v=AayDPO1A7Dg (1)

In one of her films, a mysterious, unexplainable, growth appeared on Stella's brow where before there had been nothing there.

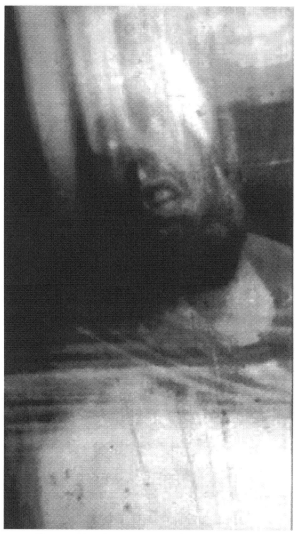

Deformed: An image of a man's face looking like a member of the Talaban.

Besides anomalies on film, Stella Lansing also obtained a few EVP-type voice anomalies on audio, as she would often tape record while on her sky watches. This is described in Dr. Schwarz's "***Book Two of UFO Dynamics***" (1983). He wrote: "In my office on April 15 to 19, 1975, Mrs. Lansing played some of her tapes and projected the accompanying films with UFO-like images (mostly clock-like formations and their metamorphoses). She had tapes with persistent rhythmic intermittent machinery-like noise; 'whooshing' followed with what sounded like a high-pitched boyish (?) rapid voice (?) saying 'at least I'll be left alone – (long pause) – drunk (?) last night.' On a tape, when she was accompanied by a friend, 'Hi!' was interjected. On one recording 'Hello' was interpolated. On another occasion, while filming, Mrs. Lansing shut off the recorder to save tape, 'and when I played it back, I heard the pause, and a voice saying, 'What are you up to?'"

In my notes from my first visit (01/05/1974) with Stella at her home in Massachusetts, I had written: "Throughout 1966 until 1969, she had a 'terrific' degree of UFO-related television and radio interference. Sounds like shortwave would burst over the TV."

Dr. Schwarz certainly felt that "paranormal photographic and audiotape techniques" could well prove highly significant to the study of UFOs. He pointed out how such things as ghostly encounters, hauntings, and poltergeist outbreaks often "seem to develop shortly after or at the time of the encounters." In addition, he noted how "witnesses often claim psychic effects, such as supposed telepathy, clairvoyance,

452

precognition, telekinesis, teleportation, materialization, dematerialization of craft and creatures, apports, causation, relief of various illnesses, and the like." (Psychic Nexus, 1980).

Three years ago, I met an "abductee" who was a textbook example of such situations that Dr. Schwarz referred to in the above paragraph. "I know for me that the paranormal activity did begin after my first abduction experience at age five and has continued ever since," Bret Oldham told me. "As a child I could never understand why so many spirits came to me and I only wanted them to leave me alone, but, as I got older and became aware of my abductions, I then began to consider the hypothesis that somehow my energy level in my body had been changed or increased by these abduction experiences and/or something in my psychic awareness had."

I have speculated that since a large portion of these reported alien/human interactions seem to most often occur at a non-verbal/telepathic level of communication, seemingly accessing neural circuits that allow for elevated or advanced psychic functioning, then possibly the reports of expanded psychic awareness and activity after such encounters is a byproduct of what was initially intended primarily for the alien/human interactional process. It may be that once certain brain sites are activated, reprogrammed and/or modified in this way then it may no longer be something that can just be easily switched off afterwards.

Dr. Schwarz also noted in his book "*UFO Dynamics*" (1983) that many UFO contactees he investigated seemed to be people with reported psychic/mediumistic abilities and that the vast majority of them also seemed to be unusually deep hypnotic trance subjects. Other researchers have also noted these patterns. "They seem to be highly susceptible to hypnotic suggestion," psychologist Dr. R. Leo Sprinkle wrote in his book "Soul Samples" (1999), adding: "They seem to experience many psychic phenomena and/or possess some psychic abilities." (We just recently discussed this and other aspects of these experiences with Dr. Sprinkle on our blog talk radio show Alternate Perceptions (http://www.liveparanormal.com/event/show-alternate.html) on 01/28/13).

Incredibly, over the last three years, since being introduced to UFO abductee Bret Oldham and his wife Gina by Sandy Nichols, founder of the Alien Research Group (ARG) of Thompson Station, Tennessee, Sandy being himself an admitted abductee, we have together and separately conducted numerous experiments and done paranormal investigations (often at sites reportedly haunted). We have all amassed hundreds of our own audio files wherein seemingly intelligent and interactive "electronic voices" (though in a few cases they were heard in the room with us!) came through on our digital recorders and over a "spirit box," which is simply a digital radio whose scanner mechanism has been disabled, thus it is on continuous scan. The theory is that the "spirits" can use the white noise to manifest to us in. Admittedly, I was initially very skeptical. In years past, I had engaged in my fair share of EVP (Electronic Voice Phenomenon) attempts going back to around 1976. My attempts were pretty dismal. I could engage in hours of audio evidence review after a recording and come up with absolutely nothing inexplicable. Now, however, I may conduct a session and in an hour or two of evidence review isolate up to half a dozen, or a dozen or more real good sections of anomalous audio!

What's the difference? One theory that some in parapsychology posited early on with regard to the EVP mystery was the theory that people with strong psychic or mediumistic abilities were better at getting positive results of this nature, but yet could help to "seed" or transmit the ability to others who might be receptive. I only know that my prior track record with this sort of thing wasn't very good at all (and that's putting it mildly) until I came to work with Bret and Gina Oldham, a couple who, I am quite convinced, both possess strong psychic abilities. Early on in our sessions we began communicating with a voice that identified itself as "John Keel," a UFO researcher who had greatly influenced my involvement in this field, and a man who I had engaged in correspondence off and on with for quite a number of years. We got some incredible interactive responses. In an attempt to convince myself that these "voices" were for real and not mere fragments of conventional radio broadcasts that were being misinterpreted, I introduced a strategy that we reproduced successfully again and again. We'd write a word or words down on an index card or sheet of paper and ask the "voices" to repeat what was written down in front of us. The response could be immediate or it might take some coaching and a couple or so minutes, but when it came through you knew that the odds were very unlikely to be coincidence or anything like that.

Faces of a group of men who were not there!

For example, I asked Keel what he could tell us about "*Jadoo*," a book he had written back in the 1950s based on his adventures in the Orient (Jadoo being a word that meant black magic) and immediately we heard a male voice come through the stereo speakers saying "'Jadoo,' eh?" Another time, that same evening (it was the one year anniversary of Keel's death, July 3, 2010), Bret asked him about Bigfoot, a subject that Keel had investigated quite extensively, and a male voice said immediately "Smuck Bigfoot, see?" and then we heard like another voice say "See," and then yet another "see." All of this in real time using the "spirit box."

Dr. Schwarz, whom I had met a couple of times (1976-77) and corresponded extensively with for over three decades, passed away on September 16, 2010. Soon I was getting "Doctor Schwarz" coming through the box. I tried to engage him in communication and as a control get him to say something that only he would have known, like the name of a book he had written, which I also had a chapter in, which was entitled "UFO Dynamics." While I thought I might have gotten it once or twice, but it was too distorted to be certain, I instead got a clear "UFO D," which occasionally he would abbreviate it that way in letters to me, when discussing that book!

Bret and Gina frequently get an apparent spirit guide/spirit technician named "Bishop" who it seems helps with sessions, and he pops up in virtually every "spirit box" event that I, my wife and daughter do at our home as well. We also get an apparent spirit named "Phillip," and occasionally "Doctor Schwarz." In a recent session (02/03/13), upon asking who was there to help us and asking for Doctor Schwarz, we got all three names within seconds, and I learned the next day that when Bret and Gina did a session that same day they also got Bishop, Phillip, and what sounded like Schwarz too.

"Pretty weird that you guys were getting all the same names that we were on the same day, and especially Dr. Schwarz showing up since we haven't heard that name in quite a while," Bret remarked after listening to some of my audio. At a Christmas Party at Sandy's (12/22/12) we all did a spirit box session together, with about a dozen people present, including some interested country music celebrities like Rodney Crowell, Claudia Church, and Michael Rojas, 2010 Academy of Country Music Awards Top Piano/Keyboard Player of the Year. Again we got these familiar names, as well as interactive responses. I asked for Doctor Schwarz and got "Doc-tor Schwarz" (first part was a little dragged out) immediately. Also, as often happens, we got a clear "fuck you," which is certainly not normal AM radio language. A pretty good number of odd anomalies were recorded that night.

We also ask for and hear responses that seemingly connect with friends and loved ones who have passed on. We get names, nicknames and first and last names, and even messages expressing love and of missing us. Bret and Gina and I have even done long-distance experiments with the "spirit box" wherein Bret and Gina would try and send me certain words and I would do the same. We'd select a certain date and time to do these experiments, and we had several successful noteworthy results. I even had a successful experiment doing this with a lady contactee in Australia whose specific message came through my "spirit box"!

Sometimes we just use a digital recorder and afterwards play back some pretty mind-boggling responses. However, generally the "voices" through "the box" are amplified and are easier to hear. This puts me in mind of the quantum physics theory of non-local reality. Even after death a part of us seems still connected to our loved ones, even though we and they are obviously now quite separated and "worlds apart," so to speak.

This gives me some measure of hope. There are things that truly can't be explained. There is more to reality than mechanistic "nuts and bolts" sterile science has allowed for.

Once again they are gone but hardly forgotten...

George Fawcett had been collecting and investigating UFO phenomena for a long, long time. In fact, his interest went all the way back to 1944, when the mysterious "foo fighters" of World War II came to his attention! He was the author of "**Quarter Century of UFOs in Florida, North Carolina and Tennessee**," published in 1975. He lectured on UFOs at almost 600 different colleges, military groups, scientific organizations, and various other gatherings here and abroad. Over the years, he authored over 100 articles for *FATE, Search, Saga, Argosy, True*, the *National Enquirer*, and my personal favorite England's *Flying Saucer Review*. He founded several major UFO groups, including the New England UFO Study Group back in 1957. I attended one of his talks for that group back around 1977. He sure could deliver a great UFO talk, and told me a very interesting personal MIB-type incident that had happened to him once. I'll have to look that up sometime and post it here at this site. Sadly George passed away on Sunday, January 20, 2013. He was 83, and lived in Lincolnton, North Carolina.

Famous remote viewer Ingo Swann also departed our world around 10:30 p.m., February 1, 2013. He was 79. Though regarded by many as an incredibly gifted "psychic," he preferred to be described as a "consciousness researcher." He is best known for his "remote viewing" work with Russell Targ and Harold Puthoff at the Stanford Research Institute. At one point, too, he also worked with New York's American Society of Psychical Research, doing out-of-body experiments. Swann was also a believer in UFOs and ET's, and I understand that he worked with a group trying to expose their presence.

References:

1. Back in 1974, with Dr. Schwarz's cooperation, I visited Stella Lansing twice myself.

INCREDIBLE ALIEN ENCOUNTERS

The first time was on Saturday, January 5th. I was accompanied by my long-time friend Jim Carey on this excursion. Jim still shares my obsession with UFOs (we did a radio show together recently). I returned home (which back then was Hallowell, Maine) around 5:00AM Sunday morning (the 6th). Later my mom had heard from an aunt how another aunt had seen a UFO that same morning! This was certainly of interest as Stella Lansing had just described to us how the UFOs might even follow her around, and cited an instance where one had followed her all the way down to Dr. Schwarz's home in New Jersey, and then too she saw it on the return trip home, back in 1973! By the time, I got down to my aunt's house to question her, which is down the hill from where I was staying with my parents, she was uncertain at that time as to whether it was Saturday or Sunday morning, but she said that she had indeed seen something in the sky that she couldn't identify. She had gotten up to go to the bathroom when she happened to glance outside and see a circle of white lights encircled by another circle of white lights moving slowly through the sky, seemingly at low altitude, going from the east towards the southwest. She heard some sort of a noise that she said was different from that of a regular plane or helicopter. She didn't seem able to describe it other than as perhaps an engine sound of some sort. The circle of white lights reminded me of Stella's film images of so-called "clockwork," images that kind of resembled the luminous points on a clock face. I decided to find out more about them. At the time, I wondered if there was a connection, and in 1976 I began getting them on my own super 8 mm film. A few others did also. Mind you, you don't see this pattern visually at the time. It just shows up on your film later. However, when I checked with Eastman Kodak, I was informed that they were caused by what they called "rivets." Edwin Austin, Supervising Photographic Specialist out of Kodak's office in Rochester, New York, explained in a letter: "Films are processed continuously by photofinishers. In order to process films continuously, he must attach the end of one film to the beginning of another. He does this by means of two rivets. As the films come off the end of the processing machine, the films are spooled up together so that the rivets come in contact with the next revolution of film. These two marks on your film were caused by those two rivets."

Neither Stella nor Dr. Schwarz seemed convinced by what I had been told, but when I examined under a bright light and under magnification my own super 8 mm film the "clockwork" actually formed physical impressions into the film itself, whereas if you turned it over and examined the other side it was smooth. Thus this fact, the fact that my own "clockwork" clustered near the end of the films (as I was told by Kodak that "rivets" would be attached end to end), and the "clockwork" would also overlap frames (defying normal optical science), all made it pretty clear to me that "rivets" was indeed the likely answer. Unfortunately, as I pressed further, to try and resolve this matter once and for all, I was informed that Kodak had discontinued the use of these "rivets." Different film specialists had told Dr. Schwarz that they couldn't explain the "clockwork" images, and though I was given an explanation from Kodak, not everyone would be convinced, it seemed, without an actual rivet in hand. Especially Stella Lansing. I even began to wonder if even that would resolve the matter once and for all.

At any rate, that was part of the story from my own involvement and perspective that I can share. There were many other anomalous phenomena reported and recorded that I cannot so easily offer an explanation for.

Jacques Vallee and Brent Raynes.

UFOs have been known to have strange and often dangerous effects on the environment. Any human eyewitness, who may accidentally get too close, may also suffer side-effects of the encounter.

THE PECULIAR SIDE EFFECTS OF UFOS – THE STRANGE UFO SAGA OF THE JAMES FAMILY

By Timothy Green Beckley

PUBLISHER'S NOTE: There are theoreticians who maintain that the presence of UFOs over the half century has given us the necessary inspiration, motivation and opportunity to forge ahead with our attempt to unravel the mysteries of the universe. Actually, what it has done is given us more to contemplate and try and figure out. A handful of researchers such as John Keel, Jacques Vallee and Paul Eno have had the foresight to head up a "modern day" search into unexplainable phenomena and offer a variety of plausible concepts for us to ponder and explore.

• • • • • • • • • •

FROM THE NY TIMES

"Scientists have found evidence of genetic damage in plants exposed to radiation from the atomic bombing of Nagasaki four decades ago. Many surviving ferns there carry radiation-induced genetic mutations in their cells, according to a team of American and Japanese botanists. The offspring of these plants show a variety of abnormalities and most do not mature successfully."

• • • • • • • • • •

If the paranormal hypothesis is valid, then without a doubt its wide-reaching effect will have a tremendous impact on our research in the years just ahead as we refocus our attention away from the extraterrestrial hypothesis it could even result in far-reaching changes and advancements in our cultural attitudes toward what seems to be the current limiting aspects of science. Over the years, I have become just as interested in what the visible effects have been on those individuals involved in a personal sense with the beings whose existence is still generally denied.

How have the percipients been "touched" by such vehicles and their occupants? Unrecognized by most researchers is the fact that over the ensuing years, flying saucers have made themselves "known" in a variety of awesome and thought-provoking ways. Well established are the instances in which unidentified airborne objects have been accused of causing blackouts and power failures.

Lights in entire communities, down to the most modest single dwellings, have flickered out due to the approach of a "foreign" apparatus of unknown origin. Ample exposure has also been given to cases in which UFOs have brought automobiles and other mechanical devices to a complete halt.

Several well-seasoned UFO researcher – writers have penned lengthy papers on this so-called EM (electromagnetic) effect. What of other, even more bizarre, irrational side-effects, traceable to disturbingly close confrontations with UFOs and their many-faceted crew members?

Despite a new respectability about this topic, there remain many factors deeply ingrained as part of the UFO puzzle which have not been openly publicized. Nor has adequate research been done to explain them. It is a documented, well-established fact that UFOs have affected or been able to alter in some way.

The growth of plant life, insects and humans.

The forces of gravity.

The passing of time and anything remotely connected with it.

The placement of physical objects.

The normal healing process.

STRANGE GROWTH PATTERNS

Mutation of butterfly after exposure to radiation.

Scientific evaluation of the Bikini atom bomb experiments some years ago established the fact that existing life forms on and near this closely-guarded South Pacific coral reef had undergone drastic transformation following the testing of two atomic warheads here in June of 1946. For years after these top secret blasts (whose mushroom clouds rose 30,000 feet) sea creatures – from the most microscopic to larger varieties – were found washed ashore, their bodies mutated in any number of ways. Marine navigators in the area even reported seeing a monstrous 66 foot shark—much larger than any ever previously seen.

On the island itself, insects were reported to have grown to tremendous proportions, six and seven times their normal size. Often they were found to have additional limbs and tentacles.

Of course the causes of these abnormalities are easily traced, scientifically. We know, for instance, that excessive radiation, especially "close-control" radiation, where atoms and molecules undergo initial changes, causes mutations to occur in nature. And certainly the radiation swept into the atmosphere by these two tremendous atomic weapons was among the most deadly ever. However, what of instances where radioactivity cannot be pinpointed as having set off the phenomenal and rapid growth of plant life, insects--and yes, even human beings?

Let us consider cases in which UFOs can be associated with such mutations. Several years ago a story was brought to my attention which, at the time, seemed incredible. So unusual was it that I neatly creased the report—which had come to me in the form of two personal letters--down the middle and placed them in the back of an unmarked file folder out of sight and for a long time out of memory It was not until recently, with the reporting of several similar cases, that I vaguely recalled the rejected episodes and retrieved them from their resting place.

· · · · · · · · · ·

Changes in growth patterns from UFO sightings -- before and after (larger plants).

During the summer of 1967, 18-year-old Jerry James, his father, mother and younger sister were driving toward California and a long-cherished vacation from their Colorado home. It was during the first night of their trip that a series of peculiar events began to transpire.

Jerry, scheduled to enter college in the fall, had taken turns with the driving chores. Finally after being on the road for more than 18 continuous hours, the family pulled their new Chevrolet pickup, behind which they towed a house trailer, onto a service station lot to refurbish themselves.

As they proceeded to stretch their limbs and catch a breath of fresh desert air, their eyes were attracted to a peculiar-looking object moving about overhead. Later, Jerry was to give me the following description of what the family had witnessed. "The object - a definite aircraft of a completely unknown type - was shaped similar to a child's top - round at the top and pointed at the bottom. It was encircled by a ring of brightly colored lights, and from out of the lower portion of the 'ship' came a beacon similar to a searchlight. This light beam passed over the area as if in search of something. We became quite shaken, moments later, when it shone directly on our trailer."

Jerry states that the object appeared to be about the size of an automobile. "Before disappearing from our view, the UFO hovered only a few feet above the top of our truck and then quite noiselessly zoomed off into the distance, and went out of sight." None of those present found it easy to believe what they had seen. The next day the James' camped off the main highway, miles from where their observation of the previous evening had taken place. "We thought we were once again going crazy when we saw a silver-looking vessel floating in from over a nearby mountain peak." This time Jerry revealed, "The UFO got so close - within 75 feet - that we could even see rivets visible in the metallic gray structure. At one point, as the orb made a direct pass at us, my mom fainted dead away. We had to use smelling salts to revive her."

Entering the back of the trailer they immediately noticed that something truly strange – well beyond their mysterious traveling companion – had come about. "Everything inside the trailer compartment was in perfect order, although when we left it the bunks had been unmade and the sink area strewn with silverware and unwashed dishes and utensils. Our beds had been put together and everything was as neat as it could be - though not as my Mom would have done it." It was then, looking around them, that Jerry noticed the most unusual feature. "On the kitchen cabinet we found a small dish with a sprouting carrot which had been placed there sometime during the last 24 hours. But something drastic and truly puzzling had happened to it, for the carrot did not resemble a carrot any longer. It had spread out, as if having grown for weeks in a tempered, professional hot house. Roots were everywhere, running outside the dish and reaching almost to the floor."

Examining the vegetable closer, Jerry and his parents and sister noticed a slimy green-colored substance on the cabinet and dish. "It was a vile smelling substance," Jerry observed, "and other than that I can't tell you much about it. One thing strange through. When I touched it with a pencil it 'ate up' the wood and lead in a matter of seconds."

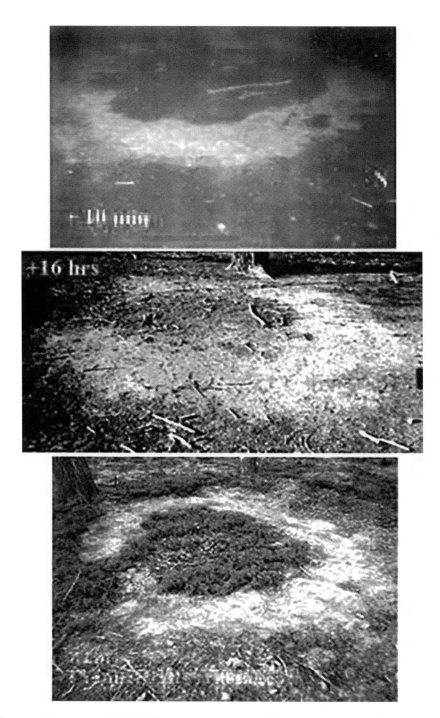

Delphos, Kansas (1971) trace case: (from top to bottom) The glowing ring taken 10 minutes after ascent, the site as it was photographed 16 hours after the event by Sheriff, the site as it appeared 3 years, 6 months after the event. - Coast to Coast AM Archive - Chief investigator Ted Phillips.

Soon after this Jerry telephoned the police, whom they hoped would investigate the series of phenomena. En route, their truck began to accelerate against the will of its driver. "Only a fractional depressing of the accelerator was enough to send the vehicle - truck and trailer - speeding along at 40 miles per hour."

But this was not all, as Jerry later confirmed. Upon arriving at the nearest gas station, the attendant proceeded to remove the gas cap. As he did out rushed an odorous and gaseous material, causing a hissing noise and bringing with it a strong smell like that of sulphur dioxide, or rotten eggs.

Even later, they discovered that the part of the truck seat where the driver sat had rotted out and the ignition key itself now glowed in the dark and had gotten soft and rubbery.

While law enforcement officials, whom they contacted, refused to believe that the James family had actually encountered a strange visitor from the depths of the universe, their insurance company was remarkably less skeptical. "They bought us a brand new truck to replace the one that had been wrecked so bad," Jerry reported. "They informed us that they had never seen anything quite like it before. What happened really had them stumped - almost as much as it had us frightened." Jerry remarked in a later communication that he was well aware that a good portion of what transpired could have been caused by a harmful dose of radioactivity. Yet, he also added that no one in his family showed the slightest symptoms of radiation poisoning. "None of us became ill afterwards. Even if the amount of radioactivity had been negligible, we should have become sick. In addition, it seems very probable that if the UFOs which passed directly overhead had carried with them some sort of contamination - enough to make the carrot root grow so widely, or the ignition key to glow and turn soft - surely it would have made us ill enough to need medical treatment. Probably we would have been quarantined in a hospital for observation. Thus I have my doubts that radioactivity was what caused these peculiar things to happen."

But if radiation wasn't the cause of this family's problems, what was? It seems more than coincidental that two UFOs were seen while all this was taking place. A careful examination of other close sightings reveals numerous instances of similar rapid "growth pattern."

Anyone who knows of additional cases where strange side effects have been noticed are welcome to report these cases which we could certainly adapt for use in further works of our high caliber research efforts.

mrufo8@hotmail.com

Missouri researcher Ted Phillips -- here with Dr. J. Allen Hynek -- has been responsible for investigating over 400 UFO trace cases.

INTERSTELLAR COMMUNICATIONS: IT COULD VERY WELL HAPPEN TO YOU (IF IT HASN'T ALREADY!)

By Timothy Green Beckley

Over the years, I have gotten some of the strangest and most bizarre letters and phone calls you can imagine. I guess, in a sense, it goes with the territory. I mean, being editor of publications like "The UFO Review, the World's Only Flying Saucer Newspaper," which had a circulation of about 30,000 on national newsstands in the late Seventies and early Eighties, and later *"UFO Universe," "UFO Files"* and *"Unexplained Sightings,"* which endured for eleven years, until the bottom fell out of the magazine business.

Every UFO and paranormal publication seemed to have folded at about the same time, and the last in-print magazine went belly up about two years ago. We still miss the Australian magazine "UFOlogist," for which we wrote for almost every issue. Today there is just the *"Fortean Times,"* which is very negative as far as UFOs go, and, from time to time, a printed issue of "Fate Magazine," just so editor Phyllis Galde can remind us they started publishing way back in 1948 and continue to "hold on." Woe is us, who don't enjoy those e-magazines as much. Though "Phenomena" out of the UK and "Encounters" in Australia do a good job, if you're addicted to your I-Pad or Kindle.

I rest my case with a couple of prime examples of these Interstellar Communications.

• • • • • • • • • •

COULD IT HAVE BEEN JUST A DREAM?

I would like to report a possible abduction. I mention the word "possible" because I think it happened when I was about seven years old. It used to be just visions that came to my mind, but now sometimes I have flashbacks and new memories of the incident come alive and the whole thing becomes more and more clear to me. This has had a great effect on my personality and for no known reason I keep reading UFO articles. I try to stop but I can't. I don't know why I keep reading the stuff. Every time I even hear the word UFO I lose my breath from a great buildup of excitement. But I don't know why I am excited about it. It's hard to explain but I'm telling you that I am going through something that I cannot explain. I really don't know if this incident was either a dream or a happening of reality. I say this because when it happened I felt like I was in a trance or state of supreme relaxation. It seemed like I was floating or something.

I think it happened when I was seven years old. I am seventeen right now and the whole thing confuses me. It was at night when I was asleep. Something awoke me from my sleep but I'm not sure what it was. I stumbled into the living room to where through the curtains I saw many glowing lights with assorted colors. I swung them open to see what appeared to be spotlights or search lights that were shining from the sky. It was then that I began to feel like I was in a trance. I opened the front door and shut it back on the way out in the front yard. At this moment I didn't know why I was outside. I felt stupid. For I was in my sleepwear and the streetlights were on. Anyone could have seen me. I felt a little more intelligent for some reason also.

After I walked out into the street I looked up in the sky and for the first time I felt my first "Last Breath Feeling." Over some nearby tree tops was the biggest and longest thing I had ever seen. It was shaped like a stretched out cigar or something. It was very shiny and there were lights present everywhere you looked upon it. It seemed to have hangers without doors on it from which smaller saucer-shaped things were swarming in and out of it. Above me were a lot of the smaller ones flying around.

Seconds later the whole area dimmed to a soft glow. I was more or less bewildered. Without warning I was stunned to feel the presence of something behind me. I turned around to see one of the saucer-shaped things land in the middle of the street about twenty feet away from me. I felt another "Last Breath Feeling."

Unexpectedly, a hatch under the craft slid to a downward position. Lights of many colors were flashing all over it. It was very difficult to look directly at it. But I think whoever was inside of it knew that also because right when I felt my eyes burn its lights dimmed to a very low magnitude. After that the hatch built up a very bright glow of white. From inside I saw a shadow of an oblong head appear. That's the last that I can remember. I woke up that next morning feeling a great bit drained of energy. It was from that day on that I became totally obsessed with the UFO phenomenon. I still am today, and the excitement never fades a bit. Night after night after that I began having dreams about UFOs continually. Dreams about seeing them and dreams about being a UFOlogist. I still have those dreams today and I match almost every single one of Aileen Edward's Characteristics of an abductee – that you printed in your first issue.

J. Trimm McKinleyville, CA

MISSING TIME

I just purchased your magazine. I had a close encounter with a UFO on 9 June 74. This happened while I was stationed at Fort Devens, Massachusetts. I had attended an ESP course at the local education center and my ESP teacher, Paul Clements, had me hypnotized to recall what I had seen. I still have the cassette that was made that night by a friend that attended the class with me. To this day I cannot reproduce the drawing that I had done under regression. I had been seeing a psychiatrist for migraines, Col. Tom Guyden, and he hypnotized me too. Both my ESP teacher and psychiatrist could not find out how I returned to the barracks that night.

This is what I remember: I was bored that night and was watching TV. The movie ICE STATION ZEBRA was on. My roommates were in that night too. I decided that I had seen the movie enough times and got dressed and went for a walk. I felt safe walking by myself on base. I walked from the barracks to the USATC&S school. To my left was the Officers' Quarters across the street; from where I was standing, the flag pole was near me.

Looking across the field I noticed a light coming above the church (at the other end of the field). It definitely was a ship. It was oval and I could see the individual colored lights revolving in a circular motion on the bottom. As it got nearer, I noticed three occupants. The center figure was standing and one sat on either side of that person. I saw the equipment surrounding them. Emblems on their clothing. I got a message telepathically: "We know you are a SHADO operative. We do not have time to contact you further at this time. We will contact you or another person later."

The next thing I remembered was waking up to my alarm clock and getting dressed for work. To give you some background: I be- longed to a science-fiction club SHADO- USCC based in California. It was an offshoot from a British TV series ("UFO"). I had grown up liking science-fiction programs, movies, books, etc. My twin and I had seen a few UFO's in Columbus, GA, while we were going to high school. When we reported them to the police and air force, they said that nothing of theirs were in the area. I no longer belong to that club (I think I let the membership run out in 1976).

A few days after my encounter, I went away for the Weekend, and, when I returned, some friends of mine said that two men in black were asking for me. I never saw or heard from those men in black. I left Fort Devens in 1976 and went to language training in Monterrey, CA. I saw some UFOs while I was on the beach with some friends. I graduated from language school and went to Goodfellow AFB, TX for intelligence school. I saw two sets of UFOs there. The first set I reported to the Air Police on base. Nothing of ours was flying nor any civilian aircraft. They made me feel ridiculous for reporting it. Needless to say that when I saw the second set of UFOs i did not report it. I would like to find out what happened from the moment they talked to me and when I woke up in the bar- racks.

I also would like to know why I cannot reproduce that picture. My friend had reproduced it for me that night in class and I tried an experiment with it. I put tracing paper (carbon) underneath and traced the picture. Nothing came out on the bottom sheet, but yet when I wrote my name diagonally across that picture that showed up on the bottom sheet of paper. I had a bad feeling about holding on to that picture and destroyed it a few nights later. Now I wish I hadn't. If you would like the cassette, I can make a copy, and if you need any corroboration of what I have said. The addresses I listed for my psychiatrist (and friend) and ESP teacher (who is a psychologist) are current. I will be looking forward to your reply. I didn't talk about this too much while I was in the military because of the ridicule.

Maria Elena Morgan Dale City, VA

ALIEN MATES

I had found your magazine, *"UFO Universe,"* the first issue, very interesting, so I bought two copies. The article by Brad Steiger really triggered my memory. At the age of 12, a strange thing happened to me. One night in May of 1967 - it was near 11:30 P.M. - when I was aroused by a blinding white light. I had thought at first that it was heat lightning, but the light seemed to fill my whole room.

I thought at first I should be afraid, but I wasn't. I felt very relaxed and at peace. A strange feeling came over me. I was no longer alone in my room. I could feel the presence of something or someone moving around in the room. That was all I really remember from my encounter.

That very same night I had a very detailed dream. I dreamed I was out walking somewhere and I found on the ground a 1906 Indian head penny. When I awoke the next morning, I could remember my dream in great detail. In the progression of that very same day, while on my paper route, I had sat down my heavy bag of papers on the first step at one of the houses I delivered to. Well, when I reached down to pull out a paper from my bag, I saw something flat and round in a freshly tilled flower bed. After I had picked it up and wiped off the dirt, there was a 1906 Indian head penny I had only dreamed of the night before. To this very day I can still remember the exact spot it was found.

Ever since that night of the blinding light I have had those kinds of dreams. I don't have them all the time, just once in a while. I now dream of a full day's events, and in the same week I will find myself repeating that day in detail at work. It is a very weird feeling to know what is going to happen before it does. I know now that the aliens that visited me did something to my mind. I have heard voices at times when there was nobody around. I have also acquired a type of cluster headaches that is very painful at times. I had had EKG's and KAT scans and doctors have found nothing to cause them. From voices I have heard lately, I am to search for others like myself who have had encounters with aliens. I am to communicate with these people and record their names for future space colonies. Those visitors that communicate with me have told me, we (meaning earthlings) are to be prepared for future evacuation of Earth.

Another encounter occurred at the age of 14. A strange man walked up to me and sat down beside me at a lunch counter in a ten cent store. The person started talking to me about UFOs. He told me that he knew that I had seen aliens in the past and that I would see more in the future. The person was holding tightly in his right hand an old, badly beaten paperback book called "Flying Saucers and the Bible." He handed the book to me and told me to read it carefully and that its contents would open my eyes to a reality that others could not fathom. The person patted my hand holding the tattered book and told me to hold on tightly to this book, it will help guide you toward a journey in the future. I looked down at the book in my hand with amazing wonder then looked up to speak to him and he was gone.

After I had read through the book, I placed it among my other books, and when I went back to get it to show to a friend, it was gone. It was nowhere to be found. To this day I still search through my things hoping it will turn up.

I am hoping I might find another copy of that book through others that have had a similar encounter. Recently, on Friday the 1st of July of 1988, I received a telepathic message from my visitors, whom I had not heard from for many years. The symbols I will write in this letter is the message given me. The message came to me while I was at work between the time of 2:30 pm and 4:00 pm. The message came with sharp pains deep within my head.

I can only speculate an interpretation, but I feel my speculation will not be far wrong. Many aliens from other worlds have made a stop on Earth to choose a human mate or companion that will soon accompany them on a journey. The journey is to that alien's planet to mate with and begin a new race of beings to inhabit newly found planets in distant galaxies able to sustain a type of human life, because soon Earth, as we know it, will be no more. Soon a great number of spacecraft will be coming to claim their new eternal companions.

Before the year 20--?, two hundred thousand humans will be removed from the Earth. I myself have been chosen as a companion to an alien female. A'yora is the name of the female. Her facial features remind me more so of an insect by the shape of her eyes and head. Even though her head may be different, the body is almost identical to a human, though they have longer toes and fingers and also they have a small five to six inch tail at the base of their spine.

My companion has only shown herself to me once. My feelings toward this female were at first questionable. But now I find myself feeling compassion for this being. Her speech is foreign to my ear, but yet it translates in my mind as if it were spoken in the King's English. I now find myself feeling alien to my own world. My wife has noticed changes in me, that she questions whether or not I am the same person she had married. The alien female is becoming more and more attractive to me, and my human wife less and less.

I am an eighteen year old girl. And I have my body chemistry. It doesn't seem long till my life here on Earth will be wiped clean from my mind and a new life elsewhere will replace it. I am now looking forward to my new life with my new companion.

D.C. Gains Toledo, Ohio

UFO SIGHTINGS IN ANTHROPOLOGIST'S FIELD NOTES

The single, unifying experience of nearly all university-trained doctoral students in anthropology has been and will continue to be fieldwork. Studying aspects of other societies in their own settings often yields an amazing array of unusual accounts. Sprinkled among the stories told to fledgling anthropologists by their informants must be many first-hand sightings of UFO's. Unfortunately, descriptions of the sightings are recounted in the language and symbolic/religious matrix of another culture, so they are difficult to recognize. They are likely to be recorded in the field notes under a catchall category, such as "magical beliefs" or "dreams and hallucinations." While conducting my own dissertation fieldwork in the Czechoslovak Social Republic back in 1972, I came across several accounts of an unusual UFO sighting that had taken place about five years earlier. I was collecting data on witchcraft and "evil eye" in a small village located in the Myjava Foothills of Western Slovakia, the easternmost province.

INCREDIBLE ALIEN ENCOUNTERS

The people living in this agricultural region have no contact with the Western media. Press coverage of UFOs in the Warsaw Pact countries is non-existent. Quite often, they even "forget" to publish news of their own airplane disasters. I am therefore fairly confident that my informants in this village were not prompted or influenced by information they had seen or read. Contagion could not have contributed to what they told me.

Since there is very little industry for miles around, the sky is exceptionally clear, so, in the absence of clouds, the stars twinkle with considerable intensity. Suddenly, out of nowhere, a revolving form appeared over the hill in back of the village's 300-year-old church. The underside was dark and completely round. A local woman, who prefers not to be named, said she could tell because it blocked out the stars where it hovered, seemingly on edge only a few hundred feet above the ground. She heard no noise whatsoever. Then the object slowly tilted down, banking in the other direction, revealing its top side. She described it as being plano-convex in cross-section with a dome on top. Ringing the dome at its base was a ribbon of light — perhaps a series of "windows."

The light was yellowish and revealed the dull gray metallic color of the surface of this object. All the while it hovered, first tilting over on one side and then on the other, it was revolving. Then, just as suddenly as it had appeared, it disappeared. As she put it, the object just got smaller and smaller. No doubt it took off at a very rapid speed. When I asked her what she thought this object was, the Registrar was evasive. I asked her if anyone else had seen it, and she listed the names of other residents for me. I then inquired about the duration of the sighting. She was uncertain, but noted that it could have been several minutes, because dogs had begun to bark and the ensuing ruckus brought their owners out into the courtyards, and that is how so many villagers came to see it. The barking dogs might indicate that the object was emitting a high-pitched frequency which would have been inaudible to the people.

Although my companion was unwilling to offer her own explanation for this sighting, she did use an expression to refer to the object. Everyone else I interviewed in this village gave me the same account and used the same expression: "letecky tanier" ("flying plate"). Over and over, I asked my informants if they had heard this expression used in newscasts or if they had read it in newspapers or magazines. No, they had not.

They formulated it by themselves. They really thought it looked like one of their dinner plates. In this part of Eastern Europe, dinner plates resemble shallow soup plates.

Janet S. Poliak, PH.D. Dept. of Sociology/Anthropology, William Paterson College, Wayne, New Jersey.

AN EERIE FUNNEL

On the night of Dec. 10, 1978, I was walking to my home from a local convenience store and I noticed that the wind was blowing all around me, but yet the air was silent. I then looked up to the sky as if "something" or "someone" told me to do so and as I did, I saw a form which resembled that of a tornado, but it was still, just there! It was black and shown clearly against the clouds.

I'm really surprised the funnel-shaped object I observed was so easy to see because it was about 7:30 P.M. and it was already quite dark. Patiently, I watched to see if anything was going to happen and something did... an orange streak of light came right down the center of the black funnel-shaped object as if it came from thin air. I sort of think it was some kind of glide path. I could be wrong since I'm no authority on the subject, only an observer. If anyone else reading this has ever had a similar experience, please notify this publication, because I would like to know of other sightings like mine.

Walter Briggs Alexandria, LA

MUTANT BEINGS

I am 31, a freelance writer and work for Southwestern Bell Telephone Co. When I was 16, I saw a UFO. It flew over our apartment building, very low. It was round and looked exactly like a wedding band, with a hole in the center, except that it had lights around the outside of the band. It was gold and gleamed. When I was younger, at the age of 12, my father and I watched Air Force jets chase a big blue light that bounded around and made 90 degree turns in its maneuvers. Even my sister and her husband in St. Clair, Missouri, told me about a UFO they saw just a few weeks ago.

Of course, I don't have any proof of these things, but I do have a telescope and a camera and would like to try and send you a few concrete things. I can't help but feel that the government has perfected some interplanetary vehicles. Why don't they inform the public? Obviously, they think people wouldn't want to pay their taxes anymore. They would want to climb into the spaceships and leave this planet. Israel and Egypt wouldn't have to be at each other's throats through eternity. They could both have all the property they wanted on another planet. And finally, I believe the government has created mutant beings for space exploration. Remember, they didn't tell the public about the atom bomb until they dropped it on Japan.

Sandra McNabt, Arnold, Mo

A UFO hovering over a town near a percipient's home.

A VERY FRIGHTENING ENCOUNTER

For your information, I have been into the flying saucer phenomenon (and most everything pertaining to it) ever since my personal close encounter back in 1955. In fact, I continue to suffer with an ailing right elbow from that incident, and the doctors are baffled and say they cannot find any type of cure.

Let me tell you a few things: I'm thoroughly pissed-off at our various government agencies, mainly the President of the United States. He has failed to live up to his promise to release all UFO data to the American taxpayers. Anyway, I hate the term UFO, as I encountered a genuine flying saucer and got close enough to throw stones at it. You people seem to have gotten on the bandwagon of constantly tying religious aspects as well as psychic phenomena with UFOs. In short, I resent this, since my experience certainly had nothing to do with religion or psychic phenomena. I faced the most frightening and strange machine that one could ever imagine and somebody was operating it. Needless to say, I am indeed very lucky to be alive today to talk about what was heading in a northwesterly direction. This was at Columbia Ranch and they didn't make a sound and were in almost a "V" formation. The sighting lasted about a minute last March 16, 1978, and happened at 9:30 A.M. My greatest wish is to have a flying saucer land right on Jimmy Carter's White House lawn. This would be the most important thing to happen in the world.

Andy Florio, Los Angeles, CA

UFOS BROUGHT ME PSYCHIC AWARENESS

Back before UFOs were being written about in the press, I had several experiences that left me with a lot of questions. Of course, I do know more about these things now than I did 35 years ago, but I am still searching for answers, the big one being— why did they pick me to be one of their guinea pigs? We stood there in the driveway not knowing why we were waiting there. Suddenly a strange light flashed into our eyes. We both jerked our heads skyward to see what was going on. We did not understand the strange craft we saw there.

Yet the sight in the sky was no greater mystery than the strange urge which had brought us to the spot from which we could see the signal flashed at us. As I recall it was a beautiful afternoon. The weather was cool. The sky mostly clear except for a very high layer of clouds in the northwestern sky. I had become very restless. I needed to get out of the yard. Dad was sitting on the front porch in the shade of a giant sycamore tree. As I walked by he got up and walked with me. This was unusual, as my Dad and I were never very close. Together we walked out the yard gate without saying a word. We turned and walked down the gravel driveway stopping at a spot apparently no different than any other. We just stood there for several minutes as if we were waiting for something. Suddenly a bright light flashed in our eyes. It was like a flash from a signal mirror. We snapped our eyes upward to see what was going on. Another flash made sure we were looking at the right spot, for there in the northern sky we saw eight strange aircraft. Those aircraft were very large and very high. They flew due west in a giant V formation.

There were four of them following the flight leader in the southern leg of the flight and three in the northern leg. Moments later we noticed another one. The ninth aircraft was following behind the vacant spot in the end of the northern leg of the flight. I believe that ninth aircraft was the command ship. I knew a lot about aircraft, having studied aircraft identification carefully. I could identify every plane in the world by sight. I had never seen any information on anything even close to the swept-wing design of those we were watching flying overhead. The nine sleek swept-wing aircrafts flew across the sky at a terrific speed. This was in 1943 during the death struggle of World War II. The propeller-driven C 47 was the elite of the cargo and transport planes. Yet, the aircraft we saw that day were flying at a speed at least four or five times the speed of the best propeller driven planes. It was not until after the end of World War II that American engineers found a model of a swept-wing bomber being tested in Germany's secret high speed wind tunnel complex at Volkenrode. Using "liberated" designs and test data, American engineers then designed and built the sleek and graceful supersonic B 47.

The first prototype of the Boeing B 47 lifted off the ground December 17, 1947. The B 47 had long slender swept-back wings of this aspect ratio for low lift and low drag, giving the plane not only excellent cruising efficiency but also a beautifully esthetic outline. The B 47 was the first plane to incorporate these advanced flight concepts here on Earth. Obviously it had been done somewhere else at least four years earlier. We watched the aircraft from the time their signal flash caught our attention at approximately 10 degrees east of due north until they disappeared over the high clouds approximately 40 degrees west of north. Even though the aircraft were at tremendous altitude, they appeared to be very large and could be seen quite clearly.

Judging by today's largest aircraft, I believe those were quite a bit larger than anything being flown today. Judging by the type of cloud formation, they were flying at approximately 20,000 feet or possibly higher. They made no noise, nor did they leave the contrails in the sky. These aircraft flew across the sky and out of sight high above a cloud layer in the northwest. Flying across the 50 degrees of the northern sky took approximately 15 to 20 seconds. There was one brief glimpse of the aircraft later as they passed over a thin spot in the clouds. Then they were gone. It was not too long after those sleek aircraft had signaled me that another even stranger thing happened. I had that feeling again. It was about ten o'clock at night, and I was drawn to a spot in the driveway very near the spot from which I had seen the strange aircraft. I was watching the sky intently. It seemed like I had to watch that one spot. I was looking directly at it when a red glow appeared and grew larger. I had the strangest thought when I saw it. I said to myself, "This one is coming to me." The red glow began moving straight east across the sky. It got to approximately the same point in the sky where I had last seen the strange swept wing aircraft when it made an abrupt turn and headed straight toward me. All the time the meteor or fireball was coming directly toward me, I knew it was not going to hurt me. I knew somebody had full control over it. I was not the least apprehensive. Later, I learned the fireball had burned through the sky and lit up parts of four states. Finally, it arched and hit the ground less than thirty feet in front of me.

Kart S. Topeka, KS

The aliens are here - some are friendly, like this member of the Ashtar Command,
as drawn by Carol Ann Rodriguez.

GONZO FLORIDA – JOHN REEVES JOURNEY TO "OTHERWHERE"

By T. Allen Greenfield

"I knew John Reeves. Quite well; visited with him any number of times with the late UFOlogist Joan Writenour, my Father Al Greenfield, my son Alex Greenfield and his mother. His story has the absurdist edge that the Joe Simonton 'pancake case' and many others have. The problem with THAT is that there were close encounters of the First and arguably Second kind among John's more or less immediate neighbors. I met some of them. Very plausible, very real-seeming. Reeves taught me – along with Ralph Lael and a few others – that context makes even the most absurdist claims more plausible."

Allen Greenfield, Author of "*God Never Does the Same Thing Twice*."

John Reeves had a life of minor adventure before moving to the then sparsely populated West Coast of Florida at the beginning of what Bob Heinlein projected as "the crazy years" - the 1960s.

Reeves had played a bit part in the classic film "*All Quiet on the Western Front*" but it was in Brooksville that the Western (Florida) 'front' came front and center to Reeves; he had moved to what I once called a 'beachhead of otherwhere'. He had a cinderblock home – some sort of abandoned store – next door to the filling station on Highway 50, just a few miles from the sinkholes that swallowed cars and trucks (and at least one bridge) whole, and just above - you guessed it, a cave system largely unexplored.

So the baseline story - the only one that most folks know (we haven't even gotten to the Billie Beer part yet, so hold onto your tin-foil hat) - is this:

John Reeves examines what he considers to be footprints left by
an extraterrestrial visitor near his Florida property.

According to the *"Night Sky"* blog, "On March 2, 1965, he decided to take a leisurely stroll through a small patch of woods near his home. The area was well shaded with large live oaks, yet the terrain of the land was sandy and full of dunes. As Reeves walked, he noticed about 300' away there was a strange object sitting on the ground. It was disk shaped and had four stilt like legs coming out of the bottom. The disk had a dome on the top and was a dull, silvery gray color. Reeves later estimated the object to be around 40' in diameter, around 9' at its thickest point. Its distance from the edge of the disk to the ground was around 3½'.

"Naturally, Reeves was quite nervous upon seeing the odd craft, he did eventually approach it, with great caution. As he walked toward the object, he could see a strange creature about 25' away. It looked unearthly, according to Reeves or almost robotic in nature. It had tight skin, luminous and light, covering its entire body.

"The being turned and started toward Reeves. It pulled from its side a small, square object, much like a camera. The creature held it chin level, and then pushed a button causing a bright, blinding flash of light to appear. Reeves, turned to run but tripped over a bush. In the process, he dropped his glasses. Reeves laid helpless on the ground, tangled in the brush. The being then walked over to the glasses and picked them up, bringing them close to Reeves. It then proceeded back to the craft, but dropped two pieces of paper along the way. The strange being entered the ship via a slat like walkway on the underside. Shortly after, the object began rotating counterclockwise, slowly at first, and then sped up drastically as it began to rise. It left the area at a rapid rate of speed. Reeves walked over to the abandoned papers and examined them. The paper was thin in consistency and contained strange writings, unlike anything he had ever seen before.

"After the encounter, Reeves went to a local radio station, bringing the odd papers with him. He was interviewed and there was so much stir publicly regarding this case, that the Air Force was contacted. According to reports, the Air Force confiscated the papers from Reeves, but did later return them to him. There was a problem though. The papers were not in their original form. These papers that Reeves received weeks after were thicker and had no writing of any kind on them."

Remember the flash, and c.f. the first "*Men in Black*" movie. Just sayin'. Nevertheless, like Joe Simonton the pancake maker to the, uhm, "stars" (mostly Sirius, seriously) once the initial 'contact' took place - flash! - and much of the rest may well be 'post super-hypnotic suggestion'. Like I said, just sayin'.

TALKING TO THE GOOD OLE BOYS OF BROOKSVILLE

So, the first thing I did on my first visit - before meeting John himself - was talk to the good ole boy who runs the gas station right next door on what was then a rather desolate roadway. I asked him about John Reeves. "Well, John's an alright guy," he said. "There was other folks around here that also saw them flyin' saucers at the same time, but John was the first, and he has all that phys'cal evidence. You know, the footprints and writing an other stuff."

"Uh-huh." I said.

Albert Greenfield at John Reeves UFO landing area.

"See these here bugs," he said pointing to a rather odd ant hill, "There weren't no such bugs here until John saw that robot thing. No they all over tha place." Indeed they were.

You need to put this all in context. Reeves had made plaster casts of the 'footprints' of the robot that came out of the saucer, and they were impressive. The only skeptical objection (and there always were, including the ridiculous aspects that researchers like Keel, or Vallee or me for that matter found most interesting) could be that he had been, earlier in life (prior to 1960) both a longshoreman and a steel worker, so although he seemed, when I met him in 1968, to be a well-meaning, sincere but befuddled guy who had a really weird experience. But he was capable of building a model of the saucer out of parts from a barbeque grill and God only knows what else, and then a full-sized albeit wooden replica of the robot's "craft". So, could he have 'faked' the robo-footprints and the casts of them? Certainly, but it seems a stretch. AFAIK, he never asked anyone for anything. Shortly before my first visit, he said alien beings had returned and taken him to the Moon.

Now, 1968 w3as the year that the first astronauts circled the Moon, but Neil and Buzz didn't set foot on the Lunar Surface until the following year. I remember the Christmas Eve circumlunar expedition only too well, because the late Jim Moseley, his daughter Betty, Tim Beckley and I were high above Brown Mountain

INCREDIBLE ALIEN ENCOUNTERS

North Carolina watching the famous Brown Mountain Lights from a remote locale, braving the icy narrow road to get a better look than the "official viewing spot" most people go to gawk at the lights. It was my second visit to the mountain, and my second interview with the "Outer Space Rock Shop Museum" contactee, Ralph Lael. Pictures were taken. Lael showed us his embalmed shrunken head (actually, a total shrunken creature) which, as Moseley remarked to Lael, reminded him of his own shrunken head in his own curio shop in Key West, the Rose Lane Gallery from his Inca grave-robbing days. Anyway, when we got back to our motel and, while Beckley was trying to explain to his mom in New Jersey why it was so cold in the Deep South (upper south, actually, high in the Smokey Mountains), "Warm weather states, but Winter there too..." he explained.

One of us turned on the TV and, there were the astronauts, reading the Bible (Genesis 1, ye curious bibliophiles) on live TV as they circled back around from the back side of the Moon (where Reeves landed, according to his account, in an alien bubble), and I thought, "Oh my stars and bars, they must be off course and doomed if they are reading scripture radioed back to Earth..." But I had forgotten the Christmas Spirit and NASA P.R. – it was better than the annual NORAD warning about the approach of Santa Claus.

The next day a Suit showed up at my room door, came in and told me to stay away from Lael, 'cause, the Suit said, Lael was a moonshiner. I must have been hypnotized or some such, because if I had been alert I would have asked the Suit, "Who the Hell are you, and how did you find my motel room?" But, at the time, it seemed normal.

Anyway, back to Brooksville, Reeves, the strange insects, the sinkholes and, Brent Raynes recently pointed out, caves with evidence of Bigfoot. As Brent related in his super online *Alternate Perceptions*, "In late November 1973, I dropped in on local resident Eula Lewis. Eula had a chilling tale of how one day, a few years earlier (1966?), she was outside her home watering a tree when she heard a strange noise like static electricity, or like someone jumping around in dry leaves. It seemed to be coming from somewhere overhead. But apparently before she could really study it further she noticed a tall creature with broad shoulders covered with dark brown hair on the edge of her property. She ran for the door, making it there just as this creature reached the edge of her small porch.

"Eula said that about three weeks later, she had a daughter-in-law who also saw a similar creature, and heard the "static" noise too.

"As happens often in UFO encounter cases, Eula's home, she said, became besieged with poltergeist type activity it seemed..."

The next year Brent relates a great story from his friend Ramona Clark that involves the (not surprising) Bigfoot/UFO connection. I won't even go into the story of the Mermaids in Weeki Wachee; this story is complicated enough. Anyway, Brent relates Ramona's account thusly, "Yeti reports from TWO TRAILERS DOWN from us last Sunday night...Wow! Banging on trailer and weird sounds...no prints in the yard." He goes on, "One very close encounter, on November 9, 1974, just five miles from her home, came in of a black haired upright creature, estimated at 8 foot tall and weighing at an estimate of approximately 400 pounds. A terrified young couple had been going down the Weeki Wachee River in an aluminum canoe and had stopped along the river bank for a little "petting." Then the man looked up, into the eyes of this creature that had a gorilla like face and huge hands, "the size of note book paper," I was informed." Petting, huh? Gray Barker, oh where are you when I need you? Gray probably formulated his 'sex and saucers' connection from the Scarberrys and Mallette raced 'at 100 miles an hour' to escape Mothman on November 15, 1966. They were in the infamous 'TNT area and likely doing some petting of their own when Mothman made his/her/its debut appearance.

John Reeves stands proudly in front of his "homemade" flying saucer.

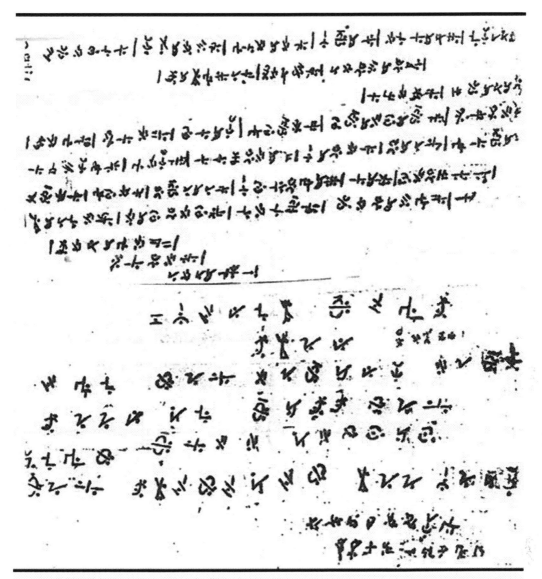

Alleged "Alien Writing" found by John Reeves at UFO landing site in Brooksville, Florida.

Now, if you are inclined to disbelieve Reeves (or Lael, or Charlie Hickson), be aware that after his initial report, which was even taken seriously by the rather hardnosed Lorenzens of the APRO, he was besieged by all kinds of attention, including a psychiatrist who found no trace of deception or delusion in Reeves, and the guy was like the Pascagoula abductees, subjected to a polygraph exam and found to be truthful insofar as he himself understood what had happene4d to him. His stories got more and more like classical contactee stories, including the later 'visitors' from the 'planet' "Moniheya." Reeves had a crystal sample nearly identical to the one

I photographed in Ralph Lael's shop, and "Moon dust" which compares favorably with the actual authentic Moon dust that astronauts encountered on the Lunar Surface from Apollo 11 on. As Keel pointed out, no one on Earth knew what the surface of Luna would be like until Neil and Buzz stepped out on the dusty surface. Make of it what you will.

There have been numerous other cases of UFOs and bird-like creatures within a couple of miles of Reeves' home. On one occasion I went with the late Joan Whritenour of the New Atlantean and her then-husband, photographer Ron Whritenour to visit John, and they introduced me to a couple, further up the Highway 50 'landing spot' and they told me a very close encounter story that they themselves experienced during the same period as Reeves' initial encounter. Technically, this salt-of-the-Earth couple had a close encounter of the First Kind, '(CE-I). This is when a UFO is within 200 yards, but it doesn't interact with the witness or environment." Whereas Reeves' experienced a Close Encounter of the Third Kind, or something beyond the scale designed by J. Allen Hynek.

Thinking it all through, in context this is among the "best of the really weird cases." I suggest that everything that happened around Reeves reinforces his own case, but I suspect, like Joe Simonton and the aliens who wanted pancakes, the ludicrous aspects are the key to the nature of the range of strange phenomena reports. Nothing that happened to John Reeves after the 'robot' "took his picture" (a flash of light) is as it seems.

Oh, I almost forgot. John's homemade replica flying saucer is no more. "'In September of 1972, the sandy dunes and woods were razed by developers. A mobile home park now sits where Reeves had his extraterrestrial encounters back in the '60s. "But the last time I visited John, the saucer was already gone. Apparently, a tornado picked it up and took it away. It turned not as it went.

John, undeterred, built an obelisk in its place with two boxes at its base. He showed me an ad he had taken out in the local newspaper advertising for a wife. Not unusual in Florida, a/k/a "God's Waiting Room." But there is the matter of the two boxes. The ad went on "Looking for a woman to marry, I have a monument and two coffins for us after we are gone."

· · · · · · · · · ·

INCREDIBLE ALIEN ENCOUNTERS

God Never Does the Same Thing Twice: Messiahs and Miracle Workers, Paperback – 2019
NEWLY REVISED EDITION

This is Allen Greenfield's gonzo book wherein Aleister Crowley and Jesus Christ wrestle for messiahood in the best two out of three tag-team match, winner take all, and where General Patton sneaks into Prague near the end of WWII to see if he can fetch the Golem in the attic of the Old-New Synagogue where it has resided these past few centuries, plus other good stuff. A long time member and facilitator of the worldwide Free Illuminist or Congregational Illuminist Movement, and past (elected) member of the Society for Psychical Research and the National Investigations Committee on Aerial Phenomena, as well as two time recipient of the "UFOlogist of the Year Award" of the National UFO Conference, T Allen H. Greenfield brings a fresh and perhaps strangely informed perspective on events which many have taken for granted their entire lives. What you were told, is what you were Sold! This New, Revised and Expanded edition has new stories as well as additional illustrations.

By T Allen H Greenfield (Author), Rorac Johnson (Editor, Introduction), Stacy Kulyk (Illustrator)

www.amazon.com/Never-Does-Same-Thing-Twice/dp/1974591646

The Complete SECRET CIPHER Of The UFOnauts, Paperback – 2018
By Allen H. Greenfield (Author), Olav Phillips (Introduction)

SECRET CIPHERS, RITUALS, CABALS, MEN IN BLACK AND THE UFO PHENOMENON.... For more than five decades, rumors have circulated amongst researcher that the UFO phenomenon is somehow directly linked to Occultism. Now, veteran UFOlogist Allen Greenfield provides proof of those connections and exposes the he UFO mystery with the discovery of hidden Secret Ciphers and Rituals used by UFONAUTS, Contactees, Occult Adepts and their Secret Chiefs who have maintained communication with Mysterious Ultraterrestrial beings who control force beyond our comprehension and human adepts, stretching from antiquity to the present moment. The entire library of magical invocation and evocation, seen in this light, is revealed to be a disguised transmission of these technologies. Now for the first time, The Complete Secret Cipher of the UFONAUTS gives you the tools to understand the ciphers and rituals, and to tap into this secret language of the ages and use it to make your own startling discoveries.

www.paranoiamagazine.com/2016/07/complete-secret-cipher-ufonauts

MIB Illustration by Carol Ann Rodriguez.

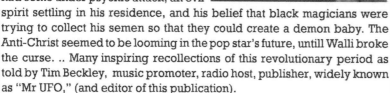

495

Made in the USA
Las Vegas, NV
04 November 2020